Infanticide

Execution of Mrs. Winsor

At Exeter,
For the barbarous murder of Mary Jane Harris's Child

Exeter, Friday.—At the usual hour this morning Mrs. Winsor expiated her crime on the gallows. Thousands assembled in front of the gaol at a very early hour, and many had walked all night to see the execution. Great commotion prevailed and it was evident that the crowd viewed the execution of a woman as a novelty, while they freely discussed the fiendish nature of the culprit, and expressed their total abhorrence of one who could make a business of murdering illegitimate offsprings.

The horrible nature of the woman's crime (which needs not to be recapitulated here) so shocked the better feelings of humanity, that when culprit and hangman stood side by side a fearful yell rose from the assembled crowd, and the excitement only ceased when the culprit, who struggled but little, ceased to exist.

You mothers all, come listen to me,
 While a dreadful tale I tell,
Of all the crimes upon this earth,
 This one does all excel.
Children slaughter'd fearlessly,
 And by a woman's hand,
Just for the sake of getting gold,
 This woman you command.

This dreadful woman, Charlotte Winsor,
 Took children in to nurse,
A devil she was in human form,
 We could not call her worse;
She would tamper with their young mother,
 With if you would like to pay,
For a few pounds, say three or four,
 I will put your child away.

Those children belong to some poor girl
 That had been led astray,
Mrs. Winsor would take them to nurse
 As long as they would pay.
She would murder them—yes, strangle them
 For this paltry gain,
By putting them between beds,
 Or pressing the juglar vein.

What must this wretch's feelings be,
 While the babes on her would smile,
She would kiss and feed him tenderly,
 And murder all the while.
She would tamper with their mothers,
 and of them beg and pray,
With get four pounds together dear,
 And your child shall die to day.

She stifled one just three weeks old,
 Jane Harris, she would say,
You will never see them after,
 They will sink in the Torquay.
Dead children tell no tales,
 And cause no more strife,
And with children smiling on her,
 She would take away their life.

No one knows this woman's crime,
 But God's all seeing eye,
But justice overtook her,
 And for these crimes she died.
The tempter and the murderess,
 As you see by these lines,
As gone to face their Maker,
 And to answer for her crime.

Frontispiece 'Execution of Mrs Winsor': a broadsheet probably printed in 1865 for the execution of Charlotte Winsor, sentenced to death for 'the Torquay Murder' (See Chapter 1).

Infanticide

Historical Perspectives on Child Murder
and Concealment, 1550–2000

Edited by
MARK JACKSON

ASHGATE

Published by

Ashgate Publishing Limited
Wey Court East, Union Road
Farnham, Surrey
GU9 7PT
England

Ashgate Publishing Company
Suite 420
101 Cherry Street
Burlington, VT 05401-4405
USA

Ashgate website: http://www.ashgate.com

British Library Cataloguing in Publication Data

Infanticide: historical perspectives on child murder and
    Concealment, 1550–2000
    1. Infanticide–History
    I. Jackson, Mark, 1959–
    346. 1'523'083'09

Library of Congress Cataloging in Publication Data

Infanticide: historical perspectives on child murder and concealment,
    1550–2000 / edited by Mark Jackson
    p. cm.
    Includes bibliographical references.
    1. Infanticide–Great Britain–History. 2. Infanticide–History.
    I. Jackson, Mark, 1959–
    HV6541.G7 I53 2002
    364. 15'23–dc21   2001041372

ISBN 978-0-7546-0318-4
Reprinted 2005, 2009

This book is printed on acid free paper.
Typeset in Sabon by Owain Hammonds, Ceredigion.
Printed and bound in Great Britain by TJI Digital, Padstow, Cornwall

Mixed Sources
Product group from well-managed
forests and other controlled sources
www.fsc.org Cert no. SGS-COC-2482
© 1996 Forest Stewardship Council
FSC

Contents

List of figures and tables   vii

Acknowledgements   viii

Notes on the contributors   ix

Abbreviations   xiii

1   The trial of Harriet Vooght: continuity and change in the history of infanticide   1
     Mark Jackson

2   Accusations of infanticide on the eve of the French Wars of Religion   18
     Luc Racaut

3   Infanticide in early modern England: the Court of Great Sessions at Chester, 1650–1800   35
     J.R. Dickinson and J.A. Sharpe

4   'The unfortunate maid exemplified': Elizabeth Canning and representations of infanticide in eighteenth-century England   52
     Amy L. Masciola

5   Bodies of evidence, states of mind: infanticide, emotion and sensibility in eighteenth-century England   73
     Dana Rabin

6   Infanticide and the erotic plot: a feminist reading of eighteenth-century crime   93
     Johanna Geyer-Kordesch

7   Infanticide, slavery and the politics of reproduction at Cape Colony, South Africa, in the 1820s   128
     Patricia van der Spuy

8   The murder of Thomas Sandles: meanings of a mid-nineteenth-century infanticide   149
     Margaret L. Arnot

9   Getting away with murder? Puerperal insanity, infanticide and the defence plea   168
     Hilary Marland

10 Images and impulses: representations of puerperal insanity
    and infanticide in late Victorian England   193
      Cath Quinn

11 The boundaries of Her Majesty's Pleasure: discharging
    child-murderers from Broadmoor and Perth Criminal
    Lunatic Department, *c.*1860–1920   216
      Jonathan Andrews

12 Legislating for human nature: legal responses to infanticide,
    1860–1938   249
      Tony Ward

13 'Nothing in between': modern cases of infanticide   270
      Julie Wheelwright

    Index   287

List of figures and tables

Figures

Frontispiece: 'Execution of Mrs Winsor', Westcountry Studies
    Library, ME 1866. (Reproduced by kind permission of
    Devon Library and Information Services)   ii

10.1 'E.R. Puerperal Mania', Hering Collection Ref. 3.
    (Reproduced by kind permission of Bethlem Royal
    Hospital Archives and Museum)   207
10.2 'E.R. Convalescence after Puerperal Mania', Hering
    Collection Ref. 3a. (Reproduced by kind permission of
    Bethlem Royal Hospital Archives and Museum)   208
10.3 'M.B. Melancholia. Infanticide', Hering Collection Ref
    22. (Reproduced by kind permission of Bethlem Royal
    Hospital Archives and Museum)   209
10.4 'Louisa L.S.', by Messrs. Barker and Parker, Bethlem Case
    Book 133, folio 61. (Reproduced by kind permission of
    Bethlem Royal Hospital Archives and Museum)   211
10.5 'Joanna C.', Colney Hatch Asylum, Ref
    H12/CH/B11/36pp29. (Reproduced by kind permission
    of Camden and Islington Health Authority and London
    Metropolitan Archives)   212

11.1 'Marjory M.', National Archives of Scotland, NAS
    HH21/48/1. (Reproduced by kind permission of the
    National Archives of Scotland)   227

Tables

3.1 Indictments for infanticide at the Court of Great Sessions,
    Chester, 1650–1800.   38

5.1 The language of emotion and conviction rates, 1723–74   84

11.1 Child victims murdered/assaulted by patients admitted to
    Perth CLD, 1857–1914.   220
11.2 Child victims murdered/assaulted by patients admitted to
    Broadmoor, 1863–1914.   220

Acknowledgements

Many of the chapters in this book were originally presented as papers at a conference held at the University of Exeter in December 1998. I am grateful to the Wellcome Trust for generously supporting that conference. The frontispiece is reproduced by kind permission of Devon Library and Information Services. Figures 1–4 in Chapter Ten are reproduced by kind permission of Bethlem Royal Hospital Archives and Museum. Figure 5 in Chapter Ten is reproduced by kind permission of Camden and Islington Health Authority and London Metropolitan Archives. Figure 1 in Chapter Eleven is reproduced by kind permission of the National Archives of Scotland.

At a personal level, I would like to thank John Smedley at Ashgate for his rapid and constructive engagement with the project, Celia Hoare and the copy-editor at Ashgate for their careful attention to the manuscript, and Jeremy Black at the University of Exeter for his support. As always, I am grateful to Siobhán, Ciara, Riordan, and Conall for creating the organized chaos that drives me to work.

Mark Jackson

Notes on contributors

Jonathan Andrews was awarded his PhD from London University in 1991. He is currently a Senior Lecturer and Wellcome University Award Holder in the History of Medicine at Oxford Brookes University. His publications include (jointly) *The History of Bethlem* (Routledge, 1997), *"They're in the Trade of Lunacy"* ... *The Scottish Lunacy Commissioners* (Wellcome Trust, 1998), and (with Andrew Scull) *Undertaker of the Mind: John Monro and Mad-Doctoring in Eighteenth-Century England* (University of California Press, 2001).

Margaret L. Arnot is a Principal Lecturer in the School of Humanities and Cultural Studies at the University of Surrey, Roehampton. Her current main area of research is gender and crime in Victorian England. She has published articles in this field, as well as co-editing (with Cornelie Usborne) *Gender and Crime in Modern Europe*, (UCL Press, 1999).

J.R. Dickinson took his BA and PhD in History at the University of Liverpool. He has worked on a number of research projects, including two major funded projects with J.A. Sharpe, the first on crime, litigation and the courts in the Isle of Man, *c.*1550–1700, and the second on a regional study of violence in England, 1600–1800. He has published articles on the history of the early modern Isle of Man, and is the author of *The Lordship of Man under the Stanleys: Government and Economy in the Isle of Man, 1580–1704* (Chetham Society, 1996). His future projects include acting as a volume editor for the New History of the Isle of Man.

Johanna Geyer-Kordesch is Research Professor of European Natural History and Medicine at the University of Glasgow. She has written books and numerous articles on women entering the medical profession and on the holistic medical theory of Georg Ernst Stahl (1659–1734). She has also published (with Fiona Macdonald and Andrew Hull) two extensive volumes on the history of medicine in the West of Scotland. Currently, she is working on a project on European natural history and its cultural impact, including its impact on women whose interest in the sciences was sometimes expressed in their own sphere, in painting, interior decoration, gardening and collecting. She is also interested in the impact of storytelling on illness and healing.

Mark Jackson is a Reader in the History of Medicine and Wellcome Award Holder in the Department of History at the University of Exeter. After qualifying in medicine in 1985, he pursued doctoral research in the social history of infanticide. He has also researched the history of feeble-mindedness in Britain and the history of allergic diseases, such as asthma and hay fever, in the modern world. His publications include *New-Born Child Murder: Women, Illegitimacy and the Courts in Eighteenth-Century England* (1996), *The Borderland of Imbecility: Medicine, Society and the Fabrication of the Feeble Mind in Late Victorian and Edwardian England,* (2000), as well as several edited volumes and numerous articles. He was Reviews Editor for *Social History of Medicine* between 1997 and 2001.

Hilary Marland is Senior Lecturer in the Department of History and Director of the Centre for the History of Medicine at the University of Warwick. She is former editor of *Social History of Medicine*, and has published on midwifery, infant and maternal welfare, nineteenth-century medical practice and alternative healing. She is currently writing a monograph with the working title *Dangerous Motherhood: Insanity of Childbirth in the Nineteenth Century*.

Amy L. Masciola is a doctoral candidate in British history at the University of Maryland. Her dissertation, '"I can see by this woman's features that she is capable of any wickedness": representations of criminal women in eighteenth-century England', addresses the material and symbolic implications of the relationship between gender, law and culture. Her awards include the Gordon Prange Award for Excellence in European History (1997–98), the Mary Savage Snouffer Dissertation Fellowship (1998–99), the American Society for Eighteenth-Century Studies/Folger Institute Fellowship (1999), and a Visiting Research Fellowship at the Lewis Walpole Library at Yale University (2001). She is currently working for the National Initiative for a Networked Cultural Heritage.

Cath Quinn is a doctoral student in the Centre for Medical History at the University of Exeter. Having previously undertaken work on asylum histories, she is now expanding her ideas on puerperal insanity to write a more extensive medical and social account of the illness. Her dissertation considers the interaction between medical, legal, social and cultural understandings of puerperal insanity and its impact on the lives of individual women from the late nineteenth to the early twentieth century.

Dana Rabin is Visiting Assistant Professor in the Department of History at the University of Illinois. She received her PhD in History at the University of Michigan in 1996. She is currently completing a manuscript entitled *Crime, the Self, and Legal Responsibility in Eighteenth-Century England* in which she explores the social and cultural history of the insanity plea and its relationship to questions of identity and sensibility during the Enlightenment.

Luc Racaut is resident lecturer for History at Crichton College of the University of Glasgow. His doctoral research, pursued in the St Andrews Reformation Studies Institute, focused on the perception and portrayal of Protestants in the Catholic polemic of the French Wars of Religion, 1557–72. He is interested in the social and cultural history of early modern France and Britain, the question of religious identity in Reformation Europe, and the role of the printing press in the elaboration of distinct identities and cultures in this period. His publications include 'The "Book of Sports" and sabbatarian legislation in Lancashire, 1579–1616', *Northern History*, 33 (1997), 73–87, and 'The polemical use of the Albigensian crusade during the French Wars of Religion', *French History*, 13 (1999), 1–19. He is currently working on a monograph entitled *Catholic Propaganda and Protestant Identity during the French Wars of Religion*.

J.A. Sharpe is Professor of History at the University of York. He has published extensively on the history of crime and punishment and, more recently, on the history of witchcraft in early modern England. His current research interests include further work on these topics, on the legal system of the early modern Isle of Man and on the Dick Turpin legend. He is also author of *Early Modern England: A Social History 1550–1760*, (London, Edward Arnold, 2nd edn, 1997).

Patricia van der Spuy is at the University of Cape Town, completing her doctoral thesis on the life of Cissie Gool, a political activist in Cape Town from the 1930s to the 1950s. Her earlier work explored the gendered nature of slavery at the Cape in the early nineteenth century, focusing on slave work, personal relationships with other slaves and those of other classes, including free workers and slaveholders, and the strategies women used to ensure the freedom of their children, if not themselves, during the era of amelioration. She has also worked as a research assistant in the Centre for Socio-Legal Research, based at UCT and Oxford, been involved in a project exploring the history of illegitimacy in Cape Town, worked as researcher for a number of school textbooks, and co-written a history reader for adult learners.

Tony Ward is Principal Lecturer in Law at De Montfort University Leicester. His historical research has centred mainly on the development of expert medical evidence, especially in relation to criminal responsibility, and he has published a number of articles in this area. Other publications include *Privatization and the Penal System* (with Mick Ryan, 1989) and *Deaths in Custody: International Perspectives* (co-edited with Alison Liebling, 1994). He is currently writing a book on state crime.

Julie Wheelwright is the author of *The Fatal Lover: Mata Hari and the Myth of Women in Espionage* (Collins and Brown, 1992) and *Amazons and Military Maids: Women Who Dressed as Men in Pursuit of Life, Liberty and Happiness* (Pandora Press, 1989). She writes regularly for several national newspapers including *The Independent, Scotland on Sunday, BBC History Magazine, The Times* and the *Vancouver Sun*. A lecturer in journalism at City University, she lives in London with her two daughters.

Abbreviations

CA	Cape Archives, South Africa
CRO	Cheshire Record Office
DRO	Devon Record Office
HH	Perth Gaol, criminal lunatic dept, case book ref./file no. [in National Archives of Scotland]
H.C. Debs.	*House of Commons Debates* [*Hansard*]
H.L. Debs.	*House of Lords Debates* [*Hansard*]
OBSP	*Old Bailey Sessions Papers*
PRO	Public Record Office
PRO CHES	Cheshire Court of Great Sessions, Crown books and rolls [in PRO]
RN	Broadmoor Register No. [in Broadmoor Hospital Medical Records Centre, Berkshire]

CHAPTER ONE

The trial of Harriet Vooght: continuity and change in the history of infanticide

Mark Jackson

At the Devon Lent assize session held at Exeter castle in March 1865, a twenty-one-year-old unmarried domestic servant, Harriet Vooght, was charged with the murder of her new-born child. The judge, in his charge to the grand jury, accepted that 'there were several circumstances tending to show that the death of the child had not been attended with any violence on the part of the mother' but, pointing to medical evidence that 'a piece of tape had been tied around the neck of the child', he directed the jury to 'find a bill for wilful murder and thus place her on her trial for the capital offence'.[1] At the trial, it appeared that on Monday 9 January, Harriet, who had been a nurse in the service of Mr Martin Strickland at Starcross near Exeter, had become ill and retired to bed early. Although her condition seemed to improve, on the Wednesday a surgeon had been called to the house to examine her. Suspicious that she had either given birth to a child or had a miscarriage, he searched the room and found a dead female child in a box. On examining the child's body, the surgeon concluded that death had been caused by strangulation but was not prepared to confirm that the child had 'ever had a separate existence from the mother'. In her defence, it was established that Harriet 'had always borne a kind and humane character' and that she had 'made clothes for the child', thereby dispelling prosecution claims that she had harboured any intent to kill it. On the balance of the evidence, the trial jury acquitted her of murder but found her guilty of concealment of birth. Harriet was sentenced to fifteen months' imprisonment with hard labour.[2]

Harriet Vooght was not the only woman to be accused of concealing or murdering her new-born child in Devon that year. At the same assize session, Margaret Enwright was also accused of murder when, after

---

[1] Details of the trial were reported in: *Exeter Flying Post* (15 March 1865), p. 8; *Exeter Flying Post* (22 March 1865), p. 7. See also the Calendar of Prisoners in the Devon Record Office (DRO) QS 34/21a.

[2] *Exeter Flying Post* (22 March 1865), p. 7; DRO QS 34/21a.

persistently deflecting the suspicions of her fellow servants and her mistress that she had recently given birth, a new-born child was found alive in a locked bag in her room. The child died a short time later and, in the light of medical evidence suggesting that the child's death might have been caused by an act of violence, Margaret was committed to gaol on 1 March 1865 to await trial for murder. At the assizes, however, the indictment was rejected by the grand jury and Margaret was released.[3] In a similar vein, Emilie Raw, a twenty-five-year-old servant from Tormoham, was committed to gaol on 1 December 1864, charged with 'endeavouring to conceal the birth of her child'. She pleaded guilty and was sentenced to three weeks' imprisonment with hard labour.[4]

Significantly, this batch of mid-Victorian trials for concealment and child murder bears striking parallels to other English cases both from the early modern period and from the twentieth century. Throughout the seventeenth and eighteenth centuries, for example, unmarried women (often domestic servants) who concealed their pregnancies and gave birth to illegitimate children alone were often suspected of murder if the children were subsequently found dead. As in the cases of Harriet Vooght, Margaret Enwright, Emilie Raw, and many other women accused of concealment and murder in England during the nineteenth century,[5] early modern trials routinely focused on the marital status of the defendant, on the evidential weight of concealment, on the preparation of child clothes as a defence against a murder charge, on the testimony of doctors as to the viability of the child and the mental and physical state of the mother, and on the character and disposition of the accused woman.[6]

---

[3] Ibid.

[4] Ibid.

[5] For discussion of the central features of infanticide trials in the nineteenth century, see for example: R. Smith, *Trial by Medicine: Insanity and Responsibility in Victorian Trials* (Edinburgh, Edinburgh University Press, 1981); L. Rose, *The Massacre of the Innocents: Infanticide in Great Britain 1800–1939* (London, Routledge and Kegan Paul, 1986); A.R. Higginbotham, '"Sin of the age": Infanticide and Illegitimacy in Victorian London', in K.O. Garrigan (ed.), *Victorian Scandals: Representations of Gender and Class* (Athens, Ohio University Press, 1992), pp. 257–88; M.L. Arnot, 'Gender in focus: infanticide in England 1840–1880' (PhD thesis, Essex, 1994); C.L. Krueger, 'Literary defenses and medical prosecutions: representing infanticide in nineteenth-century Britain', *Victorian Studies*, 40 (1997), 271–94. See also in this book Chapters Seven, Eight, Nine and Ten.

[6] For further discussion of early modern trials for new-born child murder or infanticide, see: M. Jackson, *New-Born Child Murder: Women, Illegitimacy and the Courts in Eighteenth-Century England* (Manchester, Manchester University Press, 1996); P. Hoffer and N.E.H. Hull, *Murdering Mothers: Infanticide in England and New England, 1558–1803* (New York, New York University Press, 1981); L. Gowing,

As many recent cases in England and North America have shown, the main evidential issues considered at the trial of Harriet Vooght have also been reproduced in cases of suspected infanticide in the late twentieth and early twenty-first centuries. The most striking modern case, and certainly the case that captured the greatest public and media attention on both sides of the Atlantic, was perhaps that of Caroline Beale, a young unmarried Englishwoman who was discovered in September 1994 leaving America with the body of a dead child hidden under her coat. As the investigation into, and the furore over, the death of Caroline's child (and into the recent deaths of other new-born children) demonstrate, modern judges and juries remain preoccupied with the marital status of the mother, with concealment of pregnancy and birth, with the mother's moral character, and with medical and psychological attempts to reveal her physical and mental state during pregnancy and at the moment of birth.[7]

Strikingly, apparent historical continuities in cases of suspected child murder across many centuries have not been confined to events in the courtroom. In a wider context, many of the social, legal, political and cultural concerns related to the supposed murder of new-born children also demonstrate remarkable historical constancy. For example, just as William Hunter in the late eighteenth century denounced the fathers of

---

'Secret births and infanticide in seventeenth-century England', *Past and Present* 156 (1997), 87–115; M. Jackson, 'Suspicious infant deaths: the statute of 1624 and medical evidence at coroners' inquests', in M. Clark and C. Crawford (eds), *Legal Medicine in History* (Cambridge, Cambridge University Press, 1994), pp. 64–86; Mark Jackson, 'Developing Medical Expertise: Medical Practitioners and the Suspected Murders of New-Born Children', in R. Porter (ed.), *Medicine in the Enlightenment* (Amsterdam, Rodopi, 1995), pp. 145–65; M. Jackson, 'Childbirth's mental toll', *The Times* (Tuesday 13 June 1995), 14; M. Jackson, 'Infanticide: historical perspectives', *New Law Journal* (22 March 1996), 416–20; M. Jackson, '"Something more than blood": Conflicting Accounts of Pregnancy Loss in Eighteenth-century England', in R. Cecil (ed.), *The Anthropology of Pregnancy Loss* (Oxford, Berg Publishers Ltd, 1996), pp. 197–214; M. Francus, 'Monstrous mothers, monstrous societies: infanticide and the rule of law in Restoration and eighteenth-century England', *Eighteenth-Century Life*, 20 (1997), 133–56. See also in this book Chapters Three, Four, Five and Six.

[7] For further details of the case of Caroline Beale, and of the parallels between modern and early modern cases, see: Jackson, 'Childbirth's mental toll'; Jackson, 'Infanticide: historical perspectives'; J. Wheelwright, 'A moment as a mother', *The Guardian* (13 May 1995); J. McDonagh, 'Infanticide and the nation: the case of Caroline Beale', *New Formations*, 32 (1997), 11–21; D. Campbell, *A Stranger and Afraid: The Story of Caroline Beale* (London, Macmillan, 1997); J. Wheelwright, 'Mothers who kill', *Vancouver Sun*, (4 December 1999). See also Chapter Thirteen below. On the continuation of social concerns about unmarried motherhood, see J. Lewis and J. Welshman, 'The issue of never-married motherhood in Britain, 1920–70', *Social History of Medicine*, 10 (1997), 401–18.

supposedly murdered illegitimate children as the real culprits in these
cases for having seduced and deceived credulous young women,[8] so too
mid-nineteenth-century commentators regarded women accused of
concealing and murdering their new-born children as the victims of men
who had seduced and ultimately betrayed them. Such attitudes to the
criminal responsibility of men and to the vulnerability of women, which
found expression in much contemporary literature, were partly
responsible for the persistently high acquittal rates for infanticide
throughout the eighteenth and nineteenth centuries.[9]

At another level, eighteenth-century anxieties about the increasing
leniency of juries and about the extent to which the law was no
longer acting as a deterrent in these cases were reproduced in the
mid-nineteenth century. Thus, legal debates at the time of the Royal
Commission on Capital Punishment in the 1860s about the need to
revise the laws relating to infanticide clearly echoed many of the
arguments about repealing the law nearly one hundred years earlier
in the 1770s, when proponents of reform had not only contended
that the heavy burden of guilt in the case of unmarried women
accused of murder was out of line with public sympathy for such
women but also warned that a number of legal loopholes were being
exploited by the defence in order to encourage juries to acquit. In
both periods, the overwhelming fear expressed by the judiciary, and
ultimately by the legislature, was that the sovereignty of the law was
being undermined.[10]

Within a purely English context, the nature of the evidence
considered in court, attitudes to women accused of concealing and
murdering their children, and concerns about the authority of the law
show remarkable parallels or continuities from the early modern
period through to the late twentieth century. However, within the

---

[8] W. Hunter, 'On the uncertainty of the signs of murder, in the case of bastard children',
      Medical Observations and Inquiries, 6 (1874), 266–90. See also the discussion in
      Jackson, *New-Born Child Murder*, pp. 110–32.
[9] On the sexual politics of debates about infanticide in the middle decades of the
      nineteenth century, see: Higginbotham, 'Sin of the age'; M.L. Arnot, 'Infant death,
      child care and the state: the baby-farming scandal and the first Infant Life Protection
      Legislation of 1872', *Continuity and Change*, 9 (1994), 271–311. On literary
      representations of infanticidal women, see: Krueger, 'Literary defenses and medical
      prosecutions'; J. McDonagh, 'Infanticide and the Boundaries of Culture from Hume to
      Arnold', in S.C. Greenfield and C. Barash (eds), *Inventing Maternity: Politics, Science,
      and Literature, 1650–1865* (Lexington, Kentucky, University of Kentucky Press, 1999),
      pp. 215–37.
[10] See: Jackson, *New-Born Child Murder*, pp. 158–81; Smith, *Trial by Medicine*, pp.
      143–50; G.K. Behlmer, *Child Abuse and Moral Reform in England, 1870–1908*
      (Stanford, Stanford University Press, 1982), pp. 19–20.

history of infanticide more generally, there are equally conspicuous parallels across space. As a number of detailed historical studies have shown, the central features of English trials for infanticide have been mirrored in cases from many other geographical settings. Thus, the prosecutions of women for killing their new-born children in France, Germany, North America, Ireland and Poland have shared significant features with cases from England throughout the early modern and modern periods. Whenever and wherever suspicious child deaths have been investigated and evidence assessed, the narratives of birth and death devised by suspects, communities, courts and legislatures have almost uniformly given privileged treatment to the marital status and sexual behaviour of the mother, while giving particular weight to evidence of concealment of the gestation, birth and death of the child.[11] Indeed, persistent and widespread preoccupations with the evidential weight of concealment by unmarried mothers, and with the social and legal implications of secrecy, constitute one of the most remarkable features of the history of infanticide.

There are a number of ways in which such evident historical and geographical continuities can be explained. At one level, parallels between early modern cases and cases from the nineteenth century, such as that of Harriet Vooght, can be traced to continuities in the legal framework within which women were prosecuted. Throughout the seventeenth and eighteenth centuries, single women were tried under the terms of a statute of 1624 in which concealment of death was taken as

---

[11] W. Langer, 'Infanticide: a historical survey', *History of Childhood Quarterly*, 1 (1974), 353–66; S. Faber, 'Infanticide, especially in eighteenth-century Amsterdam: with some references to Van der Keessel', *Acta Juridica* (1976), 253–67; C. Smout, 'Aspects of sexual behaviour in nineteenth-century Scotland', in P. Laslett, K. Oosterveen and R. M. Smith (eds), *Bastardy and its Comparative History* (London, Edward Arnold, 1980), pp. 192–216; Hoffer and Hull, *Murdering Mothers*; K. Wrightson, 'Infanticide in European history', *Criminal Justice History*, 3 (1982), 1–20; R. Schulte, 'Infanticide in rural Bavaria in the nineteenth century', in H. Medick and D.W. Sabean (eds), *Interest and Emotion: Essays on the Study of Family and Kinship* (Cambridge, Cambridge University Press, 1984), pp. 77–102; Marcin Kamler, 'Infanticide in the towns of the Kingdom of Poland in the second half of the 16th and the first half of the 17th century', *Acta Polonia Historica*, 58 (1988), 33–4; J. Kelly, 'Infanticide in eighteenth-century Ireland', *Irish Economic and Social History*, 19 (1992), 5–26; M.N. Wessling, 'Infanticide trials and forensic medicine: Württemberg, 1757–93', in Clark and Crawford (eds) *Legal Medicine in History*, pp. 117–44; S. Kord, 'Women as children, women as childkillers: poetic images of infanticide in eighteenth-century Germany', *Eighteenth-Century Studies*, 26 (1993), 449–66; A. Rowlands, 'In great secrecy: the crime of infanticide in Rothenburg ob der Tauber, 1501–1618', *German History*, 15 (1997), 179–99; E.C. Green, 'Infanticide and infant abandonment in the New South: Richmond, Virginia, 1865–1915', *Journal of Family History*, 24 (1999), 187–211.

evidence of murder.[12] The construction of this statute, enacted during a period of strident concerns about the rising level of illegitimacy and its impact on the poor rates, was firmly shaped by beliefs that single women (rather than married women) were concealing their pregnancies and murdering their children in order to evade the shame and punishment associated with mothering an illegitimate child. For much of the seventeenth century, effective implementation of the 1624 statute resulted in the conviction and hanging of many unmarried mothers.[13]

By the middle decades of the eighteenth century, shifting attitudes to the certainty of the medical evidence, reappraisals of the character of accused women and the emergence of new rules of evidence combined to undermine support for the 1624 statute. In the absence of an alternative verdict, the majority of single women were acquitted of murder. As a result, during the latter half of the eighteenth century, growing concern at the manner in which the terms of the statute were being ignored by juries led several commentators and members of parliament to push for reform. In particular, proponents of reform argued that the more certain application of a suitable (that is, lesser) punishment would more effectively discourage women from concealing and murdering their illegitimate children.[14]

Efforts to repeal the 1624 statute in the 1770s ultimately floundered, largely as the result of persistent judicial opposition to reforming the criminal law. However, in 1803 the statute was repealed as part of sweeping conservative reforms introduced by Lord Ellenborough. The 1803 statute returned the trials of unmarried women to common-law rules of evidence, in which the prosecution once again had to establish that a dead child had been born alive rather than being able to rely merely on evidence of concealment to prove murder. However, in cases where the murder of an illegitimate child was not proven, the statute gave juries the option of returning an alternative verdict of 'concealment of birth', for which an unmarried woman could be sentenced to a maximum of two years in prison.[15]

---

[12] 'An Act to prevent the Destroying and Murthering of Bastard Children', 1624, 21 Jac. I c. 27. For further discussion of the context in which the statute was passed, see Jackson, *New-Born Child Murder*, pp. 29–59.

[13] See: J.A. Sharpe, *Crime in Seventeenth-Century England: A County Study* (Cambridge, Cambridge University Press, 1983); J.M. Beattie, *Crime and the Courts in England 1660–1800* (Oxford, Clarendon Press, 1986); K. Wrightson, 'Infanticide in earlier seventeenth-century England', *Local Population Studies*, 15 (1975), 10–22.

[14] For further discussion of debates about reform in the 1770s, see Jackson, *New-Born Child Murder*, pp. 158–68.

[15] 'An Act for the further Prevention of malicious shooting, etc', 1803, 43 Geo. III c. 58. See Jackson, *New-Born Child Murder*, pp. 168–81.

Significantly, while the 1803 statute can be construed as a moment of change when early modern preoccupations with concealment as evidence of murder were clearly weakened, Lord Ellenborough's Act nevertheless embodied many earlier presumptions about single women, illegitimacy and concealment. These fixations – with concealment in particular – persisted in subsequent amendments to the law. In the 1828 Offences against the Person Act, disposing of the body of a dead child in order to conceal its birth, even if the child was still-born, became a separate offence for which both unmarried and married women could be imprisoned for two years, with or without hard labour.[16] In 1861, in a clause that remains in force at the time of writing, the offence of concealment was extended further to include men as well as women.[17] Although these amendments to the law can be seen as indicative of substantial shifts in attitudes towards the responsibility of men and women in these cases and towards the legitimacy of censuring the behaviour of married as well as unmarried mothers, they also mark striking continuities in legal presumptions about women who kept their pregnancies secret and concealed the births and deaths of their children.

Within the present context, it is important to recognize that the legal framework within which Harriet Vooght and many other women were tried in the nineteenth century was in many ways a powerful legacy of the 1624 statute, in which early modern anxieties about the sexual behaviour of single women, illegitimacy and concealment had been crystallized in legislation. While the impact of enduring legal formulations of new-born child murder partly explains evident similarities between early modern and modern trials for infanticide, it may also help to explain geographical parallels. Early modern and modern English legislators were acutely aware of legislation being framed elsewhere in Europe and supposedly borrowed from other jurisdictions.[18] In addition, settlers in America in the seventeenth century clearly carried with them both general Puritan concerns about sexual behaviour, illegitimacy and the morality of concealment, as well as a more particular knowledge of the terms of the 1624 statute.[19]

---

[16] 'An Act for consolidating and amending the Statutes in England relative to Offences against the Person', 1828, 9 Geo. IV c. 31, s. 14.

[17] 'An Act to consolidate and amend the Statute Law of England and Ireland relating to Offences against the Person', 1861, 24 & 25 Vict. c. 100, s. 60.

[18] It is likely, for example, that Jacobean legislators in 1624 were influenced by existing European pronouncements aimed at preventing the murder of new-born illegitimate children. And in debates on repealing the 1624 statute in the 1770s, members of parliament were clearly conversant with European laws on the subject. See Jackson, *New-Born Child Murder*, pp. 35, 164.

[19] Hoffer and Hull, *Murdering Mothers*, pp. 33–64.

Analysis of the legal parameters within which women were prosecuted for murdering their children suggests immediately another level of explanation for historical continuities. The persistent statutory emphasis on concealment and the enduring link between illegitimacy and murder reflect not only the inherent conservatism of legislatures (in which new statutes often borrowed the language and spirit of earlier legislation), but also the presence of on-going social anxieties about the economic and moral implications of the sexual behaviour of young unmarried female servants as well as the social realities for many women throughout the seventeenth, eighteenth and nineteenth centuries. In the early modern period, the pressures on young servant women to conceal their pregnancies and births – thereby raising neighbourhood suspicions of murder – derived from their fears of losing their place in service if the pregnancy was discovered and they were unable to fulfil their duties. At the same time, social and legal responses to the deaths of children in such circumstances were framed by concerns about single women, illegitimacy, rising poor rates, the preservation of family morality, the behaviour of domestic servants, the double standard of sexuality and attitudes to the role of the law. Although the nineteenth century witnessed significant social and political changes, such as sweeping revisions of the poor law in the 1830s and 1840s, these anxieties on the part of unmarried servants and their families, neighbours and employers clearly persisted. As a number of historical studies have suggested, concerns about both the sexual morality of servants and rising poor rates continued to create the context in which single women concealed their pregnancies, while at the same time such concerns consolidated the perceived links between illegitimacy and infanticide, and ensured that the majority of women accused of murdering their new-born children in the nineteenth century were domestic servants, just as they had been in previous periods.[20]

Significantly, the impact of amendments to the poor law raises the possibility that shifting social and political contexts may have resulted, paradoxically, in similar patterns of suspicion and prosecution across both time and space. From an English perspective, it is clear that by the 1860s – when Harriet Vooght was tried at Exeter – the precise climate in which women were prosecuted for murdering their new-born children had changed. In the first instance, the introduction of the new Poor Law in 1834 and its amendment in 1844 clearly made it more difficult for

---

[20] G.K. Behlmer, 'Deadly motherhood: infanticide and medical opinion in mid-Victorian England', *Journal of the History of Medicine*, 34 (1979), 403–27; J.R. Gillis, 'Servants, sexual relations, and the risks of illegitimacy in London, 1801–1900', *Feminist Studies*, 5 (1979), 142–73; Higginbotham, 'Sin of the age'; Arnot, 'Infant death'.

unmarried women not only to obtain outdoor relief but also to affiliate their illegitimate children. In addition, other concerns were appearing which altered the way suspicious infant deaths were approached by local communities, social commentators and legal authorities. Attitudes to working mothers and the care of their children were changing, novel concerns about the health and wealth of the population were emerging, the economic value of children as both capital and investment was under debate, the precise legal construction of the crime and the verdicts open to juries had changed, and there was increasing medical discussion about the mental vulnerability of women.[21] Strikingly however, these differing social, political and cultural factors appear to have reinforced, rather than displaced, the early modern connections that had been constructed between single women, illegitimacy, concealment and murder, and as a consequence such factors increased, rather than decreased, the pressures on unmarried domestic servants to conceal their pregnancies and the births and deaths of their children.[22]

Of course, the presence of historical and geographical continuities and parallels in the history of infanticide should not blind historians to equally obvious changes across time and differences across space. For example, it is clear that the history of infanticide in Japan, China, India and some other countries, where female children have apparently been routinely killed at birth more frequently than male children, follows a trajectory distinct from the Western tradition.[23] Within a more narrow British context, shifts over time are equally apparent. In the first place, it is clear that both the language and precise medico-legal focus of debates shifted from the early modern to the modern period. In the seventeenth and eighteenth centuries, doctors, lawyers, jurists and social commentators were predominantly interested in the concealed deaths of new-born (rather than older) children, partly because of the forensic problems associated with proving live birth in such cases and partly because of the perceived links between new-born child murder (as it was usually called) and a range of social problems associated with illegitimacy and unmarried motherhood.

---

[21] Many of these issues peaked in the late nineteenth and early twentieth centuries, substantially altering the social and political context in which infanticidal mothers were treated by the courts. See, for example, the discussions in: Behlmer, *Child Abuse*; A. Davin, 'Imperialism and motherhood', *History Workshop Journal*, 5 (1978), 9–65.

[22] It may also be the case, of course, that the ability of quite different social and political situations to produce similar consequences in such cases partly accounts for geographical parallel in trials for infanticide.

[23] See, for example, the brief overview in S.E. Pitt and E.M. Bale, 'Neonaticide, infanticide, and filicide: a review of the literature', *Bulletin of the American Academy of Psychiatry and Law*, 23 (1995), 375–86.

In the early nineteenth century, forensic and public interest remained focused largely on the suspicious deaths of children at birth but the term infanticide was increasingly used to describe not only the murder of new-born children but also sometimes the killing of older children. During the course of the nineteenth century, however, a number of new concerns and preoccupations arose. Although medico-legal debates about the suspicious deaths of illegitimate children at birth persisted, anxieties about the practice of 'baby-farming' and medical debates about the mitigating effects of puerperal insanity combined to concentrate forensic, media and public attention on the deaths of older, as well as new-born, children and on the actions of married, as well as unmarried, mothers.

While the courts had occasionally considered evidence of maternal insanity in the early modern period, medical testimony as to the mother's state of mind at and after the birth came to dominate Victorian debates, largely replacing medical evidence derived from the physical examination of the bodies of the mother and child.[24] Significantly, as the understanding of infanticidal women became increasingly medicalized in this way and forensic interest concentrated on puerperal insanity as a defence against a charge of murdering an older (as well as a new-born) infant, the traditional emphasis on concealment as evidence of murder began to recede. As the prosecution lawyer at the trial of Elizabeth Duff maintained in his opening speech in 1866, since the child had been fifteen months old, 'this was not a case in which the jury would be able to escape from a verdict of guilty or not guilty of murder by any reference to concealment of birth'.[25]

The meaning of the term infanticide shifted again at the start of the twentieth century, partly in response to growing acceptance of the puerperal insanity plea and partly as the result of several highly publicized trials.[26] Under the terms of the Infanticide Acts of 1922 and 1938, infanticide became a separate offence – a form of manslaughter, rather than murder. In the 1938 Act, which remains in force at the time of writing, infanticide was defined as 'any wilful act or omission' on the

---

[24] The lung test, for example, which was popular in the mid- to late-eighteenth century as a means of identifying live birth, generally fell out of favour during the nineteenth century: Behlmer, 'Deadly motherhood', 410; Jackson, *New-Born Child Murder*, pp. 84–109. On mid-Victorian approaches to the insanity defence in these and other cases, see: Smith, *Trial by Medicine*, pp. 143-60; J.P. Eigen, *Witnessing Insanity: Madness and Mad-Doctors in the English Court* (New Haven, Yale University Press, 1995); P. Guarnieri, *A Case of Child Murder: Law and Science in Nineteenth-Century Tuscany* (Cambridge, Polity Press, 1993); and Chapters Nine and Ten in this volume.

[25] *Exeter Flying Post* (14 March 1866), p. 8.

[26] See Chapter Twelve in this volume.

part of a mother which caused the death of her child under the age of twelve months, while 'the balance of her mind was disturbed by reason of her not having fully recovered from the effect of giving birth to the child or by reason of the effect of lactation'.[27] In recent years, while a variety of terms (such as neonaticide, filicide and infanticide) have been used on both sides of the Atlantic to describe the killing of children at different ages, infanticide remains the term most commonly employed by both modern commentators and historians to describe the murder of young children.

It is also clear that, over the past 400 years or so, both prosecution and conviction rates for (and indeed public interest in) infanticide have fluctuated in England. In the decades following the passage of the 1624 statute, both prosecution and conviction rates were high. During the eighteenth century, conviction rates certainly fell and there is evidence to suggest that in some areas prosecution rates also declined.[28] Although women were only rarely executed for infanticide throughout the nineteenth century, increasing numbers of women who had concealed their pregnancies and the births and deaths of their children were punished by the courts, following the introduction of an alternative verdict in 1803. In the late nineteenth century, while prosecutions and convictions remained uncommon, public and medico-legal debate was often sparked by particular crises, such as the baby-farming scandal of the 1860s and 1870s, or by outstanding cases. This pattern has persisted into the twentieth and twenty-first centuries, when occasional cases such as that of Caroline Beale have prompted lawyers, doctors, politicians and journalists to re-evaluate the particular social, political, moral and legal framework within which such crimes have been committed and judged.

Significantly, while the 1865 Devon assize sessions can be used to illustrate remarkable continuities in the history of child murder and concealment, they also highlight a critical period of change. At the same session at which Harriet Vooght was tried for murdering her new-born child, Mary Jane Harris and Charlotte Winsor were prosecuted for the murder of Harris's four-month-old son, Thomas. In February 1865, the body of a young boy was found wrapped up in an old copy of the *Western Times* near the grounds of Torre Abbey on the outskirts of Torquay. Routine police enquiries revealed that Mary Jane Harris, a twenty-three-year-old domestic servant in Torquay, had given birth in the previous October. On being questioned, Harris admitted that she had given birth to

---

[27] Infanticide Act, 1922, 12 & 13 Geo. V c. 18; Infanticide Act, 1938, 1 & 2 Geo. VI, c. 36.

[28] See Chapter Three in this volume.

a child and informed the police that she had put him out to nurse for three shillings a week with Charlotte Winsor, a forty-five-year-old married woman who lived in a cottage set back from the road between Torquay and Newton Abbot. However, Winsor clearly no longer had the child and when Winsor's grand-daughter, Selina Pratt, testified that she had not seen Thomas since one evening in early February when Mary Jane Harris had visited her grandmother's house and she, Selina, had been sent out on an errand, Harris and Winsor were arrested for murder.[29]

At the trial at the Lent assize session in 1865, a variety of evidence was presented. The testimony of several witnesses not only linked Harris to the child but also raised significant doubts about her claims that the child had recently been removed from Winsor's house to one of Harris's aunts who lived near Chudleigh. It also transpired that Harris had had a child previously by the same father, 'a well-to-do farmer' in the area. Although the medical evidence failed to establish a cause of death, the examining surgeon concluded that the child had 'died from unnatural causes'. At the end of the second day of the trial, after hearing closing speeches from the defence lawyers as well as testimony to Harris's good character from a previous employer in Teignmouth, the jury retired at seven o'clock in the evening. After deliberating for five hours, the jury was unable to agree a verdict, eight jurors apparently favouring acquittal and four preferring conviction. The jury was discharged and Harris and Winsor were returned to gaol to await a re-trial.[30]

Five months later, at the summer assizes, Harris and Winsor returned to court. The evidence presented to the jury remained much the same, except that on this occasion Mary Jane Harris had struck a deal with the prosecution counsel, Isidore Carter, and agreed to give evidence against Winsor. Harris's testimony proved influential. She claimed in court not only that Winsor had offered to kill Thomas for £5 but also that Winsor had boasted of having killed young unwanted children for money on several previous occasions.[31] According to Harris, on Sunday 9 February she had gone to Winsor's house to see Thomas.

> I went into her bedroom; the child was in the bed with her. She said, "I've made it all right with my husband. I shan't keep the child after the quarter." She said if I would give her the 5l. she would do away with the child, and asked me if I would come over one day in the week and take away the child. I said she might if she liked. I asked

[29] Details of the case are taken from: *Exeter Flying Post* (22 March 1865), p. 7; *The Times* (20 March 1865), p. 11; DRO QS 34/21a.

[30] Ibid.

[31] Details of events at the second trial are taken from: *The Times* (29 July 1865), p. 12; *The Times* (31 July 1865), p. 11; *Exeter and Plymouth Gazette*, Supplement (4 August 1865), p. 1.

her how she could do it she said she could get something at the chymist's ... I went out on the 9th to the prisoner's, and got there at half-past 3; the baby was tied in the chair, and the granddaughter playing with it. The prisoner was sitting on a stool. After talking a little time she sent the little girl out. After she was gone the prisoner said she did not do it before I came out, because if I told on her I must tell on myself, for one would be as bad as the other. I said I would never tell if we were never found out. She asked me if she should do it. I asked her how she would do it. She said put it between the bed tics. She then took the child into the girl Pratt's bedroom. I did not go. She stayed ten minutes; then came back without the baby. She asked me to look in; she said it would soon die. I looked in, and saw the bed made, but no child. The child did not cry ... The girl Pratt came back and staid a short time, but was sent out again by the prisoner to fetch some buns. The girl went out and the prisoner said she must make haste, as her girl would soon be back. She went out of the room and came back with the baby. It was dead.[32]

Under cross-examination, Harris admitted that she had seen the child 'barbarously murdered', but denied ever having given it poison (as Winsor had claimed) and insisted that she had wanted the child to live. She also testified that the child's father, Farmer Nicholls, whom she had known for a number of years, had given her some money towards Thomas's upkeep but only until the child had been taken to be looked after by Winsor.[33] Harris's statement apparently 'created the greatest sensation in a very crowded court'.[34] Winsor's defence lawyer immediately attempted to limit the damage caused by Harris's testimony, not only pointing out that Harris had much to gain by accusing his client and was therefore untrustworthy as a witness, but also insisting that it was in Winsor's financial interest for the child to have lived. Having been warned by the judge to make sure that other evidence corroborated Harris's version of events, the jurors retired to consider their verdict. After eighty minutes, they found Charlotte Winsor guilty of murder.[35] Winsor was initially sentenced to death but, after protracted arguments about the legality of the re-trial and the admission of Harris's evidence, she was eventually granted a conditional pardon and her sentence was commuted to penal servitude for life.[36]

---

[32] *The Times* (29 July 1865), p. 12.

[33] Harris also received three shillings and sixpence each week from Nicholls to look after their older child.

[34] *The Times* (29 July 1865), p. 12.

[35] *The Times* (31 July 1865), p. 11.

[36] See: *The Times* (26 January 1866), p. 5; *The Times* (10 February 1866), p. 5; *The Times* (12 February 1866), p. 10; *The Times* (13 February 1866), pp. 5, 12; *The Times* (14 February 1866), p. 12; *The Times* (24 May 1866), p. 12; *Exeter Flying Post* (14 February 1866), p. 5; *Exeter Flying Post* (16 May 1866), p. 3.

Mary Jane Harris remained in prison until she was formally acquitted by a jury, on the direction of the Home Secretary, at the Devon Lent assizes in March 1866.[37]

The Torquay murder, as it became known, was rapidly sensationalized in the local and national press and in broadsides, such as the one printed in 1865 erroneously celebrating Winsor's execution (see frontispiece).[38] Journalists regularly decried both Harris's barbarity in farming out her child to Winsor while she worked and the manner in which Winsor appeared to have made a regular trade of child murder.[39] Shocked commentators also deplored the extent to which infanticide, often referred to as 'the great crime of the age',[40] had become 'nearly as common as measles'[41] in a supposedly civilized country, and expressed their anxieties at the likely discovery of further atrocities: 'If quiet and green Devonshire discloses such villany, what would the streets of London not reveal?'[42] Such fears were prescient. After considerable public anxiety over, and medical investigation into, the prevalence of infanticide and the hidden dangers of what became known as 'baby-farming' in the late 1860s,[43] the discovery of the fatal neglect of young children being nursed by Margaret Waters and Sarah Ellis in Brixton in 1870 initiated further public uproar, precipitated the founding of the Infant Life Protection Society and the establishment of a Select Committee on Infant Life Protection in that year, and ultimately provided the momentum for the passage of the first Infant Life Protection Act in 1872.[44]

As in the case of Harriet Vooght, the trials of Mary Jane Harris, Charlotte Winsor, Margaret Waters and Sarah Ellis clearly reveal parallels between mid-Victorian debates about infanticide and some earlier preoccupations – in particular, long-standing concerns about the detrimental effects of wet-nursing and about the financial, as well as the moral, vulnerability of young domestic servants. Yet these cases, and the outcry that they generated, also reflected a constellation of

[37] *Exeter Flying Post* (14 February 1866), p. 5; *Exeter Flying Post* (14 March 1866), p. 7; DRO QS 34/23.

[38] 'Execution of Mrs Winsor', Westcountry Studies Library, Exeter, ME 1866.

[39] See, for example: *Exeter Flying Post* (2 August 1865), p. 5; *The Times* (2 August 1865), p. 9; *Exeter and Plymouth Gazette* (4 August 1865), p. 5.

[40] *Exeter and Plymouth Gazette* (11 August 1865), p. 5.

[41] *Exeter and Plymouth Gazette* (4 August 1865), p. 5.

[42] Quoted from the *Daily Telegraph* in the *Exeter Flying Post* (2 August 1865), p. 5.

[43] See, for example, J. Greenwood, *The Seven Curses of London* (Oxford, Basil Blackwell, [1869] 1981), pp. 21–38. See also D.L. Haller, 'Bastardy and baby-farming in Victorian England', http://www.loyno.edu/~history/journal/1989-0/haller.htm.

[44] For further discussion, see: Arnot, 'Infant death'; Behlmer, 'Deadly motherhood'; Behlmer, *Child Abuse*.

novel concerns that were emerging in the middle decades of the nineteenth century. The prosecution of Harris and Winsor for the death of Harris's son was fuelled by increasingly contentious debates about the ability of working mothers to care adequately for their children, about the financial independence of women, about class and gender relations, about the nurturing and preservation of healthy children for the future industrial and military strength of the nation, about the family as a legitimate site for state intervention, and about the standards of behaviour expected of citizens in a modern, civilized, industrialized society.[45]

The trials of women for child murder at the Devon assizes in 1865 therefore not only testify to evident continuities in the history of infanticide, but also shed light on a critical period of historical change. It is the central aim of this book to offer new insights into both continuity and change in the history of child murder through a series of original and detailed studies. Individually, subsequent chapters stand alone as microstudies of infanticide in particular jurisdictions at particular moments in time. Collectively, however, they provide a telling commentary on the dynamics and determinants of continuity and change in the history of child murder and concealment from the late sixteenth century through to the late twentieth century.

In Chapter 2, Luc Racaut explores accusations of infanticide during the French Wars of Religion in the late sixteenth century, and highlights three recurring features of early modern infanticide: firstly, the possibility that suspicions of infanticide could be aroused and maintained in the absence of substantive evidence of murder, that is without a dead body; secondly, the extent to which infanticide accusations were embedded in political and religious contexts; and thirdly, the manner in which concealment and secrecy were construed as suggestive of criminal activity. He also cautions against assuming that accusations of infanticide have always been directed at women.

The next three chapters explore the history of child murder during the seventeenth and eighteenth centuries, when public, medical and legal debates were largely concerned with the suspicious deaths of new-born children. J.R. Dickinson and J.A. Sharpe set the scene by charting fluctuating prosecution and conviction rates and exploring the central

---

[45] For a discussion of some of these issues and their impact, see: Davin, 'Imperialism and motherhood'; Behlmer, *Child Abuse*; J. Lewis, *Women in England 1870–1950: Sexual Divisions and Social Change* (Sussex, Wheatsheaf Books, 1984); C. Smart, 'Disruptive bodies and unruly sex: the regulation of reproduction and sexuality in the nineteenth century', in C. Smart (ed.), *Regulating Womanhood: Historical Essays on Marriage, Motherhood and Sexuality* (London, Routledge, 1992); Arnot, 'Gender in focus'; McDonagh, 'Infanticide and the nation'.

features of infanticide trials between 1650 and 1800. Drawing on their recent research on previously unused records from the Court of Great Sessions at Chester, they expose contemporary preoccupations, in particular with concealment, illegitimacy and unmarried motherhood. In Chapter 4, Amy Masciola vividly analyses how such preoccupations operated in the singular, and extremely high-profile, mid-eighteenth-century case of Elizabeth Canning, who was suspected of infanticide after disappearing inexplicably for a month in 1753. In Chapter 5, Dana Rabin explores the growing tendency in the late eighteenth century for trial juries to acquit unmarried women accused of murdering their illegitimate children and the gradual legal acceptance of psychological pleas, within the context of novel Enlightenment attitudes to emotion, sensibility and responsibility. She argues that the 'language of emotion' adopted by defendants and witnesses in the eighteenth century effectively prepared the ground for the increasing reliance on puerperal insanity as a mitigating factor in the middle decades of the nineteenth century.

In Chapter 6, Johanna Geyer-Kordesch mobilizes a rich variety of legal and literary sources, largely from Germany, to argue that the trials of women for infanticide in the early modern period (and indeed the modern period) must be understood in a broad cultural, social and political context. In particular, she is keen to emphasize that narratives of concealment of pregnancy and infanticide, whether in the medico-legal records or in literature, cannot be understood without close attention to the 'erotic plot' that has defined and constrained women at all times and in all places.

The following four chapters continue many of these themes into the nineteenth century. In Chapter 7, Patricia van der Spuy closely examines two cases that clearly remind us that, while infanticide trials in England were dominated by concerns about class and gender, in early nineteenth-century South Africa they were also fundamentally shaped by racial tensions. In Chapter 8, Meg Arnot carefully reconstructs events leading to the 1849 trial of Hannah Sandles for the murder of her two-month-old baby the previous year, maintaining in particular that such cases demonstrate the vulnerability of certain women in the face of the early Victorian criminal justice system. In Chapters 9 and 10, Hilary Marland and Cath Quinn continue some of the themes introduced by Dana Rabin, utilizing local cases as well as photographic images to explore the manner in which trials of women for child murder in the second half of the nineteenth century were transformed by growing obstetric and psychiatric interest in the clinical features, and forensic consequences, of puerperal insanity.

While debates about the mitigating effects of insanity before, during and after birth clearly had an impact in court, contemporary understandings of the natural history of puerperal insanity also influenced the subsequent management of infanticidal women in the late nineteenth century. As Jonathan Andrews demonstrates in Chapter 11, the discharge of women committed to Broadmoor and Perth Criminal Lunatic Department was determined by a wide range of biological and social factors, one of which was the possibility that a woman might relapse and re-offend. Debates about the insanity and criminal responsibility of women also contributed to the passage of the Infanticide Acts in 1922 and 1938. However, as Tony Ward argues in the penultimate chapter, reform of the law was by no means self-evident. Indeed, tensions within legal thinking clearly made the redefinition of infanticide as a non-capital offence extremely difficult to achieve on the part of the legislature.

In the final chapter, Julie Wheelwright's analysis of cases of infanticide and child abandonment in the late twentieth century revisits several key themes that run through the history of child murder in the last four centuries. As her interviews with women accused of infanticide – and with those who treat them – demonstrate, and as media portrayals of child murder highlight, modern accounts of infanticide, like their historical counterparts, continue to focus on single women, on concealment of pregnancy and unassisted delivery, and on the mental state of the mother before, during and after birth. More importantly, however, these cases also demonstrate the extent to which the evaluation of evidence and the determination of responsibility for the deaths of young children are deeply rooted in particular, but historically-mediated, social, political and cultural contexts.

Acknowledgements

I am grateful to the Wellcome Trust for funding the research on which this chapter is based. Some of the local cases discussed here were first presented at a symposium held at the University of Warwick in 2000 and I am grateful to participants at that symposium for their comments.

CHAPTER TWO

Accusations of infanticide on the eve of the French Wars of Religion

Luc Racaut

Infanticide is commonly thought to be a crime committed by women who find themselves burdened with an unwanted child. This understanding derives from work that has concentrated on trials in the seventeenth, eighteenth and nineteenth centuries. Infanticide in the medieval period and in the fifteenth and sixteenth centuries, however, remains less well known.[1] Although women were put on trial for the crime, as in the later periods, infanticide was not exclusively linked to unwanted pregnancy and poverty. On the eve of the French Wars of Religion (1562–99), for example, infanticide was associated with heresy and accusations were levelled against the Protestant community as a whole. It is interesting to note that, unlike later periods, both men and women were accused of infanticide and that the narratives indicate a collective responsibility. The accusation of ritual murder, including neonaticide – the killing of a new-born child – had been used against heretics and Jews since late antiquity. The long history of this accusation, which was used repeatedly until the early modern period, highlights the horror with which infanticide was regarded in Europe. Concealment and secrecy were prominent elements of these accusations. It is precisely because nobody knew what Protestants were doing during their secret meetings that it was possible for Catholic propagandists to accuse them of infanticide. This element of doubt, together with the fact that infanticide remained a 'hidden' crime which was often difficult to prove, constitutes a distinct element of continuity with later periods.

One cannot underestimate the importance of religion in pre-industrial Europe. The scriptures were the first port of call, and referred to infanticide in the context of pagan and sacrilegious rituals. In the Middle Ages, accusations of ritual murder, also known as the 'blood libel', were therefore turned against non-Christian Jews and heretical groups. The French Wars of Religion, which divided the country from 1562 until 1598, have often been explained along political or social

---

[1]   R. H. Helmholz, 'Infanticide in the province of Canterbury during the fifteenth century', *History of Childhood Quarterly*, 2 (1975), 379-90.

lines. It is only recently that historians have once again focused on religion in order to fully understand events during this period. The 'blood libel' constitutes an important facet of the Catholic response to Protestantism in France and provides a crucial context for the discussion of infanticide both in the late medieval and early modern periods. In this chapter, I shall explore accusations of infanticide in sixteenth-century France within the context of contemporary religious tensions.

Catholics and Protestants before the French Wars of Religion

The French Wars of Religion were marked by atrocious acts of violence which began with a massacre at Vassy in 1562 and culminated with the massacre of St Bartholomew's Day in August 1572. Recently, Denis Crouzet has argued in *Les Guerriers de Dieu* that violence was motivated by the fear of the end of time.[2] This work gives pride of place to the eschatological literature, almanacs, astrological predictions and sermons, that would have made France into a 'civilization of astrological anguish'. Crouzet's thesis has been criticized for the partial view it provides of the printed culture of sixteenth-century France.[3] Furthermore, a bibliographical survey of the printed literature of sixteenth-century France, pursued at the St Andrews Reformation Studies Institute, suggests that the astrological literature described by Crouzet does not figure as prominently as was made out.[4]

One unsuspected finding of this survey concerns the vibrancy of the Catholic response to the challenge of the Reformed message, emanating from the printing presses of Geneva in the second half of the sixteenth century.[5] An important component of this response was devoted to the systematic denigration of the Protestant cause by Catholic propagandists, including high-ranking theologians of the Faculty of Theology of the University of Paris. These authors resorted to medieval stereotypes of the heretic, borrowed from the patristic and medieval period, to capture the infamy of French Protestants. Quoting from a long list of precedents, Catholic theologians argued for the continuing

---

[2]   D. Crouzet, *Les Guerriers de Dieu: La violence au temps des troubles de religion vers 1525–vers 1610*, 2 vols (Seyssel, Champ Vallon, 1990).

[3]   L.J. Taylor, *Heresy and Orthodoxy in Sixteenth-Century Paris: François Le Picart and the Beginnings of the Catholic Reformation* (Leiden, E.J. Brill, 1999), pp. 190, 205, 212.

[4]   For further information about 'The French Religious Book Project', contact St Andrews Reformation Studies Unit at the University of St Andrews.

[5]   A. Pettegree, 'Religious printing in 16th-century France: the St Andrews project', *Proceedings of the Huguenot Society*, 26 (1997), 650–59.

persecution of Protestants at a time when the Crown was advocating measures of conciliation. These works were destined for a lay readership although the extent to which these representations of Protestants penetrated beyond the ranks of literate urban élites is difficult to establish. Catholic propagandists nonetheless aimed at manipulating the perceptions of their readership, turning Protestants into manifestations of an undying monster: the baby-killing heretic.

In the closing years of the reign of Henri II, Protestants were actively persecuted and forced to seek refuge in the anonymity of private houses. The edict of Châteaubriant (1551) made heresy a criminal offence, while the edict of Compiègne (1557) imposed the death penalty for the exercise of the Reformed religion. Persecution remained unabated after the accidental death of Henri II, as the Guise seized the reins of power and took the young king François II under their protection. Accusations in print of orgies and infanticide served to justify the persecutions. The polemical campaign intensified at the beginning of the reign of Charles IX as the regent, Catherine de Médicis, sought measures of conciliation towards Protestantism.[6]

This was a period when the Catholic majority became increasingly aware of the presence of a Protestant minority in its midst. It is marked by what were perceived as acts of provocation and defiance by the Protestants. On the night of 4 September 1557, students of the Collège du Plessis stumbled upon a clandestine Protestant meeting at a house in the rue Saint Jacques, where between three and four hundred people had gathered to celebrate the Lord's Supper. The presence of women among them inspired a rumour, which was reproduced in print by Catholic polemicists, that they had assembled there to take part in an orgy. In May 1558, between four and six thousand Protestants met every evening of a whole week in the Pré-aux-Clercs to sing psalms. The French Reformed Church was becoming more organized, and its first national synod was held in Paris in 1559. These events marked the intensification of religious divisions and the beginning of a polemical campaign to revile Protestants.[7]

The most salient point of contention between Catholics and Protestants concerned the Eucharist. Calvinists denied the real

---

[6] J.K. Farge, *Le Parti Conservateur au XVIe siècle: Université et Parlement de Paris à l'époque de la Renaissance et de la Réforme* (Paris, Les Belles Lettres, 1992).

[7] G. Baum and E. Cunitz (eds), *Histoire Ecclésiastique des Eglises Réformées au Royaume de France*, 3 vols (Paris, Fischbacher, 1883–87); A. de la Roche-Chandieu, *Histoire des persecutions, et martyrs de l'Eglise de Paris, depuis l'an 1557. Jusques au temps du Roy Charles neufviesme* (Lyon, s.n., 1563); B.B. Diefendorf, *Beneath the Cross: Catholics and Huguenots in Sixteenth-Century Paris* (Oxford, Oxford University Press, 1991), p. 50.

presence of Christ in the sacrament of the Eucharist and emphasized the symbolic nature of what they called the Lord's supper. It had been a Protestant attack on the Catholic mass in 1534, known as the Affair of the Placards, that had provoked the change of heart of François I towards evangelism. At the colloquy of Poissy in 1561, the ultimate attempt at conciliation before the outbreak of the civil wars, Theodore Beza had declared that the body of Christ was as distant from the wine and the bread as the sky is from the earth. The intractability of the Catholics and the Protestants on this particular point of contention rendered any attempts at conciliation ineffectual. The Eucharist and the Mass were at the heart of the collective religious experience of the Catholic Church.[8] By partaking of the body of Christ, communicants renewed their bond with the community at large as well as with God. The Protestant onslaught on the real presence threatened the very foundations of the communal religious experience of Catholics. During the Wars of Religion, the host was the source of much controversy and violence. Protestants pointedly derided the wafer by calling it *Jean le Blanc*, while Catholics celebrated its efficacy and ability to work miracles.[9]

It was the celebration of the Lord's supper, the Protestant response to the Catholic mass, which was at the centre of the polemical campaign to revile them. In order to avoid detection, Protestants were made to swear an oath not to reveal the names of those who took part in their ceremonies.[10] The clandestine nature of these proceedings was the source of much suspicion, just as the ceremonies of the Manichees had roused the suspicion of Augustine: 'I cannot know what you, the elect, do among yourselves. I have often heard you say that you received the Eucharist, but the moment of its reception remains hidden from me: how could I have known what you received?'[11] As with the early Christians, the Jews and the heretics of antiquity, it was the secrecy of the Protestants' celebrations that enabled the Catholics to spread stories against them. A Catholic polemicist, writing in 1560, addressed the king directly to make that very point:

> Now (if I understand correctly) after they realized that your royal majesty was offended by such insolence, they retired in caverns, forests and hidden places, where they conduct their Sabbath, and

---

[8] J. Bossy, 'The Mass as a social institution, 1200–1700', *Past and Present*, 100 (1983), 29–61.

[9] I. Backus (ed.), *Guillaume Postel et Jean Boulaese: De summopere (1566) et Le Miracle de Laon (1566)* (Geneva, Droz, 1995).

[10] Diefendorf, *Beneath the Cross*, p. 122.

[11] Augustine, *Acta Seu Disputatio Contra Fortunatum Manicheum* (Paris, Cerf, 1961), p. 137.

diabolical Eucharist, calling up from hell the superstitions of the
ancient idolaters.[12]

In the 1550s, and especially in the wake of the affair of the rue Saint
Jacques in September 1557, Protestants were accused of conducting
orgies under the cover of darkness. References to darkness, secrecy and
enclosed spaces recur in printed descriptions of the 'diabolical Sabbath'
of the Protestants. The word 'cavern' is the one most often used in these
accounts: 'caverns, forests and hidden places'; 'caverns and
subterranean hidden holes'; 'what characterizes the heretics is to have
pits, caverns and hideouts'.[13] These conventicles always took place at
night or under the cover of darkness: 'surely when you see them, you
will say that they are enemies of light as the owls are, night thieves,
blind moles, when entire companies of them throw themselves in
caverns to hide, in pits and remote places and any other hideout that
they can find'.[14]

Because Protestants gathered clandestinely at night to celebrate the
Lord's supper, Catholic propagandists were able to summon ancient
nightmares of heretics conducting a parody of the Mass, drinking the
blood and eating the flesh of a slain infant. This parody of the central
sacrament of the Christian faith had emerged during the Christian
persecutions under the Roman Empire. It had antecedents in anti-semitic
accounts of the Jewish ceremony of Passover, which were assimilated by
pagan critics of the new Christian religion.

The origins of the 'blood libel'

The ritual murder of children has deep roots in the collective memory of
the Judaeo-Christian World. The Old Testament associates the ritual
burning of children with the cult of the Canaanite fire-god Moloch.[15]
The Greeks and Romans were thought to sacrifice children to Kronos or

---

[12] J. de la Vacquerie, *Catholique remonstrance aux roys et princes chrestiens, a tous magistrats & gouverneurs de Repub. touchant l'abolition des heresies, troubles & scismes qui regnent aujourd'huy en la Chrestienté* (Paris, Claude Fremy, 1560), sigs D2v–D4r.

[13] Ibid., sigs D4r, E5v, E6v; J. Eck, *Les lieux communs de jean Ekius, contre Luther* (Lyon, Jean Marnax, 1551), sig. C4r; Antoine de Mouchy, *Responce a quelque apologie que les heretiques ces jours passés ont mis en avant sous ce titre: Apologie ou deffence des bons Chrestiens contre les ennemis de l'Eglise catholique* (Paris, Claude Fremy, 1558), sig. K1r; Thomas Beauxamis, *Histoire des sectes tirées de l'armée sathanique* (Paris, Guillaume Chaudière, 1576), p. 83.

[14] R. Ceneau, *Response catholique contre les heretiques de ce temps* (Paris, Guillaume Julien, 1562), sig. A5v.

[15] Leviticus 18: 21, 20: 2, 20: 3, 20: 4; 2 Kings 23: 10; Jeremiah 19: 5, 32: 35.

Saturn, a deity often depicted eating his own children. At the turn of the third century, Tertullian reported that 'children were openly sacrificed in Africa to Saturn as lately as the proconsulship of Tiberius'.[16] In both cases, the ritual killing of infants was attributed to a pagan cult, that of Moloch among the Canaanites and that of Saturn among the Romans. The versatility of the accusation of infanticide, associated with a hostile religious cult, points to its universal appeal as a mark of infamy. Whether these accusations had any foundations is uncertain.

It was widely believed, from the use of the word *expositio* to refer to abandonment, that Romans abandoned children to die in the wild. John Boswell, in *The Kindness of Strangers*, has argued that although the abandonment of children was a common practice in the pre-industrial world, the children were often adopted and seldom died. It seems, however, that the sale or abandonment of children did not carry the same moral stigma that it would today. The eating of children, however incredible it may seem, was also reported in cases of famine or sieges. The scriptures describe two women who had agreed to eat each other's children in turn during the siege of Samaria.[17] In Spain in the thirteenth century, it was criminal to cause a child's death by abandonment but it was legal to sell or even eat one's own child during a siege. The scriptures' condemnation of infanticide as a form of ritual sacrifice indicates that it probably did take place. The sacrifice of Isaac is the most notorious example of infant sacrifice: the willingness of Abraham to sacrifice his own son reflects its acceptance in the ancient world.[18] The intervention of the angel and the substitution of Isaac with the ram marks a watershed in this respect. The New Testament marks an even greater departure as the sacrifice of Christ on the cross can be seen as the reversal of the sacrifice of Isaac: God offers his own son in sacrifice to redeem humanity.[19]

Although both the Old and New Testament condemn it, the Romans accused both Jews and Christians of committing infanticide. Jews were accused of the ritual killing of infants under Emperor Caius: 'Appion spread the rumour against the Jews that they killed a Greek child in their temple and sucked his blood, after having fattened him for a year'.[20] The 'blood libel' dates back to at least the second century BC when the Syrians captured Jerusalem and heard that every seven years Jews carried

---

[16] Tertullian, *Apology*, chap. IX (extracted from the Christian Classics Ethereal Library at Calvin College webpage <http://www.ccel.org>).

[17] 2 Kings 6: 28.

[18] Genesis 22.

[19] J. Boswell, *The Kindness of Strangers: The Abandonment of Children in Western Europe from Late Antiquity to the Renaissance* (New York, Pantheon Books, 1988), pp. 4, 24–5, 154, 328–9.

[20] Beauxamis, *Histoire des sectes*, p. 18.

out a similar ritual in the temple.[21] During the persecutions in Rome, Christians were accused of committing ritual murder and of eating the flesh of infants. It has been suggested that the allegation of ritual murder at the hands of Christians sprang from a misunderstanding of the Christian Eucharist. The biblical entreaty, 'Whoever eats my flesh and drinks my blood has eternal life', was perhaps interpreted literally by those outside the Christian faith.[22] As we shall see cannibalism and the burning of infants to make flour and bake a simulacrum of the wafer can also be found in patristic anti-heretical literature.

The predominance of this theme suggests the emergence of a taboo regarding infanticide in the Christian world. Having been used against pagans, Christians and Jews, the accusation of ritual murder became the mark of the heretic. After the conversion of Constantine, when Christianity became the official religion of the Empire, the 'blood libel' was appropriated by the Church Fathers who used it against the first Christian heretics. Epiphanius of Salamis (315–403) first used narratives of ritual murder against the Gnostics, who were among the first challengers of Christian orthodoxy:

> In the first place, they hold their wives in common ... the next thing they do is feast ... they next go crazy for each other ... And when the wretched couple has made love ... the woman becomes pregnant ... They extract the foetus at the stage appropriate for their enterprise, take this aborted infant, and cut it up in a trough shaped like a pestle. And they mix honey, pepper, and certain other perfumes and spices ... and then all the revellers ... assemble, and each eats a piece of the child with his fingers.[23]

Epiphanius' catalogue of heresies was followed by a similar work by Augustine of Hippo (354–430) who used a variation of the blood libel against the Montanists:

> They are said to have a baleful sacrament: they make their wafer the same way they would bread, mixing flour with the blood of a one-year-old child, extracted from small puncture wounds from his whole body: if the boy dies, he is venerated among them as a martyr; if however he survives, he is held among them as a great priest.[24]

---

[21] G.I. Langmuir, 'Thomas of Monmouth: detector of ritual murder', *Speculum*, 59 (1984), 820–46, at 823.

[22] John 6: 54; N. Cohn, *Europe's Inner Demons: The Demonization of Christians in Medieval Christendom* (London, Pimlico, 1993), p. 9.

[23] F. Williams (ed.), *The Panarion of Epiphanius of Salamis*, 2 vols (Leiden, E.J. Brill, 1987–94), I, pp. 85–7.

[24] L.G. Müller (ed.), *The De Haeresibus of Saint Augustine: A Translation with an Introduction and Commentary* (Washington, Catholic University of America Press, 1956), p. 74 [Dr Peter Maxwell Stuart has provided me with a more elegant translation].

The Church Fathers provided precedents against which every subsequent heresy was compared. From the twelfth century until the fifteenth, several heretical movements were accused of the 'blood libel'. Guibert, abbot of Nogent (1055–1125), describes in his autobiography the bacchanalia of the heretics of Soissons at the beginning of the twelfth century, with a slight variation:

> In caves or other subterranean and hidden places, they hold their council. There, both men and women light some candles and go to a young girl who, bent forward, offers her behind for all to see: this is what I heard. Later on, they extinguish the lights, and shout: Chaos! Immediately, everyone grabs the person nearest at hand and makes love. If, following from this, a woman is pregnant, they return to the same place after birth: this time, a great fire is kindled, people sitting around it pass the baby from hand to hand, and then throw it into the fire where it is consumed; when it is reduced to ashes, they use it to make bread that is divided between all of them; a heretic will never repent once he has participated in such a Eucharist. If you read Augustine's list of heresies, you will find a similar account concerning the Manichees.[25]

Different versions of this story were used throughout the Middle Ages whenever the Church was faced with a wave of heterodoxy.[26] The same story was used at regular intervals against a variety of undesirable groups such as the Albigensians, the Waldensians, the Beguines and the Templars at the turn of the thirteenth century.[27] Significantly, Jews were equally persecuted during the Middle Ages and were singled out as scapegoats in times of plague. They were often accused of having kidnapped missing children to offer them in sacrifice in the ceremony of Passover. The children allegedly killed in this way became martyrs and sometimes saints and their graves were visited in pilgrimage and were the sites of miracles. Probably the most famous example of this phenomenon is the martyrdom of William of Norwich in 1144:

> the Jews of Norwich bought a Christian child before Easter and tortured him with all the torture that our Lord was tortured with; and on Good Friday hanged him on a cross on account of our Lord, and then buried him. They expected it would be concealed, but our Lord made it plain that he was a holy martyr, and the monks took him and buried him with ceremony in the monastery, and through

[25] E.R. Labande (ed.), *Guibert de Nogent: Autobiographie* (Paris, Les Belles Lettres, 1981), pp. 430–31.

[26] G. Mollat (ed.), *Bernard Gui: Manuel de l'Inquisiteur*, 2 vols (Paris, Les Belles Lettres, 1964).

[27] De la Vacquerie, *Catholique remonstrance*, sig. E7r ; Beauxamis, *Histoire des Sectes*, p. 83; Michel de Castelnau, *Mémoires* (Paris, Sebastien Chappelet, 1621), p. 7.

our Lord he works wonderful and varied miracles, and he is called St William.[28]

Another example is provided by the case of 'Little Saint Hugh' who was allegedly ritually murdered by Jews in 1254 in Lincoln, and whose grave became the site of miracles and pilgrimages. In 1235 in Fulda, thirty-four Jews were massacred around Christmas time, having been accused of the 'blood libel'; the authors of the massacre went as far as carrying the bodies of the alleged victims to the emperor to prove that the Jews lusted for blood.[29] In Trent in 1475, Jews were judged for the killing of a child (who shortly became 'Blessed Simon, martyr'), and were accused of having drawn blood for the purpose of celebrating Passover.[30] Later accusations, which focus on the drawing of blood, show a clear kinship to the stories of antiquity.[31]

Medieval accusations of infanticide went hand in hand with monastic idealization of children's virginity as a mark of purity and innocence. The medieval catalogue of saints included many infants whose sanctity derived from their virginity. Hayward has argued that 'children were thought to possess an almost angelic and pre-lapsarian purity in both body and mind by virtue of their virginity, and the monastic life was frequently conceived as a means of preserving this condition or of returning to it'.[32] According to John Boswell, there was a lapse in child abandonment in the twelfth century as monasteries often welcomed abandoned children as oblates.[33] In the hagiography of early Christian Europe, royal children killed by ambitious relatives were often made into Christian martyrs.[34]

Strikingly, the 'blood libel' had lost none of its potency in the early modern period when Catholics used it against Protestants. Natalie Davis has described how children were often involved in acts of cruelty against Huguenots, and Crouzet has argued that they carried out God's will in all innocence and purity.[35] By contrast, the accusations of ritual murder

---

[28] Langmuir, 'Thomas of Monmouth', p. 820.

[29] G.I. Langmuir, *Toward a Definition of Antisemitism* (Oxford, University of California Press, 1990), pp. 263–81.

[30] R. Po-Chia Hsia, *Trent 1475: Stories of a Ritual Murder Trial* (New Haven, Yale University Press, 1992), p. 4.

[31] Boswell, *Kindness of Strangers*, pp. 352–6; G. Langmuir, 'The knight's tale of young Hugh of Lincoln', *Speculum*, 47/3 (1972), 459–82; A.C. Gow, *The Red Jews: Antisemitism in an Apocalyptic Age 1200–1600* (Leiden, E.J. Brill, 1995).

[32] P.A. Hayward, 'The idea of innocent martyrdom in late tenth- and eleventh-century English hagiology', *Studies in Church History*, 30 (1993), 81–92, at 88.

[33] Boswell, *Kindness of Strangers*, p. 296.

[34] Hayward, 'The idea of innocent martyrdom', p. 83; Boswell, *Kindness of Strangers*, p. 139.

[35] N. Davis, *Society and Culture in Early Modern France* (Cambridge, Polity, 1987), p. 184; Crouzet, *Guerriers de Dieu*, I, p. 88.

of innocent children in diabolical ceremonies made the Protestants all the more detestable.

The use of the 'blood libel' against Protestants

Comparison between Protestantism and the heresies of late antiquity and the medieval period was a common staple of anti-Protestant polemics. Two Fundamental Church Councils (Nicaea in 325 and the fourth Lateran Council in 1215) defined orthodoxy in the face of the heresies that marked these key periods of Church history. The heretics condemned at these councils became indistinguishable from one another in the minds of the Catholic authorities and were used as precedents to condemn further heresies. To all intents and purposes, all heretical groups were related and any new heterodox movement would immediately be added to the family tree of heresy. Augustine had described the tree of heresy and the great medieval summae perpetuated this image and passed it on to the sixteenth century.[36] For example, Bernard of Luxembourg's *Catalogus haereticorum omnium* (1522) and Alphonso de Castro's *Adversus omnes haereses* (1534) catalogue heresies along the principles laid down by Augustine.[37]

From the outset of the Reformation, Catholic theologians compared Protestants with what they saw as their medieval counterparts. For example, in 1537, the Catholic controversialist George Witzel described the Lutherans in those terms: 'the sects of this age have great affinity with the old … . The similarity of nature and behaviour is in all points obvious'.[38] In order to fuel their arguments, Catholic theologians also translated and borrowed heavily from Church Fathers' treatises against heretics.[39] The translator of an edition of the work by Vincent of Lérins, *Pour la verité et antiquité de la foy catholique* (1563) thought that no modern author could be as eloquent, or brief, on the subject of heresy.[40] When George Witzel compared the doctrine of salvation by

---

[36] M-M. Fragonard, 'La détermination des frontières symboliques: nommer et définir les groupes hérétiques', in R. Sauzet (ed.), *Les Frontières religieuses en Europe du XVe au XVIIe siècle* (Paris, J. Vrin, 1992), pp. 37–49.

[37] B. von Luxemburg, *Catalogus haereticorum omnium* (Köln, E. Cervicorni, 1522).

[38] G. Wicelius, *Libellus de moribus veterum haereticorum* (Leipzig, N. Wolrad, 1537) published as G. Witzel, *Discours des moeurs tant des anciens hérétiques que nouveaux Lutheriens & Calvinistes auquel leur resemblance est clairement demonstrée* (Paris, Claude Fremy, 1567), p. 5.

[39] Optat, *Histoire du schisme, blasphemes & autres impietez des Donatiens* (Paris, Federic Morel, 1564).

[40] Vincent de Lérins, *Petit traite de Vincent Lerineuse pour la verité et antiquité de la foy catholique* (Paris, Vascosan, 1563).

faith with the Manichees' beliefs, he was echoed by the French authors who wrote against the Calvinists.[41] This argument was used, for example, by Nicolas Durand, Chevalier de Villegagnon, who compared the doctrine of predestination to the dualism of the Manichees.[42] Thus all heretics were interchangeable and were guilty of the same crimes. Crucially, infanticide played a large role in the stereotyping of heretics.

At the beginning of the sixteenth century, the 'blood libel' was influentially relayed by Desiderius Erasmus in his book *Liber de Sarcienda Ecclesiae* (1533):

> But these examples are all in the past. Surely much more to be deplored is that within recent memory there have been discovered nightly gatherings at which, after praise has been given to God, the lights are extinguished and the men and women consort in promiscuous love. Or the ceremonies in which mothers freely hand over their infants to be butchered, and even watch serenely the horrid crime, so persuaded are they that their children will thus find a high place in heaven ... . This madness seems to have taken its origin from the heresy of the Valentinians, who made the Eucharist from flour mixed with the blood of an infant. This blood they would draw from small pinpricks, and if in the process the child died, it was venerated as a martyr.[43]

Whether this passage was inspired by a contemporary rumour that circulated in Paris about a sect that sucked the blood of infants is unclear.[44] But the use of the 'blood libel' by Erasmus gave it a degree of credibility, and subsequent authors cited it as a precedent. Stanislas Hozius, a Polish cardinal, refers to Erasmus as his source in his *Des sectes et heresies de nostre temps* (1561):

> I only mention in passing the 300 who, after having sung praises to God, extinguished all the lights, and copulated with one another like animals ... . And another sect (that is mentioned by Erasmus) amongst whom mothers bring their own children to be killed, and consider lightly such a horrible sacrifice ... . Can anybody think of

---

[41] Witzel, *Discours des moeurs*, pp. 22–5.

[42] Nicolas Durand, *Lettres du Chevallier de Villegaignon sur les remonstrances, a la Royne Mere du Roy la souveraine Dame, touchant la Religion* (s.l., s.n., 1561), sigs B3r–v.

[43] Desiderius Erasmus, *Liber de sarcienda Ecclesiae concordia deque sedandis opinionum dissidiis* (Basel, J. Froben, 1533); reproduced in J.P. Dolan, *The Essential Erasmus* (New York, New American Library, 1964), pp. 442–3.

[44] L. Lalanne (ed.), *Journal d'un bourgeois de Paris sous le règne de François Premier (1515–1536)* (Paris, J. Renouard, 1854), p. 429; Nicolas des Gallars, *Seconde apologie ou defense des vrais chrestiens, contre les calomnies impudentes des ennemis de l'Eglise. Ou il est respondu aux diffames redoublez par un nommé Demochares docteur de la Sorbonne* (s.l., s.n., 1559), sig. B7r.

something more abominable, hateful, and horrible than that?[45]

A Frenchman, Antoine du Val, referred to Erasmus as a precedent of what he inferred had occurred at the assembly of the rue Saint Jacques in September 1557:

> Our Calvinists are like those heretics: after having sung psalms and other songs, they put out the lights: as for what they do after that, I refer you to what was done in Paris, in the night of 4 September 1557, in the great rue Saint Jacques, where there were more than 500 heretics assembled ... who after the candles were put out, mixed together indiscriminately, men and women, to make love. Erasmus adds in his book on the admirable concord of the church that far worse was done at these nocturnal meetings, where fathers willingly offered their own children to be sacrificed, seeing such horrible crime favourably, believing that their children, thus killed, became martyrs.[46]

By using this story, Catholic polemicists associated Protestantism with a long line of heretics and sought to justify their persecution at a time when Protestantism threatened to take over the body politic. The use of the 'blood libel' against the Protestants of the rue Saint Jacques must be seen in the context of centuries of characterization of heretics, which had become ingrained in the culture of western Christendom. The story had become an integral part of the institutionalized Church's response to heresy and Catholic authors were effectively perpetuating medieval persecution mechanisms.

Protestant reactions to the 'blood libel'

It is difficult to gauge what Catholic polemicists tried to achieve by using the 'blood libel' against Protestants and whether it had the intended impact on their audience, which remained fairly limited. It provoked, nonetheless, a vigorous response from the Protestants and fuelled a flurry of polemic that contributed to the definition of Protestant identity. Because the 'blood libel' had been used against early Christians, Protestants argued that their persecutions were as unjust as those of the Early Church martyrs. This enabled them to make a case for the martyrdom of the victims of the persecutions under the reign of Henri

---

[45] Stanislas Hozius, *Des sectes et heresies de nostre temps: traicte composé premierement en Latin, par reverend Pere en Dieu monseigneur Stanislas Hozie, Evesque de Varme en Pouloigne, dedié au roy de Pouloigne, & nouvellement mis en François* (Paris, Vascosan, 1561), pp. 166–7.

[46] Antoine du Val, *Mirouer des Calvinistes et armures des chrestiens pour rembarez le Lutheriens & nouveaux evangelistes de Genève* (Paris, Nicolas Chesneau, 1562), p. 9.

II. Martyrdom was a keystone of Protestant identity, and it was propagated from Geneva through the numerous editions of Jean Crespin's *Histoire des Martyrs*, from 1554 onwards.[47] The most revealing exchange took place between Nicolas des Gallars, who was minister in Paris during the affair of the rue Saint Jacques, and the Dean of the Paris Faculty of Theology, Antoine de Mouchy.[48]

Des Gallars made a point of indicating the pagan origins of these accusations: 'Is it not the same accusation that was used against Christians in the past, saying that they killed little children to eat them?'[49] Des Gallars pointed out the similarity with the accusations against which Tertullian wrote his *apologia* during the persecutions of Emperor Trajan in the second century:

> We are called abominable from the sacrament of infanticide and the feeding thereon, as well as the incestuous intercourse, following the banquet, because the dogs, that overturn the lamp, (our pimps forsooth of the darkness) bring about the shamelessness engendered by our impious lusts.[50]

Unlike any minority group against which the accusation had been used before, Protestants were able to turn it to their advantage. By drawing attention to the use of the accusation against the Early Church martyrs, Protestants were legitimizing their cause. Another Parisian minister, Antoine de la Roche-Chandieu, recounts in his *Histoire des persecutions* (1563), that des Gallars' arguments had been decisive:

> Doctors of the Sorbonne tried to respond to this argument: but the stupid brutes, as is their custom, could only uncover their own ignorance in this matter. One named Mouchy, deducing without any proof from a learned decree that we are heretics, spends the whole book discussing the punishment of heretics and concludes that they must be burned.[51]

Whether in response to the Protestants' arguments or not, there is evidence that Antoine de Mouchy attempted to substantiate his claims with first-hand accounts of clandestine meetings. The controversy that had been roused by the affair of the rue Saint Jacques in 1557 was

---

[47] J. Crespin, *Histoire des Martyrs* (Geneva, Jean Crespin, 1582).

[48] Des Gallars, *Seconde apologie*; P. Feret, *La Faculté de Théologie de Paris et ses Docteurs les plus célèbres: Epoque Moderne XVI–XVIIIème siècle*, 6 vols (Paris, A. Picard & fils, 1900–09), II, pp. 51–5; De Mouchy, *Responce a quelque apologie*, sigs F2r–v, F4r–v, J8v, K1v.

[49] Des Gallars, *Seconde apologie*, sigs D8r–v; Baum and Cunitz, *Histoire Ecclésiastique*, I, pp. 143–4.

[50] J.E.B. Mayor (ed.), *Tertullian: Apologeticus* (Cambridge, Cambridge University Press, 1917), p. 27.

[51] De la Roche-Chandieu, *Histoire des persecutions*, sig. d1v.

intensified during the short reign of François II, which was dominated by the infamous duc de Guise who stepped up religious persecution. This period coincided with an unprecedented wave of persecution that lasted from August 1559 to March 1560 and culminated in the purge of royal officials and high-ranking civil servants. In addition to accusations in print, there is evidence that the Cardinal of Lorraine, the duc de Guise's brother, conspired with de Mouchy to add credibility to these stories at court.[52] According to Protestant sources, Antoine de Mouchy received the testimony of two young apprentices who claimed to have been taken to a Protestant meeting by their master. They were coaxed into revealing the names of those who had taken part and to testify that an orgy, such as was described in the polemic, had indeed taken place. Antoine de la Roche-Chandieu provides a detailed account of the testimony of one of the apprentices:

> The apprentice told the judges that it was his master who had led him to the assembly. As he was so prompt to denounce his master, great promises were made to him in exchange for the names of those he saw there, and he enumerated everyone without exception, adding that the rumours about the assemblies were true, that people copulated freely once the candles were put out.[53]

According to another account, one of the apprentices even claimed to have had sex two or three times with one of the daughters of the lawyer in whose house this orgy had taken place.[54] The Cardinal of Lorraine brought the two apprentices to Catherine de Médicis in an attempt to convince her that the stories disseminated in print by de Mouchy and others were true.[55] Theodore Beza's *Histoire Ecclesiastique* (1580) adds that the Cardinal of Lorraine drew parallels with a number of medieval heresies, mirroring printed polemic:

> The Cardinal, for his own part, did not miss an opportunity to use their testimony. With their written confession in hand and the two apprentices at his tail, he went to the Queen Mother, to describe to her at length the content of their confession with great exclamations, leaving nothing out so that those of the religion were portrayed as the most odious and abominable creatures that had ever lived. So that nothing would be missed, he embellished his

---

[52] Diefendorf, *Beneath the Cross*, pp. 55, 135; Théodore de Bèze, *Histoire Ecclesiastique des Eglises Reformes au Royaume de France*, 3 vols (Antwerp, Jean Remy, 1580), I, p. 228; Lancelot du Voisin de la Popelinière, *L'Histoire de France enrichie des plus notables occurances survenues ez Provinces de l'Europe & pays voisins*, 2 vols (s.l., s.n., 1581), I, fol. 147v.

[53] De la Roche-Chandieu, *Histoire des persecutions*, sigs x7r–x8r.

[54] Bèze, *Histoire Ecclesiastique*, p. 234.

[55] Anon, *La Maniere d'appaiser les troubles, qui sont maintenant en France, & y pourront estre cy apres: A la Royne mere du Roy* (s.l., s.n., 1561), sig. B2r.

account with all the things that various heretics had done in the past, accusations which had been suggested by the devil to cast a shadow on the light of the Gospel, from the time when it had started being preached in secret, because of the persecutions of the pagan and idolatrous emperors.[56]

According to the *Histoire Ecclesiastique*, Catherine de Médicis would have been swayed by the testimony of the two apprentices but was advised to have them cross-examined.[57] The cross-examination of the witnesses revealed that they had been lying, and the whole matter was dropped. There is evidence, however, that despite the denial of the false witnesses the belief that Protestants took part in orgies survived. Penny Roberts has uncovered the case of a city councillor of Troyes who escaped prosecution in 1562 by arguing that his only reason for attending a Protestant meeting was the hope of taking part in such an orgy:

> A few were imprisoned in the gaol of the palace where they stayed awhile. The *conseiller* de Pleurre was one of them. Being brought before those gentlemen of the court of the *Parlement* to be interrogated, he confessed so that he could be let out of prison. He had attended a Protestant assembly and sermon to fulfil his carnal desire and have sex with the woman of his choice, thinking that the rumour was true, that women gave themselves freely at those assemblies. But having seen and understood that this was false, and not having found what he was looking for, he had resolved not to go there again. The court released de Pleurre, trying hard not to laugh out loud.[58]

Furthermore, the myth of orgiastic Protestants was mixed with the horrible reality of the Parisian persecutions during which times children were left abandoned on the streets of Paris. Lancelot du Voisin de la Popelinière's history of France recounts how preachers on street corners rekindled the 'blood libel' by pointing at these children as those the Protestants had intended to eat during their orgies:

> One could not walk through the streets without coming across soldiers armed with swords who roughly led all kinds of male and female prisoners. Poor little children were left in the streets, crying of hunger, and no one rescued them for fear of being arrested. People paid less attention to them than they would dogs, such was the Parisians' contempt for the Protestant faith. To encourage the hatred of the Parisians, there were people at street corners who told them

[56] Bèze, *Histoire Ecclesiastique*, p. 236.

[57] Ibid., p. 237.

[58] P. Roberts, *A City in Conflict: Troyes during the French Wars of Religion* (Manchester, Manchester University Press, 1996), p. 84 n. 64; BN Dupuy MS 698 (Pithou), fol. 243v (I have to thank Penny Roberts for the transcript of this document).

that the heretics gathered at night to eat those little children and copulate with one another when the candles were put out, after having eaten a pig instead of the Paschal lamb and committed together an infinity of incest and infamous deeds: and people believed it as if it was true.[59]

Again, it is difficult to determine the circulation of the 'blood libel' and whether it had any credit amongst the Catholic population of Paris. Another Protestant author, however, remarks that the 'blood libel' lost credibility and that the Catholic switched to more credible accusations of rebellion.[60] Indeed, in March 1560, a small Protestant army attempted to kidnap the young king François II, which provoked a second salvo of Catholic propaganda. After the outbreak of the French Wars of Religion in 1562, when the Protestant Prince of Condé seized Orleans, the accusation of political disobedience was more credible and perhaps more justified. Nonetheless, the 'blood libel' appeared once more on the eve of the massacre of Saint Bartholomew and was used against Italians, mirroring the rumour that had circulated in 1532.[61] This points to the universality of the 'blood libel' that was used indiscriminately against Jews, heretics, Protestants and Italians in the course of almost two thousand years.

Conclusion

I have suggested in this chapter that the 'blood libel' was used against minority groups throughout antiquity and the Middle Ages. Catholic authors who disseminated these accusations in print after the affair of the rue Saint Jacques were merely setting a medieval persecution mechanism into motion. As it had successfully been used against heretics and Jews in the past, the expectation was that it would work once more, against Protestants. The Protestants were able to respond to these accusations and turn them to their advantage by drawing on comparisons with the Early Church martyrs. Furthermore, the agenda of

---

[59] La Popelinière, L'Histoire de France, fol. 148v.

[60] Augustin Marlorat, Remonstrance a la royne mere du Roy, par ceux qui sont persecutez pour la parole de DIEU. En laquelle ils rendent raison des principaux articles de la Religion, & qui sont aujourdhuy en dispute (s.l., s.n., 1561), sigs. B5v–B6v.

[61] H. Heller, 'The Italian Saint Bartholomew: assassins or victims?' (unpublished paper given at the Sixteenth-Century Studies Conference, 1999); Le Tocsain contre les massacreurs et auteurs des confusions en France (Reims, 1579) in L. Cimber and F. Danjou (eds), Archives curieuses de l'histoire de France (Paris, Beauvais, 1835), 1ère série, 7, p. 27.

Catholic polemicists like Antoine de Mouchy had coincided with the royal policy of persecution during the reigns of Henri II and Francis II. But when the latter died in 1560, the ten-year-old king Charles IX was put under the tutelage of Catherine de Médicis who started implementing conciliatory measures. After the appointment of Chancellor Michel de l'Hôpital, the policies of the regent's court were increasingly at odds with the Faculty of Theology and the Parlement of Paris. Printed accusations of infanticide were gradually replaced by accusations of rebellion and civil disorder, which were easier to substantiate, especially after the outbreak of the French Wars of Religion.

In the early modern period, infanticide was not exclusively associated with women and unwanted pregnancies. The killing of a new-born child was also regarded as a collective ritual, perpetrated by heterodox groups under the cover of darkness. To the modern reader, the 'blood libel' may seem little more than a folk tale, but in the highly volatile context of sixteenth-century France it could have dire consequences for the groups against which it was used. In the eyes of Catholic polemicists, it served to justify further persecution of heresy, in the same way that it had been used against Jews across the ages. On the eve of the massacre of St Bartholomew's Day, it was used even against Italians, whose wealth and influence at court attracted popular hatred. Before becoming a crime which could be ascribed to poverty and to the opprobrium associated with pregnancy outside marriage, infanticide constituted a universal mark of infamy with which one could brand all undesirable groups.

CHAPTER THREE

Infanticide in early modern England: the Court of Great Sessions at Chester, 1650–1800

J.R. Dickinson and J.A. Sharpe

The murder of new-born children was a phenomenon which attracted considerable comment in early modern England. A year or two before the important 1624 infanticide statute, the clergyman and moralist William Gouge, in his large treatise on family life, described infanticidal mothers as 'lewd and unnatural'.[1] Two years after the statute was passed, the Cheshire justice of the peace Sir Richard Grosvenor described infanticide as 'a sinne which cries for vengeance and rather then it shalbe undiscovered God will worke miracles'.[2] Occasional evidence of community disquiet can be added to such statements by educated or elite commentators. Thus in 1645 a number of the inhabitants of Terling in Essex, headed by their godly minister, petitioned the county bench about an infanticide carried out by Elizabeth Codwell, which they described as an 'unnaturall and barbarous murther ... the guilt whereof we are anxious not to contract', expressing their hopes that 'so horrid a crime may not escape the hand of justice'.[3] There would therefore seem to be considerable justification for Keith Wrightson's commenting on 'the enormous symbolic significance which infanticide had acquired in European culture' by the early modern period, and the way in which it 'had been identified as an unnatural act'.[4] Certainly, the offence is now regarded by historians of early modern crime as one of the distinctive offences of the period. Most European states enacted legislation which defined infanticide as a separate offence, which became one of the more salient forms of female criminality in the early modern period. Infanticide was a more sex-specific crime than witchcraft, that other offence so closely associated

---

[1] William Gouge, *Of Domestical Duties: Eight Treatises* (London, 1622), p. 507.

[2] Richard Cust (ed.), *The Papers of Sir Richard Grosvenor, 1st Bart (1585–1645)* (Record Society of Lancashire and Cheshire, 134, 1996), p. 22.

[3] Essex Record Office, Quarter Sessions Bundles, Q/SBa 2/57.

[4] Keith Wrightson, 'Infanticide in European history', *Criminal Justice History*, 3 (1982), 1–20, at 15.

with women, and it is probable that what might be termed an 'infanticide craze' in early modern Europe led to the execution of at least as many women as did the more familiar European witch-craze.[5]

Discussion of infanticide raises some difficult definitional issues. The term was seldom used in early modern England, and, as Mark Jackson has commented, an alternative term, such as new-born child murder, might be more appropriate and certainly less anachronistic.[6] Moreover, as the contributions to this collection demonstrate, infanticide – at least as a legal concept – has been defined differently in different cultures and in different periods. In this chapter, however, we will follow the usage current among most historians of early modern England, and use the term to mean the killing of new-born children at the time of their birth.[7] Yet problems remain even when following this restricted usage. In 1624 parliament passed 'An Act to prevent the destroying and murthering of bastard children', which specifically targeted 'lewd women that have been delivered of bastard children'. This legislation, aiming to negate the obvious defence in infanticide cases that the child in question had been born dead, made it a capital offence to conceal the death of a new-born illegitimate child.[8] Thus between 1624 and the Act's repeal in 1803 'infanticide', as the term is understood by most historians of England, in fact covered two offences: the murder of new-born children; and the concealment of illegitimate children who had been born dead.

Again as contributions to this volume demonstrate, there are various ways in which infanticide as an historical phenomenon can be approached. Our intention here is to analyse it as a criminal offence tried before the courts, and to trace variations in its treatment over a fairly long time-span. Despite the importance of infanticide as a characteristic early modern offence, and also one which can be

---

[5]   Alfred Soman, 'Deviance and criminal justice in Western Europe, 1300–1800: an essay in structure', *Criminal Justice History*, 1 (1980), 22–3. The point about witchcraft executions holds good for Cheshire, where only seven women were executed as witches, all of them between 1631 and 1675: James Sharpe, *Instruments of Darkness: Witchcraft in England 1550–1750* (London, Hamish Hamilton, 1996), p. 122.

[6]   Mark Jackson, *New-Born Child Murder: Women, Illegitimacy and the Courts in Eighteenth-Century England* (Manchester, Manchester University Press, 1996), pp. 6–7.

[7]   Keith Wrightson, 'Infanticide in earlier seventeenth-century England', *Local Population Studies*, 15 (1975), 10–22; R.W. Malcolmson, 'Infanticide in the eighteenth century', in J.S. Cockburn (ed.), *Crime in England 1550–1800* (London, Methuen, 1977), pp. 187–209; Jackson, *New-Born Child Murder*; Laura Gowing, 'Secret births and infanticide in seventeenth-century England', *Past and Present*, 156 (1997), 87–115. Peter C. Hoffer and N.E.H. Hull, *Murdering Mothers: Infanticide in England and New England 1558–1803*, (New York and London, New York University Press, 1981), differ in defining infanticide as the killing of children up to nine years old.

[8]   21 Jac. I c. 27.

interpreted as a specifically female form of criminality, there have been comparatively few studies which have attempted to analyse fluctuations in the prosecution of infanticide and its treatment over time. This is in some measure due to problems in the survival of court records upon which such an analysis might be based, especially for the seventeenth century. Most studies of serious crime in early modern England have, indeed, been based on the records of the Home or South-Eastern Circuit of the assizes, whose indictment rolls, although imperfect, do provide something like a continuous run of relevant records from the early years of Elizabeth onwards.[9] This chapter will however be based on the records of the Court of Great Sessions of Chester and is the product of a broader study of violence in that county in the seventeenth and eighteenth centuries.[10]

Cheshire was a palatinate county, enjoying independent jurisdiction, and the records of the Court of Great Sessions, which appear to run in an almost unbroken series from the fourteenth to the nineteenth centuries, constitute the best source for the reconstruction of the prosecution of serious crime in the early modern period. The importance of these records has only recently been realized, and they form the basis of two important doctoral theses currently being prepared for publication.[11] The Court of Great Sessions met twice annually, in spring and autumn sessions, and its workings were essentially similar to those of the assizes in other areas: the clerical staff of the court formatted and organized documents in the same manner as clerks of assize, and the law being applied was that current in the rest of England. For our purposes, the most important records are the Crown books, in which a précis of all the business of each session of the court was noted, and the rolls, which contain indictments, recognizances and (in limited numbers from the early eighteenth century onwards) depositions.[12] We have decided,

---

9   Public Record Office (PRO), Clerks of Assize Records, Home Circuit indictments, ASSI 35.

10 ESRC Award Number L133251012, 'Violence in early modern England: a regional study'. This project ran under the auspices of the ESRC's Violence research programme.

11 Steve Hindle, 'Aspects of the relationship between the state and local society in early modern England with special reference to Cheshire c.1590–1630' (PhD, Cambridge University, 1992); Garthine Walker, 'Crime, gender and the social order in early modern Cheshire' (PhD, Liverpool University, 1994). For some preliminary comments on the prosecution of serious crime at the Court of Great Sessions between 1580 and 1709, see J.A. Sharpe, *Crime in Early Modern England 1550–1750* (London, Longman, 2nd edn, 1999), pp. 82–93.

12 The records consulted for this essay were Crown books, PRO CHES 21/4–7, and rolls, PRO CHES 24/127/1 to 24/179/5. A gap for the period 1711–57 is partially filled by a slightly imperfect Crown book covering the years 1714–40 held in the Cheshire Record Office (CRO), CR 580.

for the purposes of this chapter, to restrict our investigations to the period 1650–1800. Preliminary investigations suggest that the situation in the earlier seventeenth century, complicated as it was by the impact of the 1624 Act, deserves a separate study which we hope to complete at some future point.

Prosecutions and verdicts

Cheshire was a front-line county in the First Civil War, and consequently for much of the 1640s the normal machinery of administration was disrupted and the Court of Great Sessions did not sit. By 1650, however, county administration was running smoothly again and the court had resumed its meetings. Between that date and the end of the eighteenth century, as Table 3.1 demonstrates, the court tried 112 cases of infanticide, involving some 123 persons accused as principals. Prosecutions were too few to make analysis by decade meaningful, and hence they have been grouped into three blocks each of fifty years. This process reveals a clear pattern. Over half the total prosecutions were in the period 1650–99. The period 1700–49 witnessed less than half the prosecutions experienced within the previous fifty years, and prosecutions roughly halved again between 1750 and 1799. The 1680s experienced the highest level of prosecutions (eighteen), but during the eighteenth century no decade experienced more than eight prosecutions and the average for that century was about five per decade. Overall, then, the Cheshire evidence would suggest a situation in which infanticide was – on the strength of formal prosecutions at the Court of Great Sessions – a crime fairly regularly prosecuted in the later seventeenth century but which, in statistical terms, declined steadily over the eighteenth century.

Table 3.1 Indictments for infanticide at the Court of Great Sessions, Chester 1650–1800.

	Cases	Acc.	Hanged	Rep./P.	Acq.	Acq./HoC	Ign.	Un	Other
1650–99	63	72	20	5	25	4	7	4	7
1700–49	31	33	4	1	15	–	7	4	2
1750–1800	18	18	3	–	12	–	–	–	3
Totals	112	123	27	6	52	4	14	8	12

Key: Acc = persons accused; Rep/P = reprieved or pardoned; Acq = acquitted; Acq/HoC = acquitted but sent to house of correction; Ign = ignoramus; Un = unkown or unclear.

The outcomes of cases also indicate a declining severity in the attitude of the courts. Twenty-seven of those accused of infanticide (some 22 per cent) were executed, but twenty of these suffered in the period 1650–99. Within this period the most severe decade was the 1680s when – in the course of what looks like a local infanticide wave – there were eighteen indictments involving twenty accused, ten of whom were executed (though one was possibly reprieved). Surviving documentation leaves no indication why this situation obtained. The prosecutions were scattered throughout the decade, and although seven of the capital sentences were the product of five cases tried in 1680–81, the remaining three came in 1686–87.[13]

The three executions in the first decade of the eighteenth century all arose from prosecutions at the spring 1701 sessions of the court, and may well have been prompted by a need to combat what was perceived as a sudden upsurge in infanticide cases: a fourth case, whose outcome is uncertain, had been tried at that sessions, and two others had come before the court in the previous year.[14] Similarly, the last woman in our sample known to have been hanged – Sarah Sant, executed and anatomised after the spring session of 1778 – may have been the victim of another local panic over infanticide. Coroners' inquests returned to that session include one on the body of an unknown new-born child found drowned and, in the jury's opinion, murdered at Wincham, and one on the child of Esther Barnes of Sproston, who had given birth in secret, wrapped the child in 'a certain piece of featherbed ticking', and thrown it into a privy where it died. Barnes had fled, the killer of the Wincham child was unknown, and the court was probably anxious to make an example of the one infanticidal mother in custody.[15] It was probably a sense of particular heinousness which lay behind another late capital conviction, that of Sarah Dean, a Congleton spinster, in 1755. Dean had apparently slit her child's throat from ear to ear, thus precluding any claim that it had died accidentally.[16]

Apart from the higher levels of capital convictions in the 1680s, the only other peculiarity in the court's treatment of infanticide suspects came in the 1650s and 1660s. In those decades the court frequently inflicted what might be described as supplementary punishments upon persons acquitted of infanticide or even those whose indictments had been returned *ignoramus* by the grand jury. Under a statute of 1610, mothers of unborn illegitimate children could be sent to the house of

---

[13] PRO CHES 21/5, fols 186v, 208, 280, 290.

[14] PRO CHES 24/163/6.

[15] PRO CHES 21/7, fols 58v, 59–59v, 60. Sant's case attracted the attention of the regional press: Jackson, *New-Born Child Murder*, pp. 2–3.

[16] PRO CHES 24/163/6.

correction for a year.[17] It was either awareness of this legislation, or a more general desire to punish women of loose morals, which led to Jane Hodgkin and Elizabeth Baxter being sent to the house of correction after being acquitted of infanticide at the spring 1653 session.[18] In the next decade, Thomas Massey was sent to the house of correction until the next session of the court after being acquitted at the July 1664 session.[19] George Amery, an accessory, and Mary Jones were both sent to the house of correction for a month and bound over to keep the peace after acquittal at the spring 1666 session, and Elizabeth Beckett was sentenced to three months after the indictment against her had been returned *ignoramus* in 1667.[20]

Worse fates were suffered by Emma Highfield and Margaret Wyatt, both tried in September 1661. Wyatt was acquitted, and the indictment against Highfield returned *ignoramus*, yet the two women were not only sentenced to a short period in the house of correction, but were also to be whipped,[21] while Joan Frances, acquitted in 1666, was ordered simply to be whipped.[22] It was obviously felt that some form of supplementary punishment was needed even after an indictment was rejected. In another case in 1657, a woman acquitted of infanticide and the father of the child were both bound over to answer the justices of the peace for fornication.[23] Such practices seem to have ended with the 1660s, and they do not seem to have been resorted to in Cheshire or other areas in the eighteenth century. It is, however, noteworthy that the early Restoration regime in Cheshire seemed happy to continue penal attitudes which might more readily be associated with the 'Puritan' rule of the 1650s. Whether coincidentally or as a conscious echo of earlier practices, the Act of 1803 – which repealed the 1624 statute – prescribed two years in the house of correction or the county gaol as the punishment for an unmarried mother concealing the birth of a child, if she was acquitted of murder.[24]

---

[17] 7 Jac. I c. 4, 'An Act for the due execution of divers laws and statutes heretofore made against rogues, vagabonds and sturdy beggars, and other lewd and idle persons'.

[18] PRO CHES 21/4, fol. 286v.

[19] PRO CHES 21/5, fol. 20.

[20] Ibid., fols 52v, 67.

[21] PRO CHES 21/4, fol. 418.

[22] PRO CHES 21/5, fol. 46v.

[23] PRO CHES 21/4, fol. 374v.

[24] 43 Geo. III, c. 58, 'An Act for ... repealing a certain Act, made in England in the twenty-first year of the late king James the First, intituled an Act to prevent the destroying and murthering of bastard children'. The repeal of the 1624 infanticide statute was only one of the matters dealt with in this piece of portmanteau legislation, which also, interestingly, made it a felony to administer to pregnant women substances aimed at causing abortion.

Here, as in other samples,[25] those accused of infanticide were overwhelmingly spinsters. The Crown books, on which we have mainly depended in this initial survey, are inconsistent in noting whether infanticidal mothers were married, but those cases where it has been possible to ascertain this status include fifty-eight spinsters (unfortunately the records of the period give no details of their employment or occupation), four widows and eight married women. Men figured very rarely as principals in infanticide prosecutions. Thomas Massey was acquitted in 1663 for involvement in the death and concealment of Frances Goodwyn's child, Goodwyn herself probably being hanged.[26] Similarly Richard Dodd, a clergyman, was acquitted when Mary Tailor was hanged for killing the child he had supposedly fathered on her in 1672.[27] Alice Morris, spinster, and Thomas Bettilly, yeoman, were both acquitted when charged with killing and concealing the death of Morris's child in 1694,[28] while Robert Whicksted, a Nantwich gentleman, and Alice Davies both had the indictments against them found *ignoramus* when they were accused of murdering Davies's child in 1696.[29] Overall, indictments suggest that men were very rarely thought to have been involved in the deaths of these illegitimate children, and were extremely unlikely to be convicted.

A slightly more complex picture emerges with infanticides carried out by married women, although even here the murder was normally carried out by the mother alone. In 1654 Ursula Wright, the wife of Richard Wright of Congleton, fled after killing a new-born female child.[30] Five years later, Dorothy the wife of John Fairbrother, a Brereton husbandman, was acquitted of killing her new-born child.[31] Sarah Worrall, the wife of Peter Worrall of Little Leigh, had the indictment against her found *ignoramus* when she was charged with infanticide in 1711.[32] Conversely, the only two men known to have been hanged for infanticide in our Cheshire materials were both apparently married to the infanticidal mothers. This was probably the case with William Ball, charged at the September 1681 session – together with a woman

---

[25] J.A. Sharpe, *Crime in Seventeenth-Century England: A County Study* (Cambridge, Cambridge University Press/Past and Present Publications, 1983), p. 136; J.M. Beattie, *Crime and the Courts in England, 1660–1800* (Oxford, Clarendon Press, 1986), p. 114; Jackson, *New-Born Child Murder*, p. 29.

[26] PRO CHES 21/5, fol. 20.

[27] Ibid., fol. 126; CHES 24/138/2.

[28] PRO CHES 21/5, fol. 335. The inquest, noted at ibid., fol. 336v, showed that the dead child was found in Bettilly's house.

[29] Ibid., fol. 350v.

[30] PRO CHES 21/4, fol. 299.

[31] Ibid., fol. 408v.

[32] PRO CHES 21/5, fol. 421v; CHES 25/151/6.

described variously as Elizabeth Ball or Elizabeth Kendricke – with killing Elizabeth's new-born illegitimate child. Both were sentenced to death, although it is possible that the woman was reprieved.[33]

At the same session, Jonathan and Sarah Whoretopp were accused of killing the new-born illegitimate child of Margery Priest, the indictment revealing that the child was killed by Sarah, with Jonathan, described as a husbandman, acting as accomplice. The case is a most unusual one, in that the killing was not carried out by the child's mother, who was apparently not accused of complicity. We have no details of the motives at play in this case, although we do know that the couple were executed.[34] Infanticides committed by married couples would be more difficult to detect – and possibly more difficult to prove before the courts – than those carried out by single women, although some of the cases involving infanticide by married women must have involved considerable emotional pressures. Thus in July 1711 an inquest was held at Bredbury on the body of a child which had been conceived before marriage (and hence, according to the wording of the relevant entry in the Crown book, illegitimate) and allegedly murdered by Lydia, the wife of Joseph Wagstaffe. The mother shortly afterwards had committed suicide.[35] As so often, one is left reflecting how the terse wording of official documentation conceals an ocean of human tragedy.

Contexts

Infanticide was essentially a secret act, most often carried out by the mothers of the children involved in isolation. This raises considerable problems with both the detection rate in general and the circumstances under which individual cases might be discovered and brought to law. Certainly, the Cheshire coroners' inquests include regular, although hardly numerous, references to the discovery of infant deaths, the victims usually having been killed or left to die by unknown persons. Unfortunately, the wording of these inquests, at least before the mid-eighteenth century, rarely stated whether these children were new-born,

---

[33] Ibid., fol. 208.

[34] Ibid., fol. 208; the relevant indictment, PRO CHES 24/141/5, says that Sarah broke the child's neck and that Jonathan acted as accomplice.

[35] PRO CHES 21/5, fol. 421v; CHES 24/151/6. There appears to have been some confusion here, for although the entry in the Crown book was insistent that the child was a bastard under English law, both legal sources and local opinion would have held that an illegitimate child was one which was born, rather than conceived, out of wedlock. For a brief discussion of this point and of the relevant legal texts, see Jackson, *New-Born Child Murder*, pp. 43–5.

although it would seem to be a safe inference that they generally were. By the later eighteenth century, coroners' juries seem to have been explicit when they investigated such deaths: typical examples might include what was described as a new-born bastard male child, lately murdered by person or persons unknown, found at Witton in June 1780, or the new-born child whose death was investigated at Lawton in February 1795, murdered by a person unknown but presumed to be 'a single woman' who had suffocated the child in a linen cloth.[36] Such cases remind us that the infanticides which led to formal prosecution were an uncertain but probably small proportion of the total that were committed, but they can hardly form the basis of any statistical survey.

As we have noted, it is possible – on the basis of the wording of the 1624 statute, the comments of contemporary moralists and occasional archival evidence of community disquiet at the discovery of a dead new-born child – to argue that infanticide was regarded with a particular horror. Conversely, as the Cheshire records demonstrate, it is also possible to discover scattered but intriguing evidence of friends and family rallying to help the mother through childbirth, and to assist in concealing the dead child subsequently. Thus Ellen Anderton, accused of infanticide in 1663, escaped with the aid of nine people, their efforts being negated by (as the Crown book entry put it) 'the prisoner being mett with'.[37] Evidence of family involvement came to light in a case in 1656, when Amy Hancocke of Alsager was allegedly assisted in concealing the death of her illegitimate child by John, Richard, and Elizabeth Hancocke 'by burryeing the same in a private manner' in John Hancocke's house'.[38] In general, accessories to infanticide seem most often to have been relatives, while it is probable that a number of married women who assisted infanticidal mothers were sisters, the change of surname that came with marriage masking from us this connection. Relatives were, of course, the people who would naturally be called on in a crisis like childbirth. When Elizabeth Fisbie *alias* Fusackerly of Aldford went into labour in the early hours of 14 July 1732 she called on another woman living in her house, a labourer's wife

---

36 PRO CHES 21/7, fol.73v; CHES 24/178/3.
37 PRO CHES 21/5, fols 2–3v.
38 PRO CHES 21/4, fol. 351v; CHES 24/131/4. As the authors of an important regional study of crime in eighteenth-century England have pointed out, many infanticidal mothers may well have gone undetected because of 'the support which some women derived from their family which shielded them from scrutiny at the crucial moment': Gwenda Morgan and Peter Rushton, *Rogues, Thieves and the Rule of Law: The Problem of Law Enforcement in North-East England, 1718–1800* (London, University College London Press, 1998), p. 40. For some interesting comments on family attitudes in a closely related issue, the seduction of young women, see Susan Staves, 'British seduced maidens', *Eighteenth-Century Studies*, 14 (1980–81), 109–34.

named Joan Pearson, and asked her 'to send for her brother and sister John and Hannah Dodd who lived a little way higher in the said town of Aldford'. There is a constant sense that family solidarity, for those in a position to call upon it, would overcome any sense of horror about infanticide and produce assistance for infanticidal mothers.[39]

For women without such support, concealing infanticide was more difficult. Sometimes, indeed, birth came so unexpectedly as barely to make it an option. On 14 August 1756 Mary Thomas *alias* Turner was making hay in a field at Neston when 'she found violent panes [pains] and pangs of labour came upon her and considering that her sister was out, the door of the house locked and afraid that none of her neighbours would take her in in the condition she found herself to be in', she went 'for decency sake' into a neighbouring barley field where she gave birth to a child that was, as she claimed, born dead. But the owner of the field, Daniel Parsons, 'looking at his barley saw a woman cowering down between the barley and the hedge side'. He went across to her and, on asking Thomas what she was doing, she answered that she was 'doing her needs'. He told her it was 'a very improper place' for such an exercise, but as he followed her out of the field he noticed a 'large quantity of blood'. He went home, told his wife what he had seen, and asked her to come and help him investigate, which they did, finding the corpse of a new-born male child.[40]

Most women charged with infanticide did not give birth as publicly as did Mary Thomas, and the discovery of the children they had borne and whose bodies they had attempted to conceal sometimes came to light days or weeks after birth. A typical case was that of Esther Hayes, a servant girl who was tried in 1731. Her employer, John Lancaster, the vicar of Bowden, told how on 6 December 1730 one of his sons came to him and said that his younger brother had seen something which he described as an adder, but which the older child described as 'like a serpent and had four feet and nails'. Lancaster went to investigate, and found 'the dead body of a male infant dragged out of a ditch by a dogg or some sort of vermin'. He sent for his wife and his 'next neighbour', Isaac Bracegirdle, to look at the corpse and then, as he recounted:

> he recollecting a remarkable illnesse that happened to the said Esther Hayes his servant about five weeks before and the body of the child buryed so near to his dwelling house seeming to have been buried for so long a time, it gave him great cause of suspicion that the said Esther Hayes had privately brought forth the said child whereupon he sent for a constable to take her into custody.[41]

---

[39] PRO CHES 24/157/5.

[40] PRO CHES 24/164/3.

[41] PRO CHES 24/157/4.

A similar chance discovery led to the trial and execution of Sarah Dean in 1755. A Congleton labourer named James Bason recounted how, returning from his 'house of office' one morning, he noticed what he thought was a pig in 'the brook lying betwixt his own garden and Mr Antrobus's meadow'. Noticing it again the next morning, he 'went down to see what it was and took a cow rake and pulled it out of the brooke and found it was a dead female child'. He called to Antrobus and John Vawdrey, Sarah Dean's employer, who were walking in the meadow. A justice of the peace was alerted, rumours that Dean was with child were apparently rife, and a midwife was ordered by the justice to examine the girl, who admitted giving birth five days previously and hiding the body under the floor of a privy.[42]

Many pregnant servant girls, like Dean, gave birth in their employers' houses and – in the short term at least – attempted to hide the bodies of the dead children in their rooms, frequently in their beds. According to her mistress, Margaret Cliff, who was tried in 1760, 'from Saturday until Tuesday following ... kept her bed as a sick person'. The mistress went to Cliff, and said 'I'll beg you'l be plain and tell me the truth what really ails you', upon which the girl burst into tears and, on further questioning, confessed that she had given birth. The body of the child, wrapped in two handkerchiefs, was found hidden under Cliff's bed.[43] In 1728 much the same set of circumstances led to the trial of Anne Trevor. Her mistress, Elizabeth Halwood the wife of Thomas Halwood of Audlem, 'having reason to suspect she had been delivered of a child', searched Trevor's room and 'found two male children which were rapt up in an apron & found about the bed which were then both dead'.[44]

Such cases demonstrate the capacity, perhaps remarkable to the modern observer, for women to keep their pregnancy secret until a very late stage. It was obviously important for a young woman in this situation to maintain such secrecy. But on occasion the circumstances under which a birth might pass unnoticed by other members of an infanticidal mother's household were remarkable, as was the physical and psychological resilience shown by the woman in question. Indeed Sarah Dean's employer, the Congleton baker John Vawdrey, told how the morning after she had given birth he called her at seven o'clock 'and she got up and made a fire and then went to ... milk the cow and suckle the calf and serve the swine as usual and did everything that was necessary to be done in and about the house'. Dean, like many other women in her condition, was the subject of rumours, and both Vawdrey

---

[42] PRO CHES 24/163/6.

[43] PRO CHES 24/165/4.

[44] PRO CHES 24/156/2.

and his wife had questioned her about them yet seemed satisfied with her denials. Vawdrey's wife indeed declared that 'she never suspected or apprehended the said Sarah Dean was or ever had been with child until she was apprehended and searched as aforesaid': the girl had been with them for nearly three years, and was regarded as a good servant.[45]

Other similar accounts reveal a world of gossip and rumour, in which the moral conduct and physical appearance of women were made a matter of comment among other women in the community. Further investigation of this evidence would illuminate such matters as attitudes to pregnancy, attitudes to sexual honour and the workings of the politics of reputation in the period. That the eye for physical evidence could be exercised in unusual circumstances was proved in the investigation of Martha Roberts, a pauper from Toft, in 1748. Elizabeth Robinson told how Roberts had come to her 'to borrow a pair of stays of her in order to go to Over Knutsford Fair on Whitsun Tuesday'. Robinson lent her the stays which, according to Robinson, 'the said Martha Roberts said were then a handful too wide for her'. Three weeks later Roberts again wanted to borrow the stays but this time, as Robinson's deposition tells us, 'the said Martha Roberts on trying the said stays said they were too little for her, upon which this examinant told the said Martha Roberts that she was with child'. The baby was eventually born in a 'boghouse' belonging to the farm where Roberts was employed doing needlework.[46]

The discovery of dead children was followed by the involvement of officialdom: parish constables and justices of the peace, certainly, but also doctors and midwives. Medical evidence generally acquired a greater importance as the eighteenth century progressed, and the Cheshire records demonstrate that medical practitioners were regularly called in to examine newly discovered dead babies. In the case of Sarah Dean, for example, a surgeon and apothecary named James Barrat, having heard conflicting rumours that the body of her child had been savaged by rats or had had its throat cut, was able to confirm the latter opinion.[47] Midwives were, of course, also heavily involved at this point, and were either called upon by worried householders or ordered to carry out searches by local officials.

Essentially local women with experience in childbirth, midwives often occupied a liminal position between official and community values, and their statements deserve more detailed attention than can be given to them here. On occasion they seem to have carried out fairly detailed investigations. When Elizabeth Jackson of Shocklach was involved in

---

[45] PRO CHES 24/163/6.
[46] PRO CHES 24/162/4.
[47] PRO CHES 24/163/6.

the investigation of the death of the child of Dorothy Maddock – who had herself died, possibly as a result of poison administered by the child's father – she asked detailed questions of another member of the household, Elizabeth Taylor, about who had cut the umbilical cord and what had happened to the afterbirth, for example.[48] Another midwife, Mary Hobson of Tarporley, had the disquieting experience of having her daughter, also called Mary Hobson, being charged with infanticide: she denied both knowledge of her daughter's condition and delivering the child.[49] Midwives, one senses, might have had some control over the definition of a suspicious birth. Hester Pixey, widow, a midwife giving evidence in the Anne Trevor case in 1728, told how she had examined the two dead children, 'and looking upon it as a miscarriage she this examinant took the s[ai]d children and buried them at the back side of the same house', recovering them the next day she 'being inform'd that she ought not so to have done'. It is possible that many dead children were quietly disposed of on this basis.[50]

The vividness of such depositional evidence and the obvious emotional impact of infanticide cases have together led historians to consider the topic in the light of community attitudes, or as a means of illuminating the wider experience of women in early modern England.[51] The undoubted importance of such issues should not, however, obscure the fact that more work needs to be done on the treatment of infanticide cases by the courts, and by the officials and jurors on whose running the courts depended. We have already noted changes in levels of prosecution and in verdicts, but behind these lie shifting official attitudes to the crime of infanticide which can only be inferred from a close study of coroners' inquests and indictments.[52] Although our investigations into these sources are still at a preliminary stage, it is clear that official attitudes were potentially of considerable importance, detailed examination of which might reveal clues to regional variations in levels of prosecution and conviction rates.

Certainly the wording of inquests seems to have changed. In the later

---

[48] PRO CHES 24/158/4.

[49] PRO CHES 24/157/5.

[50] PRO CHES 24/156/2. As such cases remind us, early modern midwives are in need of detailed research: for two important discussions of this subject, see David Harley, 'Ignorant midwives – a persistent stereotype', *Bulletin for the Society for the Social History of Medicine*, 28 (1981), 6–9; and idem, 'Historians as demonologists: the myth of the midwife–witch', *Social History of Medicine*, 3 (1990), 1–26.

[51] Notably Gowing, 'Secret births and infanticide'. See also the discussion of infanticide as a female crime in Morgan and Rushton, *Rogues, Thieves and the Rule of Law*, pp. 112–7.

[52] For an extended discussion of this issue, see Jackson, *New-Born Child Murder*, pp. 133–57.

seventeenth century, it seems to have been commonplace for coroners' inquests to adopt a wording which included both the possibility of murder and of concealment, a formula which in effect specified that a child had been murdered but, even if it had not, concealment brought the child's mother under the 1624 statute. The subsequent indictment, however, would select either murder or concealment as the issue.[53] Doubtless concealment continued to carry considerable evidential weight throughout the eighteenth century, but even by the early part of that century it had ceased to be much noted in official documentation. Both inquests and indictments generally focused on the actual killing of children. Inquest juries also seemed increasingly willing to return verdicts that children had been born dead. Anne Trevor's two children were described as having been born 'abortivos et mortuos',[54] while a number of inquests in the years 1737–50 noted that children had been born dead, a verdict that had been comparatively rare previously.[55] In 1760, indeed, the jury called to view the dead child of Margaret Cliff, who claimed that the child had died when it had been dropped from her bed accidentally at birth, declared 'but whether the said female child was still born or whether destroyed in the birth or how or in what manner the said female bastard child came to her death the jurors cannot pretend to say'.[56] An equivocal attitude towards evidence in infanticide cases was clearly running throughout the judicial system by this point.

Conclusion

Our investigations on records from the Court of Great Sessions at Chester are at an early stage, and we are thus better placed to raise problems than to solve them within the compass of this chapter. It seems, however, that the general profile of infanticide as a prosecuted offence in our Cheshire sample is similar in many ways to that sketched out in an important introductory essay of 1977.[57] The victims of

---

[53] For example, PRO CHES 24/143/4, where the inquest on the body of the illegitimate child of a widow named Alice Stonehouse was equivocal as to whether the issue was concealment or murder, but a subsequent indictment stated clearly that on 14 March 1686 Stonehouse 'did stop, choake and strangle' the child. She was sentenced to death. Conversely, for evidence of a woman being indicted (albeit subsequently acquitted) a few years later for concealment, which was also noted as the issue on the relevant inquest, see documentation on Elizabeth Howard, PRO CHES 24/146/3, CHES 21/5, fols 329v, 330v.

[54] PRO CHES 24/156/2.

[55] CRO CR 580, fol. 95v; PRO CHES 24/160/5 (two cases); PRO CHES 24/162/7.

[56] PRO CHES 24/165/4.

[57] Malcolmson, 'Infanticide in the eighteenth century', p. 192.

infanticide were normally killed by their mothers, men were rarely involved, most of these mothers were unmarried, they were generally drawn from the lower orders, many of them being servants, the child victims were normally killed at birth, and the sex of the baby was irrelevant. It was probably a combination of things – shame, confusion and entrapment in a terrible logic, which was set in motion once the initial decision to conceal pregnancy had been made – which led to new-born child murder. Although this pattern appears to have persisted, by the mid-eighteenth century people seemed to understand the circumstances in which infanticide became possible and had developed a conventional wisdom for dealing with it.

As we have stressed, the infanticides which came to court can only have been a sample, and possibly a skewed sample, of those carried out, while one suspects that a comparison of eighteenth-century materials with those from the seventeenth century might indicate a more complex situation in the earlier period. At the very least, any woman contemplating infanticide must have had a clear grasp of the alternative. Margaret Cliff gave birth to a child she claimed was born dead in 1760. Asked if she would have killed the child had it been alive:

> she rung her hands and said as God is my witness and I have a soul to be saved I would not have done a thing for all the world but rather have gone begging from door to door with the child upon my back.[58]

Many unmarried mothers, one suspects, would have regarded this as far too daunting a prospect.

The Cheshire data also follow a similar trajectory of accusations to that found in such other samples as are available. The situation in the first half of the seventeenth century, both for Cheshire and nationally, remains obscure. One sample that does exist, for Essex between 1620 and 1680, demonstrates a high level of capital convictions, with thirty-one from eighty-four accused being executed, over a third of them in the most severe decade, the 1630s.[59] This would suggest that in Essex there was a movement over the seventeenth century away from a period of harshness following the enactment of the 1624 statute. These figures also contrast sharply with comparable data for women charged with non-infanticidal homicide, which suggests that only six from a total of forty-nine were hanged over the same sixty-year period.[60] Data produced by John Beattie for Surrey between 1660 and 1800 suggest a curve of accusations similar to that found for Cheshire, with indictments

---

[58] PRO CHES 24/165/4.
[59] Sharpe, *Crime in Seventeenth-Century England*, table 15, p. 136.
[60] Ibid., table 12, p. 124.

at their highest in the late seventeenth century, then roughly halving between 1700 and 1750, and halving again in the second half of the eighteenth century.[61]

This eighteenth-century pattern is confirmed by figures for London and Middlesex derived from the *Old Bailey Sessions Papers*. Analysis of this source for the years 1707–27 reveals forty accused, of whom seven were executed; and another source for 1764–87 gives eighteen accused, of whom only one suffered death.[62] On the Northern Assize Circuit, conversely, perhaps indicating other as yet undiscovered regional variations, levels of indictments for infanticide remained fairly level throughout the eighteenth century.[63] The Northern Circuit records, however, demonstrate the common pattern of low levels of conviction and execution for infanticide after the early eighteenth century: of some 200 women accused of infanticide between 1720 and 1800 only six were found guilty, two of whom were hanged.[64] Our Cheshire materials would therefore seem to match a national trend. It should, however, be remembered that the high levels of accusation and conviction in the 1680s preclude any simple model of steady decline, while we are also left with the task of investigating the peculiar circumstances which lay behind the fate of those few women who *were* executed during the eighteenth century.

Existing literature suggests that complex transitions underlay the eighteenth-century decline of infanticide's special status as a horror-provoking crime: changing attitudes to women; changing attitudes to children; a sharpened concern about rules of evidence in the criminal courts; and a shift of emphasis within Christianity which emphasized rational religiosity rather than hell-fire. The complexity is agreed upon, although the exact significance of these and the other factors which led to the decline of prosecutions and convictions for infanticide, and to the repeal of the 1803 statute, are matters of contention. If this chapter has done little to illuminate these large shifts, it has at least deepened our knowledge of infanticide as a criminal offence tried before the English courts through an initial investigation of a hitherto largely unexplored but important body of archival materials. Clearly, we are adding one piece to the mosaic of varied evidence and varied interpretations that form the history of infanticide as a broad cultural phenomenon. But it is undeniable that further research into these Cheshire materials will add an important regional and institutional

---

[61] Beattie, *Crime and the Courts in England*, table 3.6, pp. 115–6.
[62] Hoffer and Hull, *Murdering Mothers*, table 3.1, p. 73.
[63] Jackson, *New-Born Child Murder*, p. 26, n. 61.
[64] Ibid., p. 3.

dimension to our understanding of the handling of infanticide prosecutions by the courts. It will also illuminate the lived experience of the women who were prosecuted, and that of their employers, kinsfolk, friends and neighbours. These women participated in small but intense dramas that together constitute the core of the history of infanticide in early modern England.

CHAPTER FOUR

'The unfortunate maid exemplified':[1] Elizabeth Canning and representations of infanticide in eighteenth-century England

Amy L. Masciola

On New Year's Day 1753 Elizabeth Canning, an eighteen-year-old servant, visited her aunt and uncle, Alice and Thomas Colley, at their home in Salt-Petre Bank in the East End of London. She arrived at about eleven o'clock in the morning after visiting her mother and younger siblings in Aldermanbury Postern.[2] Canning 'dined and supped' with the Colleys, and at nine o'clock that night it was time for her to return to her master's house. Her aunt and uncle accompanied her as far as Houndsditch where they left her at about half-past nine. They returned home and went to bed. Some time between eleven o'clock and midnight there was a knock at the door. It was Canning's mother's apprentice, James Lord. Elizabeth was missing! Her master, Mr Lyon, had gone to Mrs Canning's house at nine o'clock and again at ten o'clock, looking for his servant. Mrs Canning in turn sent her apprentice to the Colleys' house and they assured him that they had last seen the young woman at Houndsditch on her way home to Lyon's. The search for Canning continued throughout the night. The next morning, before dawn, the apprentice returned to the Colleys' house along with Mrs Canning. There was still no sign of Elizabeth.[3]

---

[1] Anon., *The Unfortunate Maid Exemplified in the Story of Elizabeth Canning* (London, Corbett, 1754).

[2] A map of these locations is included in Lillian de la Torre, *Elizabeth is Missing* (New York, Knopf, 1945), pp. 8–9. Aldermanbury Postern was then on the edge of London, about half a mile from the Guildhall; Salt-Petre Bank is now Dock Street, a little to the east of the Tower of London. It was a journey of about two miles.

[3] T.B. Howell (comp.), *A Complete Collection of State Trials*, vol. XIX (London, Hansard, 1813), pp. 474–95. My account of Canning's disappearance is based on the testimonies of Alice and Thomas Colley, Elizabeth Canning senior and James Lord at Canning's trial for perjury in May 1754. The account in the *State Trials* is unusually lengthy at 205 pages (cols 283–692). One late-nineteenth-century scholar claimed that Canning's trial 'was probably the first criminal trial to last more than a day and that it "established the principle that in cases of misdemeanour the Court may adjourn and the

Over the next four weeks, Mrs Canning placed three separate advertisements for her daughter in the *London Daily Advertiser*. She 'went to all the agents and places where [she] could think of, fearing some casualty', including the Wood Street Compter, the city prison for minor offenders, and she consulted a conjurer in the Old Bailey. The only clue to the younger Canning's whereabouts was a statement by a woman in Bishopsgate Street that she had heard a young person scream from inside a moving coach at night around the first of the year. This led Mrs Canning to suspect that her daughter, being 'a sober body', had been 'forced away in a coach'.[4] Her second advertisement mentioned this incident and asked that the coachman or anyone else who had heard the scream come forward. Mrs Canning must have feared for her daughter's chastity as well as her life. The story of a young single woman's disappearance would certainly have raised questions for her family, her neighbours, her employers and those who read about her in the first newspaper advertisements. It was not unheard-of for young women to be abducted and forced into prostitution in the city or, for that matter, for single women to become pregnant and leave their jobs and neighbourhoods in order to lie in secretly.[5]

Four weeks later, on the evening of 29 January, there was a knock at Mrs Canning's door. It was her daughter. The young woman was weak and bleeding from a cut above one ear. Lord, the apprentice, was shocked at her appearance and later testified that 'she was e'en almost dead, as black as the chimney-stock, black and blue. She was dressed up with an old bit of an handkerchief round her head, and an old dirty ragged bed-gown, what they properly call a jacket'.[6] Canning told her family and friends an extraordinary tale that night.[7] She alleged that two men had robbed and beaten her near Bedlam Wall in Moorfields after she left her aunt and uncle on 1 January. After knocking her out with a

---

jury may separate".' See Malvin Zirker (ed.), *An Enquiry into the Causes of the Late Increase of Robbers and Related Writings* (Middletown, Conn., Wesleyan, 1988), p. cx, n. 6. Zirker's introduction is a useful discussion of the case and Henry Fielding's role.

4 *State Trials*, XIX, pp. 482–5, 489.

5 Randolph Trumbach, *Sex and the Gender Revolution: Vol. 1: Heterosexuality and the Third Gender in Enlightenment London* (Chicago, University of Chicago Press, 1998), pp. 136–53.

6 *State Trials*, XIX, p. 491. The apothecary who examined Canning the day after she came home said that 'she was extreamely low and weak; I could scarcely here [sic] her speak, her voice was so low, and her pulse scarcely to be felt with cold sweats'. *Old Bailey Sessions Papers* (hereafter referred to as *OBSP*), Feb. 1753, 115.

7 On the story Canning told that night and how it differed from the accounts she later gave, see Judith Moore, *The Appearance of Truth: The Story of Elizabeth Canning and Eighteenth-Century Narrative* (Newark, University of Delaware Press, 1994), pp. 24–50.

blow to the head, the two men had carried her about ten miles north of London along the Hertfordshire road to Enfield Wash.[8] The men 'carried her into an house where she saw in the kitchen an old woman and two young women'. The old woman 'took hold of her by the hand, and promised *to give her fine cloaths if she would go their way*'. She understood this 'expression' to mean she should become a prostitute, and she 'utterly refused to comply'. The woman then used a knife to cut off Canning's stays and 'forced her up an old pair of stairs ... threatening that if she made the least noise or disturbance', the old woman 'would come up and cut her throat'. Canning remained in the upstairs room for four weeks with only a 'large black jug, with the neck much broken, filled with water, and several pieces of bread, amounting to about the quantity of a quartern loaf' to sustain her. She finally broke out of a window at about half-past four on the afternoon of 29 January and 'got back to her friends in London in about six hours, in a most weak and miserable condition, being almost starved to death'.[9]

On 1 February, when Canning had recovered enough to travel, a group of men that included her master Lyon and several neighbours took her to Enfield Wash to identify her captors. Once inside the house, Canning said she recognized two old women, Susannah Wells and an old gypsy who was lodging there, Mary Squires. Despite Canning's earlier statements in which she had mentioned one old woman – not two – and had not referred to a gypsy, Squires and Wells were arrested. They were tried together at the Old Bailey, London's central criminal court, on 21 February, Squires for assaulting and stealing Canning's stays and Wells for harbouring a known felon. The two women insisted that they had never seen Canning before she came to the house at Enfield Wash to identify them; and Squires claimed that she had been in the west of England in early January. Their defence was not enough to convince the jury, and both women were convicted. Squires was sentenced to hang while Wells was sentenced to six months in jail.[10]

---

[8]   Canning told her former master, John Wintlebury, that she knew she was in a house on the Hertfordshire road because she recognized the Hertford coachman as he drove past. *State Trials*, XIX, p. 510.

[9]   My account of Canning's story is based on Henry Fielding, *A Clear State of the Case of Elizabeth Canning* (London, Millar, 1753) reprinted in Zirker (ed.), *An Enquiry*, pp. 287–8. According to the prosecution in her 1754 trial for perjury, she did not mention the gypsy woman until she had arrived at the house at Enfield Wash. She may have said that she knew the old woman's name was Wills or Wells, although some witnesses claimed that a neighbour, Mr Scarrat (who had supposedly visited Mother Wells's house), suggested that name to her when she said she had been in a house on the Hertfordshire road. See *State Trials*, XIX, pp. 498–9.

[10] *OBSP*, Feb. 1753, 108–17.

The matter was far from resolved, however. Sir Crisp Gascoyne, the Lord Mayor of London and one of the judges who had presided at Squires's and Wells's trial, took a personal interest in the case.[11] He was dismayed by the guilty verdicts and launched his own investigation into Squires's alibi. He sought out and paid for the testimony of witnesses in the west of England who claimed that they had seen Squires and her children in Dorset in late December and early January. Gascoyne was able to gather enough evidence in favour of Squires to win her a full pardon and release from jail on 21 May. In the meantime, he had issued a warrant for Canning's arrest on perjury charges on 13 March and an enormous pamphlet war had erupted, with partisans on each side. The noted painter and essayist Allan Ramsay claimed in May 1753 that the Canning story was 'the conversation of every alehouse within the bills of mortality'. In 1760 the novelist Tobias Smollett wrote in his *History of England* that the case had 'divided the greater part of the kingdom, including the rich as well as the poor, the high as well as the humble, ... [and] became the general topic of conversation in all assemblies, and people of all ranks espoused one or the other party with as much warmth and animosity as had ever inflamed the Whigs and Tories'.[12] Those in favour of Squires called themselves Egyptians (from the supposed origin of the gypsy race)[13] and Canning's 'friends' referred to themselves as Canningites.[14]

---

[11] There were already pamphlets in circulation at this point and Canning's disappearance had been discussed in the newspapers. Zirker says that a broadside entitled *The Case of Elizabeth Canning* was published early in February 1753 'to encourage contributions to prosecute a "nest of villains"'. Zirker (ed.), *An Enquiry*, p. 293, n. 1.

[12] Allan Ramsay, *A Letter to the Right Honourable the Earl of ——* (London, Seddon, 1753); reprint entitled *On Elizabeth Canning* in *The Investigator* (London, Millar, 1762), p. 38 – the 'bills of mortality' covered central London. Tobias Smollett, *The Complete History of England* (London, Baldwin, 1760) quoted in Moore, *Appearance*, p. 194.

[13] A gypsy is 'a member of a wandering race (by themselves called Romany), of Hindu origin, which first appeared in England about the beginning of the sixteenth century and was then believed to have come from Egypt'. Also, 'a contemptuous term for a woman, as being cunning, deceitful, fickle, or the like, a 'baggage', 'hussy', etc.' *Oxford English Dictionary* (1989), vol. VI.

[14] More than fifty pamphlets and broadsides with either Canning or Squires in the title are listed in the British Library catalogue. See Hugh Amory, 'The virgin and the witch: an exhibition at the Harvard Law School library' (1987) for a list of publications and prints in chronological order and Lillian Bueno McCue, 'Elizabeth Canning in print', *University of Colorado Studies*, 2 (October 1945), 223–32. It is not clear whether suspicions of Canning emerged before or after Gascoyne launched his investigation. His actions probably fuelled the pamphlet war among several prominent men including himself, Henry Fielding, John Hill, Dr Solas Dodd, Dr Daniel Cox and the artist Allan Ramsay. See Zirker's introduction in *An Enquiry*, p. cii, n. 2, for a discussion of this élite debate and the animosity among the participants.

Representations of Canning and her alleged captors were constructed orally in the streets of London, in coffee-houses and pubs, and eventually in the courtroom at the Old Bailey.[15] They took visual and written form in the prints, trial accounts, pamphlets, broadsides, ballads and newspaper accounts that began to circulate shortly after she reappeared.[16] And whether for or against Canning, all of the commentators on the case took advantage of a common set of stereotypes to make their arguments. They used dichotomous representations of the ideal woman (quiet, chaste and domesticated) and the evil woman (scolding, promiscuous and savage) to construct a coherent narrative out of the mass of conflicting testimony.[17]

On the one side, Canningites were persuaded that the two older women were guilty of theft, kidnapping and prostitution because of images constructed in early news reports and the Old Bailey trial account. For them, Canning's youth, chastity and 'Englishness' were the visual and symbolic markers of virtue.[18] And Squires's vagabond status, old age, physical ugliness (culturally defined, to be sure) and racial otherness marked her as the evil woman.[19] On the other side,

---

[15] Mr Nares, defence counsel at Canning's 1754 trial for perjury, claimed that 'I do not believe there is an individual in this great city that has not heard of this affair, nor hath a company met for one single evening, where this was not a subject matter of conversation'. *State Trials*, XIX, p. 463.

[16] See Amory, 'The virgin and the witch' and Bueno McCue, 'Elizabeth Canning in print'. An engraving of Canning was published as early as 3 March 1753 and one of Squires came out on 14 March. For a description of prints related to the case, see Frederic George Stephens and Edward Hawkins, *Catalogue of Prints and Drawings in the British Museum: Political and Personal Satires*, vol. III, pt II (London, Trustees of the British Museum, 1870–1954).

[17] On the changing notions of ideal womanhood, see Nancy Armstrong, *Desire and Domestic Fiction: A Political History of the Novel* (New York, Oxford University Press, 1987), pp. 59–95; Felicity A. Nussbaum, *The Brink of All We Hate: English Satires on Women, 1660–1750* (Lexington, University of Kentucky Press, 1984), pp. 77–93; and Anthony Fletcher, *Gender, Sex, and Subordination in England, 1500–1800* (New Haven, Yale University Press, 1995), pp. 376–413.

[18] On gender and English identity in mid-eighteenth-century England, see Ruth Perry, 'Colonizing the breast: sexuality and maternity in eighteenth-century England', *Journal of the History of Sexuality*, 2:2 (1991), 204–34; and Felicity A. Nussbaum, *Torrid Zones: Maternity, Sexuality, and Empire in Eighteenth-Century English Narratives* (Baltimore, Johns Hopkins University Press, 1995), pp. 1-21.

[19] This chapter is part of a project that explores representations of criminal women in early-eighteenth-century England. My research on Elizabeth Canning examines how all three women – Canning, Squires and Wells – were constructed in the press and pamphlets. Stereotypes were used by partisans on both sides in the debate over Canning's whereabouts. Squires was portrayed repeatedly as a witch; artists and writers suggested that she had flown to London on a broomstick and that this explained why witnesses saw her in both Dorset and London in early January. The sinister image of the gypsy was also used to great effect by Fielding and others. Squires

Egyptians filled in the void left by Canning's absence with narratives that revolved around sex and crime: prostitution, abortion and infanticide.[20] Still, the 'truth' about Canning's whereabouts was never revealed and the case has been a source of scholarly and popular interest for 250 years largely because it remains an unsolved mystery. Writers have continued to revisit the case in the form of histories, historical fictions and even a travel guide. Most have attempted to reconstruct the events of 1 January 1753 and to deconstruct the various stories that Canning and others told on and after 29 January, in order to solve the mystery of her disappearance.[21]

In the twentieth century, a variety of both popular and scholarly books and articles on the case appeared. Some of them took a distinctly misogynistic tone, as in Edmond Pearson's 1936 assessment of Canning; he called her 'one of those pretty little liars, who are so often found among girls between the ages of twelve and twenty. Many a man has

---

and her children were depicted as dark, sub-human, monstrous and naturally criminal in an effort to paint them as the obvious villains. And although Susannah Wells admitted that her reputation was not spotless, there was little evidence that her house was a brothel. Yet she was always portrayed as an old bawd and brothel-keeper set on expanding her operation. See my forthcoming dissertation, '"I see by this woman's features that she is capable of any wickedness": representations of criminal women in eighteenth-century England' (PhD thesis, University of Maryland, 2001).

20 Of the three, only infanticide was a felony. Abortion did not become a statutory crime in England until 1803. Prostitution was prosecuted as a vice by magistrates throughout the eighteenth century. All three were considered to be violations of standard Christian behaviour, as was the illicit sex that each represented. See: Angus McLaren, *Reproductive Rituals: The Perception of Fertility in England from the Sixteenth Century to the Nineteenth Century* (London, Methuen, 1984), pp. 113–44; and Tony Henderson, *Disorderly Women in Eighteenth-Century London: Prostitution and Control in the Metropolis, 1730–1830* (London, Longman, 1999), pp. 86–103.

21 However, late-eighteenth- and early-nineteenth-century writers were more interested in the contemporary obsession with Canning than in arguing for one side or the other. According to Smollett the furore over a lowly servant girl revealed something central to English national identity. He claimed that the case was 'a dispute in itself of so little consequence to the community, that it could not deserve a place in a general history, if it did not serve to convey a characteristic idea of the English nation.' He explained that the 'genius of the English people is perhaps incompatible with a state of perfect tranquility' and if there was not enough to occupy them the English sought 'provocations' wherever they might be found. For Voltaire, Canning's case was a shining example of the 'glorious vindication of English justice and compassion'. He contrasted Canning's treatment with the 'prejudice and superstition of his own country' where in 1762 Jean Calas had been falsely accused, tortured and executed for his son's murder. Smollett, *History*, cited in Moore, *Appearance*, p. 194; John Treherne, *The Canning Enigma* (London, Cape, 1989), p. 158; and F.M.A. Voltaire, *Histoire d'Elisabeth Canning, et des Calas* (London, Jean Nourse, 1762), reprinted in *Oeuvres Completes de Voltaire* (Paris, Dupont, 1824). For a thorough analysis of the literature on Canning, see Moore, *Appearance*, pp. 192–239.

gone to prison, or even swung in a noose, because of the tales told by girls, like Elizabeth Canning'. F.J. Harvey Darton's reconstruction of the gypsies' alibi in *Alibi Pilgrimage* is a nostalgic traveller's guide to the route the Squires family claimed they took from Somerset to London in the first half of January 1753. And Josephine Tey was inspired by Arthur Machen's anti-Canning account, *The Canning Wonder*, to write a novel set in twentieth-century Britain. In *The Franchise Affair*, published in 1948, Tey transformed Canning into Betty Kane, a 'cold-blooded and deliberate' liar who accused two innocent women of kidnapping her and forcing her to wait on them in exchange for food.[22]

In 1989 John Treherne, a retired Cambridge entomologist, wrote *The Canning Enigma*. Treherne's popular account received critical attention and reflected fresh interest in Canning, particularly among literary scholars. In a 1991 article, Arlene Wilner analysed Henry Fielding's Canningite pamphlet in order to illustrate the apparent 'incongruity between the complex social vision of [Fielding's] novels and the rigid conservatism of [his] pamphlets'. She argued that in his social and legal writings Fielding sought to assimilate 'history to mythology' and to explain, justify and make 'coherent within established structures of thought events that are potentially disruptive and subversive'.[23] Wilner's work marked a shift away from the impulse to solve the mystery.

In 1994 Judith Moore published the first scholarly monograph devoted to Canning. In *The Appearance of Truth: The Story of Elizabeth Canning and Eighteenth-Century Narrative*, Moore conducted a close reading of several texts in order to reach a 'final resolution to the case's contradictions'. Her analysis was influenced throughout by her conclusion 'that Elizabeth Canning's whole story was true' and 'that she reported its contents as accurately as she was able to, and that the defects in her recollection were of the sort common to human fallibility'. Moore argued that Canning's class or servant status, rather than her sexuality, underlay the controversy that surrounded her. In contrast, Kristina Straub argued in a 1997 article

---

22   Edmund Pearson, 'The first great disappearer' in *More Studies in Murder* (London, Arco, 1953, repr. from New York, 1936), p. 204, quoted in Moore, *Appearance*, p. 209; F.J. Harvey Darton, *Alibi Pilgrimage* (London, Newnes, 1936); Arthur Machen, *The Canning Wonder* (London, Chatto and Windus, 1925); Josephine Tey, *The Franchise Affair* (London, Peter Davies, 1948); and Moore, *Appearance*, pp. 225–33.

23   Roy Porter, 'Review of *The Canning Enigma*', *Times Literary Supplement*, (22 December 1989), p. 1408; John Biffen, 'Stays of execution', *The Sunday Times*, (14 January 1990), features section; and Andrew St George, 'Flirting with truth', *Financial Times* (6 January 1990), p. 15; Arlene Wilner, 'The mythology of history, the truth of fiction: Henry Fielding and the cases of Bosavern Penlez and Elizabeth Canning', *Journal of Narrative Technique*, 21:2 (spring 1991), 185–201, at 185 and 190.

that the case 'helped to crystallize particular constructions of feminine sexuality that formed part of broader patterns of thought and feeling about the British social order'. Like Wilner, Straub felt no urge to debate Canning's guilt. For her, representations of Canning revealed patriarchal attempts to define middle-class femininity and to control female sexuality within that context.[24]

In this chapter, I also want to reject the notion that the case demands a solution. The important question for us is not Where was Canning? but rather, What do the many stories about, or representations of, Canning mean? In the introduction to her study of another notorious case, Cynthia Herrup articulated the importance of shifting one's perspective away from the verdict (or resolution) in legal case studies. She explained that:

> Once [she] asked not *if* Castlehaven was guilty, but why knowing if he was seemed so important, [she] realized the source of [her] discomfort: [she and her] audiences ... had been searching not for an ending, but for a beginning. Certainty about the verdict would offer us a way of seeing, a filter through which to assess all other information. Trials, after all, are supposed to provide closure or at least its illusion; if that closure remains elusive, later commentators are expected to provide it.[25]

I shall argue that an analysis of representations of Canning provides an ideal case study precisely because there was no satisfactory conclusion. Studying Canning frees us from the verdict, from our urge to focus on 'what really happened'.

What better lens through which to examine the construction of the villainous or infanticidal servant – or indeed the chaste English maid –

---

24 Moore, *Appearance*, pp. 21 and 256; Kristina Straub, 'Heteroanxiety and the case of Elizabeth Canning' *Eighteenth-Century Studies*, 30:3 (1997), 296–304, at 296.

25 Cynthia Herrup, *A House in Gross Disorder: Sex, Law, and the 2nd Earl of Castlehaven* (New York, Oxford University Press, 1999), p. 6. On the usefulness of criminal trials and biographies to historians, see: Lincoln Faller, *Turned to Account: The Forms and Functions of Criminal Biography in Late Seventeenth- and Early Eighteenth-Century England* (Cambridge, Cambridge University Press, 1987); Natalie Zemon Davis, *Fiction in the Archives: Pardon Tales and Their Tellers in Sixteenth-Century France* (Stanford, Stanford University Press, 1987); and Joy Wiltenburg, *Disorderly Women and Female Power in the Street Literature of Early Modern England and Germany* (Charlottesville, University of Virginia Press, 1992). On the use of case studies or microhistories, see: Edward Muir and Guido Ruggiero (eds), *Microhistory and the Lost Peoples of Europe: Selections from Quaderni Storici* (Baltimore, Johns Hopkins University Press, 1991); Edward Muir and Guido Ruggiero (eds), *History from Crime: Selections from Quaderni Storici* (Baltimore, Johns Hopkins University Press, 1994); and Martin J. Wiener, 'The sad story of George Hall: adultery, murder, and the politics of mercy in mid-Victorian England' *Social History*, 24:2 (May 1999), 174–95.

than a case riddled with contest and contradiction? That contest among elite and ordinary Londoners alike generated an unprecedented amount of printed material that described and debated the life and behaviour of a lowly maid-of-all-work. This chapter will focus only on those pamphlets published from March to the end of July 1753 in order to chart the emergence of a narrative that portrayed Canning as an infanticidal woman. It will draw connections between contemporary understandings of the cunning, criminal servant maid, the typical infanticide, and Canning's absence or independence from male supervision. By taking a microhistorical approach, my study further contextualizes the lives of domestic servants and reveals the power of representations of criminal women, even on the lives of apparently innocent women.

The story that Canning told upon her return – or rather the one that circulated as gossip and in print immediately after her reappearance – emphasized her chastity by stressing her refusal to be drawn into prostitution by the women at Mother Wells's house, who were portrayed in stark contrast as savage and promiscuous. But, in the absence of conventional evidence, many observers and writers began to speculate on Canning's whereabouts. They constructed their narratives from pre-existing stereotypes attached to servant maids and single women. Images of Canning reveal the contradictions inherent in the female servant's position. She was always already a suspicious figure, regardless of her reputation, and any exercise of freedom or independence from male authority could cement her criminal identity. Much of the negative discourse surrounding servants focused on secrecy, concealment and, to use Fran Dolan's words, dangerous familiarity.[26] That discourse shaped and reflected employers' and authorities' anxiety about servants' ability to hide their true (criminal) identities. Virtuous servants with good characters were as vulnerable to accusations, if not more so, because all servants were represented as essentially criminal.[27]

---

[26] Frances E. Dolan, *Dangerous Familiars: Representations of Domestic Crime in England, 1550–1700* (Ithaca, Cornell University Press, 1994).

[27] The dichotomous stereotype of the virtuous servant maid who was frequently victimized by her master or fellow servants is epitomized in Samuel Richardson, *Pamela* (London, Kingman, 1741). Historians and literary scholars who study domestic service have focused largely on female servants' victimization. Historians of crime, and infanticide in particular, have focused on servants' precarious economic position, their vulnerability to sexual advances by masters and fellow servants, and the consequences of pregnancy (i.e., dismissal or infanticide). See: Bridget Hill, *Servants: English Domestics in the Eighteenth Century* (Oxford, Clarendon, 1996), pp. 93–114; and R.W. Malcolmson, 'Infanticide in the eighteenth century' in J.S. Cockburn (ed.), *Crime in England, 1550–1800* (Princeton, Princeton University Press, 1977), pp. 187–209.

The stereotype of the cunning, criminal servant maid affected the lives of well-behaved domestic servants. Elizabeth Canning was, by many accounts, one such servant – at least until 1 January 1753.

The virtuous servant as potential infanticide

Early-seventeenth-century legislators had constructed a profile of the murderous mother in a 1624 statute that targeted 'lewd women that have been delivered of bastard children'.[28] The law made concealing the birth of a new-born bastard later found dead a capital offence, and thereby solidified the association of new-born child murder with single women and with social and sexual disorder.[29] By the early eighteenth century, concern about the rising number of young women flooding the city to work as domestics was linked with a perceived infanticide epidemic to cement an image of the infanticidal servant. The connection between the two images – servant and infanticide – was strengthened by increasing concerns about the social and sexual regulation of young, single women.[30]

This was the cultural context in which Canning lived and worked for Mr Lyon. Before him, she had been servant to Mr Wintlebury for eighteen months. In many ways, she was a typical servant maid. Domestic service was the most important source of employment for young, single women in London from the late seventeenth through to the mid-nineteenth century.[31] It was probably one of the more attractive

---

[28] 21 James I, c. 27 (1624). For a discussion of the history of infanticide in early modern England, see: Laura Gowing, 'Secret births and infanticide in seventeenth-century England' *Past and Present* 156 (Aug. 1997), 87–115; Marilyn Francus, 'Monstrous mothers, monstrous societies: infanticide and the rule of law in Restoration and eighteenth-century England,' *Eighteenth-Century Life*, 20 (1997), 133–56; Mark Jackson, *New-Born Child Murder: Women, Illegitimacy and the Courts in Eighteenth-Century England* (Manchester, Manchester University Press, 1996); J.M. Beattie, *Crime and the Courts in England, 1660–1800* (Princeton, Princeton University Press, 1986), pp. 115–24; Peter C. Hoffer and N.E.H. Hull, *Murdering Mothers: Infanticide in England and New England, 1558–1803* (New York, New York University Press, 1981); and Malcolmson, 'Infanticide in the eighteenth century'.

[29] Dolan, *Dangerous Familiars*, p. 129.

[30] For the history of single women, see Amy Froide, 'Singlewomen, work, and community in Southampton, 1550–1750' (PhD thesis, Duke University, 1996); Judith Bennett and Amy Froide (eds.), *Singlewomen in the European Past, 1250–1800* (Philadelphia, University of Pennsylvania Press, 1999).

[31] On the history of domestic service, see Tim Meldrum, 'Domestic service, privacy, and the eighteenth-century metropolitan household', *Urban History*, 26:1 (1999), 27–39; idem, 'London domestic servants from depositional evidence, 1660–1750: servant–employer sexuality in the patriarchal household' in Tim Hitchcock, Peter King

occupations available to single women, whose wages outside service
were always lower than men's and barely met subsistence levels. David
Kent argues that single women chose service over other occupations,
and may have chosen to remain in service rather than marry, because of
the freedom and security it offered them. According to Kent, 'the female
servant was independent ... . Her wages may have been low, as they were
for all women workers, but they were the wages of an independent
woman and not those of a supplementary wage-earner'. Servants in
London appear to have taken advantage of the high demand for their
labour by changing jobs frequently. About fifty per cent of the women
in Kent's sample stayed in their positions for only one year and only
twenty-five per cent stayed three or more years.[32]

Many servants lived with the families for whom they worked. They
were privy to the personal habits and secrets of their masters and
mistresses; they had access to their employers' belongings, and they were
familiar with their bodies. Servants dressed their masters and mistresses,
laundered their clothing, emptied their chamber pots and prepared their
food. And yet they were expected to remain in the background –
impervious to their surroundings. As women living within the household
and among the family, but not *of* it (as had been the case in the
seventeenth century), they posed a sexual and criminal threat.

Indeed, by the eighteenth century the context and forms of domestic
service had changed. Relationships among servants and their employers
were no longer familial, rural and customary; rather, they had become
contractual, urban and based on wage labour. The proportion of women
in London who were single had increased during the seventeenth century
as apprenticeship opportunities for men declined and the demand for
female domestic servants rose. Women outnumbered men in London by

and Pamela Sharpe (eds), *Chronicling Poverty: The Voices and Strategies of the English
Poor, 1640–1840* (London, Macmillan, 1997); Paula Humfrey, 'Female servants and
women's criminality in early eighteenth-century London' in Greg Smith, Simon
Devereaux and Allyson May (eds), *Criminal Justice in the Old World and the New:
Essays in Honour of J.M. Beattie* (Toronto, Centre of Criminology, University of
Toronto, 1998); Peter Earle, 'The female labor market in London in the late
seventeenth and early eighteenth centuries' in Pamela Sharpe (ed.), *Women's Work: The
English Experience, 1650–1914* (London, Arnold, 1998), pp. 121–47; Bridget Hill,
Servants: English Domestics in the Eighteenth Century (Oxford, Clarendon, 1996);
Patty Seleski, 'Women, work, and cultural change in eighteenth- and early nineteenth-
century London' in Tim Harris (ed.), *Popular Culture in England, c.1500–1850* (New
York, St. Martin's, 1995), pp. 143–67; D.A. Kent, 'Ubiquitous but invisible: female
domestic servants in mid-eighteenth-century London', *History Workshop Journal*, 28
(1989), 111–28; Sarah Maza, *Servants and their Masters in Eighteenth-Century France*
(Princeton, Princeton University Press, 1983); J.J. Hecht, *The Domestic Servant Class
in the Eighteenth Century* (London, Routledge and Kegan Paul, 1955).

32 Kent, 'Ubiquitous but invisible', 115.

as much as 100 to 77 by 1695. And by the 1690s approximately eighty per cent of domestic servants in the City were women. These numbers had not changed significantly by the 1750s.[33] The growing number of young single women with disposable income and the opportunity to change jobs at their own whim, as well as their familiarity with the lives and bodies of their employers, was a source of anxiety for employers and authorities. That anxiety contributed to a widespread perception that the criminal underworld of theft, prostitution and infanticide was largely populated by domestic servants.[34]

Daniel Defoe shaped and reflected the attitudes of middling employers toward their servants. In 1725, he claimed that 'there have always been thieves and whores, who get into people's houses, under the characters of honest servants, even with design to rob the families . . . [but] there were never so many such as now'. He was particularly critical of young women who he said dominated the sessions papers and 'with instances of servant maids robbing their places, this can be only attributed to their devilish pride; for their whole enquiry now a days, is how little they shall do, how much they shall have'. He complained of 'the abuses insensibly crept in among us, and the inconveniences daily arising from the insolence and intrigues of our servant wenches, who, by their caballing together, have made their party so considerable, that everybody cries out against 'em'.[35] Middling people were increasingly dependent upon female servants and, at the same time, were suspicious of the knowledge that servants had about their employers' personal and financial habits.

Just as young, single women were flooding the metropolis in search of domestic work, authorities and social critics insisted there was an

---

[33] This critical demographic shift helps explain why so many of the women prosecuted for felony at the Old Bailey were servants. Roger Finlay, *Population and Metropolis: The Demography of London, 1580–1650* (Cambridge, Cambridge University Press, 1981), pp. 140–41. See also Peter Earle, *City Full of People: Men and Women of London, 1650–1750* (London, Methuen, 1994), pp. 39–40; and idem, *The Making of the English Middle Class: Business, Society, and Family Life in London, 1660–1730* (Berkeley, University of California Press, 1989), p. 219.

[34] In 1713, Parliament passed legislation that directly targeted 'divers wicked and ill-disposed servants' who were 'encouraged to commit robberies in houses by the privilege, as the law now is, of demanding the benefit of clergy' (12 Anne, c. 7 [1713]). The statute made the theft of goods worth 40 shillings from a house, whether or not the owner was within, a non-clergyable felony. Nonetheless, it appears that relatively few women were actually tried under the 1713 statute in the years following its passage. Beattie found that only 150 men and 100 women were tried in Surrey under the 1713 statute in his sample. J.M. Beattie, 'The criminality of women in eighteenth-century England', *Journal of Social History*, 8 (1975), 80–116.

[35] Daniel Defoe, *Everybody's Business is Nobody's Business* (London, 1725), pp. 4, 7 and 13.

infanticide epidemic in the city. In July 1713, Joseph Addison lamented in the *Guardian* that 'there is scarce an Assizes where some unhappy wretch is not executed for the murder of a child. And how many more of these monsters of inhumanity may we suppose to be wholly undiscovered, or cleared for want of legal evidence.'[36] In 1729, Defoe claimed that 'not a sessions passes, but we see one or more merciless mothers try'd for the murder of their bastard-children'.[37] Accounts of infanticide trials were widely circulated in the *Old Bailey Sessions Papers* as well as in newspapers and pamphlets, and commentators wrote at length about the perceived epidemic. Women who secretly killed their children were monsters lacking natural feminine tenderness. But, perhaps just as disturbing, they had attempted to conceal their illicit sexual behaviour and, it was thought, many had been successful. There appears to have been as much concern among commentators about single women's sexuality going 'wholly undiscovered' as there was for the lives of innocent infants.

And yet, according to Addison, child killers acted out of a contradictory desire to maintain a virtuous appearance and to support their children: 'It is certain, that which generally betrays these profligate women into it, and overcomes the tenderness which is natural to them on other occasions, is the fear of shame, or their inability to support those whom they give life to'.[38] Infanticide was the result of both virtue and vice. Where did one end and the other begin? Bernard Mandeville wrote in 1732 that servants who had been protective of their honour for years were still susceptible to temptations and could easily find themselves in a very difficult position. A woman could be modest, religious and hard-working, and still succumb to the advances of a deceitful man. Mandeville's infanticidal servant was 'wicked' and 'cruel' precisely because of her 'good parentage', diligence, modesty and faith. 'The fear of shame' pushed servants to commit murder. Murderous servants walked a fine line between villainy and virtue in the public imagination. A well-behaved servant with a good character, like Canning, was as susceptible, if not more so, to

---

[36] Joseph Addison, *Guardian*, 105 (13 July 1713). Portrayals of infanticides shifted dramatically from the early seventeenth century, when women were often depicted as monstrous child killers, to the late eighteenth century, when they were increasingly portrayed either as virtuous victims of men's deceit or as insane. See Jackson, *New-Born Child Murder*, pp. 110–32, and Dana Rabin (Chapter Five) in this volume.

[37] D. Defoe, *Augusta Triumphans*, (London, Roberts, 1729, 2nd edn), pp. 16–17. See also idem, *The Generous Projector: or, a Friendly Proposal to Prevent Murder* (London, Dodd and Nutt, 1731); and idem, *The Great Law of Subordination Consider'd; or, The Insolence and Unsufferable Behaviour of Servants in England Duly Enquir'd Into* (London, Harding, 1724).

[38] Addison, *Guardian*.

accusations of promiscuity, pregnancy or infanticide as a woman with a bad reputation.[39]

Reforming politicians and social critics such as Addison, Mandeville and later the surgeon and man–midwife William Hunter assumed that women with poor reputations or no need to secure an employer's recommendation had less motive than reputable domestic servants to conceal their pregnancies and murder their illegitimate children.[40] The image of the infanticide constructed in the sixteenth and seventeenth centuries as a poor, single woman had combined with the image of the virtuous domestic servant.[41] The predominance of service as an occupation of single women during the eighteenth century – combined with the fact that the 1624 statute targeted single women for prosecution – helps explain the high proportion of servants among defendants. The public perception that poor, unmarried women were killing their new-born children at an alarming rate was widespread, even though the average number of women tried for infanticide at the Old Bailey remained consistent at less than two per year throughout the eighteenth century and few women were convicted after the 1720s.[42] The Canning case reveals the power of the image of the virtuous servant maid turned infanticide.

Images of Elizabeth Canning as infanticide

If Canning's story was a lie, where had she been? Although most writers hesitated to call Canning explicitly an infanticide, the rumours that she had been lying-in in her absence were widespread in the streets of London, and writers often referred to those 'slanders' in their re-tellings

---

[39] See the discussion of Mandeville in Jackson, *New-Born Child Murder*, pp. 110–32.

[40] William Hunter, 'On the uncertainty of the signs of murder, in the case of bastard children', *Medical Observations and Inquiries*, 6 (1784), 266–90.

[41] Whether female servants were more likely to commit infanticide than men or women in other occupations is impossible to know. Trial accounts in the *OBSP* suggest that they were certainly more likely to be prosecuted for the crime. Of 105 women tried for infanticide at the Old Bailey between 1714 and 1803, sixty percent were identified as servants; in thirty-five percent of cases no occupation was listed (although in a portion of those it appeared that the accused was a servant); and only five percent listed other occupations, for example, prostitute or labourer, or stated that the accused was unemployed. Amy Masciola, 'Infanticide at the Old Bailey, 1714–1803', (MA thesis, University of Maryland, 1994).

[42] Francus, 'Monstrous mothers'. For discussions of the decline in infanticide indictments and convictions, see Beattie, *Crime and the Courts*, p. 115; Hoffer and Hull, *Murdering Mothers*, pp. 71, 73–4, 80; Jackson, *New-Born Child Murder*; Malcolmson, 'Infanticide in the eighteenth century,' p. 197; and J.A. Sharpe, *Crime in Early Modern England, 1550–1750*, (New York, Longman, 1984), pp. 61–2.

of her story. Debate in the newspapers was vigorous and pamphlets were published at a rate of one or two per week throughout the spring and summer of 1753.[43] *The Case of Elizabeth Canning Fairly Stated* was published on 13 March, three weeks after Squires's and Wells's convictions and on the same day that Gascoyne issued a warrant for Canning's arrest. The anonymous author claimed that Canning had 'given a false information, that there is no truth in the evidence she gave against Squires and Wells, and that she forged this story purely to conceal her own criminal transactions in the dark'. And although Squires and Wells had been convicted, the writer claimed that 'it must be confessed there have been some all along, who have suspected a snake in the grass, and notwithstanding this fair outside, that there was a worm at the root, which in the end would bring this fine superstructure to the ground'.[44] The pamphlet attacked both Canning's 'friends' and Henry Fielding, the well-known magistrate and novelist who had taken her statement on 7 February and had issued warrants for Squires's and Wells's arrests. The author implied that Canning's friends had taken up her cause and established a prosecution fund for their own profit and not 'to assist her in carrying on the prosecution, [or] as some recompence for the unheard of hardships she had undergone, and as a reward for so resolutely maintaining her virtue in the midst of so much danger'.[45] According to the author, the Canningites saw in their young charge an opportunity to make money and at least £300 had been collected already.

This early anti-Canning pamphlet argued that Canning lied about her whereabouts to conceal her 'own criminal transactions' and suggested that the motivation of either her captors or her defenders, or both, was financial. And yet, she was not the primary villain in this version. Rather it was Fielding, Canning's wealthy patrons and her captors and co-conspirators who were the real criminals. Canning was portrayed as a servant maid with a good character who was kidnapped and manipulated by a series of criminals and powerful men. Most of the early anti-Canning accounts took a similarly ambivalent position, constructing Canning as virtuous even as they marked her as a liar and a cheat. But, at the same time, the accounts alluded with increasing prominence to the more sinister narrative of Canning as infanticide, thus playing on widespread fears of an organized underworld populated by cunning servant maids.

---

[43] Amory, 'The virgin and the witch'.
[44] Anon., *The Case of Elizabeth Canning Fairly Stated* (London, Cooper, 1753); Amory, 'The virgin and the witch'.
[45] Anon., *Case of Elizabeth Canning*, p. 14.

Fielding responded to *The Case of Elizabeth Canning Fairly Stated* immediately with a pamphlet entitled *A Clear State of the Case of Elizabeth Canning* published on 20 March. In Fielding's account Canning embodied youth, simplicity and chastity – all of the qualities most prized in a female domestic servant. Throughout the pamphlet, he referred to her as 'little girl', 'poor little girl' and 'poor simple child'. He emphasized her chastity, youth and general good character, and suggested that the best judges of that character were the people for whom she had worked in service:

> Will they believe this of a young girl, hardly 18 years old, who hath the unanimous testimony of all who ever knew her from her infancy, to support the character of a virtuous, modest, sober, well-disposed girl; and this character most inforced by those who know her best, and particularly by those with whom she hath lived in service?[46]

To her youth and simplicity, Fielding added ignorance, another quality of the ideal servant. He claimed that 'the girl can scarce be supposed wicked enough, so I am far from supposing her witty enough' to come up with such a story. He continued, 'this girl is a child in years, and yet more so in understanding, with all the evident marks of simplicity that I ever discovered in a human countenance'.[47] Fielding endeavoured to portray Canning as a dull-witted, virginal and hard-working servant in response to the rumours that were spreading in London and beyond that she was no idiot, but rather a cunning deceiver. He expressly denied rumours that she had spent the month with a lover, saying 'it could not be a lover; for among all the cruelties, by which men have become infamous in their commerce with women, none of this kind, can, I believe be produced.'[48]

On 29 March, John Hill, the essayist and long-time opponent of Fielding, responded with *The Story of Elizabeth Canning Considered*. He argued that Canning was a liar and speculated that she had indeed been with a lover: 'Not with a Lover certainly, say you! . . . Eighteen, let me remind you, is a critical age; and what would not a woman do, that had made an escape, to recover her own credit, and screen her lover'.[49] Hill suggested that Canning might have done anything, even commit a crime, to protect her reputation. A young woman with 'credit' was suspicious because that credit was so important to middling employers. Reputable working women were economically dependent upon their fragile reputations and thus protective of them to the point of fraud or even infanticide.

---

[46] Fielding, *Clear State of the Case*, p. 293.
[47] Ibid., pp. 293–4.
[48] Ibid., p. 292.
[49] J. Hill, *The Story of Elizabeth Canning Considered* (London, Cooper, 1753), p. 24.

Three weeks later, on 20 April, Doctor James Solas Dodd published a Canningite pamphlet entitled *A Physical Account of the Case of Elizabeth Canning* in which he proposed to explain her physical condition before and after the ordeal and whether or not her version of events was medically plausible. As evidence for her abnormal bodily functions, he explained that 'she for five preceding months had had the common female benefit totally obstructed'.[50] According to Dodd, her failure to menstruate for five months was the result of sleeping on the damp stone kitchen floor so that she would hear the watchman and wake in time to do her work. Observers who were already suspicious of Canning took this last piece of information as proof that she had been pregnant when she disappeared. Even as Dodd produced 'scientific' evidence in support of Canning's version of events, he had to construct her as a hard-working servant in order to shift the focus away from her menstruation and her sexuality.

News that Canning had not menstruated for five months before her disappearance fuelled rumours that she had been lying-in secretly. On 9 June, Daniel Cox published *An Appeal to the Public, in Behalf of Elizabeth Canning*. His purpose was to prove Canning's good character by a consideration and refutation of the various slanders against her. His pamphlet was one of the first to address, in print, the rumour that Canning had given birth to a child during her absence. Cox had met with Canning alone on 30 March to question her about her health. He asked her:

> whether before her going from home on new-years day she had been regular in her courses? She replied without any kind of hesitation, that she had not had them for about five months before. That one night being up at washing when she was out of order, she took cold and they ceased, nor had returned again but since she came home: this is no uncommon case with servants who are obliged to dabble in cold water.

Like Dodd, Cox was careful to associate obvious signs of pregnancy with Canning's domestic work, deflecting attention away from her sexuality and onto her reputation as a hard-working servant. He went on to address the rumours that were being 'cruelly suggested', that she was hiding a 'private lying-in' during her absence. According to Cox, if she had been

> cunning enough to have devised her whole extraordinary story, in order to cover a private lying-in, ... she would have been artful enough to have concealed a circumstance, which might have

---

[50] James Solas Dodd, *A Physical Account of the Case of Elizabeth Canning* (London, Bouquet, 1753), p. 7.

countenanc'd a suspicion, that the obstruction had been of longer duration, and had arisen from some other cause than what she had alledged.[51]

Cox articulated the set of assumptions that were likely to have arisen in the public mind when confronted with the news of Canning's failure to menstruate for five months. People would not, according to Cox's scenario, immediately equate the five-month hiatus with an abortion, but rather, they would assume that the 'obstruction had been of longer duration' and that she had given birth to a child and rid herself of it somehow. A more logical counter-argument to the 'lying-in' rumours would have been to use the revelation about her menstruation as proof of her innocence by simply pointing out that five months was not long enough to carry a child to term.

Cox interviewed Canning again in early April to investigate a rumour that a midwife had examined her shift and had concluded that 'it was too clean to have been worn so long as had been pretended'. He questioned Mrs Canning about the midwife's visit to her daughter. She said the midwife had indeed come a few days after Canning's return to examine the shift, and had said that 'she would make oath, that from the appearance of the shift the girl had had no commerce with men, nor any distemper, or other discharge, for that the shift was free from all kind of stains'. He examined Canning again on 9 and 15 May, and took Frances Oakes, a midwife, with him on the second visit. He had Oakes examine Canning alone and then he examined her breasts and belly himself; the two professionals agreed that she had never had a child. Finally, he had two local women, Mrs Woodward and Mrs Rossiter, who were friends and neighbours of the Cannings, examine her. They came to the same conclusion that the doctor and the midwife had. Cox and Dodd attempted to overcome sexual gossip with scientific evidence and with references to Canning's reputation as an honest, hard-working servant. Ironically, it was Canning's most ardent defenders – Fielding, Cox and Dodd – who repeatedly introduced her sexuality and criminality in print. By responding to the rumours of Canning's pregnancy, they said what anti-Canning writers had not been willing to say yet.

A ballad published in early July entitled *The Devil Outdone* responded to Cox's pamphlet and suggested that Canning was no innocent, young virgin. It made explicit the charges that her defenders were so eager to dispel and that her more 'reputable' critics had only been willing to hint at:

---

[51] Daniel Cox, *An Appeal to the Public, in Behalf of Elizabeth Canning* (London, Meadows, 1753), pp. 19–20.

I'll tell how a Girl was met, stript, and knock'd down,
And carried an Airing ten Miles out of Town.

By Men who first plunder'd her under a Wall,
Then stole her to rob her of — Nothing at all;
They sought not a Maiden-head, for if they had
They went to the wrong Shop to find it, Egad.

My Pen is grown weary, or else I wou'd tell ye
How a sapient Physician has grop'd at her Belly,
And how the grave Doctor has taken great Pains
To demonstrate that People may write without Brains;

And has blabb'd out a Secret, from which may be guess'd,
That a Cuckoo (five Months before) laid in her Nest,
And that her Pr-t-ct-s may learn, to their Shame,
That she has miscarry'd — I mean of her Aim.[52]

The balladeer played with Cox's careful construction of Canning's story, candidly claiming that she was pregnant when she disappeared. He took literally Canning's assertion that she had not menstruated for five months and suggested that she had miscarried or procured an abortion.

Allan Ramsay, whose paintings were hanging in the new Foundling Hospital, published a pamphlet on 27 June entitled A Letter ... Concerning the Affair of Elizabeth Canning. According to Ramsay, Canning, a servant with a good reputation, had disappeared on 1 January in order to end an unwanted pregnancy and rid herself of the child. His pamphlet contains the clearest articulation of the stereotype of the infanticidal servant. This stereotype corresponded with the early portraits of the typical infanticide in works by Addison, Defoe and Mandeville. He argued that

> it may not be amiss to hint to them that there are such distempers as lyings-in and miscarriages, to which young servant-maids of eighteen are very much subject; distempers that will hold them as long, and reduce them as low as has been related of E. Canning, especially if attended and nursed in the manner we may easily suppose her to have been. It may not be amiss to hint, that thirteen shillings and six-pence, with the sale of a gown and pair of stays, is hardly more than sufficient to defray the expences of such an operation; even altho' no part of it was expended in a christening, a wet nurse, or a coffin, which, not to continue any idea of horror in your Lordship's imagination, might have been all provided by that most humane institution, the Foundling-Hospital.[53]

---

52 Anon., The Devil Outdone (London, Wright, 1753).
53 Ramsay, Letter to the Right Honourable, p. 20. See John Brewer, The Pleasures of the Imagination: English Culture in the Eighteenth Century (London, Fontana, 1997), pp. 226–7.

Ramsay suggested that Canning's gown and laces had not been stolen, but that she had sold them to pay an unscrupulous midwife. There had been no need for a christening, wet-nurse or coffin because Canning had concealed the birth, death and body of the infant, rather than abandoning it to the Foundling Hospital. Ramsay portrayed Canning as a good servant turned whore, liar and infanticide. For him, her good character was evidence against her. The problem for Canning and her supporters was that her detractors could use her good character against her, because the virtuous servant was as susceptible to sexual temptation as other women and more likely to hide the results of illicit sex with murder.

Conclusion

Gascoyne pressed perjury charges against Canning and she was finally tried in May 1754, almost a year and a half after her disappearance. She was convicted of wilful and corrupt perjury and sentenced to be transported to the American colonies.[54] In August 1754, she departed for Connecticut where she eventually married, had at least one child, and died in 1773.[55] As far as we know, she never changed her story. Although the jury decided that she had lied about her whereabouts and had falsely accused the gypsy, her prosecutors did not need to establish a plausible explanation of her disappearance in order to make their case. Thus the mystery was never 'solved' to anyone's satisfaction. I have shown that it is the *mystery* that makes Canning's case so important. The mystery has encouraged writers to keep retelling the story ever since. Those retellings (like this retelling) reveal the preoccupations of their culture.

Possible explanations for Canning's disappearance that emerged in print included infanticide, abortion, seduction and abandonment, miscarriage, prostitution, treatment for venereal disease, and fraud for monetary gain. Each of these explanations, except perhaps the last, shared an assumption that Canning was a sexually active servant with secrets to conceal. That assumption did not emerge from a vacuum, but reflected the widespread perception that female domestic servants were essentially criminal. That perception was based in part on the unique material conditions of the late seventeenth and early eighteenth centuries. A nascent middle class sought more female servants to

---

[54] The jury returned a verdict of 'guilty of perjury, but not willful and corrupt' but the judge would not accept their verdict and sent them back to deliberate further. They finally returned a verdict of 'willful and corrupt perjury'. *State Trials*, XIX, 669–70.

[55] Moore, *Appearance*, pp. 173–4.

accomplish the myriad tasks associated with its new domestic life. As the demand for female servants appeared to outpace the supply, employers grew increasingly wary of servants' power to control their own personal and professional lives. Women who exercised even a small degree of independence were a threat to the social order. Within this context, the apparently virtuous servant was as dangerous as her disreputable sister because she might be successfully concealing her true criminal identity. Representations of infanticidal servants reflect both the early seventeenth-century preoccupation with single women's illicit sexual behaviour and new anxieties about a growing class of independent women dangerously familiar with their employers' property, bodies and secrets. By the eighteenth century, employers were concerned not only with single women's ability to conceal the bodies of their dead infants but also with their servants' ability to conceal their true characters.

Acknowledgements

Versions of this chapter were presented at the North American Conference on British Studies in 1997 and 2000; at a symposium on the history of infanticide held at Exeter in 1998; and at the Folger Institute's spring 1999 seminar, 'Going to Law'. I would like to thank the participants of those meetings for their helpful questions and suggestions. I would like to extend special thanks to J.S. Cockburn, Amy Froide, Gay Gullickson, Cynthia Herrup, Mark Jackson, Dana Rabin and Shelley Sperry for their thoughtful critiques.

CHAPTER FIVE

Bodies of evidence, states of mind: infanticide, emotion and sensibility in eighteenth-century England

Dana Rabin

Recent research has shown fairly conclusively that conviction rates for infanticide dropped sharply in England during the eighteenth century.[1] Scholars have suggested that the jury's sympathy with the plight of unwed mothers and the discomfort of legal authorities with the harsh statute of 1624 together accounted for this phenomenon.[2] This chapter seeks to deepen these arguments by outlining the social and cultural context in which leniency and dissatisfaction with the 1624 statute emerged, through an examination of the culture of sensibility in eighteenth-century English society and in legal discourse. I will explore the relationship between the language of the mind that resonated in the English courtroom throughout the eighteenth century and jury verdicts in cases of infanticide. This comparison will illustrate evolving definitions of the crime and its perpetrators.

As the 'most specifically female crime',[3] infanticide can serve as a case study, allowing us to examine the changing relationship between the emotions, the body and the State, as revealed in the courtroom dialogue

---

[1] The term infanticide, as Mark Jackson has argued, can be seen as vague and anachronistic. Almost all of the cases discussed here involved the death of a new-born infant and none refer to the death of a child older than one year of age. Mark Jackson, *New-Born Child Murder: Women, Illegitimacy and the Courts in Eighteenth-Century England* (Manchester, Manchester University Press, 1996), pp. 5–6. The drop in convictions is described in J.M. Beattie, *Crime and the Courts in England, 1660–1800*, (Princeton, Princeton University Press, 1986), pp. 113–24; Peter Hoffer and N.E.H. Hull, *Murdering Mothers: Infanticide in England and New England, 1558–1803* (New York, New York University Press, 1981), pp. 65–91; Jackson, *New-Born Child Murder*, pp. 133–4; and R.W. Malcolmson, 'Infanticide in the eighteenth century', in J.S. Cockburn (ed.), *Crime in England 1550–1800* (London, Methuen, 1977), pp. 196–8. Jackson points out that the drop in convictions accompanied a rise in grand jury dismissals of accused women and in findings of natural death or still-birth by coroners' juries.

[2] Beattie, *Crime and the Courts*, pp. 120–4, Jackson, *New-Born Child Murder*, pp. 133–50.

[3] J.A. Sharpe, *Crime in Early Modern England* (New York, Longman, 1999), p. 157.

among defendants, witnesses, victims, judges and jurors during the eighteenth century. I will focus on trial accounts in which defendants – or witnesses on their behalf – submitted a defence that referred to the emotional or mental state of the accused as their primary explanation for the crime. These defences described the accused as 'insensible', 'agitated in mind' or 'confused'. They are significant because they were exceptions to the popular, formulaic and mostly successful 'preparation defence'. My goal is not to speculate on the outcome of any specific case; instead this exceptional testimony will show growing preoccupations with states of mind, the emotional causes of crime and sensibility.

How was the emergence of such states of mind related to the understanding of the body? I shall argue that during the latter part of the eighteenth century the state of the defendant's mind became so privileged – both by defendants and by jurors and other legal authorities who heard testimony about infanticide – that evidence about the body no longer determined the outcome of a trial. This is especially intriguing in light of the copious evidence presented about the body by expert witnesses such as male and female midwives, surgeons and coroners.[4] Attention to the language of emotion in these infanticide cases, often more curt and elliptical than the physical evidence, recast the crime and the criminal. Inside the courtroom, psychological pleas redefined the motives for infanticide and contributed to the decline of its association with concealment and secrecy. Outside the courtroom, these pleas reflected society's new attitudes about emotion and responsibility.

Infanticide, marital status and insanity

The attitude of legal authorities toward women who committed infanticide was determined primarily by the marital status of the accused. Married women were charged with murder, and they were often acquitted when they claimed to have suffered temporary insanity. Single women accused of infanticide in the seventeenth century were tried under the 1624 'Act to prevent the destroying and murthering of bastard children'. This statute presumed that any mother of a bastard child who concealed its death was guilty of murder unless she could establish by the oath of at least one witness that the child had been

---

[4] For medical presence in the courtroom, see Michael Clark and Catherine Crawford (eds.), *Legal Medicine in History* (Cambridge, Cambridge University Press, 1994) and Thomas Forbes, *Surgeons at the Bailey: English Forensic Medicine to 1878* (New Haven, Yale University Press, 1985). Mark Jackson examines the growing medical discourse surrounding infanticide in *New-Born Child Murder*, pp. 60–110.

stillborn.[5] The statute claimed to address the problem of 'lewd women' and asserted that they committed these crimes 'to avoid their shame' and 'to escape punishment'. The statute and its enforcement suggest that in the seventeenth century infanticide by an unmarried woman was considered a reasoned, premeditated (though immoral and criminal) act, undertaken to preserve her reputation and her economic well-being. Such motives were not considered in the trial of a married woman accused of killing her baby because married women ordinarily seemed to lack any incentive to conceal the birth of a child.[6]

In his discussion of 'the defects of idiocy, madness and lunacy' in his *Pleas of the Crown*, Matthew Hale (1609–76) treated the crime of infanticide as a special case within the category of insanity. He cited a 1668 trial at the Old Bailey in which a married woman 'having not slept many nights fell into a temporary phrenzy, and killed her infant in the absence of any company'.[7] After a good night's sleep, the woman 'recovered her understanding', and had no recollection of her acts. The jury was instructed that

> if it did appear, that she had any use of reason when she did it, they were to find her guilty; but if they found her under a phrenzy, tho' by reason of her late delivery and want of sleep, they should acquit her.[8]

The jury was further cautioned that:

> had there been any occasion to move her to this fact, as to hide her shame, which is ordinarily the case with such as are delivered of bastard children and destroy them; or if there had been jealousy in her husband, that the child had been none of his; or if she had hid the infant, or denied the fact, these had been evidences that the phrenzy was counterfeit.[9]

Based on her 'honesty and virtuous deportment' and 'many circumstances of insanity appearing to the jury', the defendant was found not guilty.[10]

Hale specifically included the category of married mothers who committed infanticide among his examples of exculpatory mental states.

---

[5] 'An Act to prevent the Destroying and Murthering of Bastard Children', 1624, 21 Jac. 1, c. 27.

[6] The children of married women were not automatically charged on the parish; married women who had a bastard child were seldom exposed as long as the mother's husband could be accepted as the father.

[7] Matthew Hale, *History of the Pleas of the Crown*, ed. Sollom Emlyn, 2 vols (London, 1736), vol. 1, p. 36.

[8] Ibid.

[9] Ibid.

[10] Ibid.

Married women who killed their new-born babies were considered *a priori* different from mothers of illegitimate children who committed the same crime. The law assumed that married mothers were not driven to their crimes by the same desperate or deviant motives as unmarried women. Infanticide by married women was considered so shocking and so unlikely that the only motive assigned to it was insanity.[11]

Mary Dixon's trial at the Old Bailey in 1735 confirmed the widespread application of Hale's recommendation in the eighteenth century. Dixon, a married woman, was indicted for murdering her infant son by throwing him into the house of office. The testimony that followed the description of the crime included varied language about Dixon's state of mind during the crime. Dixon testified that 'my senses went from me and I did not recover my self, nor know what I did or said'.[12] Several witnesses corroborated Dixon's claim that she suffered some sort of mental haze immediately after the discovery of the crime. Phoebe Webster told the court that Dixon was 'weak and faint' on the morning that the baby was found. When she asked 'how she could be so barbarous, and why she did not call for help', Dixon answered only 'because I was wicked'. Mrs Morgan reported that Dixon 'made no answer' to her questions and that she was 'seemingly very weak', but Morgan asserted that she could not say 'whether she was out of her senses or not'. Mrs Bousset said that she 'could find no sense in her' and that when she called the midwife, both women 'thought she was dead'.[13] Mary Dixon was acquitted.

According to legal commentary, an acquittal based on insanity rested on proof that the defendant lacked an evil intent when he or she committed the crime. In practice, proof of insanity was measured by the individual perpetrator's history of peculiar behaviour or the inexplicable nature of the crime itself. Dixon's testimony – so unusual in an insanity defence in which the prisoner usually said nothing – addressed the

---

[11] Hale's exception, inconsistently applied, reflected a belief not uncommon in the seventeenth century that childbirth could be the cause of temporary insanity. Women who used the language of emotion to explain infanticide in the eighteenth century certainly traded on this belief. For more on the well-established link between infanticide and insanity in the nineteenth century, see: later chapters in this volume; Shelley Day, 'Puerperal insanity: the historical sociology of a disease', (PhD thesis, Cambridge, 1985); and Roger Smith, *Trial by Medicine: Insanity and Responsibility in Victorian Trials* (Edinburgh, Edinburgh University Press, 1981), pp. 143–60.

[12] Mary Dixon, *Old Bailey Sessions Papers* [henceforth *OBSP*], July 1735, p. 145. For further discussion of these sources, see: John Langbein, 'The criminal trial before the lawyers', *University of Chicago Law Review*, 45 (1978), 263–316: idem, 'Shaping the eighteenth-century trial: a view from the Ryder sources', *University of Chicago Law Review*, 50 (1983), 1–136.

[13] Mary Dixon, *OBSP*, July 1735, p. 145.

question of intention directly. She told the court: 'I was under no temptation of being so barbarous, for I had a good husband who was able to maintain the child; and I had at the same time one child living of four years old'.[14] Unlike more typical cases involving insanity, none of the witnesses mentioned that Dixon had a history of peculiar behaviour and the prisoner took the stand and spoke at length about her crime and her state of mind. These two variations on the usual, successful insanity defence reveal the special status of infanticidal insanity which was assumed to be temporary, caused in Hale's words by 'a phrenzy'.[15]

Unmarried women seldom used the insanity defence when confronted with infanticide because a plea of insanity would entail some implicit admission of guilt, and if unsuccessful, would lead to immediate conviction and possible execution. Instead, these women used 'loopholes' in the statute of 1624 to make their defence. Single women accused of infanticide testified that the baby was born dead, that the baby died immediately after birth because they were delivered alone, that they had not concealed the pregnancy, and that they had prepared for the delivery and the birth of the child. Their stories were usually confirmed by a woman in the community who told the court that she knew about the pregnancy and that the mother had made some arrangements for the lying-in and had prepared necessary provisions for the child such as items of clothing. The testimony in these cases was entirely uniform, formulaic and generally successful: it usually resulted in the mother's acquittal.[16] Elizabeth Turner, indicted for murdering her child in June 1734, told no one that she was pregnant and at first denied the crime when a body was found in a box in her employer's cellar. Although Turner said nothing in her own defence, a witness on her behalf testified that when she was at Newgate, Turner's coat was stolen 'for garnish money' and sewn in it they found 'baby things'. These included a shirt, a cap, a stay, a forehead cloth and a biggin. Based on evidence of these 'preparations', Turner was acquitted.[17]

By about 1715, a dramatic drop in convictions for infanticide had taken place. The preparation defence had become the legal mechanism by which the courts negotiated this crime. Of the women tried for infanticide at the Old Bailey during the eighteenth century, 85 per cent were acquitted and there were no convictions for infanticide after 1774. Juries and judges may have felt an implicit sympathy for the accused,

---

[14] Ibid.

[15] Hale, *Pleas of the Crown*, vol. 1, p. 36.

[16] Beattie, *Crime and the Courts*, pp. 120–4 and Malcolmson 'Infanticide in the eighteenth century', pp. 197–8.

[17] A biggin is a child's bonnet or head covering. Elizabeth Turner, OBSP, June 1734, p. 136.

who were mostly young working women with few means to support a
child.[18] They may have rejected the presumption of guilt written into the
statute of 1624 as William Blackstone (1723–80) did when he wrote
that the law 'savours pretty strongly of severity'.[19] Nevertheless, the
legal fiction by which the crime was negotiated – the preparation
defence – affirmed the statute of 1624 and the legal system that
produced it.[20] This legal mechanism accepted the statute's definition of
infanticide as a crime and mounted a defence based on a refutation of
concealment, the issue around which the statute revolved.

What about exceptions to the preparation defence? Why in the face
of such a successful strategy would accused women argue anything
else? In this chapter, I shall examine those cases in which defendants
presented evidence of emotional turmoil to explain their behaviour.
Unlike women who brought a preparation defence, they
acknowledged the crime and sometimes even admitted their role in the
murder. In their defence, they drew upon new epistemologies of
emotion that reveal the preoccupation with self and sensibility in the
second half of the eighteenth century. Such testimony played on the
implicit sympathy evident in most trials for infanticide. By demanding
that the court's sympathy be made explicit, however, this testimony
called into question the statute of 1624: it redefined the accused as
insane and the act of infanticide as *prima facie* proof of insanity, rather
than crime. The implications of this testimony were devastating to the
1624 statute and led to its repeal in 1803; however, the language of
emotion had much more destabilizing implications for the legal system
in general because it threatened to redefine all crime as insanity by
linking all behaviour to psychological motives for which the defendant
took little or no responsibility.

In cases of infanticide the language of emotion had a significant
effect. The association of the sanity of a woman accused of the crime
with her marital status underwent a dramatic shift during the eighteenth

---

[18] Jackson, *New-Born Child Murder*, pp. 113–28. Jackson's analysis also considers
the opposition to humanitarian accounts, which emerged at the end of the
eighteenth century.

[19] William Blackstone, *Commentaries on the Laws of England: Vol. 4 Of Public Wrongs*
(Chicago, University of Chicago Press, 1979), vol. 4, p. 198. John Beattie argues that
a rejection of the 'crudity' of the statute of 1624, its presumption of guilt and the way
the offence was 'formulated and punished' accounted for the drop in the accusation
and conviction rate – Beattie, *Crime and the Courts*, p. 124. Mark Jackson gives a
detailed explication of the statute and changing laws of evidence and standards of
proof in *New-Born Child Murder*, pp. 145–51.

[20] Although the preparation defence was the most common, some women also claimed
the child was stillborn or that the child had died during or immediately after birth.
These other defences did not exclude a preparation defence.

century. Medical literature articulated a remarkable change in the attitudes toward single women accused of infanticide: both the assumption of guilt and the assumption of criminal intent were questioned by doctors. By the end of the eighteenth century, the crime itself became evidence of madness that required little or no supporting testimony of marriage or mental alienation.

William Hunter's lecture to the members of the Medical Society in July 1783 (published posthumously in 1784) reflected this change of opinion. Hunter (1718–83) was a renowned physician, anatomist, surgeon and man–midwife. After training in Edinburgh and London, he specialized in surgery, later becoming the leading obstetrician in England. His patients included Queen Charlotte, to whom he was appointed physician extraordinary in 1764. In his lecture, entitled 'On the uncertainty of the signs of murder, in the case of bastard children', Hunter warned his colleagues against 'early prejudice' in cases that looked like infanticide and reminded them that the act could not be considered a murder unless it was

> executed with some degree of cool judgement, and wicked intention. When committed under a phrenzy from despair, can it be more offensive in the sight of God, than under a phrenzy from a fever, or in lunacy?[21]

Hunter pointed to the diagnosis of temporary insanity when he reminded his audience that

> in making up a just estimate of any human action, much will depend on the state of the agent's mind at the time; and therefore the laws of all countries make ample allowance for insanity. The insane are not held to be responsible for their actions.[22]

Hunter suggested instead that single women 'with an unconquerable sense of shame' who found themselves pregnant out of wedlock might be 'overwhelmed with terror and despair' until their 'distress of body and mind deprives them of all judgement and rational conduct'.[23] He speculated that these women were driven by a 'violently agitated' mind experiencing 'a conflict of passions and terror', and that in this state 'an irrational conduct may appear very natural'.[24] The shame of such a pregnancy drove one of his patients to suicide when she was 'struck with panic and lost her judgement and senses'.[25] Hunter explained the deaths

---

21 William Hunter, 'On the uncertainty of the signs of murder, in the case of bastard children', *Medical Observations and Inquiries*, 6 (1784), 271.

22 Ibid., p. 268.

23 Ibid., pp. 272–3.

24 Ibid., p. 278.

25 Ibid., p. 279.

of seemingly healthy babies born to women delivered alone 'distracted in ... mind, and exhausted in ... body, [who] will not have strength or recollection enough to fly instantly to the relief of the child'.[26]

Hunter's speech signalled a change in the attitude of the medical community with regard to the effects of pregnancy out of wedlock on the mind of the mother. He argued that the very motives cited in the statute of 1624, shame and fear, produced mental distress leading to 'phrenzy'. The clear connection between concealment, murder, and reason on which the assumption of guilt was based was complicated by Hunter's introduction of another factor – an 'agitated' mind – to which he attributed the crime and for which he did not believe the accused should be held responsible. For Hunter, the villain was not the infanticidal mother, whom he thought 'weak, credulous and deluded', but rather the father of the child who 'is really criminal'.[27] Hunter concluded that:

> every humane heart will forget the indiscretion or crime, and bleed for the sufferings which a woman must have gone through; who but for having listened to the perfidious protestations and vows of our sex, might have been an affectionate and faithful wife, a virtuous and honoured mother, through a long and happy life.[28]

Hunter's interpretation of the crime of infanticide and its causes is a strong example of the humanitarian narrative defined and deconstructed by Thomas Laqueur.[29] Hunter stripped the women accused of infanticide of all agency granted to them, however peremptorily, by the statute of 1624. He transformed them into passive victims of male seducers and redefined them as insane. This redefinition nullified their intention and their criminal and moral responsibility. The humanitarian narrative was especially effective for furthering the cause of medical professionalization, and Hunter referred often in his text to his vast clinical experience which conferred his unique authority and ability to diagnose and treat these women.

The language of the mind as excuse

How do we account for this dramatic shift in the discourse of infanticide during the eighteenth century? Although William Hunter

---

[26] Ibid., pp. 288–9.

[27] Ibid., p. 269.

[28] Ibid., p. 270.

[29] Thomas Laqueur, 'Bodies, details, and the humanitarian narrative', in Lynn Hunt (ed.), *The New Cultural History* (Berkeley, University of California Press, 1989), pp. 176–204.

articulated this change, it was not the medical community that directed the fall in the conviction rate of single women accused of infanticide, nor did physicians first redefine the relationship between infanticide, single women and insanity. I want to suggest that one reason for this novel association of infanticide by unmarried women with insanity rests in the development of pleas of non-responsibility permeated with a language of emotion and the mind. In this 'language of the mind', which appeared increasingly in the Old Bailey trial transcripts from the 1720s and the 1730s, circumstance and sensibility began to emerge as ever-present themes. By claiming that they were 'not sensible', 'agitated in mind', 'almost distracted', 'stupefied', 'confused' and 'delirious', defendants and witnesses explained a wide range of emotional states from confusion to delusion and insanity. They fashioned pleas of diminished responsibility based on popular perceptions of mental distress which differed significantly from exculpatory insanity as defined by the law and in legal commentary. This language and the larger interest in sensibility convinced those participating in the courtroom dialogue – from the defendants and witnesses to judges and prosecutors – that the women accused of infanticide had no criminal intention of murdering or hurting their children and that they should not be held responsible for the crime.

This language of emotion and excuse was initiated by defendants themselves, and it was part of a larger trend in legal discourse that permeated trials for offences as varied as theft, arson, sedition and murder. In the eighteenth century, the narratives of excuse presented by common people in pre-trial depositions and trial testimony reveal a new interest in 'psychology' and the social pressures that might interfere with the defendant's judgement and capacity for self-restraint. Defendants introduced evidence about emotional distress to argue for mercy; their words often resonated with the jury's search for grounds on which to mitigate.[30] This trend was documented by those observers of English courts who wrote extensively about their anxieties about the legal system and the destabilising influence of defendant-initiated pleas that drew on the language of mental incapacity to widen the established parameters of the excuse of insanity. For these reformers, arguments for mitigation based on broadened conceptions of mental illness created a further disjuncture between legal prescription and legal practice. Their perception of the prevalence of this language of emotion exacerbated

---

[30] The language of excuse is the subject of my dissertation, '"Of Persons Capable of Committing Crimes": Law and Responsibility in England, 1660–1800', (PhD thesis, University of Michigan, 1996).

their concerns about the trend toward unsystematic mitigation and their calls for legal reform and 'certain punishment'.[31]

Defendants and their families had always tried to influence the courtroom dialogue. In their appeals for acquittal or mitigation they introduced evidence about extenuating circumstances and details particular to their situation. During the eighteenth century, the traditional excuses found in depositions and trial transcripts were inflected with a vocabulary of mental incapacity that sought mitigation on the grounds that the defendant was not in a fully responsible state of mind when the crime was committed. This new language of excuse necessitated an admission of guilt, and it often attributed the crime to uncontrolled passions and emotions that overwhelmed the offender's reason and self-control. These appeals to the psychological motives for crime may or may not have been heeded by juries. The discretion that permeated the English legal system precludes any systematic correlation between the evidence and the verdict in a given case; nevertheless, the efforts of defendants to excuse their criminal behaviour with appeals to a language of mental incapacity were as visible to contemporaries as they are to today's historian.

Using infanticide as a case study, one can trace the trend toward a rich and varied language of excuse. What is particularly interesting about infanticide is that the preparation defence was already so effective for single women by the second decade of the eighteenth century, judging by the way the conviction rate had dropped.[32] The insanity defence was generally the preserve of married women and it simply did not serve the purposes of single women whose crime was used as evidence of their sanity, reason and malicious intent, and who were almost assured an acquittal using the formulaic preparation defence.

---

[31] For more on the English movement for legal reform in the eighteenth century, see: Leon Radzinowicz, *A History of English Criminal Law and its Administration from 1750: Vol. 1, The Movement for Reform, 1750–1833* (London, Stevens and Sons Limited, 1948); Beattie, *Crime and the Courts*, pp. 450–618; Thomas A. Green, *Verdict According to Conscience: Perspectives on the English Criminal Trial Jury, 1200–1800* (Chicago, University of Chicago Press, 1985), pp. 267–317; and Rabin, 'Of Persons Capable', pp. 279–348.

[32] Conviction rates were high in the years immediately after passage of the Act of 1624 and even in the late seventeenth and early eighteenth centuries. By the middle of the 1720s, however, Beattie notes 'a striking shift in attitudes' towards the women accused of infanticide. Beattie, *Crime and the Courts*, pp. 118–19, 122. Mark Jackson's findings for the Northern Circuit qualify Beattie's conclusions. Jackson suggests that prosecutions may not have fallen at the same rate all over the country. His evidence demonstrates that suspicions of murder persisted throughout the eighteenth century and continued to undermine public sympathy for those women accused of infanticide. Jackson, *New-Born Child Murder*, pp. 13–14.

This study is based on a set of 110 indictments for infanticide tried at the Old Bailey in London between 1714 and 1803.[33] Most of the women in this sample were indicted under the 1624 statute. Of the 110 women tried for infanticide, 93 were acquitted and 17 were convicted and sentenced to death.[34] Of the 110 cases, the language of emotion and excuse was introduced in 22 cases. Of these, 13 resulted in an acquittal while 9 resulted in a conviction. These numbers suggest that despite the general acceptance of the insanity defence for other crimes, it was never the most common line of defence in infanticide cases and it was less successful than other pleas.

What can this small sample tell us? It is the exceptions to the commonly-used preparation defence that shed light on changing perceptions of the crime, the criminal and the self during the eighteenth century. In 22 cases from the sample, single women attributed their behaviour immediately before, during or after birth to a form of insanity or mental turmoil, rather than denying the concealment of their pregnancy or asserting that the child was born dead. My data show that throughout the eighteenth century an increasing number of single women introduced language of emotion at their trials, thereby broadening the insanity defence.[35] While such insanity pleas were unsuccessful in the first part of the century, the language of emotion became more successful as the century wore on.

Mary Radford's trial for infanticide saw the first introduction of the language of emotion in 1723.[36] The presence of such language increased in the 1720s and 1730s with eight of the cases that included language of emotion taking place in those two decades. Of the nine pleas of emotion brought to the Old Bailey before 1745, six ended with a conviction.[37] Of

---

[33] This study begins in 1714 when the complete set of microfilmed records of the Old Bailey begins; the study ends in 1803 with the repeal of the statute of 1624 under Lord Ellenborough's Act. I wish to thank Amy Masciola for sharing her data set with me.

[34] Of the 17 women found guilty, only one, Ann Terry, was certainly pardoned and transported to the colonies for life. Others may have been pardoned, but this information is not consistently noted in the OBSP.

[35] My definition of an insanity defence includes any allusion to emotional turmoil that might compromise mental capacity and influence behaviour. I considered this language from anyone participating in the courtroom dialogue.

[36] Mary Radford's trial was the 22nd case of infanticide tried at the Old Bailey between 1714 and 1723. No language of emotion was introduced to excuse the crime and no insanity pleas were made in the first nine years of the sample. The frequency of the language increased thereafter. The second instance of such language of emotion was in Pleasant Bateman's successful use of the insanity defence just a month after Radford's conviction in February 1723.

[37] The ninth case that introduced language of emotion before 1745 was Ann Terry's conviction in May 1744. Terry's pardon may be seen as a herald of changing reception of the defence of insanity.

the three acquittals, two of the defendants were married women. After 1745, the success – but not the incidence – of the insanity plea increased. Between 1745 and 1774, nine women presented evidence of insanity; six were acquitted. Of those six, none was married. After 1774, four women introduced the insanity plea and, like all other women tried for infanticide after that date, they were acquitted.[38]

Table 5.1 The language of emotion and conviction rates, 1723–74.

	convictions	total acquittals	married women acquitted
1723–45	6	3	2
1746–74	3	6	–

[38] In the light of increasing acceptance of pleas of emotion in the latter half of the eighteenth century, Jane Cornforth's conviction in 1774 seems strange. But compared to other insanity defences, it is not surprising that her plea was unsuccessful. Cornforth's insanity was introduced at her trial by Mary Jarvis, the mistress of the workhouse where she was brought after the crime was discovered. None of the seven witnesses who appeared on her behalf corroborated Cornforth's insanity. No one made any mention of her mental capacity before, during or after the crime. For more on the insanity defence, see: Joel Eigen, 'Intentionality and insanity: what the eighteenth-century juror heard', in William Bynum, Roy Porter and Michael Shepherd (eds), *The Anatomy of Madness: Essays in the History of Psychiatry: Vol. 2, Institutions and Society* (London, Tavistock Publications, 1985), pp. 34–51; idem, 'Delusion in the courtroom: the role of partial insanity in early forensic testimony', *Medical History*, 35 (1991), 25–49; idem, *Witnessing Insanity: Madness and Mad-Doctors in the English Court* (New Haven, Yale University Press, 1995); Rabin, 'Of Persons Capable', pp. 86–155; Nigel Walker, *Crime and Insanity in England: Vol. 1, The Historical Perspective* (Edinburgh, Edinburgh University Press, 1967); idem, 'The insanity defence before 1800', *Annals of the American Academy of Political and Social Science*, 477 (1985), 25–30. For more on attitudes to insanity in the early modern world, see: A. Fessler, 'The management of lunacy in seventeenth-century England: an investigation of Quarter-sessions records', *Proceedings of the Royal Society of Medicine*, 49 (1956), 901–907; Michael MacDonald, *Mystical Bedlam: Madness, Anxiety, and Healing in Seventeenth-Century England* (Cambridge, Cambridge University Press, 1981); Roy Porter, *Mind-Forg'd Manacles: A History of Madness in England from the Restoration to the Regency* (London, Athlone, 1987); Peter Rushton, 'Lunatics and idiots: mental disability, the community, and the Poor Law in North-East England, 1600–1800', *Medical History*, 32 (1988), 34–50; Akihito Suzuki, 'Lunacy in seventeenth- and eighteenth-century England: analysis of quarter sessions records', Part 1, *History of Psychiatry*, 2 (1991), 437–56; idem, 'Lunacy in seventeenth- and eighteenth-century England: analysis of quarter sessions records', Part 2, *History of Psychiatry*, 3 (1992), 29–44.

Bodies of evidence

What was the language of emotion and how did defendants (or their witnesses) portray their states of mind during the crime? There are two different categories of testimony about mental states in infanticide trials. The first and more traditional excuse explained the crime as a consequence of the mother's long-standing mental deficiency.[39] In the second category, witnesses or defendants associated the crime of infanticide with the experience of childbirth, specifically the pain of labour. They likened their state of mind to a 'phrenzy' or temporary insanity.

References to a woman's mental deficiency were rarer than descriptions of post-partum insanity. Although Mary Radford made no reference to her mental state at her trial in 1723, her mistress and several other witnesses 'gave the prisoner the character of a very silly creature; that she was a half natural, and that her mother was so before her'.[40] Sarah Allen claimed that she was out of her senses when she committed the crime in 1737 while an unnamed witness in her defence told the court that 'the prisoner always was a silly, giggling creature'.[41] One witness called Ann Terry 'foolish' while another described her as 'a very silly foolish girl, not capable of taking care of herself ... I believe sometimes she is not *compos mentis*'.[42] The juries in all of these cases rejected the claims of congenital infirmity and found the women guilty. Given that evidence of idiocy was usually more acceptable than evidence of insanity, because judicial authorities believed they could verify its authenticity more easily, the convictions in these cases suggest that the jurors were not convinced by the severity of the women's conditions.

The second category of cases associated insanity with childbirth and the pain of labour. In 1723, Pleasant Bateman claimed that 'she was ill, and was in a fit when she was delivered, and had not her senses'.[43]

---

[39] The tests for idiocy were set out by Anthony Fitzherbert (1470–1538) in *La Nouvelle Natura Brévité*, (London, 1534), 233(b). According to Fitzherbert an idiot would be unable to count to twenty, name his parents or state his own age. 'But if he knows letters, or can read by the instruction of another, then he is no idiot'. For more on the diagnosis and treatment of idiocy in early modern England, see: MacDonald, *Mystical Bedlam*; Richard Neugebauer, 'Treatment of the mentally ill in medieval and early modern England: a reappraisal', *Journal of the History of the Behavioural Sciences*, 14 (1978), 158–69; Rabin, 'Of Persons Capable'; and Rushton, 'Lunatics and idiots'.

[40] Mary Radford, *OBSP*, January 1723, p. 26. Radford was sentenced to death.

[41] Sarah Allen, *OBSP*, October 1737, p. 204. Allen was found guilty and sentenced to death.

[42] Ann Terry, *OBSP*, May 1744, p. 116. Ann Terry was found guilty and sentenced to death. She was later pardoned and transported to the colonies.

[43] Pleasant Bateman, *OBSP*, February 1723, p. 4. Bateman was acquitted.

Elizabeth Ambrook did not testify in her own defence, but at her trial in 1735 her sister-in-law told the court that when she asked Elizabeth why she threw her baby out of the window, Elizabeth responded that 'she did not know what she did, for thro' the extremity of pain she thought the room was on fire when she threw it out'.[44] At her trial in 1769 Sarah Hunter said 'I awaked in the morning and found there was a child: that frighted me very much. I was not sensible what I did. I can give no account how I did it'.[45] In 1771 Elizabeth Parkins said she was 'taken very bad over night'. She explained in her defence: 'I went to cut the string to ease myself: I was deprived of my senses, and do not remember any thing that I did'.[46]

What did these defendants say about their level of responsibility for the crime given their description of their mental states? Pleasant Bateman explained that 'she had made provisions for the child'. She called one of the witnesses for the prosecution who confirmed that she had made preparations five or six months before the birth and that 'she had several fits but a few days before, and she was not able to help herself in an hour's time after'.[47] When a midwife examined Mary Shrewsbury in 1737, she asked 'how she could cut her child's throat so barbarously?' Shrewsbury insinuated that an external force had prompted her crime when she replied that 'the devil had given her strength, and not God'.[48] At her trial in 1755 Isabella Buckham said 'I was not in my senses; I do not know what I said or did. Had I been in my senses I should have been very loth to have parted with it'.[49] In this unusual defence, Buckham spoke for herself: while she admitted that she had indeed killed her child, she denied that her actions were criminal. Diana Parker made a similar claim in her trial in 1794. She told the court 'I did not mean to make away with the child, I did not know what I was about. Here are some things that I made for the child; a shift, cap, etc'.[50]

In all of these cases the defendant made a narrow claim about the state of her mind during the crime itself. Each argued that the actual fact of childbirth produced a mental state similar to a 'blackout' during

---

[44] Elizabeth Ambrook, *OBSP*, January 1735, p. 25. Ambrook was found guilty and sentenced to death.
[45] Sarah Hunter, *OBSP*, June 1769, p. 314. Sarah Hunter was acquitted.
[46] Elizabeth Parkins, *OBSP*, April 1771, p. 203. Parkins was acquitted. When the court asked her supervisor, Thomas Stevenson, if Parkins was 'in her right senses', he opined, 'I did not think so, I will assure you'.
[47] Pleasant Bateman, *OBSP*, February 1723, p. 4.
[48] Mary Shrewsbury, *OBSP*, February, 1737, p. 68. Mary Shrewsbury was found guilty.
[49] Isabella Buckham, *OBSP*, December 1755, p. 17. Isabella Buckham was acquitted.
[50] Diana Parker, *OBSP*, September 1794, p. 1067. Diana Parker was acquitted.

which she had no control over her behaviour. The women's descriptions gave the impression that they did not remember this time and that they could take no responsibility for their actions. They did not deny that a murder took place, but they argued that their behaviour was not criminal because they lacked intent. They established the temporary nature of their insanity by introducing evidence about the preparations they had made for the birth of their child before the onset of labour.

As the century passed, the court showed increasing interest in the state of the defendant's mind at the time of the crime. Some of this interest came from the defendants' counsel – who appeared in an increasing number of cases in the course of the eighteenth century – but some of the questions about the woman's mental capacity came from the judge or jurors.[51] In Hannah Perfect's trial in 1747, the court and counsel for the defence questioned Mary Millet, a servant, about the details of the crime. The counsel for the defence then introduced a line of questioning about the state of the prisoner's senses to which Millet responded: 'I believe she was stupefied'. The court then intervened to pose the question: 'You believe she had not the government of her understanding?' Millet answered, 'No, I believe she had not'. Counsel for the defence followed this question with one about whether Perfect was 'a sensible woman at other times'. Millet responded that Perfect was 'a very sensible young woman' and that her general character was that of a 'very sober, honest girl'.[52]

At her trial in 1781, Elizabeth Harris said nothing in her own defence, but several witnesses responded to questions put to them by her counsel about her state of mind. The midwife at the trial, Sarah Tuffnel, was asked if the prisoner seemed 'much confused or afflicted' to which she replied that 'she seemed to give very odd answers at times, as if she was not quite right in her head'.[53] In the trial of Elizabeth Jarvis in 1800 the defence counsel asked Robert Whitfield, a surgeon who examined the child, whether 'A woman in strong labour is not always possessed of her

---

[51] A defendant's right to counsel was augmented in the course of the eighteenth century, but it was not until 1836 that the right to counsel was extended to all aspects of trial for felony. See Beattie, *Crime and the Courts*, pp. 353–62; idem, 'Scales of justice: defence counsel and the English criminal trial in the eighteenth and nineteenth centuries', *Law and History Review*, 9 (1991), 221–67; Green, *Verdict According to Conscience*, pp. 267–317; Langbein, 'Criminal trial before the lawyers', pp. 282–3; idem, 'Shaping the criminal trial', pp. 123–34; idem, 'The prosecutorial origins of defence counsel in the eighteenth century: the appearance of solicitors', *Cambridge Law Journal*, 58 (1999), 314–65; and Stephen Landsman, 'The rise of the contentious spirit: adversary procedure in eighteenth-century England', *Cornell Law Review*, 75 (1990), 498–609.

[52] Hannah Perfect, *OBSP*, February 1747, p. 83. Hannah Perfect was acquitted.

[53] Elizabeth Harris, *OBSP*, May 1781, p. 268. Harris was acquitted.

faculties of reason?' Whitfield responded, 'Not always'.[54] In these examples, the line of questioning attempted to tie the state of the woman's senses to her labour and drew a distinction between her character and mental capacity when she was in labour and when she was not. This line of questioning paralleled the argument made by women accused of infanticide about the effect of labour on their senses.

The court's interest in the defendant's state of mind mirrored Hunter's medicalized explanation for infanticide. Hunter explained that the woman with 'an unconquerable sense of shame' who 'pants after the preservation of character' would be 'overwhelmed with terror and despair' when she found herself pregnant out of wedlock.[55] As a result of the emotional stress of concealing the pregnancy and trying to preserve their reputations, these women 'are overtaken sooner than they expected'. He accounted for their behaviour by pointing to 'their distress of body and mind [which] deprives them of all judgements and rational conduct; they are delivered by themselves ... in their fright and confusion ... insensible of what is passing'.[56] Hunter's assessment of the circumstances leading to the act of child murder legitimized the narratives that emerged in the trials by placing them in a medical context. It redefined infanticide as the natural, almost predictable, result of the physical and emotional distress experienced by single women during pregnancy and childbirth.

States of mind

This narrative of infanticide articulated by women in the courtroom and appropriated by physicians like Hunter had devastating implications for the statute of 1624, and for criminal law in a more general way. This kind of testimony insisted on a shift in the legal mechanism with which the crime was ushered through the system: it traded on the insanity defence rather than the preparation defence. This new understanding of the crime invalidated the assumptions of the statute of 1624 and presented a serious problem for the legal system by introducing an explanation for crime as an excuse for it. Courtroom observers worried that if applied more broadly, this language could lead to the equivalence of all crime with insanity and open the possibility that no one would be held responsible for any criminal behaviour. Hale had clearly been aware of this problem:

---

[54] Elizabeth Jarvis, OBSP, July 1800, p. 80. Jarvis was acquitted.

[55] Hunter, 'On the uncertainty of the signs', p. 272.

[56] Ibid., p. 273.

> For doubtless most persons that are felons of themselves [such as suicides], and others are under degree of partial insanity, when they commit these offenses: it is very difficult to define the indivisible line that divides perfect and partial insanity, but it must rest upon circumstances duly to be weighed and considered both by the judge and jury, lest on the one side there be a kind of inhumanity towards the defects of human nature, or on the other side too great an indulgence given to great crimes.[57]

In the case of infanticide the problem posed by the language of emotion was resolved by the repeal of the 1624 statute in 1803 and by the embrace of a narrative of temporary insanity for single women faced with a pregnancy outside marriage. The nature of the excuse, its application to a relatively small group of defendants and the implicit sympathy on which it depended allowed its acceptance in court. By admitting this excuse and defining its parameters, the legal system may have prevented the admission of other excuses that built upon the language of emotion.

The increased use of the plea of emotion in depositions and trial transcripts in the 1730s and 1740s, and its acceptance by juries during the latter part of the century, coincided with the emergence of the language and culture of sensibility.[58] By the mid-eighteenth century 'sensibility', which had referred to physical sensitivities, came to mean an emotional and moral faculty: it denoted a special and admirable susceptibility to one's own feelings and the feelings of others. As Adela Pinch has remarked, this period was marked by a 'fascination with trying to account for where feelings come from and what they are'.[59] The relationship between emotion and morality preoccupied the literature of sensibility, which was at its most influential and widespread

---

[57] Hale, *Pleas of the Crown*, vol. 1, p. 30.

[58] The work on sensibility is tremendously rich and provocative. See: Nancy Armstrong, *Desire and Domestic Fiction: A Political History of the Novel* (Oxford, Oxford University Press, 1987); G.J. Barker-Benfield, *The Culture of Sensibility: Sex and Society in Eighteenth-Century Britain* (Chicago, University of Chicago Press, 1992); Barbara Benedict, *Framing Feeling: Sentiment and Style in English Prose Fiction, 1745–1800* (New York, 1994); R.F. Brissenden, *Virtue in Distress: Studies in the Novel of Sentiment from Richardson to Sade* (New York, Harper and Row, 1974); Alan T. McKenzie, *Certain, Lively Episodes: The Articulation of Passion in Eighteenth-Century Prose* (Athens, University of Georgia Press, 1990); John Mullan, *Sentiment and Sociability: The Language of Feeling in the Eighteenth Century* (Oxford, Oxford University Press, 1988); Adela Pinch, *Strange Fits of Passion: Epistemologies of Emotion, Hume to Austen* (Palo Alto, Stanford University Press, 1996); Janet Todd, *Sensibility: An Introduction* (London, Methuen, 1986); and Ann Jessie Van Sant, *Eighteenth-Century Sensibility and the Novel: The Senses in Social Context* (Cambridge, Cambridge University Press, 1993).

[59] Pinch, *Strange Fits of Passion*, p. 2.

from the 1740s to the 1770s.[60] Although novels are the best-known expression of the culture of sensibility, philosophical essays, newspapers, sermons and crime pamphlets also shared these preoccupations.

According to Pinch, 'the era of sensibility defined relations between middle class British men and women and their social others: Indians, slaves, the poor, and the mad'.[61] These relations were modelled in the literature of sensibility, which assumed that life and literature were directly linked. In its capacity to teach, it 'showed people how to behave, how to express themselves in friendship and how to respond decently to life's experiences'.[62] An examination of the reception of the language of emotion in court serves as a good test of this hypothesis and its implications beyond literature.

The language of emotion in court met with a mixed response and one wonders why it was not embraced immediately by juries. One explanation certainly lies in the fact that the acceptance of an insanity plea for infanticide would have had a destabilising effect on the law and would necessitate the repeal of the statute of 1624. An extra-legal explanation might call on the chronology of sensibility. The translation of the crime of infanticide from a premeditated act into the result of mental illness coincided with the height of the production and consumption of fiction concerned with sensibility. The production of pleas of emotion was connected with cross-class concerns about feeling, emotion and self.

The change in the reception of the pleas of emotion may bear relation to the changes in the didactic message conveyed by the cult of sensibility. Eighteenth-century writers of sensibility had inconsistent views of sensibility and class. While some saw sensibility as a shared, equalizing characteristic that crossed lines of class, for others 'it was the property more or less exclusively of the higher and more genteel orders'.[63] The latter conception of sensibility may account for the rejection of the narrative of emotion expressed in the pleas of poor single women accused of infanticide. As the century progressed, however, the narrative of insanity and infanticide became the property of poor, single women as well. In the context of the culture of sensibility, it was received as sincere and inevitable.[64]

---

[60] Todd, *Sensibility*, p. 9. The 'era of sensibility' lasted from the end of the seventeenth century until the beginning of the nineteenth.

[61] Pinch, *Strange Fits of Passion*, p. 11.

[62] Todd, *Sensibility*, p. 2.

[63] Ibid., p. 13.

[64] The question of how this narrative was created and its relationship to the development of the self is the subject of my forthcoming book: D. Rabin, *Crime, Legal Responsibility and the Self in England, 1660–1800*.

The individual self may not have been defined as part of the identities of the lower orders at the beginning of the century and may account for jury resistance to the narratives of emotion in the 1720s and 1730s. However, by the middle and late eighteenth century having a sense of oneself meant recognising the subjectivity of the other. This acceptance of a working-class subjectivity by middle-class judges and juries was not an act of beneficence on their part. Their acknowledgement of the feelings and the suffering of the poor affirmed their own superior sensibility and especially their belief that their own compassion was only attained though contact with suffering. This suffering could be acknowledged as such if a single woman were defined as the passive victim of male seduction and insanity rather than as an active, premeditating murderess.[65]

The eighteenth-century courtroom became one site in this exchange of sensibility. It was the place where defendants performed their emotional repertoire, acting out their roles as archetypal victims. Judges and jurors responded to these sentimental narratives by affirming their own superior sense of self and sensibility. The acceptance of pleas of emotion from women accused of infanticide, starting in the middle of the eighteenth century, reflected a new epistemology of emotion: it made explicit the sympathy that existed for women accused under the statute of 1624.

Conclusion

This chapter seeks to deepen our understanding of the decline in convictions for infanticide in the eighteenth century. While scholars have pointed to the jury's sympathy with the single women accused of this crime, consideration of the culture of sensibility and its emphasis on experience, emotion and sympathy explains the defences made by the accused and suggests reasons for their acceptance by judges and juries. The development of narratives of excuse, spoken in the language of emotion, demonstrates the influence of sensibility on people of all social ranks of early modern English society and reveals a dynamic that existed between the single women accused of infanticide and those who heard their stories.

The concept of sensibility had a distinct effect on what was said in court. Their use of the language of the mind may suggest that single women were caught up in this new understanding of self and sensibility along with their masters and mistresses. When confronted with the

---

[65] Van Sant, *Eighteenth-Century Sensibility*, pp. 16–59.

crime of infanticide, they had to find a way to explain the accusations and their guilt to themselves and to their community. The preparation defence did not serve this purpose. These alternative explanations rested on the reconstruction and narration of experience and emotion and involved some admission of guilt. This admission diverted attention away from the concealment and secrecy that had formerly defined the crime.

Defendants may also have known that the culture of sensibility affected the reception of their pleas. The development of the language of sensibility led to a fall in conviction rates. Justices of the peace who presided over the deposition process, and judges and jurors who listened to these pleas in court, must have been influenced by the 'era of sensibility'. My sample of Old Bailey trials suggests that as the eighteenth century progressed, juries became more open to pleas of emotion in place of, or along with, the preparation defence. This increased association of infanticide, insanity and single women in the second half of the eighteenth century set the stage for what Roger Smith describes as 'the legally exculpatory attitude towards [all] infanticidal women' in the nineteenth century.[66]

For other crimes, there was a price to be paid for the acceptance of a link between infanticide and insanity. While eighteenth-century concerns with emotion and sensibility ushered in the acceptance of the defence of insanity in 1843, the M'Naghten Rules circumscribed the language that could be used to describe mental states and dictated harsher punishments for those found insane.[67] In the nineteenth century, medicalized and criminalized descriptions of patients replaced the permeable language of the eighteenth century, which had allowed defendants and others who spoke on their behalf to broaden Hale's category of exculpatory mental states and to define them as temporary and unrelated to the defendant's true self and sensibility.

Acknowledgements

I want to thank Clare Crowston, Amy Froide, Craig Koslofsky, Mark Jackson, Amy Masciola, Randall McGowen and Kathryn Oberdeck for their suggestions and advice. A previous version of this chapter was presented at the North American Conference on British Studies.

---

[66] Roger Smith, *Trial by Medicine*, p. 147.
[67] I wish to thank Professor Scott Brophy for this insight.

CHAPTER SIX

Infanticide and the erotic plot: a feminist reading of eighteenth-century crime

Johanna Geyer-Kordesch

'Don't touch me', she said, taking a step backward. She refused to be doomed. As long as she was on her side of the door she would be safe. Cunningly he began his transformations, trying to lure her into his reach ... Then he stood looking at her sadly; he was wearing a turtle neck sweater ... 'Let me take you away,' he whispered. 'Let me rescue you. We will dance together forever.' ... Once she had wanted these words, she had waited all her life for someone to say them ... 'No,' she said. 'I know who you are'.[1]

This 'gothic' confrontation is one of many in Margaret Atwood's ingenious novel *Lady Oracle*. Gender relations are turned upside down as the woman is given the active voice and the power to refuse. But an older prototype resonates through the modern feminist portrayal: the danger and allure of Bluebeard. The original was a fairy tale, an eighteenth-century favourite published in Charles Perrault's Mother Goose Tales of 1694. Bluebeard is fascinating because he is not what he seems. Cast in the old mould of the trickster figure, the powerful shape-changer whose real character and intentions the storyteller will unlock, this handing-down of the story provides succeeding generations with the 'key' knowledge that unveils his evil. Bluebeard seems a good match, at first, in the traditional story of love and marriage, a man of virile charm and enough worldly goods to provide a stylish life and the contentment of material comforts. Only the ambiguous quest for a separate female identity – which is, often enough, negatively portrayed as insatiable female curiosity – reveals him a monster. His 'gothic' power lies in his sexuality, as a consumer of women or as a consummate womanizer. Each wife turns the 'key' on this secret, to find revealed a promiscuous, impersonal sexuality – and death as its price.

Angela Carter's fairy tale, *The Bloody Chamber*, builds on this Bluebeard archetype,[2] but she uses this same theme to different effect.

---

[1] As quoted from M. Atwood, *Lady Oracle*, in Susanne Becker, *Gothic Forms of Feminine Fictions* (Manchester, Manchester University Press, 1999), p. 183.

[2] Angela Carter, *The Bloody Chamber And Other Stories* (London, Vintage, 1995): 'The Bloody Chamber', pp. 7–40, first published in 1979.

His virile seduction is also a tale of female sexual collusion. The young
bride finds her own sexuality unlocked in response to his suave
masculinity. Sensual pleasure spills over to her rich enjoyment of his
worldly goods and possessions. The bride not only has, but sensually is,
the lustre and pleasure of the pearls he gives her. The sensual implicates
Carter's heroine in the erotically dangerous and in sexual satisfaction.
Sexuality is as seductive as sympathy and love in the rite of passage from
virgin to lover.

The loss of innocence and the transition to responsibility and identity
in the key phase from girlhood to womanliness, provide the focus for
this essay. How female sexuality and its consequences are negotiated in
a past reaching to the present is crucial to this transition. There were
many acceptable and socially condoned variations governing female
choice. Acceptable choices included, of course, the suitable marriage in
which provision for the bride was not unhinged by a groom profligate
with money or with sexual favours. Surprisingly they also included – as
we shall see – bearing illegitimate children. Nor was spinsterhood,
contrary to its derogatory image, a despised solution. Where the social
provision for women broke down was at a point where projections
about gender clashed with female reality. Proven child murder was
irreconcilable not just with the law and its legally defined punishments,
but with how women were idealized. The honourable woman and what
she must seem determined a labyrinth of hopeful or destructive choices.
If a woman seeking marriage, the cornerstone of traditional female
existence, killed her child, she was doing more than murdering a new-
born baby. It is this theme of murder in its widest connotations,
including that of a suicidal desperation to acquiesce in a judicial
scapegoating, that will pull together a considerable breadth of material
in this chapter, ranging from literature through social history and from
a focus on Prussian and Scottish sources to comparisons with some
contemporary cases.

Child murder, I want to maintain, was a final deed of revulsion by a
few that called into question the trajectory of coming-of-age and
entering the state of marriage. This is also the fulcrum on which a final
consideration of this paper turns: were and are there alternative
solutions to marriage and having children? Why have they not been seen
as a positive foil for a female destiny? Has historiography concealed the
'true' revulsion with a gendered fate by not sufficiently considering the
complex palette of women's lives? Marriage was predominant as an
economic and social determinant for women's lives. But it was far from
ideal and perhaps a trap to be sprung.

Social expectations are rarely liberating. Often they plot a restricting
sense of alternatives. In this chapter two of these, the erotic plot and the

marriage plot, reflect potentially destructive, but socially highly desirable, choices in women's lives. The erotic plot highlights the sexual potential of female passion, but curtails it by the expectation that romance will lead to marriage. This is the classic Mills and Boon story-line of surmounting the obstacles to a happy end; this story-line may be trivial, but the conspiracy to curtail women to romantic success is not. Of vital importance is an historical exploration showing women transcending either the use of sexual wiles or marital teleology. This can go badly wrong, as it did with child murder. But the purpose of investigating crime in historical perspective should be to deconstruct expectations. Redefining the boundaries of gender roles must also be to relocate historical thinking.

The 'key' to the Bluebeard murders is the shared marriage bed. Here the erotic plot does not lead to a romantic happy ending. The tale of Bluebeard restates it as dangerous, as a potential horror story. Susanne Becker has suggested that these confrontations, where women confront marriage as only one aspect of their possible lives, 'emphasise the multiple subject-in-process'.[3] This means that, as these stories unfold, the various plots relating to passion, sexuality, love, violence and marriage undergo different and often parallel exposition, all open to the scrutiny of the reader, and, by way of 'gothic' improbabilities, allow these multiple solutions to become part of the fabric of reflection and escape.[4] 'Rescue' – with its often unresolved endings – depends, in the feminist version, on the woman extricating herself from the marriage plot and its over-riding dependency on male provision or male sexual desire.

In the eighteenth century in such countries as Prussia and Scotland, escape from gendered expectations had a different scale of choices, as the female plot of wooing, marriage and children was played out in the narrower confines of stricter social parameters. But whatever the time and place, how much freedom was given to women defined the meaning and tragedy of infanticide. Letters and ballads – whether rock ballad or folksong – still tell of the erotic plot and the meaning of courtship. The anger, joy, romance and frustration poured out in diaries or correspondence usually echo the alluring ring of 'we shall dance forever together' – as enticing in the eighteenth century as in modern courtships. But the ability to say 'No', given the spell cast by this gendered destiny, was – and is – a much more difficult lesson, even more difficult when transformed from an individual fate to that of a culturally acceptable choice.

---

3   Becker, *Gothic Forms*, pp. 183–5.
4   Ibid.

Stories – and her story – unlock history in new ways. The recasting of an old story can inscribe a fairy tale with gendered wisdom. As women talk to women – a strand of her story developed with feminist aspirations – a skein of knowledge is woven, of a kind that may have moved Angela Carter to resolve the climax of her Bluebeard story with a mother's incisive intervention, converting an old significant warning into a modern feminist tale of resurgence. Read as a story meant to suggest how a girl comes to understand how to be a mature woman, the mother figure balances the pitfalls of instinctual sexuality. Her actions successfully hold at bay male sexual exploitation. Just as Bluebeard is about to savour the next killing of his latest wife, the trophy of his sexual prowess, and just as the tide rushes to cut Bluebeard's island from the mainland, the mother rides her black horse through the closing gates and raises her pistol to shoot dead this Bluebeard, and every Bluebeard, and save her daughter. In Carter's modern tale, the female reader can reinterpret her choices and accept identification with an active and powerful female figure.

Infanticide, concealment and the law

In the eighteenth century, prosecution for infanticide marked the point when a young woman entered a process which ultimately would annihilate her as a respectable member of her family or village. The legal machinery would strip her of privacy, honour, a home, employment, kinship ties and reputation – and, if convicted, her life. Several aspects of early modern infanticide trials offer feminist readings. The first concerns the disparity between the fictionalized characterization of the child-murderess and her real existence in the trial literature. Another concerns the concealment of pregnancy outside marriage. A majority of convictions were made for both concealed pregnancy and infanticide.

Prosecution at law enforced the role of women as married sexual consorts because it punished illicit sexual transgression. Making concealed pregnancy a crime reinforced a very narrow band of behaviour. The forced disclosure of sexual relations and the public humiliation of the inquisitional process did not present women as innocent or honourable. The trials became a showpiece of the wrongfulness of female behaviour. At the level of individual fate, however, each woman was caught in the despair forced on her by her trial. Her private road to hell then became a public allegory of the rights and wrongs of gendered behaviour. The history of legal reform does not dwell on how codifying crime enforced gendered roles. Most of it tends to record Enlightenment changes at law as progressive.

Milder sentencing or fewer convictions are perceived as an achievement of reform ideologies. The story of female crime becomes the story of victims at law and their liberation by far-sighted and concerned legislators.

The latter half of the eighteenth century did see progressively milder punishments and even the eventual abolition of the death sentence for infanticide. But there are some serious caveats to be emphasized in such a narrative of reform. Infanticide trials had much in common with witchcraft trials. These too were seen to be challenged through liberal arguments by top consulting jurists disclaiming the existence of the devil or using forms of madness (depression or melancholia) as a mitigating medical diagnosis, pitting a scientific ideology against superstition.[5] Expert testimony from the medical profession was often used to argue 'rational' reform of criminal law. Enlightenment became synonymous with a distancing from the 'folklore' of superstition. Advances in medical science benefited men as active and in command as surgeons or male midwives while reinforcing the dependency of women. Childbirth itself was increasingly advertised by medical men as dangerous and in need of male surgical expertise. The traditional practices of the midwife were branded 'ignorant'.[6]

Codification in law for the criminal offence of infanticide was defined for the first time in the *Constitutio Criminalis Carolina* of 1532, the penal code used in most of Europe. The inquisitional procedures defined by the *Constitutio* punished the violent killing of a live infant by an unmarried mother.[7] Causing the death of children within marriage was not a legally distinct offence. Disclosed pregnancies that led to marriage were not criminalized, nor were they unusual. Being with child could significantly reinforce an intent to marry.[8] Thus only concealed pregnancies – and single mothers accused by employers, neighbours,

---

[5] See J. Geyer-Kordesch, 'Whose Enlightenment? Medicine, witchcraft, melancholia and pathology', in R. Porter (ed.), *Medicine in the Enlightenment* (Amsterdam, Rodopi, 1995), pp. 114–29.

[6] I have explored the tensions between male and female midwifery in regard to the licensing of surgeons in Glasgow in my chapter on midwifery in J. Geyer-Kordesch and Fiona Macdonald, *Physicians and Surgeons in Glasgow: The History of the Royal College of Physicians and Surgeons of Glasgow, 1599–1858* (London, Hambledon Press, 1999), pp. 253–92.

[7] Michael Alberti, *Commentatio in Constitutionem Criminalem Carolinam Medica* (Halle, Waisenhaus Verlag, 1734).

[8] See, for example, Rebekka Habermas (ed.), *Das Frankfurter Gretchen, Der Prozess gegen die Kindesmörderin Susanna Margaretha Brandt* (Munich, Beck Verlag, 1999), pp. 13–14, where she cites the illegitimacy rate in Frankfurt as 5 per cent of all births at the end of the eighteenth century. Women could also prosecute for alimony in cases of illegitimate children.

family members and others, and brought to the attention of officialdom
– were targeted. In making the concealment of pregnancy a criminal
offence, the sexual activity of unmarried women came under legal
scrutiny. Where there was no means of reintegrating an unmarried
woman and her illegitimate child into a community, openly or through
a discreet absence, her conduct was made public. She was pilloried
through a criminal investigation as a warning against immoral female
behaviour. Thus she was made an outcast by the legal proceedings
opened to investigate her life and actions. Her death became a symbolic
sacrifice to a public code of morality and this was as significant as the
death of the child.

Michael Schmidt in his excellent book, *Genossin der Hexe*, delves in
some detail into the recorded criminal cases of infanticide, citing recent
studies that show low trial rates.[9] He calculates that under 10 per cent
of all criminal executions were for infanticide in the area covered by the
Carolingian code until the end of the eighteenth century.[10] For the
German cities that Richard van Dülmen investigated (Augsburg,
Nuremberg, Frankfurt-am-Main, Danzig, Ulm, Memmingen) only 7.8
per cent of all criminal executions were for infanticide, but this rose to
46.36 per cent of all death penalties involving women.[11] Infanticide was
clearly the crime for which women were put to death most often. Van
Dülmen suggests that the criminalizing of infanticide from the middle of
the seventeenth century onwards was a product of an increasing
vigilance on sexual morality by the Protestant churches.[12] Schmidt
calculates that at a conservative estimate 30,000 women were executed
for infanticide between 1500 and 1800 in Germany. While witchcraft
prosecutions included some men, the crime of infanticide was
exclusively female. Schmidt points out that infanticide prosecutions
went on for a century longer than witchcraft trials; and witchcraft trials
involved clustering, often concurrent with witchcraft crazes, while
infanticide trials were a product of normal judicial prosecutions.

Schmidt emphasizes the links between the witch and the child-
murderess. In both cases illicit sexuality was central. Prosecutions for
witchcraft regularly involved interrogation on pacts with the devil and
sexual copulation. Infanticide, too, was prosecuted through an
inquisition and torture. Confessions regularly described how the devil

---

[9]   Michael Schmidt, *Genossin der Hexe: Interpretation der Gretchentragödie in Goethe's
      Faust aus der Perspektive der Kindesmordproblematik* (Göttingen, Altaquito Verlag,
      1985). I quote from Schmidt's arguments on pp. 22–39.
[10] Ibid., p. 23.
[11] Richard van Dülmen, *Frauen vor Gericht. Kindsmord in der frühen Neuzeit* (Frankfurt
      am Main, Fischer-Taschenbuch Verlag, 1991), p. 60.
[12] Ibid., p. 74.

whispered to the defendant urging her to kill the child.[13] Schmidt has uncovered a valid and important aspect of the scapegoating of women for 'sexual' crimes by linking witchcraft and infanticide. The projection of evil by embodying it as the devil was very real for these women, particularly when ideological and social pressures became irreconcilably oppressive. The fear and attraction of sexuality was double-edged. It was a natural response and in no way evil as such, but in the context of the moral and authoritarian gendering of 'temptation' it became an act defining the boundary between the chaste and morally good, and the wicked and fallen woman. Many infanticide cases show women of marginal status, but also some from respectable households,[14] who were sexually abused while employed or under the same roof as male relatives or having undergone what today we call date rape. The men involved in these cases as judged by the criminal records were singularly elusive, whilst simultaneously effusively documenting the life and 'criminal' actions of women. The law did not prosecute the men who made the women pregnant and their evidence in infanticide cases usually took the form of disclaimers. A frighteningly high number of the fathers named were related to the women, resonating with today's statistics on domestic violence, rape or child abuse.

Many infanticide cases show the emotional isolation of the pregnant women. In a grotesque publication that Schmidt cites, Protestant ministers who attended women before their execution presented them as pious converts to chastity and religion. These 'wretched, illiterate and degraded women',[15] as Schmidt describes them, were presented as paragons of atonement and remorse when facing death, lending themselves to an imagery of sentimentalized womanhood. One was described with pastoral pride as so modest that she even asked if exposing her neck to the executioner might violate her modesty.[16] Schmidt sees this transformation of real women into saccharine confections as the religious beatification of the guillotine's victims ('*Sakralisierung der Opfer des Schafotts*').[17] Secular and religious writing of this kind constructed the feminine as dependent, contrite and

---

[13] Schmidt, *Genossin der Hexe*, p. 29.

[14] Profiles of the child-murderess are given on the basis of records in specific sovereign territories cited in: Markus Meumann, *Findelkinder, Waisenhäuser, Kindsmord. Unversorgte Kinder in der frühneuzeitlichen Gesellschaft* (Munich, Oldenbourg Verlag, 1998), pp. 117–25; Otto Ulbricht, *Kindsmord und Aufklärung in Deutschland* (Munich, Oldenbourg Verlag, 1990), pp. 25–84; Kerstin Michalik, *Kindsmord. Sozial- und Rechtsgeschichte der Kindstötung im 18. und beginnenden 19. Jahrhundert am Beispiel Preussen* (Pfaffenweifer, Centaurus-Verlag Gesellschaft, 1997), pp. 55–71.

[15] Schmidt, *Genossin der Hexe*, p. 38.

[16] Ibid.

[17] Ibid.

in need of supervision.[18] The economically marginalized and powerless child-murderess – whose pregnancy in these cases was caused by seduction, rape or romantic collusion – was recast in the mould of the chaste female saint. Pious edification began to erect a female image of weakness, innocence and holy chastity. Remorse meant reinstating the confines of gender expectations.

In Prussia there were frequent decrees on infanticide. Under Frederick William I infanticide was punishable by *säcken*, which meant sewing the woman into a sack and throwing her into a river while she was still alive. Although his successor Frederick the Great forbade *säcken*, he issued a decree in 1756 warning Prussian civil servants not to disregard earlier legal directives whereby pregnancies outside marriage were to be notified to town officials by family members, neighbours or holders of public office.[19] This of course heightened tendencies to gossip about single women and their courtship, and encouraged overt surveillance. The decree of 1756 is often seen as a liberal benchmark and praised fulsomely.[20] It dispensed with a basic legal requirement, proving live birth, which eased cases where violence was not proven, and it finally abolished torture as a means to confession. What it did not do was to relieve pressure on single women who consented or were lured into sexual intercourse. If an illegitimate pregnancy was suspected it had to be notified by law to a midwife. By law the father of the child was also held to notify town officials if he knew of pregnancy. This latter rule may have been on the books but had no practical results. These legal measures did not extend to the financial support of the mother and the child, however.

The legislation of 1756 penalized the single woman by making her pregnancy a criminal offence pursued at law, while the state did nothing at all to alleviate the social or economic distress of women.[21] The willingness to prosecute for concealed pregnancy and infant murder remained. Only the argument that notification might save a child seemed better than unqualified criminalization. The threat of public exposure remained because the law enforced notification of 'illegitimate' pregnancy. The risk of the 'erotic plot' was still squarely placed on the law's potential criminal, the woman.

In 1794, the *Allegemeine Preussische Landrecht* converted punishment by decapitation to *Staupenschlag* (public whipping at the

---

[18] On shaping the feminine through attribution of particular characteristics not directly connected with sexuality, see Rozsika Parker, *The Subversive Stitch: Embroidery and the Making of the Feminine* (London, The Women's Press, rev. edn 1996).

[19] See Schmidt, *Genossin der Hexe*, p. 32.

[20] Ibid., p. 33.

[21] Schmidt, *Genossin der Hexe*, pp. 33–4.

stake and imprisonment in the workhouse). Bavaria repealed the death sentence for other categories of crime in 1813, but it took until 1851 to revoke capital punishment for child murder. In France, severe punishment for infanticide remained until 1832 when mitigating circumstances were allowed before the courts.[22] Austria introduced liberal laws in 1803, repealing the death sentence, but in 1810 the new penal code common to Catholic France and Austria was introduced, once more calling for capital punishment. In Scotland, infanticide was criminalized between 1609 and 1809, following the European pattern.

Between 1700 and 1850 the legal prosecution of infanticide in Europe was not effectively liberalized, even though punishments were modified, as single mothers were still prosecuted under the criminal law and little was done to help single mothers with illegitimate children. The foundling hospitals had high death rates and partook of moral condemnation, separating mother and child. As the object of state vilification and moral crusades by so-called enlightened writers as well as religious reformers, female sexuality outside marriage – the 'erotic plot' – was condemned as evil, wrong and, if the woman became pregnant, open to public scapegoating in both Protestant and Catholic countries.

The public ritual of death and thus the public impact of trials for child murder are well documented in the case of Susanna Margaretha Brandt.[23] Rebekka Habermas details the extensive juridical involvement of the patrician families of Frankfurt-am-Main. The men of these families were judges, town officials, lawyers appointed to the defence and civil servants who administered the many stages of investigating and bringing a child-murderess to trial. Other historians have remarked on how the execution as the resolution of the trial highlighted the symbolic needs that early modern legal ritual was meant to satisfy.[24] Consistent with this ceremonial need, Susanna Brandt was not just executed. Her punishment was not seen as a private or individual crime, but a public offence. A scaffolding was erected on the main square, military guards were mounted on the walls and city gates, companies of soldiers detailed to keep onlookers in line, and a great crowd was expected.[25] Two ministers kept a night vigil with Brandt, and at six o'clock in the morning on 14 January 1771 the senior judge came to the gaol to read

---

[22] Beat Weber, *Die Kindesmörderin im Deutschen Schrifttum von 1770–1795* (Bonn, Bouvier Verlag, 1974), pp. 10–13.

[23] Habermas (ed.), *Das Frankfurter Gretchen.*

[24] See: Richard van Dülmen, *Theater des Schreckens, Gerichtspraxis und Strafrituale in der frühen Neuzeit* (Munich, Beck Verlag, 1985), pp. 121-44; and Klaus Kastner, *Literatur und Wandel im Rechtsdenken* (Stuttgart, Richard Boorberg Verlag, 1993).

[25] Kastner, *Literatur und Wandel,* p. 36.

the death sentence out to her. He then took a red cane, broke it in two and threw it down in front of her. This signified the official consensus to end her life. She was so frightened at this that she shook all over for several minutes.[26]

Several men, including the town scribe Dr Cloudy, the pastors Willemar and Zeitmann, the judge Raab and two officials, then sat down with Susanna Brandt to eat the *Henkersmahlzeit*, her 'last supper'. It was fulsome: soup, red cabbage, 3lb sausages, 10lb beef, 6lb fish, 12lb dressed veal roast, a bowl of sweets, 30 pieces of bread and two black loaves (*Hospital Leibbrodt*) and 8½ measures of 1748 wine.[27] Dr Cloudy ate nothing, the ministers and the judge very little, but the town officers ate of every dish. Brandt only had a glass of water 'which she drank completely'.[28] Susanna Brandt was then escorted to her place of execution dressed in her death robes ('*Todten-Kleid*'). These were white: white cap, white linen jacket and skirt, white gloves. She was tied to the executioner's chair and amid prayers she was beheaded.[29]

Even more so than the inquisitional procedure of the trial, this was a thoroughly public act. Susanna Brandt was no longer just an individual: she stood for public remorse and her own transformation to someone whose heavenly salvation was now assured. Hence her white attire, attesting to her purity and hope of redemption. The ritual of the execution held all in thrall. Only her involuntary shivers as the staff of her life was symbolically broken speak of other feelings before she was led to the scaffold.

Demographic distribution and comparative conviction rates (between male and female crime) do not disclose the ideological impact of gendered criminal prosecutions. Men and women involved in crime are not given the voice of their sex or their gendered predicament when their fate is disclosed only statistically. The relationship between crime and social – or indeed criminal – penalties incurred through gendered expectations is subtly altered by seeing it through a demographic lens. In this agenda, as with insanity, 'equating' women with men shows that fewer females were confined, convicted or punished particularly in the early modern period.[30] With equality seemingly upheld by comparing the absolute numbers of crimes of violence committed by men and women respectively, the agenda of gender comparisons is subtly

---

[26] Ibid., p. 36.
[27] Ibid., p. 37.
[28] Ibid.
[29] Ibid.
[30] Overall statistics on crime, particularly violent crime, show these crimes to be primarily committed by men. In the early modern period, women were statistically less involved in crime.

changed. It looks as if women were spared in criminal prosecutions. And it then becomes easy to discount an analysis based on how gender issues were perceived. The category gender becomes a means of tabulating a difference based on numbers. These figures can then be subsumed into 'big-picture' discussions where the dominant area of interest is not specifically gender related, such as economic or political change. Social history then retains analytical categories more congenial to its pursuits, such as the rural/urban, or Catholic/Protestant divide and its delineation of social trends. These are sociological questions which continue to dominate major work on witchcraft, childbirth and women's diseases.

Unfortunately the sociological emphasis on 'facts' and their relation to social trends has tended to devalue the work of interpretation. If a historian turns to feminist literary criticism it is to find truly imaginative readings of history and the gendering of women's life experience in the past.[31] It is to these readings I owe the following attempt to interpret what child murder may have meant to women of the eighteenth and early nineteenth centuries who saw no alternative except to kill. To agree with one's own death sentence is to admit to a deep dissonance between life and aspiration or to a deep sense of moral failure. There are two central narratives in women's gender expectations, the 'marriage plot' and the 'erotic plot'. In the life stories of women these two plots are often intertwined. In the prelude to child murder they are definitive way-stations. To go to the gallows for child murder can be read as a negation of both choices, despite the public rituals of remorse at an execution. To kill a child is to pronounce a judgment on sexuality, passion, love and marriage as being potentially dangerous and destructive.

Suicide and the erotic plot

Few have sought to explain one of the most obvious findings of pre-trial interrogation: the stubborn silence of women questioned about being pregnant. I want to argue that through this staunch denial of pregnancy – which seems contradictory because admission would have paved the way for some kind of rescue of mother and child – gendered expectations were starkly and openly called into question. This behaviour was female-orientated and spoke to a public increasingly

---

[31] See, for example: Becker, *Gothic Forms*; Joanna Russ, *How to Suppress Women's Writing* (London, The Women's Press, 1983); Carolyn Heilbrun, *Writing a Woman's Life* (London, The Women's Press, 1989); Cheryl Bernard and Edit Schlaffer, *Viel erlebt und nichts begriffen: Die Männer und die Frauenbewegung* (Reinbek bei Hamburg, Rowohlt Verlag, 1985).

divided over the deterrent effect of showcase morality. If the law wanted
an example of 'perverse' women (child-killing), then the infanticide
herself fitted the bill: but her case also proved the inhumanity of
executing single mothers.[32]

In the reform debate and in novels and plays, the infanticide sets a
regressive pattern in terms of a womanly image. As a public scapegoat,
however, she comes to represent the ultimate negation of women's
confinement to the female plot. Infanticide caused social turmoil. It
divided opinions, and created animosities, and was played out as a
public tragedy, as the pre-trial interrogations show. Child murder was a
conscious, although passionately negative act. Bringing to trial meant
the whole tragedy floodlit, as it were: hidden sexual abuse, romantic
misjudgement or coercion, power relationships between men and
women, the double standard and the conflicts of class and kinship. On
the scaffold the infanticide became an icon, a sacrificial victim of several
systems of betrayal and fear, not least those of Church and state. As a
reversal of the ideological intention of authority to force women to
conform, it liberated them in the awfulness of a public trial and
execution. The folk ballad retold the bravery of women climbing the
scaffold and sang of the pitfalls of courtship. New novels and plays
made women innocent and accused the faithless lover. Female sexuality
was now discussed, although still condemned as the work of the devil.

Female sexuality and its legitimate realization is at the centre of the
'erotic plot'. The 'erotic plot' however – throughout most of her story –
was the gateway to achieving financial security and social status through
its 'happy ending', marriage. But female sexuality and passion have their
own momentum culminating, often enough, in 'illicit' sex, the female
risk in courtship, which endangered the reputation and happiness of a
woman. The double standard, judging women differently from men
engaged in the same actions or circumstances, was deeply rooted in the
sexual codes of behaviour of the time.

The destructive dissonance between gender expectations as
phantasized in the erotic plot and reality was played out dramatically
in the eighteenth century. The suicide that became paradigmatic – for
the gap between romantic aspirations and a cruel pragmatism that in
effect devalued female desire and ambition – was that of Karoline von
Günderrode (1780–1806). She died by her own hand when twenty-six
by plunging a knife through her heart. She was not pregnant nor was
she a child-murderess. But her suicide made clear that there was female
resistance to the compromises of a powerless role. Günderrode was a
writer on the verge of the limited literary career open to women: she

---

[32] The killing done by men in the name of courage in war is also a gendered expectation.

was publishing her works under a pseudonym. Her poems and plays were already displaying the sure touch of other emerging (male) Romantic writers. Her letters and her study of natural philosophy were equal in style and imaginative depth to her male peers.[33] Her suicide, however, made public the impossibilities and contradictions of a female sense of romantic freedom. She could voice the same complex aesthetic and embrace the same ideology on the page, but she could not change the expectations of gender even in what seemed then to be an avant-garde movement.

Günderrode fell in love with the Heidelberg University classicist and professor, Friedrich Creuzer, who befriended many of the Romantics but was, unlike most of them, without a private income. He was married to a woman he did not love but on whom he was entirely dependent in practical matters, from the provision of meals to the household accounts. Sophie Creuzer was older than he and the former wife of his deceased professorial mentor. He is recorded as saying he married her out of gratitude. As the writer Christa Wolf has remarked, here was the typical middle-class soap opera with all the roles typecast: the lover who won't accept the consequences; the wife who defended a possession, her husband; the intimate friend and go-between, Susanne von Heyden, who passed on letters and arranged clandestine meetings; the adviser, Friedrich Karl von Savigny, loyal, concerned, pragmatic, but fearful; plus the gossips, female confidantes, spectators and the clueless.[34]

As the situation became hopeless, friends counselled compromise. Creuzer's intimates told him how Karoline couldn't possibly run a household: she was too intellectual and had no dowry to speak of, one of the reasons her aristocratic family placed her in a Damenstift (lay religious foundation for unmarried ladies). Creuzer withdrew. Günderrode too tried to compromise, sublimating her vision of love and sexual honesty. But her imagination rebelled, as did her integrity. She insisted her vision was indivisible from what she was and what lovers ought to be. As one of the few women who articulated the meaning of philosophical principle in her own writings, she could not sacrifice her imaginal values. Her work was about her ability to love, even tragically, and she insisted this was a romantic freedom possible for women. She refused to subjugate her mind to pragmatism. To her the erotic plot had

---

[33] See Markus Hille, *Karoline von Günderrode* (Reinbek bei Hamburg, Rowohlt Taschenbuch Verlag, 1999).

[34] Wolf uses the comparison of 'burgerliches Trauerspiel' which, to give the same sense for today's English-language readers, can be translated as 'soap opera'. For the full quotation that I have paraphrased, see Karoline von Günderrode, *Der Schatten eines Traumes, Gedichte, Prosa, Briefe, Zeugnisse von Zeitgenossen,* Herausgegeben und mit einem Essay von Christa Wolf, (Darmstadt, Sammlung Luchterhand, 1981), p. 36.

a powerful meaning beyond the sexual: it meant 'true love', synonymous with a female identity not coerced into marketable marriage. Romantic love was here equivalent to a female ability to choose a man and lifestyle outside the socially prescribed gender roles. He, on the other hand, was able to compartmentalize.

Those around her, the intelligentsia of Weimar and German Romanticism, including Johann Wolfgang von Goethe, Friedrich von Savigny, the lawyer and civil servant, other prominent men, and experienced older women, expressed a genuine horror over Günderrode's unwillingness to accept an ordinary female fate. The Duchess Anna Amalia of Saxe-Weimar, benefactress to Goethe and Friedrich Schiller, dryly remarked on hearing of Günderrode's suicide: 'Idealism has often brought Charon [the god of the Underworld] this kind of tribute'.[35] Even more dryly, Friedrich von Savigny, her first love, to whom Günderrode had been devoted and who married another, commented: 'How sad it would be if all our mistakes were to have such tragic endings'.[36]

Günderrode's suicide can be read as a classic example of the failure of the erotic plot for women. Suicide is the ultimate negation of the ability to live life in fulfilling and sustainable terms. To have stylized romantic love as an ultimate end failed the woman who believed it to be an escape from conventional constriction. Its failure was lethal but alternatives were not available, such as fulfilment through a career. Only sexual denial or the marriages of convenience stood open. Women needed to use the erotic plot to carry them beyond the crippling alternative of continuing girlhood innocence. Susanne von Heyden, the romantic go-between, fell for the erotic plot in its unhealthy idealizing of the victim. In an onrush of grief at Günderrode's death, she turned Günderrode into a female icon, the same beatification that Goethe created with the tragic death of the betrayed infanticide, Gretchen. The lonely girl of 26 with serious literary talent and ambition, and no support for it, became a wronged angel. Von Heyden wrote to Günderrode's brother about her suicide: 'her knife pierced to the heart of this angel. She could not live without love, her whole identity dissolved in the tediousness of life ... only the most intimate love could have kept her alive; when this died her heart too had to stop beating.'[37]

Such hyperbole enhanced the role of romantic passion and made Günderrode a figure of heroic proportions, although she paid with her

---

[35] Hille, Karoline von Günderrode, p. 148.
[36] Ibid.
[37] Susanne von Heyden to Hektor von Günderrode [Karoline's brother], letter of 28 July 1806, in von Günderrode, Der Schatten eines Traumes, 1981, p. 255.

life. Friedrich Creuzer, on the other hand, as Christa Wolf very nicely points out, lived to be 87 – surviving Sophie, his capable housewife – and took another, younger model when he married a second time. Karoline was never mentioned by him again. Her letters to him were burnt, his were preserved, not out of piety but for legal reasons. They demonstrated that he did everything to avoid 'illegitimate' sexual relations. The letters contained his caveats on the relationship and were a testimony to his virtuous abstinence for most of the time, proving his willingness to put work before venality.[38]

How ironic, then, to read of a current television remake of *Anna Karenina*, who committed suicide because of her affair with the vain and superficial Vronsky. In the remake, sexuality and passion are presented as fulfilling for women – a simplification, surely, of the original. This makes light of Anna Karenina's suicide and its judgment on a passion gone wrong. Helen McCrory, who plays the character Anna Karenina, explained to *Guardian* readers why this nineteenth-century heroine still appeals to twenty-first-century women:

> When viewers first see Anna, they are aware of the elements of her existence – she is a society hostess, an obedient wife, a good mother – but they don't know who she is. Nor does anyone in the story because they don't bother to ask. But loneliness isn't dependent on the century: there are many women today who feel isolated. They don't feel they express themselves in the way they want to, they don't look the way they want to, they are not doing the job they should be doing. Anna is a woman who feels all those things and decides her passion to be loved is greater than her fear of being alone and afraid all her life ... For the first time in her life, Anna is pursued by a man who tells her that she is loveable, that she is beautiful, intelligent and sexual. Everyone understands that need to be loved.[39]

Women's fulfilment seems still to be equated with the erotic plot. These classic female heroines abound in grief and tragedy, and wrongly make mature friendship or marriage look second-best.[40] No matter that erotic heroines are unable to cope, unlike Creuzer who married to get the washing and shopping done. This fiction of a fulfilment through the erotic plot is implicated in child murder. One cannot, as the judicial process is indeed constrained to do, and as many historians find methodically correct, examine the crime on admissible factual evidence alone. Child murder must refer to the possible narratives of women's lives: their striving towards happiness

[38] Ibid., p. 47.
[39] Helen McCrory, 'All about Anna', *The Guardian*, G2, (9 May 2000).
[40] On the value of supportive marriages, unexplored in women's biographies, see Heilbrun, *Writing A Woman's Life*, p. 83 ff.

and security within the pitfalls of the gender plot, or their often doomed attempts to circumvent it.

The post-coital erotic plot involves guilt and failed womanhood. It shows how difficult it is to square the circle of women's gender expectations. The first woman to be executed in Arkansas for more than 150 years was tried for killing her two children in 1997.[41] 'Riggs, 28, waived her right to appeal and prevented her lawyer from applying for clemency, saying that she could not live with the guilt of the murders and wanted to be reunited with her children in heaven'.[42] Riggs' defence lawyer made the astute comment that: 'It started out as a suicide and ended as a suicide. She killed her children and tried to kill herself.'[43] Doctors testifying for her said 'she had been severely depressed as a result of sexual abuse as a child, a series of failed relationships with men, lack of money, and lack of self-esteem because of her obesity'.[44]

If the erotic plot were to impart a positive impulse, it would be by embracing the power of the outlaw. By accepting the power of illegitimacy (of the illicit), of women being sexually able and willing, the suicidal heroine and her unrequited passion would be dethroned. In life, as in fiction, suicide is indicative of destructive choices. In Carolyn Heilbrun's valuable book, *Writing a Woman's Life*, she discusses a feminist version of the erotic plot, namely the liberation possible in being a 'fallen' woman. Losing 'virtue' and 'reputation' enables a woman who has a solid grip on her passions to escape gendered expectations. The 'fallen woman' does not have to waste energy 'opposing the only narrative available ... the conventional marriage or erotic plot'.[45] Heilbrun cites Harriet Vane, Dorothy L. Sayer's fictional heroine. She stands convicted of murder, and is saved by Lord Peter Wimsey, a man convinced that women deserve equal terms, who then lends the crucial helping hand to free her. Heilbrun writes:

> Here is a woman who has, metaphorically speaking, killed and abandoned her lover when she outgrew him. So realistic, so 'unfeminine' is her scorn of him that she is tried for his literal murder in *Strong Poison*, a fate society might well mete out to a woman who treats a man as men have ever treated their woman lovers.[46]

Confessional women's writing did not emerge sufficiently strongly to enable the public rejection of motherhood and marriage until the 1970s. The 'suicide' poetry of Anne Sexton and Sylvia Plath opened a dark

---

[41]   See: 'Mother executed for killing her children', *The Guardian*, (4 May 2000).
[42]   Ibid.
[43]   Ibid.
[44]   Ibid.
[45]   Heilbrun, *Writing A Woman's Life*, p. 48.
[46]   Ibid., p. 57.

discourse which eventually made room for more diverse solutions and different endings. Divorce and 'failure' were addressed by Adrienne Rich, Denise Levertov and many other feminists such as Kate Millett, Gloria Steinem and Germaine Greer. The twentieth century has been described as 'the first in which women were seeking to find themselves rather than find a husband.'[47]

Infanticide, literature and the erotic plot

Infanticide is a theme that has never ceased to stir both the imagination and conscience. It was absorbed quickly into literary forms: the oral tradition embodied in the ballad, street theatre and the play, and the longish novels read at leisure by the middle classes. With such a rich presence in legal, social and symbolic reality, infanticide has much to convey. But a gendered dissonance in the portrayal of women makes for completely different readings.

In German literature of the late eighteenth century, as Beat Weber tells us,[48] the theme was the spiritual rebirth or transformation ('*innere Wandlung*') of the female sinner. She was changed for the better because she came to understand her sin and expressed regret over killing an innocent child. This genre of literature had moral lessons at its core. The more pathetic the heroine and the greater her redemption from sin, the better the lesson. Female conformity remained the objective. The 1770s and 1780s saw a plethora of plays and literary ballads on infanticide published. But in these writings child murder was by no means a rebellion against the failed erotic plot, but an act motivated by the fear of public humiliation and the loss of 'female honour' ('*Geschlechtsehre*'). This explanation was also a recurring theme in the case evidence.[49] The loss of honour and female redemption as motive and solution to a gendered fate amounted however to nothing more than a circular argument.

The trial and the moral high ground of literature only reinforced an existing code of behaviour laid down by authority. The punishments meted out by Church and state were designed to imprint exactly this message. Legal codification saw child murder as abhorrent precisely because it violated a mother's bond to her innocent child.[50] Female behaviour was enforced through specified punishments, particularly the criminal offence of concealing pregnancy. Female sexual honour and

---

[47] Richard Reeves, 'If you go down to the gender ghetto today', *The Guardian*, G2, (5 July 2000), p. 7.

[48] Weber, *Die Kindsmörderin*, p. 3.

[49] Ibid., p. 7.

[50] Ibid., p. 8.

identity was equal to sexual abstinence. There was to be no sexual appetite outside marriage – although in reality this was patently untrue. The plays and treatises on infanticide, conversely, played up the weakness and seduction of innocent girls. This may have struck at draconian criminal prosecutions, but did not empower women or bring about a clearer understanding of the social dynamics of scapegoating a frightened woman who did not want to be pregnant.

Literary redemption emphasized the acceptance of idealized motherhood. The rejection of motherhood itself was still outside the pale. The bond to the child was idealized as 'natural' and underwritten by the sentiments of educators; one can think of Jean Jacques Rousseau and his lessons on the female role in *Emile*, but also of the fashionable portraits of society ladies with idealized pretty children.[51] As the reverse of the 'natural', the rejection of children was unmistakably unfeminine.

The leading society writers of the time, such men as Johann Wolfgang von Goethe and Sir Walter Scott, portrayed infanticide with idealized fervour and a distinct disregard for the facts. Both men were trained in law and had experience of infanticide cases. Goethe was familiar with case records and was involved in a plea for the death penalty.[52] However, their heroines were the heady stuff of females fallen, but redeemed by remorse, whose errant men returned just too late (the child had been killed in an agony of grief) to construct a happy ending, at least in the sense of a fulsome moral lesson. The audience was speedily confronted with the consequences of sin. Weakness was the character trait most applauded in women because it showed infanticide as an aberration from the feminine, not as its angry or confused rejection. A girl had loved imprudently, had been swept off her feet by a lover, and despair led to child murder. This was the plot. The seducer now came back remorsefully in the last scene to show the error of men's sexual ways.

A male life is a life of considered choices 'called up because of a sense of ultimate arrival. Even the drunken Hemingway arrives in the narrative of his drunken life.'[53] How men's lives are portrayed, even in the event of mistakes and wrong doing, seems more positive, given an involvement with public affairs rather than 'private' life. Certainly the hero arrives back in the final act having been away to do other important things. The narrative in the famous infanticide dramatizations of the 1770s was still confined to male action, while the

---

51 The work of two painters of the period is representative:: Elizabeth Vigée Le Brun and Johann Friedrich August Tischbein. Both were society portrait painters. Even Meissen porcelain had figurines called 'the happy family'.

52 Habermas (ed.), *Das Frankfurter Gretchen*, p. 28.

53 Carolyn Heilbrun, *Women's Lives: The View from the Threshold* (Toronto, University of Toronto Press, 1999), p. 96.

stay-at-home single mother passively endured despair and familial recrimination. This discourse on female dependency was reinforced in Goethe's *Faust* and Sir Walter Scott's *The Heart of Midlothian*. These two powerful examples of the dramatization of infanticide extol female virtue and female action only within the confines of duty. Carnal knowledge or gendered rebellion is ignored or tainted with evil – as illicit sexuality – and the seduced meet an ultimate scary doom. Love has a male focus when heroines are idealized.

Ballads and street theatre – *Bänkelgesang*, where the storyteller performed in public places standing on a bench and intoned a story pointing to picture sequences – included many infanticide themes.[54] These were the oral folk narratives raided for conversion to high literature. We owe collections on 'folklore' to this 'borrowing'. Original folk ballads were used by Goethe and the Storm-and-stress movement. Ballads were collectors' items and were notoriously 'cleaned' of sexual and 'offensive' content, as were the fairy tales collected by the Brothers Grimm.

For example, a ballad called the *Three Riders* was cited in a work on Goethe because he used it as a source. The focus on its conversion to high literature lets the critic who traced it completely miss its horrific message of rape. J.M. Rameckers in his book on infanticide and the ballad describes this ballad's theme as seduction, somehow glossing over its tale of prostituting and raping an innkeeper's daughter. The ballad tells of three riders stopping at an inn. They negotiate with the woman innkeeper to buy her daughter for their pleasure. The mother goes upstairs to 'sleep' while the ballad records the cries of the daughter, its refrain the insistent: 'mother, mother I am now lost'. Her 'loss' is her rape! Her 'mother' has sold her for sexual gratification. It is chilling to read Rameckers's commentary – after he has missed the tragedy and protest of this ballad – on the literary attitude to child murder: 'They [*the writers of the Storm-and-stress movement*] felt a deep sympathy for these unlucky girls and often recorded their feelings.'[55] In the literary recasting of the *Three Riders* the warning on rape and lack of protection for women in public houses is lost. The cautionary power of the ballad is recast in sugary sentiment or middle-class distancing as 'folklore'.

The ballads in raw form sentimentalized very little. Like the tales of doom which were messages of warning told on the streets, their mission was to help the unwary by recording the worst. Deborah

---

[54] J. M. Rameckers, *Der Kindesmord in der Literatur der Sturm-und-Drang Periode. Ein Beitrag zur Kultur- und Literaturgeschichte des 18. Jhts.* (Rotterdam, 1927), pp. 146–7.

[55] Ibid., p. 149.

Symonds makes the point that women were proud to sing ballads like 'Mary Hamilton' in Scotland.[56] This ballad is a bold statement, in that a woman who has killed her child fully acknowledges her act. She accepts responsibility and is proud to walk to the scaffold. 'Mary Hamilton' makes no claims on innocence. Ballads had a proven female provenance in Scotland and they 'tell of murder, pregnancy, jealousy and infanticide'.[57] They also confirm that courtship was seen as a 'deadly and serious business'.[58] Ballads signalled the dangers for single women who were in employment as servants or in the rural economy. The newly productive agricultural reforms in Scotland toward the end of the century made courtship even more precarious, as Symonds points out, producing a dangerous instability in marginal and subsistence agricultural communities.[59] This impacted on social patterns that often allowed pregnancy before marriage, but presupposed employment and stability.

Symonds shows effectively that the economics of change undermined the place of women and that this may have made the risks of courtship that much more dangerous for women who were caught out. She sharply compares the different agendas in the infanticide trial of Isobel Walker in 1738 and its fictional use in Sir Walter Scott's novel. The criminal trial was an affair of the village. It was neither gentle nor compassionate. After the body of the baby was found, the suspect, Isobel Walker, was soon flushed out. She was 'judged by her neighbours in the light of local rumours of courtship and illicit sexuality'.[60] Isobel Walker denied infanticide in the first instance, as she had denied her pregnancy, despite 'several months of rumour and chiding'.[61] As the village women surrounded her they physically assaulted her and said they would justify her claims of not having given birth by inspecting her. They squeezed her breasts and found milk. At this point Isobel confessed a birth, but still claimed the dead baby was not hers.[62]

In this awful scenario of accusation and denial several characteristics of these types of cases emerge. The village judgment includes women who try to go easy on the suspect and understand that the judicial process is stacked against the accused. They try to mitigate its inevitable harshness. Other women seek the downfall of the accused, most

---

[56] Deborah Symonds, *Weep Not for Me: Women, Ballads and Infanticide in Scotland* (Pennsylvania, Pennsylvania State University Press, 1997).

[57] Ibid., p. 9

[58] Ibid.

[59] Ibid.

[60] Ibid., p. 184.

[61] Ibid.

[62] Ibid., pp. 184–6.

probably because of village jealousies and kinship rivalries. There is little moral eulogizing in the records. The documents are full of evidence, adding the sickening details of murder and usually ignoring motivation or circumstance as mitigating factors. Most of the women accused were respectable. It was ordinary women who were thus sucked into the slow and tortuous grip of the trial.

The outstanding characteristic of many of these cases is the denial of pregnancy. Even giving birth is denied. Isobel Walker asserted against all probability that the dead baby was not her baby. What the village gossip had traded for months was denied by the woman whose body must have given her warning signs. But there is room to suppose the signs of pregnancy were not well understood. A further important characteristic in child murder is the remoteness of the father. The father of Isobel's child was named by her. He claimed that he had 'heard about the child' but not from Isobel. He maintained she denied being with child.[63] Isobel was convicted, but was later pardoned. Talk had it that her half-sister Helen obtained the pardon. This aspect of the story was picked up by Walter Scott and it became the focus of his novel *The Heart Of Midlothian*, published in 1818.

Scott's novel is entirely different from the questions raised by the case of Isobel Walker, most prominent among them her denial of her pregnancy and her ultimate exclusion from the village. Walker appears typical of the denial of pregnancy as a last defiant act by a woman deserted because she could not fulfil the marriage plot. Scott's novel skates over this dark centre of self-destruction. His story even denies that infanticide took place. Effie Dean, the unmarried mother, never kills her child. This is indicative of Effie never acting decisively, although Scott embroils her in all 'the creeping rot of illicit sexuality'.[64] Scott punishes illicit sex by sentencing to various evil ends those characters prone to venality. Effie ends badly in a convent, even though she weds her lover. Her *alter ego*, and the heroine, is her competent older half-sister Jeanie Deans, the sister who saves her. Symonds describes this Jeanie as 'so very, very good'.[65] Jeanie is 'a model woman, and arguably a model of bourgeois womanhood'.[66] By choosing a woman character as the heart of his novel Scott turns his hand to the bonding of domestic virtue with womanhood. As Symonds disparagingly remarks: 'In the course of her journey [*to London, to effect Effie's pardon*] Jeanie becomes a model of good sense and

---

[63] Ibid., p. 190.
[64] Ibid., p. 194.
[65] Ibid., p. 193.
[66] Ibid.

honesty to hundreds of gawking Englishmen ... she also persuades the Duke of Argyll that she is virtue incarnate'.[67] Not only does Scott's novel put Jeanie on an unassailable pedestal of virtue, but in doing so it hides the real female despair that drove child murder. It was the failure of the marriage plot, amongst the insecurities of unemployment and subsistence economies or migrant labour, that made a pregnant woman despair. Scott's Effie was not faced with the 'hardship, necessity and poor judgement' that drove to infanticide, but is cast in the mould of the bourgeois romance, where the concealment of crime is 'the result of rash behaviour and great passion'.[68]

Romance plays to a male imagination. Its unreal presence destroys an understanding of the ignorance and fear faced by a woman isolated in an unwanted pregnancy. The fear raised by insisting on the 'virtuous' women undermined every woman's right to sexuality, as well as the ability to come to terms with illegitimacy. The great bugbears of 'innocence' and 'romantic passion' and 'virtue', all nicely lined up, were magnified by the lessons of fiction. The message of the infanticide cases was the opposite: had these 'ugly sisters' not appeared, the woman might have coped.

The evidence for a safe journey through the difficulties of being an unmarried mother is borne out by the statistical facts on high rates of illegitimate births. In Scotland these were not unusual. As Deborah Symonds remarks, 'most failed courtships and casual sexual encounters simply resulted in illegitimate births, which plagued various Scots communities with startling regularity throughout the seventeenth, eighteenth and nineteenth centuries'.[69] In Germany, illegitimacy was also tolerated, although most works on infanticide do not seem to treat these figures. Habermas explains that as long as a father acknowledged the child as legitimate, it didn't matter when it was conceived. In rural communities illegitimacy was seen as less of a problem than in middle-class circles.[70] Other strategies were also available, such as abandoning children to foundling hospitals.[71]

Like Walter Scott, Goethe based his literary treatment of infanticide

---

[67] Ibid., p. 194.

[68] Ibid., p. 199.

[69] Ibid., p. 2. Symonds cites the statistics for Stirlingshire: 15 women were investigated for infanticide between 1637 and 1820 while 1,955 women gave birth to illegitimate children between 1637 and 1747. Five per cent of all births were illegitimate in Scotland in this period.

[70] Habermas (ed.), *Das Frankfurter Gretchen*, pp. 12–13. See also Schmidt, *Genossin der Hexe*, p. 26 ff.

[71] On child welfare in Germany, see Markus Meumann, *Findelkinder, Waisenhäuser, Kindsmord* (Munich, Oldenbourg Verlag, 1995).

on an actual case. Susanna Margaretha Brandt killed her illegitimate child on 1 August 1771 in Frankfurt-am-Main.[72] She was beheaded on 14 January 1772 when she was 23 years of age. No one can know the inner despair of Susanna Brandt. But it surfaced in a stubborn death-defying refusal to admit her pregnancy to others. Like Isobel Walker, she suffered the indignity of bodily inspection. Her married sisters Maria Ursula and Maria Dorothea wanted to be sure she was telling the truth. Neither they, nor a doctor called in to 'touch' her, could say so conclusively, although she must have been six months pregnant by this time.[73] She gave birth in the inn *Zum Einhorn* (At the sign of the Unicorn) on the day she was dismissed from employment there as a servant. She fled to Mainz, but returned the next day, arrested at the city gates of Frankfurt because a wanted poster sought her arrest. She was 'dressed in a checked Berlin flannel skirt and a red-brown cotton jacket, with a white apron, tall and slim in stature'.[74]

Her pregnancy was most certainly unanticipated; possibly she was raped while drunk. The father was Dutch, either an apprentice to a jeweller or a merchant, who had left for St Petersburg before Christmas.[75] In her confession she recalls she was given wine, then 'pulled onto a bed and there was molested sexually'.[76] Her sexual plight is immaterial to her indictment for infanticide; sexual coercion was at most seen as incidental to the murder charge. She discovered she was pregnant – if indeed she admitted this to herself – just as she realized the father would never return. She could never make good her lost sense of self. Her pregnancy was perceived as alien. It was no part of her: she denied it all together, most of all to herself. About Eastertime, she had the sensation 'as if a stone was rolling from side to side' in her stomach.[77] The child was obviously unreal to her, and the first time she spoke about her pregnancy was in her cross-examination. No emotional connection seems to have existed between the person Susanna, the tall, slim woman, and the alien fate of her pregnancy and the murder of the child.

Habermas does not explore this inner alienation, but she does highlight how the juridical proceedings were both alien and incomprehensible to an uneducated woman. Susanna was caught in a legal mechanism where she often said the wrong things because what was important to her was not important to the trial.[78] While she was still

---

[72] Habermas (ed.), *Das Frankfurter Gretchen*, p. 15.
[73] Ibid., p. 33.
[74] Ibid., p. 16.
[75] Ibid., p. 13.
[76] Ibid., p. 32.
[77] Ibid., p. 33.
[78] Ibid., pp. 32–6.

trying to comprehend what had happened, the lawyers and judges gathered evidence. The statements they recorded were seen as conclusive and the outcome was unavoidable. The defence was only allowed to speak with the accused very late in the proceedings.[79] None of the male judges actually met the accused until near the end of the case. After her conviction they only met to fulfil ritualistic formulae, such as participating in her last supper.

Goethe wrote his *Urfaust* – the first version of the play *Faust* – in 1774, three years after Susanna Brandt's beheading. The centrepiece of the drama is the so-called *Gretchentragödie* (the tragedy of Gretchen). The devil Mephistopheles arranges the trysts between Faust and Gretchen with whom Faust has fallen in love. The inevitable happens and Gretchen kills the child of this union. The most famous scene is the one in which Faust returns to free Gretchen from the dungeon where she awaits death. Mephisto is the lord of darkness and his carriage and horses must fly before the light of day. It is his magic that will ensure her escape. Gretchen is nearly mad, recalling the deaths directly and indirectly caused by Faust's courtship and illicit seduction: those of her mother, her brother and her child. As Faust tries to pull her from the prison she tells him his hand is sticky with the blood of their child. She imagines the sharp blade that will be put to her neck and the bloodlust of the crowds. And at the last moment, although he invokes the sensual joy of their love and wants her to fly with him, she pulls back. She rejects him, saying she shudders to be near him. With this she accepts her criminal sentence. In the final versions of *Faust* written in the 1790s, Goethe adds the words 'she is saved' just as another voice utters the verdict 'she is condemned' (in German this is a play on words: '*gerettet*' and '*gerichtet*'). This scene of the play usually shows Gretchen illuminated by a heavenly radiance, as do later book illustrations.

Goethe's *Faust* is a play about the redemption of *man* from temptation. The 'fallen woman' is an episode in a protracted process of the male quest: Faust's bargain with the devil centres on whether Faust will find satisfaction in the varied and rich episodes he experiences in his lengthy life. Gretchen is only a waystation in his pilgrimage from sensual delights to spiritual transcendence. The fallen woman redeemed by her willingness to die as she renounces him is as far away from the confusion and bewilderment of women accused of infanticide as is the juridical process into which their young lives were bled. The men who made them pregnant hardly bothered about them in the real world. In the recorded cases men stay well clear of the trial proceedings except for witness statements. The men themselves were never put on trial.

---

[79] Ibid., pp. 25–6.

The story of Anna Maria Ohnmais, the daughter of a respected town official (*Schultheisz*) in Uhlbach in southern Germany contradicts the beatification of Gretchen in Goethe's *Faust*. Where Gretchen is redeemed and raised to an icon of 'the eternally feminine' ('*des ewig-weibliche*'), Anna Maria is lost, an abused daughter frightened and lonely at what may be happening to her. She choked her child to death on 31 October 1784. The father was a married uncle staying in the same house. Thea Koss wrote *Kindesmord im Dorf* ('Child Murder in the Village')[80] because she wanted to reconstruct Anna Maria's motives. Anna Maria was the daughter of wealthy parents with prospects of marriage and security. But her pregnancy was soon gossiped about and her body, as Koss writes 'became the centre of village interest'. 'Whispers, speculation and close observation' followed her everywhere.[81] Everybody in the village knew she no longer menstruated.[82] The minister asked her directly whether she was pregnant. She denied this to him, her father and her sister.

Reading back from the evidence taken for the trial, circumstances emerge that go some way to explaining Anna Maria's situation. Two years before her pregnancy her mother had died. Anna Maria loved her father and yet feared him. This love of her father and the fear of disgracing him 'didn't diminish her feelings of guilt and hopelessness; rather they increased her fear'.[83] Koss sees this fear of her father, even though he does not disown or disinherit his daughter, as the probable motive for killing the child: 'His threat that his daughter may no longer call him father was her reason for committing the crime, as she stated in her confession.'[84]

The man who impregnated her claimed he was drunk. She said she slept with him only once; he stated it was more often, obviously in an attempt to discredit her. He was not called to account, nor was he fined for *Unzucht* (illicit sex). Anna Maria remained silent on the subject of this liaison with a married uncle, probably out of fear, familial shame and defencelessness. The onus was on her for losing her virtue. The unwillingness to admit her pregnancy triggered the murder as it had done in the cases of Isobel Walker and Susanna Brandt. The motive for child murder that Koss suggests is riveting, as it disclaims the influence of passion and romance. For her the immediate family and its place in the village is ultimately the reason Ohnmais murdered her child. Anna

---

[80] Thea Koss, *Kindesmord im Dorf, Ein Kriminalfall des 18.Jahrhunderts und seine gesellschaftlichen Hintergründe* (Tübingen, Silberburg Verlag, 1994).
[81] Ibid., pp. 14–15.
[82] Ibid., p. 17.
[83] Ibid., p. 29.
[84] Ibid., p. 28.

Maria's silence was a defence not against being accused of illicit love, but against all her family ties collapsing. Familial and gender expectations were the immediate pressures that broke Anna Maria.

In Virginia Woolf's influential essay, *Three Guineas,* she reminds us that women's activities were still severely restricted by equating the feminine with modesty at the end of the nineteenth century. Woolf describes these limitations by the example of Gertrude Bell in 1892. She 'went with Lizzy, her maid, to picture exhibitions; she was fetched by Lizzie from dinner parties; she went with Lizzie to ... Whitechapel.' Chastity was invoked to prevent her from studying medicine, from painting from the nude as required for art schools, from reading Shakespeare, from playing in orchestras, or from walking down Bond Street alone. Gertrude Bell 'had reached the age of 27 and married without ever having walked alone down Picadilly.'[85] 'Lizzie' is hardly commented on, but chastity imposed itself as the straight and narrow path for her too.

Whatever their social class, women met the same dilemmas. Jane Austen touches on them in *Sense and Sensibility* (first draft 1797; published 1811) seven years before Scott's novel and while Goethe was revising *Faust.* Straitened circumstances made marrying off daughters a precarious undertaking. Marianne and Elinor, the sisters Dashwood, embody two sides of the Janus face of female choice. Marianne, like Effie Dean, defies advice and follows inclination: she insists sentiment and passion are guides to female well-being and chooses the flamboyant, articulate and good-looking Willoughby. His womanizing – known by Colonel Brandon, his rival, but not revealed to the sisters – has already compromised Brandon's ward. What passion without prudence can lead to is amply shown, and ruefully retracted. Marianne nearly dies of influenza caught while foolishly paying tribute to romantic memories. She wants to catch sight of Willoughby and is engulfed in a powerful storm. The real and the symbolic convey Austen's judgment on the romantic illusion. Willoughby denies his courtship of Marianne, and Marianne must see to her own fate. Austen's corrective is to grant Marianne a suitably sensible alternative: she merely has to endure, or learn to love, an older husband of means (Colonel Brandon). But it could have been so much worse.

Elinor adheres to the conventions and steers a course of deprivation hard on the edge of spinsterhood. She must learn the humiliation of knowing that the man she loves, Edward Ferrars, is unsuitably engaged and honours his very silly fiancée's indiscretions by remaining silent.

---

[85] Virginia Woolf, *Three Guineas* (London, 1937), pp. 165–8, as quoted in Russ, *How to Suppress Women's Writing,* pp. 25–6.

This code of honour is rigorous, and not – to my mind – part of Austen's admired irony. Male honour does credit to Edward's character, retiring and reticent as it may be, in that he does not lightly break his word. Austen must here have uttered the silent prayer of all unmarried women. So many of the infanticide cases document a broken promise of marriage or being abandoned outright.

What the recent film version of *Sense and Sensibility* brings out especially strongly is the close relationship between Elinor and Marianne. They come to understand – and exchange – the closeness of their disparate views and actions. Elinor recognizes Marianne's need for truth and poetry; Marianne comes to understand prudence. When Marianne is severely ill and near death and nothing seems resolved for the sisters, Elinor pleads with her not to die, for she knows that prudence and goodness cannot live without passion and feelings. Elinor comes to value the natural richness of feeling she had learned to suppress.

Medical testimony and the determination of guilt

In a newspaper report on an infanticide case from *The Guardian*, the girl was described as slovenly and drunk.[86] She was a single mother. The prosecution lawyer insisted that the jury 'put emotion aside'. Obviously the woman could not cope, found the female trajectory to be impossible. The law judges not on compassion, but on fact. The crime, on one level of analysis, ultimately evolves from the murderous capacity of the social fabric to punish rather than redeem.

The punishment is that of deterrence, relying on an amplification of the actual criminal prosecution, as the judicial machine 'puts emotion aside'. The prominent eighteenth-century juris-consultant Christian Thomasius says somewhere that the witch in witchcraft trials is the judiciary. He threw this bolt of emancipatory lightning at the law because he wanted to blitz its inquisitional procedures. The backbone of the witchcraft trial was the confession. The same applied to all infanticide cases, as did the means to this confession, torture. Thomasius's reasoning exposed how the judge was also the jury, a judicial contravention: through the pressure to confess, the confession was assured and the 'witch' was produced. Witchcraft trials needed what they could not, on evidence, have: proof of a pact with the devil. Therefore the exacted confession, rather than evidence, produced the 'truth' of sexual and malicious depravity.[87]

---

[86] *The Guardian*, (21 April 2000).
[87] Christian Thomasius, *Vom Laster der Zauberei. Über die Hexenprozesse* (Munich, Deutscher Taschenbuch Verlag, 1986), pp. 108–217.

The comparison of infanticide to witchcraft trials lies in the judicial procedure. Both show the same *Inquisitionsprozess* at work. Criminal proceedings were initiated through accusation or the finding of a corpse, and conviction relied on inquisitional protocols, medical expert-witness testimony, and the use of torture for confessions. Judicial certainty was achieved by an exhaustive process in which the full weight of officialdom descended on the accused, usually an unmarried domestic servant in her twenties experiencing a first birth. The loopholes possible in this process – post-partum melancholia, still-birth – or inadvertent death – were largely blocked by the very means that exonerated women from witchcraft prosecutions, namely factual expert testimony. The protocols of medical evidence in the *consilia* (model excerpts of trial records for medical practitioners and jurists) are among the most voluminous in this type of publication.[88] If the few voices raised in Germany against witchcraft trials between 1630 and 1700 were medical and questioned, for one thing, the evidence, and for another, the destruction of the beauty of the created body through torture, this could have applied even more to infanticide cases. As the ascendancy of medicine as a science capable of establishing material proof asserted itself unequivocally in the eighteenth century, its expert-witness testimony in large measure helped convict infanticides.[89]

In a case against the domestic servant of 'Goldsmith B' on 26 February 1743 in the jurisdiction of the city of Magdeburg, it emerged that the infant was born in secret at 6 p.m. and hidden in a manure heap.[90] The accused, Johanna Dorothea Bossen, twenty-three years old, states 'how on Monday, February 25 in the evening at approximately 7 p.m. she bore a child while standing in the courtyard, not far from the privy, the baby shooting out from her quite suddenly onto the paving stones.'[91] Her statement adds that she then shoved the child into the manure pile and hit it twice with a manure fork. The infant was retrieved, bathed by a midwife, the umbilical cord was bound; they tried to warm the child, but it was already weak. The medical report notes a laceration on the head.

---

[88] Michael Alberti, *Systema Jurisprudentiae Medicae* (Halle, Schneeberg, Fulda, Leipzig, 6 vols, 1725–47). See also J. Geyer-Kordesch 'Medizinische Fallbeschreibungen und ihre Bedeutung in der Wissensreform des 17. und 18. Jhts', *Medizin, Gesellschaft und Geschichte*, Heft 9 (1991), 7–19.

[89] On the medical examination of the dead bodies of children and its difficulties, see: Mark Jackson: 'Developing medical expertise: medical practitioners and the suspected murders of new-born children', in Roy Porter (ed.), *Medicine in the Enlightenment* (Amsterdam, Rodopi, 1995), pp. 146–55.

[90] Michael Alberti, *Systema Jurisprudentiae Medicae Tomo Sexto* (Leipzig and Goerlitz, Marchen Bibliopolam, 1747), Casus II, pp. 7–14. The details of the case given below are taken from this case documentation.

[91] Ibid., p. 13.

The infant died the following night. The autopsy report of 26 February 1743 was written by the town physician, Johann Dehne and the surgeon Johann Tobias Wolff. It reveals that the child was male, *partus perfectus et maturus* (perfect and mature at birth), the umbilical cord was tied properly, and two concussions without penetration of skin or bone were in evidence. However a fracture of the skull had also occurred (this is presented in great anatomical detail), and there was little blood in the rest of the body. The cause of death was either loss of blood or a head injury. The latter is the point of doubt which resulted in a request for the *consilium* (an expert witness statement).

Michael Alberti, the medical expert witness, excerpts other relevant points from the interrogation documents: firstly, that the accused knew she was pregnant (the criminal offence of concealing a pregnancy); secondly, that she left the child in the manure (neglect); and, thirdly, that she admitted she wished to kill the child (malicious intent). The *responsum Facultatis Medicae Halensis* follows in full. Its conclusions are the following: if the accused told the truth, then the concussion resulted from the infant's fall to the courtyard paving. The use of violence (the manure fork), however, contributed to the death, as did the 'squalor of the manure and the cold and rough weather, while the baby was suffering loss of blood through the untied umbilical cord'.[92] It is noted that the accused admitted to wishing to kill the child. The verdict of the *consilium*, signed 8 April 1743, was that death had resulted from these multiple causes. The accused was beheaded.

In this case and all other infanticide cases the doctors had to decide three points:

1. whether a live birth had taken place
2. whether the infant was mature at birth
3. whether there was evidence for wilful murder, such as concealment of pregnancy, unattended birth, neglect of the child or intent to kill.

The Alberti cases in his *consilium* compilations show that the medical evidence usually coincided with the legal specifications and worked toward convicting the suspect. No one can deny high moral purpose in the trial testimony of Michael Alberti. He tried his best to distinguish supportable medical evidence from amorphous or ambivalent conclusions. But straightforward and conclusive medical evidence also bolstered his overt aim, to make a case for the validity of medical knowledge. He made no concessions to social causes or the plight of single mothers.

---

[92] Ibid.

Neither the law nor medicine went beyond its narrow brief. The efficacy of the lung-test was discussed in the medical literature, but not even its newly admitted uncertainty was used as a rule to gain acquitals. Infanticide prosecutions were not made more lenient through medical evidence, but rather through a public debate on the stage, in journals, in ballads and other literature from 1770 onwards. A man with a more lenient heart and less moral rigour, Johann Heinrich Pestalozzi, a Swiss reformer at the end of the eighteenth century, aired publicly the problem of a 'victim' crime, the pitfalls evident in impossible marriage terms and the abandonment of women to criminal prosecution for an event whose determining circumstances lay elsewhere.[93]

In terms of the Enlightenment it seems an important point to make that medico-judicial reform banished the pact with the devil as phantasmagorical, while at the same time its emphasis on factual proof was used to convict in infanticide cases. From the documentation in the case collections it seems that men were not brought to account even though fornication and adultery were criminal offences and had obviously taken place. Pestalozzi gives a clue as to why this was so in his 1783 publication *On the Law and Infanticide. Truths and Dreams, Research and Images.* He castigates clever legal manoeuvres which could invalidate marital promises, even though the woman was under the illusion of security and, as was the custom between those betrothed, slept with the man.[94] The impression the Alberti cases give is that men will do much to push the blame on women when faced with legal prosecution.[95] One of them, implicated as an accessory in infanticide, even stated the child was alive when he exposed him on an icy riverbank, destroying the argument of a still-birth put forward by his lover.[96]

Escape from the erotic plot

Codes of moral behaviour crammed women's lives into the depressing alternatives of married propriety or misbehaviour. Propriety meant marriage and marriage meant that a father no longer had to pay the upkeep of his daughter. The plight of married women is robustly put by

---

[93] Johann Heinrich Pestalozzi, *Über Gesetzgebung und Kindermord. Wahrheiten und Träume, Nachforschungen und Bilder* (Frankfurt am Main and Leipzig, 1783).

[94] Ibid., pp. 13–21.

[95] Alberti, *Systema Jurisprudentiae Medicae Tomo Sexto*, Casus III: 'Infanticidum suspectum per vim capiti inflictam, commissum', pp. 14–39.

[96] Ibid., and other cases in Alberti, *Systema Jurisprudentiae Medicae Tomo Sexto*, which I combed for infanticide cases.

Joanna Russ as she explains their middle-class status being solely dependent on male economic provision: 'It's commonly supposed that poverty and lack of leisure did not hamper middle-class persons during the last century, but indeed they did—when these persons were middle-class women. It might be more accurate to call these women attached to middle-class men, for by their own economic exertions few middle-class women could keep themselves in the middle class; if actresses or singers, they became improper persons.'[97]

Marriage was by no means an affair of the heart: it was an act of prudence, negotiated and enforced by parental vigilance. One of the first women novelists in Germany, Sophie von La Roche, was forced to abandon her love match with her Italian tutor. Her father made her burn all letters and mementoes. She was made to marry the respectable civil servant and courtier von La Roche. She and her husband maintained the polite and distant marriage conventional for their day.

The sister of Johann Wolfgang von Goethe, Cornelia, was married off to a successful civil servant at one of the minor German courts. A semi-fictional biography speculates about her wasted life, as it is a particularly poignant story of a well-educated, interested, spontaneous, witty and talented woman, who had to follow her stodgy and respectable husband, and arrange his household and entertain. She died in 1777 aged 26, in childbirth. Sigrid Damm writes:

> Always determined in her fate by others, by her father, her brother Wolfgang, her husband Johann Georg Schlosser ... she broke apart in the conflict between her own wishful projections for her life and the conventions forced on her.[98]

Maximiliane von La Roche, the daughter of Sophie von La Roche, the novelist, was another young woman doomed to waste her talents. She was very well educated privately, and so intelligent and lively that Goethe was one of her keen admirers. At seventeen she was married off to a successful expatriate Italian merchant, much older, Peter von Brentano, who already had five children from a previous marriage. She had to manage his large household and help with his business. Maximiliane, like Cornelia, died an early death, her unused talents inherited by her two famous children, Bettina and Clemens von Brentano, who became established authors of several books still in print.

One successful strategy to escape the marriage plot was to remain a spinster. Susanna Katherina von Klettenberg, daughter of a patrician Frankfurt family and the model for Goethe's 'beautiful soul' in his

---

[97] Russ, *How to Suppress Women's Writing*, p. 7.
[98] Sigrid Damm, *Cornelia Goethe*, (Insel Taschenbuch, Frankfurt-am-Main, 1992).

CHAPTER SEVEN

Infanticide, slavery and the politics of reproduction at Cape Colony, South Africa, in the 1820s

Patricia van der Spuy

Although childbirth is a significant personal experience for women, it is also a social event bound up with the maintenance and reproduction of social order.[1]

In the summer heat of November 1821, the decomposing corpse of a new-born *wit kind* (white child) was discovered in the rural town of Graaff-Reinet, near the eastern frontier of the British Cape Colony. The discovery of the body in this Calvinist, Dutch-speaking, slave-holding community of fewer than two hundred households set in motion an investigation which resulted in the arrest and indictment of three women.[2] Anna Sauer, sixteen years old, unmarried daughter of Johan Nicolaas Sauer, was arrested along with Rosalyn van de Kaap, aged about thirty, one of Sauer's three slaves, and a Khoekhoe *waschmeid*, Philida, about fifty years of age.[3] The first two were charged with the

---

[1] J. Murphy-Lawless, 'The obstetric view of feminine identity: a nineteenth century case history of the use of forceps on unmarried women in Ireland', in Alexandra Dundas Todd and Sue Fisher (eds), *Gender and Discourse: The Power of Talk* (New Jersey, Norwood, 1988), p. 177.

[2] Official documentation and numerous private records pertaining to the Cape Colony from the beginning of colonization are lodged in the state archives in Cape Town, referred to as the Cape Archives. All primary sources for this chapter are to be found there. The main sources for Anna Sauer are: CO (Colonial Office) 2633, no. 110: letter from *Landdrost* A. Stockenstrom to Colonial Secretary C. Bird, 20 November 1821; GH (Government House) 49/22, criminal and civil pleadings, 1822 April–July, p. 32 ff; ZP 1/1/28, microfilm of CO 48/60: letter from Lord Charles Somerset to Earl Bathurst, 28 April 1823; CJ (Court of Justice) 816, no. 17: criminal sentences; 1/GR (archives of Graaff-Reinet) 3/27: judicial declarations, 1821–22.

[3] Registration of birth became mandatory only from 1894. These ages are those given by the women themselves: Cape Archives (CA): 1/GR 3/27, no pagination. People indigenous to the Cape were known to the settlers as 'Hottentots' (herders) or 'Bushmen' (hunter-gatherers). Philida was labelled 'hottentot'. Today the term used for 'Bushmen' is 'San', and for 'Hottentot', 'Khoekhoe'. These categories describe life-style (Khoekhoe people are primarily herders), not national groups. Among Khoekhoe today are the Xun, Khomani and Khwe peoples. See *The South African San Institute Annual Review, April 2000–March 2001* (Cape Town, South African San Institute, 2001).

provision or taking of abortifacients, and with *kindermoord* (child-murder, a term which included the murder of infants).[4] Philida was charged with complicity – as Rosalyn's *man*, Letjou, would have been, had he not died in the interim.[5]

This case was unique, because it involved both a settler woman facing a charge of infanticide and evidence of a co-operative network of women from a cross-section of Cape society. The District Secretary, Theodorus Muller, was present at the interrogation of some witnesses and suspects, including that of Anna herself. Ironically, in January 1822, in the midst of this investigation, Muller was publicly accused of having forced his stepdaughter (unnamed in the report) to submit to an abortion, twelve years earlier.[6] The informer was his now son-in-law, Christoffel Rothman, who included this allegation in a list of complaints against Muller, including the physical abuse of slaves. It can hardly be coincidental that the younger man chose this moment to bring to light actions normally deeply hidden within patriarchal families. Not only had the Sauer case brought to the forefront issues of reproduction in this town, but the wider socio-political context permitted an engagement with patriarchal politics.

The patriarchy of Cape Colony

In the 1820s, Cape society was struggling to adapt from a relatively self-regulating patriarchy under the Dutch East India Company (VOC), to a paternalist British colony confronted with the imminent demise of slavery. Formerly private issues of patriarchal control were being forced into the public domain. Since the British take-over of the Cape Colony in 1806, the government had become gradually but increasingly interventionist. The year 1828 was to see an overhaul of the administration and the abolition of Khoekhoe indenture; 1834 witnessed the ending of slavery, preceded by various ameliorative laws.[7] Certainly, under the government of the VOC in the eighteenth century, the authorities had intervened if settlers'

---

[4] CA: 1/GR 3/27, no pagination: '*Verbaal gehouden ... contra 1. Anna Dogter van den Burger Johan Nicolaas Sauer ... te zaake van hey gebruiken van middelen ter afdrijving van den vrucht waarmede zy beswangerd was en ter zaake van kindermoord.*' Despite the problems with using the term 'infanticide', which was not a specific crime at the Cape, I use it in this chapter to refer to the killing of neonates.

[5] Ibid.

[6] CA: CO 2641, letters received from Graaff-Reinet, 31 January 1822, Stockenstrom to Bird, no pagination.

[7] Although slavery was officially abolished in 1834, slaves had to endure a further four years of 'apprenticeship' before they were actually freed on 1 December 1838.

treatment of workers was perceived to be unacceptably abusive. The relationship between slaveholder and slave had been regulated by law and the operation of a moral economy.[8] Slaves could complain against their masters, and many did so, with varying degrees of success.[9] On the other hand, bar murder, relations between husbands and wives, or parents and children, were beyond the concern of the VOC. They have also tended to be treated by historians as unproblematic.[10]

Under British colonial government, slavery came under closer scrutiny by the authorities. Official slave registers were instituted with the establishment of a Slave Office in 1816. In 1823, before the Sauer case was complete, the governor introduced his own set of amelioratory regulations, which included permission for slaves to marry (under very limited conditions).[11] Amelioration and emancipation were confused in the minds of both slave and settler.[12] Slaveholding patriarchs were losing authority over their 'families': the apparent loss of control over slaves threatened to undermine patriarchal authority more broadly. As patriarchs were being forced to cede authority over slaves to a foreign, paternalistic state, so slaves, young men and settlers' daughters challenged the rights of slaveholders and fathers.[13]

---

[8] W. Dooling, *Law and Community in a Slave Society: Stellenbosch District, South Africa, c.1760–1820* (Communications no. 23/1992, Centre for African Studies, University of Cape Town, 1992); R. Ross, *Beyond the Pale: Essays on the History of Colonial South Africa* (Johannesburg, Witwatersrand University Press, 1993), pp. 155–65.

[9] Ross, *Beyond the Pale*, pp. 156–7.

[10] Ross, *Beyond the Pale*, takes a demographic approach to the 'white' population. Historians of the eighteenth- and nineteenth-century Cape have tended to be more interested in 'inter-group' relations than in examining settler familial dynamics. See, for example, R. Elphick and H. Giliomee (eds), *The Shaping of South African Society, 1652–1840* (Cape Town, Maskew Miller Longman, 1989) and R.C.-H. Shell, *Children of Bondage: A Social History of the Slave Society at the Cape of Good Hope, 1652–1838* (Johannesburg, Witwatersrand University Press, 1994). However, there are signs that younger scholars are turning to examine gender relations within settler families (British, not Dutch), in the face of criticism of elitism. See, for example, N. Erlank, 'Letters Home: the Experience and Perceptions of Middle Class British Women at the Cape 1820–1850', (MA diss., University of Cape Town, 1995); K. McKenzie, 'Replacing Wollstonecraft's models: gender, honour and colonial political rights in middle-class Cape Town, c.1800–1850', (paper presented to the IFRWH Conference, University of Melbourne, 1998).

[11] P. van der Spuy, 'Slave women and the family in nineteenth-century Cape Town', *South African Historical Journal*, 27 (1992), 50–74.

[12] P. van der Spuy, '"Making himself master": Galant's rebellion revisited', *South African Historical Journal*, 34 (1996), 1–28.

[13] Two large-scale worker rebellions – the only two on record – took place in this period. For an examination of the gendered dynamics of subaltern resistance to patriarchy, see van der Spuy, '"Making himself Master"'.

Attempted abortion and the killing of infants were covered by a criminal ordinance, under which Anna, Rosalyn and Philida were tried, but which Theodorus Muller did not have to face.[14] The law did not distinguish between child murder and other forms of murder, and death was the only possible penalty. It was only in 1845 that new legislation allowed mothers of dead babies to be convicted of concealment of birth instead of child-murder, and so to avoid the death penalty. From 1845, sentences became relatively lenient, with women judged guilty of concealment of birth receiving sentences of a year or two.[15] Cape government officials of the *ancien regime* were proud of a local foundling tradition, and chose to imagine that infanticide was exceedingly rare. It was believed that unwanted babies were abandoned rather than killed, to be taken in and cared for by God-fearing families. It was only after the Dutch lost control of the Cape to the British that the first orphanage was established, by the Dutch Reformed Church, in 1811.

In 1817, a British visitor to the Cape, Mr R. B. Fisher, wrote to William Wilberforce in England asserting that infanticide was widespread and unreported at the Cape.[16] He alleged that he had seen three infant corpses and had heard of the discovery of 'no less than 13 murdered infants lying on the Beach without any enquiry having been instituted as to the manner in which they lost their lives'.[17] No indication was made of the status of these corpses, whether slave or free, black or white. The Colonial Secretary demanded an investigation. The members of the Cape Court of Justice, the Fiscal, and the Burgher Senate (mostly Cape-Dutch officials who had sworn allegiance to the British) responded with hostility. They seemed to take the accusations as a personal affront to their honour.

---

[14] 1/GR 3/27, Judicial declarations 1821–22, no pagination: '*Zaak ... contra De Slavin Roselyn.*'

[15] Thanks to Professor Helen Bradford of the University of Cape Town for this unpublished information. For some sense of the numbers of indictments, see P. Scully, *Liberating the Family? Gender and British Slave Emancipation in the Rural Western Cape, South Africa, 1823–1853* (Cape Town, David Philip, 1997), p. 134, n.1. The reasons for changes in the law at the Cape – and their relationship to British law – have not yet been examined. For an insightful examination of the British case, see Jackson, *New-Born Child Murder.*

[16] G.M. Theal, *Records of the Cape Colony*, (London, Government Printers, 1902), vol. 11, p. 346: Letter from Lord Charles Somerset to Earl Bathurst, 19 May 1817. For the details of his complaint, see ibid., pp. 173 ff: Letter from R.B. Fisher to Earl Bathurst, 4 Southampton Place, Euston Square, 13 September 1816, and enclosure: to William Wilberforce. Fisher claimed to be 'younger brother to the Bishop of Salisbury, and am extremely well known to ... Sir John Cradock and Mr Pitt, Member for Crickdale' (ibid., pp. 174–5). Apart from infanticide, he claimed knowledge of unbridled incest and miscegenation (ibid., pp. 176–7).

[17] Ibid., pp. 176, 346.

From the united testimony of all these authorities ... from the
indignation with which so foul an accusation has been received, and
from my own observation of the strictness with which crimes, when
they unfortunately do occur, are impartially prosecuted, I may
venture to pronounce Mr Fisher's allegations gross and unfounded
misrepresentations.[18]

The Chief Justice, J.A. Truter, reported that since 1800 'only' eight
inquests had been performed on infant corpses. If anything like the
number of corpses alleged by Fisher had been lying around, surely 'it
must have attracted the attention of the public' and thence the Court of
Justice, and this had not occurred.[19] Therefore Fisher must have grossly
misrepresented the facts. Truter concluded his report, underlining the
difficulty in establishing infanticide in that period, with the assertion that:

> even supposing ... that all eight infants ... came alive into the world
> (which in two cases only fully appeared) ... the crime of infanticide
> is not more prevalent in this Colony than elsewhere, on the contrary,
> there are several examples of new born children having been placed
> in such situations that they must be found, and who have
> accordingly been taken up and properly provided for.[20]

The history of infanticide at the Cape has been approached in a
haphazard manner. Few historians of Cape slave society have examined
infanticide at all, but Robert Shell's *Children of Bondage* devotes a page
to the subject, concluding that 'there is little evidence that it played any
significant role in reducing the count of newborn slaves, although the
practice surely existed'. He does not discuss the possibility of settler
infanticide.[21] After emancipation, all infanticide cases studied have been
of subaltern women, mostly unmarried.[22] As in Victorian Britain, most
infants that featured in infanticide or concealment cases were
illegitimate. However, as long as slavery existed at the Cape, the concept
of legitimacy was irrelevant to the majority of subaltern women. At the
time of the cases examined here, slaves could not marry. Even after the

---

[18] Ibid., pp. 344–5.

[19] Ibid., p. 346.

[20] Ibid., p. 346: Letter from J.A. Truter to Lord Charles Somerset, 27 March 1817.
Theal, in translating the word '*kindermoord*' into English, chose the term
'infanticide', a British category of crime which correctly described the murders to
which Truter was referring.

[21] Shell, *Children of Bondage*, p. 314. Ross's *Beyond the Pale* has a section devoted
to the 'white' family, but does not mention the possibility of infanticide. Elphick
and Giliomee's classic, *The Shaping of South African Society*, has no index entry
for infanticide.

[22] Scully, *Liberating the Family?*, pp. 134 ff. Her interpretation ignores the legal context;
her cases cross the 1845 threshold, but this is not mentioned. 'Subaltern' here refers to
people from the subordinate groups in society; these women were neither peasants nor
proletarians, but were mostly slaves or ex-slaves, San or Khoekhoen.

ameliorative regulations of 1823, prerequisites for marriage included the consent of their masters and Christian baptism. Few, if any, slaves married before emancipation.[23]

Slave infanticide, then, meant something quite different from slaveholder infanticide, or indeed the killing of babies by working women in Victorian Britain. For slaves, no shame could be attached to childbirth – slave women were expected to reproduce (although they were not generally considered 'breeders' as was the case in other British slave societies), and there were no economic pressures to kill their babies: their survival was the slaveholder's responsibility. Although as Shell suggested, slave infanticide probably did occur, the death of most slave babies was arguably due to forced neglect, especially where the mothers were wet nurses for their mistresses.[24] In one case, a slave woman named Hester van de Kaap tried to drown herself and her three children, aged from infancy to nine years old. Her relationship with her mistress was intimate and had become too exploitative for her to bear.[25] Following Barbara Bush, I would expect slave infanticide to have been political, a sign of the immense psychological strain of slavery.[26]

In the case of settler women, too, it seems clear that infanticide was rare, although it is true that it tended to be hidden within families, thus reducing its chance of appearing in court records. Most women married, often while they were young: pre-marital pregnancy could be accommodated and the offspring legitimated after marriage. Nevertheless, as the cases discussed here demonstrate, reproduction was not always welcome in settler society: both subaltern and settler women knew of ways to 'bring down the courses' and to abort unwelcome pregnancies. The former practice was considered legitimate (with the permitted sale of relevant patent medicines), which makes the second more difficult to discover.[27] One of the most interesting aspects of the

---

[23] van der Spuy, 'Slave women and the family'.

[24] Shell paints a more positive picture of such women in *Children of Bondage*, chapter 10. For a more caustic view, see P. van der Spuy, '"What, then, was the sexual outlet for black males?": a feminist critique of demographic representations of women slaves at the Cape of Good Hope in the eighteenth century', *Kronos*, 23 (Nov 1996), 43–56.

[25] Hester could not play the role of subservient, passive, dutiful slave. Although she claimed that she worked so hard that she was forced to neglect her children, her attitude was particularly insolent and disrespectful. Rather than acting against the cause of her oppression, however, Hester introverted her aggression and tried to kill herself and her three youngest children. She was executed for their murder. See Theal, *Records*, vol. 16, pp. 379–95: Letter from Lord Charles Somerset to R. Wilmot, 20 October 1823, with enclosures.

[26] B. Bush, *Slave Women in Caribbean Society 1650–1838* (London, James Curry, 1990), chapter 7.

[27] Helen Bradford, 'Herbs, knives and plastic: 150 years of abortion in South Africa', (paper presented to the Africa Seminar, Centre for African Studies, University of Cape Town, 11 April 1990).

Sauer case is the discovery of a broad network of women – slave, Khoi, settler – who bore and could share this knowledge. An undercurrent of women's co-operation existed within a society which operated on the surface in rigid hierarchical terms (even within settler society).[28] It is possible that unmarried daughters were relatively open to such networks; after marriage wives may have become more aloof. Certainly, slaveholding women of all ages constantly interacted with slave women in the intimacy of slaveholders' homes, and subaltern women who worked intimately with settler women knew their secrets. As the case of Anna Sauer demonstrates, this knowledge empowered subaltern women, who might literally hold the power of life and death over women in the slaveholding class.

An exploration of the cases of Anna Sauer and Martha Boshof[29] urges a re-examination of settler women's position and roles in eighteenth and early nineteenth-century Cape slave society. Some historians posit a powerful position for settler women, owing to their relative scarcity:[30]

> Few, if any, Cape European women remained spinsters ... In short, there were few economic constraints to keep settler women at the Cape from marrying and having lots of children.[31]

Their supposed empowerment follows from the assumption that because there were fewer settler women than men, women could choose whom to marry, and thereby enrich themselves.[32] This ignores power relations within families, and the key dynamic of age, in addition to gender.

Writing in the early nineteenth century, a British army officer at the Cape, Robert Semple, remarked that

> women are sometimes married here very early, sixteen years being fixed upon as the most general age at which they become wives, and often mothers; and ten, twelve and even eighteen children are not uncommonly the produce of one marriage.[33]

---

[28] The rigid hierarchies of rank within settler society are well established in South African historiography, reflected in such things as where one could sit in Church and the acceptable size of one's funeral procession. See, for instance, Ross, *Beyond the Pale, passim.*

[29] Cape settler women retained their 'maiden' names even after marriage. Boshof was Martha's father's name.

[30] Shell, *Children of Bondage*, p. 291.

[31] Ibid., p. 301.

[32] Ibid. In addition, women were in a better position at the Cape concerning rights of inheritance; ante-nuptial contracts were also possible under the Roman Dutch legal tradition which operated at the Cape. Roman Dutch law has remained the basis of common law in South Africa.

[33] Robert Semple, cited in Shell, *Children of Bondage*, p. 300. See also Ross, *Beyond the Pale*, p. 130.

Robert Ross's quantitative research for the eighteenth century confirms Semple's impression: of a sample of 279 women, most married at 17 years of age. He found that men tended to be on average five years older than women and he suggests that 'the relatively young ages of marriage at the Cape provide ... evidence for the hypothesis that the majority of men were able to escape from the control of their parents at a relatively young age and set up on their own'.[34]

Whereas early marriage may have empowered young men, this was not necessarily the case for women. Indeed, one could argue to the contrary that the younger the women, the greater the parental pressure to enter into unwelcome marriages. Teenage girls did not always choose their husbands, as the discussion of the case of Martha will demonstrate. High rates of marriage need not imply the empowerment of Cape settler teenage girls. Almost one hundred per cent nuptiality rates may reflect the power of parents to exact obedience from daughters.[35]

The cases of Anna and Martha provide a rare opportunity to glimpse those women most profoundly silent in South African slave historiography: slaveholders' daughters, the young, unmarried 'white' women of whom unceasing reproduction would be demanded, but only after marriage.[36] Both young women were slaveholders' daughters, but their fathers occupied different places on the social scale. J.N. Sauer was a widower of no significant social standing, who had only three slaves, and only three children (Anna and two sons). Theodorus Muller, on the other hand, was more stereotypically patriarchal, presiding over fifteen or sixteen dependent children (under the age of twenty-five) at one time, of greater wealth and high status in the community, as District Secretary of Graaff-Reinet.[37]

A European visitor to the Cape in the early nineteenth century described Graaff-Reinet in disparaging tones, which nevertheless allow us insight into this settler community:

> The total seclusion of the colonists from general intercourse with the world, and with civilised life, their own confinement to the little circle of their families ... are very disadvantageous to them ... and

---

[34] Ross, *Beyond the Pale*, p. 131.

[35] It was arguably only in the remarriages of widows that women indeed 'made their ... marital choice skillfully' and relatively freely. See Shell, *Children of Bondage*, p. 292.

[36] In the past decade much has been written on slave women: see, for example, van der Spuy, 'Slave women and the family'; J.E. Mason, 'Fit for freedom: the slaves, slavery, and emancipation in the Cape Colony, South Africa, 1806 to 1842', (PhD diss., Yale, 1992); P. van der Spuy, 'A Collection of Discrete Essays with the Common Theme of Gender and Slavery at the Cape of Good Hope, with a focus on the 1820s', (MA diss., University of Cape Town, 1993); Shell, *Children of Bondage*.

[37] In 1816 (the first year of slave registration) Muller was the registered owner of nineteen slaves, CA: SO 6/69: Slave Register, 'M', Graaff-Reinet.

notwithstanding their simplicity of manners, their general purity of morals, and their ignorance of many of the greater crimes to which the European nations are subject, they appear ... much rather under an unfavourable than a favourable point of view. Selfishness, lawlessness, hardiness, intolerance, and a thirst for revenge, are the reigning vices in their character, which will perhaps hardly be thought atoned by a disposition to be easily satisfied ... a firm adherence to truth, and a great respect for religion. But what is most to be deprecated in the character of some among them, is the harshness with which they treat their slaves and Hottentots, and in others, the bitterness and irreconcilable animosity with which they carry on their differences among each other.[38]

This was not a community in which one could happily have children out of wedlock. Anna Sauer and Martha Boshof, finding themselves pregnant, chose to resolve this dilemma in quite different ways.

Narratives of infanticide: Anna Sauer and Rosalyn van de Kaap

Anna Sauer was sixteen years old, when she was arrested for attempted abortion and the murder of her new-born baby in November 1821.[39] Although she admitted only the pregnancy and birth, the evidence presented by others – the majority of whom were subaltern women – drew a convincing picture of the desperation of, and options open to, a young unmarried settler woman facing the shame of bearing a bastard. Together, the women's *declaraties* weave a tale about women. Men – without whom there would have been no story – do not feature, although they lurk in the background. What is striking is the particular women who people this tale, and the relationships that developed between them. All except Anna herself were either slaves or Khoekhoe workers.

This narrative of Anna Sauer has been constructed from various sources, although there are huge gaps in the archival record.[40] The main

---

[38] H. Lichtenstein, *Travels in Southern Africa, in the Years 1803, 1804, 1805 and 1806* (Cape Town, van Riebeeck Society, 1930), pp. 377, 380.

[39] The precise date of birth/death is unclear, but the women were interrogated from 23 November 1821. The corpse had apparently been undiscovered for about three weeks. CA: 1/GR judicial declarations 1821–22, no pagination: 'Zaake van den Landdrost van Graaff Reinet ... in Cas Crimineel contra De Slavin Roselyn [*sic*] van Johan Nicolaas Sauer'

[40] CA: CO 2633 no. 110: letter from *Landdrost* A. Stockenstrom to Colonial Secretary C. Bird, 20 Nov. 1821; GH 49/22, criminal and civil pleadings, 1822 April–July, pp. 32 ff: 'In appeal from a Sentence of the Worshipful Court of Justice bearing date 2nd day of April 1822'; ZP 1/1/28, microfilm of CO 48/60: letter from Lord Charles Somerset to Earl Bathurst, 28 April 1823; CJ 816, no. 17.

source was the local 'judicial declarations' of suspects and witnesses, interrogated by a member of the Court of Justice.[41] He would ask a formal set of questions, starting with name, age and so on, and then allow the woman to reply to the allegations of others, and to tell her own story: seldom what she had done, more often what she had seen or overheard. It was at this stage that District Secretary Muller's signature appears as witness to the proceedings. From the declarations the final list of suspects was drawn up and a case was constructed.

The case was tried by the Court of Justice in Cape Town, although no records of the trial itself appear to survive. Anna must have been tried separately from Rosalyn and Philida, because there is no record of her sentence in the Court of Justice archives, whereas the sentences of Rosalyn and Philida, both convicted, are recorded jointly.[42] From this one might have concluded that Anna had avoided prosecution; certainly others had been eliminated from the inquiry. However, correspondence between the Cape and British governments reveals that Anna was indeed brought to trial, and convicted of attempted abortion and *kindermoord*.[43] It is also through these records, and those of the Appeal Court, that we may discover that all three women were convicted and that Rosalyn and Anna were sentenced to death. Philida was sentenced to stand beneath the public gallows with a rope around her neck, and to be beaten. Then she was to be branded, placed in irons and forced to spend the rest of her life on Robben Island.[44] The governor, Lord Charles Somerset, reduced her sentence to time served, thus effectively pardoning her. Both Anna and Rosalyn appealed. Anna was eventually acquitted – on the argument that 'Nature could not have leapt' and turned her into a murdering monster: she must have been unaware of what was going on.[45] Rosalyn served five years' imprisonment. Her life was saved by the argument that, as a slave, she had had no choice but to obey her mistress. Thus, both women were saved by the myth that their behaviour did not represent a challenge to slaveholding society.

---

[41] CA: 1/GR 3/27.

[42] CA: CJ 816, no. 17.

[43] This correspondence was part of a vast archive of records in the Public Records Office in Britain, transcribed by the Cape archivist, G.M. Theal, in the early part of this century and published as *Records of the Cape Colony*. This is the first source to which historians of this period turn. Theal does not provide the full transcript of correspondence, which reveals the fate of Rosalyn as well as Anna – perhaps he did not consider it significant (he was more concerned with 'politics'), but I was able to trace the original on microfilm.

[44] CA: CJ 816, no. 17. This was a typical sentence under the Dutch East India Company in the eighteenth century, for a fairly serious offence. See Ross, *Beyond the Pale*, p. 163.

[45] CA: GH (Government House) 49/22, criminal and civil pleadings, 1822 April–July, pp. 32 ff.

Anna could be dismissed as a mere child (of only fifteen), and Rosalyn was shown to be an exemplary slave.[46]

The declarations provided the evidence on which Anna was convicted. Remarkably, every deposition bar Anna's and that of the local chemist was that of a subaltern woman, either slave or Khoekhoe: a member of the slaveholding class was convicted of murder on the word of subaltern women – the body itself provided no clues due to the advanced stage of decomposition. Although the women's stories do not always agree (each woman being concerned to deny her own involvement), it is possible to construct a scenario of Anna's probable journey from amenorrhoea to the death of her baby. The tales told by slave and Khoekhoe women reveal the limits of possibility for someone in Anna's position. They also throw into confusion simplistic notions of powerful white women lording it over subaltern women, their power quite literally devolving through white male household heads.[47] Instead, in this particular case, a young 'white' woman's reputation and life were placed in the hands of subaltern women. Initially they carried her, and then they let her fall.

Anna Sauer's mother had died some time within the previous six years, after the birth of her youngest child. It is possible that she died in childbirth, though we cannot say precisely when she died.[48] Married women played an important part in Cape communities in cementing ties of friendship and support, partly via the practice of 'visiting'. Sauer's lack of a wife may have served to alienate him from Graaff-Reinet society. This might also have been true for Anna, his only daughter. There is no hint in any of the various records in this case that Anna felt able to turn to anyone within the settler community, including her father or grandmother, for support or even advice. The only people she could turn to were subaltern women – and their support proved tenuous, although it was not the women of her own household who betrayed her.

According to the official slave register, Sauer had three slaves at the time of the infant's death: Rosalyn, her child, and an adult male, Letjou.[49] The Khoekhoe woman, Philida, also worked in Sauer's household as cook.[50] Rosalyn described her own occupation, not as

---

[46] van der Spuy, 'Gender and slavery', chapter 4.

[47] Mason, 'Fit for freedom', chapter 3.

[48] Death notices were instituted only in 1834.

[49] CA: SO (Slave Office) 6/74, folio 43: slave register of Johan Nicolaas Sauer. In 1817 Sauer registered two slaves, Roselyn [sic] and Letjou. Three children are listed as having been born to Rosalyn, two of whom died. The only other slave recorded was registered in 1823 and sold two years later.

[50] CA: 1/GR 3/27, declaration of Philida.

slave, but as needlewoman – she could have added confidante and midwife.[51] She was about thirty years of age and had a family of her own. Witnesses referred to Letjou, the man who helped Rosalyn bury the baby's corpse, as her husband. As slaves, they could not have married legally.[52] Letjou died of unknown causes some time between the discovery of the body and the interrogations. Rosalyn had given birth three times since the establishment of slave registration in 1816. Her first baby, 'Letjou 2', had died the day he was born, in 1817. Her second child, Cesar, born in 1819, survived, while her third, François, was born on 7 October 1821 – shortly before Anna gave birth – and died six days later.[53] Rosalyn was charged with the murder of Anna's baby, but no inference was drawn from the death of her own infants. Her own struggle with childbirth and infant death was ignored, invisible, irrelevant.

However, Rosalyn's pregnancy was highly significant from Anna's perspective. She had already given birth to at least two babies, whereas presumably this was Anna's first pregnancy. Given the absence of a mother or other female relative in whom Anna felt she could confide, Rosalyn was the obvious choice of confidante, someone whose reproductive knowledge Anna might trust. Moreover, Rosalyn was acquainted with infant death. Anna Sauer had not menstruated for four months. She turned to Rosalyn for help to 'bring down the courses'.[54] We do not know how either woman interpreted amenorrhoea, whether or not they equated it with pregnancy. Most settler girls would have learnt about their maturing bodies from mothers or other older female relatives. Anna may have relied on Rosalyn for such knowledge.

Rosalyn sought out Mina, a Khoekhoe woman who worked for Sauer's neighbour, Gabriel du Toit. Mina, a cook, was known for her home-made remedies. As one historian of abortion has noted, '[i]ndigenous people ... knew the veld best'.[55] Rosalyn approached Mina, who duly provided a concoction.[56] This failed to restore Anna's monthly cycle, so she sent Rosalyn to buy 'Hoffman's Drops' from the local chemist. He later claimed that he had had no idea that this preparation was intended for Anna – Rosalyn had claimed it was

---

51 CA: 1/GR 3/27, declaration of Rosalyn.
52 van der Spuy, 'Slave women and the family'.
53 This is evident from the slave register, but was not mentioned in any of the records I have traced: CA: SO 6/74, folio 43; SO 5/1 No.138, folios 378, 394 and 400.
54 CA: 1/GR 3/27.
55 Bradford, 'Herbs, knives and plastic', p. 3.
56 CA: 1/GR 3/27: declaration of Roosje, Mina's fellow Khoisan worker, that Mina 'Rabas had gekookt en er van een bottel ... aan Rosalyn had gegeven om aan Antje Sauer te bezorgen'.

for her free sister, who lived beyond the colony's border – or that it might have been used as an abortifacient. Indeed, it is unclear whether or not Anna saw the *kraam-middel* (cramp medicine) in that light.[57] This concoction having failed, Mina then tapped into her own network of women healers. She reportedly contacted a 'free black' woman named Marie who visited Anna and applied some form of ointment and massage.[58]

It soon became clear, if it was not before, that Anna was pregnant. The records do not reveal the father of her baby – none of the declarations even hinted at his identity, and there is no indication that he was investigated. It is clear that Anna was not engaged to marry, because had this been the case her baby would have been legitimated; there would have been no *schaamte*.[59] She may have been subjected to rape or incest. This possibility is supported by the silence of Anna's father. According to Philida, Sauer was told of the pregnancy, but chose to ignore it. He never seems to have questioned Anna. Despite the fact that he was in the house at the time of her labour and her baby's birth, just rooms away, he feigned deafness and did nothing. The fact that Anna felt that she could turn to nobody in the slaveholding community supports the possibility of incest. Her father played no part in the proceedings at all, according to the extant documents.

Given that marriage was out of the question for Anna, other options presented themselves to her. She considered keeping the baby, but was apparently dissuaded by Rosalyn, who reminded her of the shame of illegitimacy for settler women.[60] Wayne Dooling has argued for the existence of a shared moral economy between slaveholders and slaves in the rural district of Stellenbosch in this period.[61] Rosalyn's behaviour in this case suggests that slaves were fully aware of the moral and social norms of settler society, but it does not indicate that they shared those values. Rosalyn could sympathize with Anna's shame, but it was never her own experience. She viewed her own pregnancy quite differently. As slaves were excluded from the legal institution of marriage, their children were by definition 'illegitimate'; the condition carried none of the connotations for Rosalyn that it carried for Anna.[62] Rosalyn's awareness of Anna's sense of shame underlines the extent to which

---

[57] CA: 1/GR 3/27: declaration of Philida; declaration of Frederik Willem Ernst (14 January 1822).

[58] Ibid. See also the deposition of Marie, 15 December 1821.

[59] CA: 1/GR 3/27: declaration of Philida.

[60] Ibid.

[61] Dooling, *Law and Community*.

[62] See van der Spuy, 'Slave women and the family'.

subaltern women penetrated the mind and morals of settler society, yet without sharing them.[63]

Rosalyn observed, most acutely, given the irrelevance of this ritual for subaltern women: 'Who will visit you if you have a [bastard] child?'[64] Formal visiting between settler women constituted a central locus of settler women's lives, establishing networks of respectability, knowledge and support. For Anna, exclusion from such a network would leave her alienated, given the absence of female siblings and her mother. Although she had been born in Graaff-Reinet, and had lived there all her young life, there is not a single mention in any of the case records to suggest that she was on intimate terms with any settler women. The picture that emerges is of a lonely, frightened young woman.

Having decided against keeping her baby, Anna Sauer considered giving the baby away to her grandmother (we do not know whether maternal or paternal), who would then be expected to rear it. This was certainly an option, in the foundling tradition, although unfortunately there has been no research around this issue at the Cape.[65] The literature of the eighteenth- and nineteenth-century Cape typically ignores the plight of unmarried mothers. No reason is given for Anna's decision not to send the baby to her grandmother. Perhaps she preferred to keep the pregnancy and birth a secret – and if it seemed to her that this was possible within her own family, this suggests a great deal about the burden of silence in the Sauer household. In any case, Anna's decision implies an absence of familial support. Her predicament could have been so extreme because of her father's widowed status, which makes it difficult to generalize to families where mothers were present.

Having rejected grandmotherly care for her baby, Anna asked Rosalyn what she should do. Philida claimed to have overheard their conversation. According to her, Rosalyn's immediate response to Anna's question was 'kill it'. Whereupon '*Antje*' (little Anna), '*mijn kleyn nonje*' (my little mistress) 'fell silent'.[66] Whether or not the women planned to

---

[63] For slave women, the important distinction as far as children were concerned was not legitimate/illegitimate, but free/slave. Bearing a slaveholder's child was potentially a means of gaining freedom for one's children, and at times for oneself. Once the office of Slave Registrar had been established in 1823, a great many slave women complained that they had entered into sexual relationships with their masters 'on the promise of freedom'. Children had often resulted, and their mothers now claimed that freedom. In numerous cases, slaveholding men were shamed into granting their slave children freedom, and, in some cases, the freedom of slave mothers too. See van der Spuy, 'Gender and slavery'; Mason, 'Fit for freedom'.

[64] CA: 1/GR 3/27.

[65] Sandra Burman at the University of Cape Town's Centre for Socio-Legal Studies is in the process of examining issues around illegitimacy in Cape Town's history.

[66] CA: 1/GR 3/27: declaration of Philida.

kill the baby, Anna depended on Rosalyn to help with the birth. The use of subaltern women as midwives was doubtless common in settler households, especially in frontier towns like Graaff-Reinet. The authorities had tried to regulate midwifery, precisely because it had been dominated by slave and Khoekhoe women. 'Legitimate', registered midwives were sworn to discover the name of the father of illegitimate children, and to report the same to the local magistrate.[67] Anna may have wanted to resist such an eventuality, if she had the choice – which is unlikely, given her circumstances.

It is impossible to unravel precisely what happened when the baby was born. It seems that the infant was alive and died subsequently. One account had it that Rosalyn hit the baby on the head with a rock, after having nearly strangled it to stop it from screaming.[68] Anna claimed to have been '*buite kennis geraakt*' (insane, literally, torn from knowledge or understanding): she did not know what was happening, and therefore could not be held responsible. She did not know whether the baby was alive or dead.[69] Philida was present; it seems that she took the child and wrapped it in an old dress, but did not know if it was alive or dead. Later, when the child had definitely died, Rosalyn took it and asked Letjou to dig a hole in the garden. They buried the body.[70] Their secret depended on the silent support of a subaltern network that extended beyond the domain of the Sauer household. Had they been able to contain all knowledge within the subaltern 'family', the corpse would never have been discovered.

Anna's profound vulnerability, and ultimate exclusion from subaltern community, was revealed when the network which had supported her untangled. Mina, the Khoekhoe provider of abortifacients, lived and worked on the other side of a wall which separated the garden of Sauer from that of his neighbour, Gabriel du Toit. Mina had admitted to having been sweet-talked by Rosalyn into providing '*een bottel goed*', but 'of the use I knew nothing'. The underlying implication seems to have been that she thought she was giving Rosalyn the preparation for her own use, which seems to have been acceptable. She claimed no knowledge that it was for Anna. On the day of the baby's death, Mina and another Khoekhoe servant, Roosje, were peering over the wall into Sauer's garden. They observed Letjou and Rosalyn bury an object. Curiosity overcame them, and they scaled the wall to investigate further. It is not unlikely that they were expecting precisely what they found –

---

[67] C.G. Botha, *Collected Works, vol. II: History of Law, Medicine and Place Names in the Cape of Good Hope* (Cape Town, van Riebeeck Society, 1962).

[68] CA: 1/GR 3/27: declaration of Philida.

[69] Ibid., declaration of Anna Sauer.

[70] Ibid., declaration of Letjou.

the corpse of a 'white' baby. According to their testimony, they put two and two together. Duty-bound or, certainly, fully aware of settler public morality, Mina decided to expose the body to public view. Interestingly, she waited approximately three weeks in the midsummer heat, by which time the body had decomposed to a great extent. Nevertheless, Mina and Roosje then dug up the corpse and drew du Toit's and the authorities' attention to it, thereby exposing Anna and Rosalyn to public scrutiny and condemnation.

We have no way of discovering why Mina betrayed Rosalyn and Anna. As with so much in this story, the records do not allow unqualified answers. Had Mina remained silent, the corpse and the killing – and perhaps the pregnancy itself – would never have been discovered. Although she had been part of a support network at one stage, she clearly felt no obligation to care for other women – of the class of slave or slaveholder – when it no longer suited her. She claimed that she had not realized at the time that she was committing a crime and later deliberately exhumed the body and placed it where it would be discovered.[71] However, the motives of Khoekhoe and slave women for disclosing the crimes of their masters and mistresses are never self-evident or unambiguous. In this case there may have been conflict between Mina and Rosalyn or Philida which could have led to Mina's exposing the body. It is unclear whether or not Mina foresaw that Rosalyn and other workers would be implicated in the killing – and spoke out in order to save herself, or to avenge herself for some undisclosed matter.

Anna entered the historical record only through this case, whereafter she returned to historical obscurity. Her name is excluded from the widely-used published genealogical source, De Villiers' and Pama's *Genealogies of Old South African Families*.[72] The genealogies were compiled largely from baptismal and burial records, and it is unclear why Anna does not appear as Sauer's child. Perhaps her involvement in this case secured her obscurity for posterity. We do not know how she was received by the Graaff-Reinet settler community, or her own immediate family, having been condemned to death, and then on appeal acquitted, of the murder of her baby. She was probably rendered 'unmarriageable' and may well have been excluded from her father's house. With the end of the trial, Anna Sauer disappears from history.

On the other hand, it proved possible to trace Rosalyn's life after the trial, partly through the records of the Slave Office. Having served five

---

[71] Ibid., declarations of Rosalyn and Mina.
[72] C.C. De Villiers and C. Pama, *Genealogies of Old South African Families*, 2 vols (Cape Town, A.A. Blakema, 1982).

years' imprisonment, Rosalyn was apparently returned to Sauer. She approached the Slave Office in Cape Town in 1828, requesting assistance to purchase her manumission.[73] As she could only raise 100 Rixdollars, the Guardian of Slaves, George Rogers, did not consider the case worth pursuing. Sauer told Rogers that he had already sold her to look after a Mr De Villiers's children (Rogers did not note the irony of such an occupation for someone convicted of killing her mistress's baby). According to Sauer's slave register, however, she was transferred to a Mr Baks in Cape Town, and was eventually manumitted on 23 July 1829, the purchase price having been paid by a free man named Morat of Bengal.[74] We do not know what became of Rosalyn's child.

Challenging patriarchy: Martha Boshof and Christoffel Rothman

Early in 1822, as Theodorus Muller (District Secretary of Graaff-Reinet) and Andries Stockenstrom (*Landdrost*, or magistrate) were investigating the killing of Anna Sauer's baby, Muller's son-in-law, Christoffel F. Rothman, presented Stockenstrom with a list of complaints against his father-in-law. One of these was '[t]hat the Said Secretary had attempted to cause one of his Step Daughters (now the wife of the Informer) who was pregnant before Marriage, to miscarry'. Muller had apparently wanted to prevent Martha's marriage to Rothman.[75] Rothman had waited more than ten years. Perhaps in the light of Anna Sauer's case and the wider political context, he felt that the time was right to expose his father-in-law.

Stockenstrom was shocked that Rothman could want such an intimate family matter to be dealt with publicly, or indeed that Rothman should abandon his filial duty to protect the reputation of his father-in-law, despite the fact that his other complaints alleged Muller's brutal flogging of a slave, as well as treason. The magistrate seems not to have seen the irony in his different approaches to the cases of Anna Sauer and Muller. He attempted to persuade Rothman to drop the complaints, considering it scandalous that a son should take his father to court.

> I was thunderstruck and could hardly Consider the Man in his Senses ... I would admit of no Secret Calumny against any one, but particularly against one in Mr Muller's Situation, and that Coming

---

[73] CA: SO 3/3 no. 138, report of the Guardian of Slaves, 6 June 1828; SO 5/1 day book, Guardian of Slaves no. 138: pp. 378, 394, 400.

[74] CA: SO 6/8; SO 12/13, manumissions.

[75] CA: CO 2641, letters received from Graaff-Reinet, 1822: 31 January 1822. Stockenstrom to Bird, no pagination. See also CA: CO 2463 no. 13.

from so near a Relation ... Having pointed out to Rothman ... the impropriety of Such Conduct from a Son to a Father, he insisted.[76]

The young woman, unnamed in the complaint, but according to De Villiers and Pama's *Genealogies* Martha Maria Boshof, aged fifteen,[77] had wanted to marry Rothman against her stepfather's specific demand that she marry another man. This may explain why she became pregnant: the only way to remove the stigma of an illegitimate child was to marry the father, and the man whom Muller had chosen as Martha's husband would have been unwilling to marry her, pregnant with another man's child.

Muller insisted that she abort. It appears that he took for granted his right to interfere in, and indeed to direct, his stepdaughter's life, and Stockenstrom expressed no outrage in this regard.[78] There is no mention in the records of Muller's wife, or any suggestion that she might have played a role in the matter. She was certainly alive at this time, outliving Muller when he died in 1827.[79] Whatever role she did play remained private. Her name was Regina Rog (also spelt Rogge and Roche), widow of Martha's father, Jacobus Nicolaas Boshof.[80] It is possible that she was fully involved in trying to force Martha to abort but, if so, there was no reason for Rothman to complain against her. For Rothman this was an issue of patriarchal politics: the complaint represented a young man's attempt to unseat an older, more successful patriarch, and the women who were central to the story were neither named nor permitted to speak.

Theodorus Muller was very much more of a recognizable patriarch than was J.N. Sauer. In 1810, at the time of the alleged attempted abortion, Muller's household consisted of his wife Regina and their eight children, plus a number of children from Regina's previous marriage.[81] There were possibly fourteen 'children' in the household, ranging in age from two to twenty-four years.

This case underlines the importance of patriarchal control over childbirth and suggests that unwanted children would normally be

---

[76] CA: CO 2461: 31 January 1822.

[77] De Villiers and Pama, *Genealogies*, p. 606.

[78] Muller does not appear to have considered his attempt to force her to terminate her pregnancy as immoral. Because such attitudes were part and parcel of familial control, they are very difficult to discover and impossible to quantify.

[79] CA: SO 6/69, Slave Register, Theodorus Muller.

[80] Regina was in her mid-forties at the time of the attempted abortion, having borne fourteen children, eight after her marriage to Muller, the last one having been baptized in 1808 (De Villiers and Pama, *Genealogies*, p. 73).

[81] Regina had married first at about sixteen years of age, and had had children more or less non-stop until 1808.

dealt with within the patriarchal family. Had Rothman not decided to complain, the attempted abortion would have been contained within the domestic domain, never to have entered the historical record. Significantly, although Muller had insisted on the abortion, he played no other overt role in the process, which was controlled by women. His stepdaughter was sent to her grandmother who was expected 'to persuade her to abort, by giving her herbs, vinegar' and other abortifacients.[82] The grandmother in question must have been Regina's mother, a woman in her mid-sixties; Muller's parents were in Europe. That Martha was sent to her maternal grandmother suggests her own mother's complicity. In any case, both Martha's experience and that of Anna Sauer point to the importance of grandmothers in reproductive strategies in this period.

As with Anna Sauer, all attempts at abortion failed, and Martha gave birth to a baby girl. We know nothing of the process whereby Muller came to allow Martha and Rothman to marry; perhaps he considered that marriage to Rothman would remove the chances of a scandal in this small community. They married in December 1810, and baptized their baby, Maria Elisabeth Johanna, in the same month.[83] Rothman, who had been living in the countryside near Graaff-Reinet, moved into town and set up home with Martha.[84] They had five children, but Rothman was never as wealthy or powerful as his father-in-law, and clearly never forgave him for trying to prevent his marriage with Martha.[85] He saw his opportunity in 1821 and took it, but did not take into account the deep-seated respect which the magistrate held not only for Muller himself as a high-ranking official, but for the 'correct' behaviour between a son and a father. Stockenstrom seems to have succeeded in burying the case. Despite Rothman's insistence that the British government be informed – hence Stockenstrom's letter to Colonial Secretary Bird – I have found no evidence that the matter was taken any further. Stockenstrom did not recognize the irony of pursuing Anna Sauer, Rosalyn and Philida for attempted abortion, while dismissing the same accusation in the case of Theodorus Muller.

---

[82] CA: CO 2461: Stockenstrom to Bird, 31 January 1822.
[83] De Villiers and Pama, *Genealogies*, p. 797.
[84] CA: J (Opgaaf) 133, tax register, Graaff-Reinet, 1810. This included the rural sub-districts of Graaff-Reinet as well as the town: Rothman lived in one called Camdebo; J 257, Graaff-Reinet, 1821.
[85] De Villiers and Pama, *Genealogies*, p. 797.

Conclusion

The stories of Anna Sauer and Martha Boshof suggest a range of reproductive strategies, and the importance of reproductive politics, in Cape slave society in the early years of the nineteenth century. Pregnancy and illegitimacy held different meanings for different women, both across classes and within the slaveholding class itself. For Anna this was a source of deeply felt shame, whereas for Martha it was a sign of resistance to patriarchal control. Although Anna's response was perhaps typical, Martha demonstrated that she could use the scandalous potential of illegitimacy in a high-ranking family to her advantage. Nevertheless, Martha was powerless to protect her pregnant body from her stepfather's demands that she undergo an abortion; she was fortunate not to have lost her baby. There is no doubt that she was supported throughout her trials by her lover. On the other hand, Anna reminds us of the intense alienation experienced by young women who had no such support. Whether or not her father had raped her, he abrogated any responsibility for his daughter or her child. Anna Sauer's birth-experience, unlike Martha's, stripped her of any power or authority in her household (for Martha it provided her with a household of her own), and nearly cost her her life. For young unmarried settler women, meanings of illegitimacy varied: Martha's pregnancy seems to have been a deliberate strategy to enable her to marry the man of her choice. She welcomed her child and what it meant for her life, whereas Anna's unwed pregnancy was deeply fearful.

In the experience of both Anna and Martha, separated by ten years, various abortifacients failed; it seems that many of the 'remedies' available to Cape women were ineffective. Nevertheless, it is clear that both indigenous and older settler women were recognized as bearers of knowledge of abortion. The fact that a man of Muller's position automatically referred Martha to her grandmother – someone within the family – for an abortion suggests a great deal about patriarchal strategies of birth control. On the other hand, Muller, one of the wealthiest and most powerful men in the district, was unable to prevent either the birth of Martha's and Rothman's child, or their marriage. Within a family, the head of which seemed to have such control over women's bodies, a positive ending was possible for a vulnerable young woman.

This chapter has argued that the bodies of young settler women were sites of resistance to traditional forms of patriarchal authority in Cape slave society, at a time when patriarchy was felt to be under threat. Anna's body became a stage on which subaltern women could exercise power and authority, thus overturning traditional hierarchies. In the case of Martha, the battle was more cleanly fought, almost as a duel between a patriarch and a younger challenger.

These cases reflect the changing nature of Cape colonial society, as colonists had to come to terms with new conditions under British rule. In this period of flux and uncertainty, where boundaries of authority had become blurred and increasingly contested, less powerful members of Cape society – Mina (otherwise profoundly powerless) and Rothman – forced the attention of the government on the personal lives of seemingly more powerful settler men and women. At the same time, both Anna and Martha took steps to control their own fate. Patriarchs living on the very frontiers of the colony were being forced to recognize the increasingly interventionist stance of the British colonial government *vis-à-vis* not only their slaves but also other members of their 'families'. What happened to unmarried settler daughters' babies in as distant a district as Graaff-Reinet became a topic of public concern to the colonial governments in Cape Town and London.

The authorities had traditionally relied on the 'state in miniature', the patriarchal settler family, to police female sexuality.[86] This was particularly the case with settler women. In the nineteenth century, with the British takeover, this changed. As Pamela Scully has noted, focusing on the 1840s:

> The killing of infants in the rural Western cape surely happened before the 1840s, yet the records are mostly silent on this action. The apparent increase of crimes such as infanticide ... reflects in part the penetration of British legal discourse into new terrains of social life in the empire. In the course of the nineteenth century, marriages, deaths, family relationships, and sexual activities all came under the legal spotlight in both the metropole and the colonies.[87]

That spotlight was already shining in the 1820s.

Acknowledgements

This chapter is based on the material researched for a chapter of my master's dissertation at the University of Cape Town. I am indebted to the University of Cape Town and the HSRC for funding. Thanks to those who commented on the dissertation: Nigel Worden, Helen Bradford, Robert Ross and Pamela Scully. Thanks to Lindsay Clowes and Helen Bradford for comments on later versions.

---

[86] See, for example, K. Elks, 'Crime, Community and Police in Cape Town 1825–1850', (MA diss., University of Cape Town, 1986), chapter 1.

[87] Scully, *Liberating the Family?*, p. 135.

CHAPTER EIGHT

The murder of Thomas Sandles: meanings of a mid-nineteenth-century infanticide

Margaret L. Arnot

Convictions of women for murdering their young children were rare in England in the nineteenth century.[1] Yet the extraordinary can reveal a great deal about the ordinary, and were it not for the fact that Hannah Sandles's chosen solution to the unwanted burden of her illegitimate baby was an unusual one, we would know nothing about her at all. The justification for telling her story is twofold: it is interesting in itself as a piece of social history, a slice of 'history from below'; and it serves as a focal point for exploring the meanings that were woven around her circumstances by mid-nineteenth-century commentators. I have elsewhere explored some aspects of Victorian new-born child murder[2] and 'baby-farming' where young children died at the hands of those who were not their parents.[3]

While killings of babies older than new-born by their mothers were often accompanied by some circumstances similar to those surrounding neo-natal murder – in particular, the poverty and severe constraints of single motherhood – there were also differences significant enough for the historian to warrant a separate discussion here. While new-born child murder could sometimes be a form of late abortion in Victorian England, the murder of a two-month-old baby whose birth and name had been registered was not. While the mother of a new-born infant might well have managed to repress acknowledgement of its existence as a

---

[1] Hannah Sandles was one of only three women convicted at the Sussex Assizes between 1840 and 1880 for murdering their own children.

[2] Margaret L. Arnot, 'Understanding women committing newborn child murder in Victorian England', in Shani D'Cruze (ed.), *Everyday Violence in Britain, 1850–1950* (London, Longman, 2000), pp. 55–69.

[3] Margaret L. Arnot, 'Infant death, child care and the state: the baby-farming scandal and the first infant life protection legislation of 1872', *Continuity and Change*, 9 (1994), 271–311.

worthwhile to write to her from the Chailey Union workhouse – where she went to give birth in 1848 – requesting sixpence to help her on her way to London.[13] Whether or not this assistance was forthcoming is not entirely clear, yet it is significant that the amount requested was actually quite insufficient to support a woman and two children on a journey from Chailey to London, let alone pay for their conveyance. Certainly, the relationship between Hannah and Louisa was important in some way to both of them: Louisa was reportedly 'in great affliction at the result of her Mother's Trial' and had enquired by mail whether she could see her mother.[14] The relationship was certainly not intimate in all respects, however, for Hannah Sandles considered it crucial that her daughter not discover her late pregnancy, and managed to conceal the fact of it – and of her new child – from her daughter. It was her daughter to whom Hannah turned for assistance when she returned to London from Chailey, for she was found living in the same vicinity – with the same landlady as her daughter – when the police traced her a few days after the body of an infant was found in a well in Chailey, Sussex.

As to her son from her first marriage, Joseph, it seems that he too was grown up and living in London, but there is no mention of any contact between Joseph and his mother. Of Hannah's apparently large number of siblings, only two received mention in the records: a sister (according to the evidence, her only sister) who had not seen Hannah for some considerable time, although she lived at Isfield, only three and a half miles from Chailey; and a brother and sister-in-law, the latter of whom Sandles took into her confidence about three months before the child was due. Although this was not necessarily the full extent of Hannah's social and kin networks,[15] it seems likely that the general picture that emerges from the trial and consultation of the parish register can be relied upon: Sandles had only sparse and fragile kin relations.

Hannah Sandles entered the Chailey Union workhouse at the end of March 1848.[16] At this stage she was probably about six months pregnant and entered the workhouse in preparation for the birth of her child. It was common for women with few resources to go to the workhouse to give birth, and it is significant that a number of infanticide cases involved women who had been recently confined in workhouses.[17]

---

[13] 'The Chailey murder', *Supplement to the Brighton Guardian* (28 March 1849), p. 3, col. 2, evidence of Charlotte Simmons.

[14] Letter from John M. Cobbett, counsel for the prosecution, to Sir George Grey, home secretary, 27 March 1849, PRO HO 18 252/34.

[15] The picture here results mainly from the prosecution efforts to round up witnesses.

[16] Computed from evidence in several depositions, PRO ASSI 36/6.

[17] A survey of all cases appearing in the Central Criminal Court sessions papers between 1840 and 1880 discovered the following cases: Mary Furley (1844), *Central Criminal*

Hannah Sandles's early resort to the workhouse also suggests that she may have been anxious at this stage to conceal her pregnancy from her friends and family. Certainly, a number of witnesses from the workhouse stated at the trial that they had heard Sandles say that she hoped the child would die, or that she hoped it would not survive the birth. Someone else reported hearing her say to the child after it had been born that she wished that God had taken him.[18] Commentators at the time found these expressions quite understandable in her situation, explaining them in terms of shame at her moral lapse, of which the child was stark evidence. The source of her anxiety as the birth approached needs consideration.

Social practices relating to marriage, extra-marital sexual liaisons and the children resulting from them are central to understanding the practice of infanticide during the nineteenth century. It seems obvious that lack of social, economic and moral space for women with children born out of wedlock would contribute towards the practice of infanticide. Yet some work in social history has suggested that the picture of Victorian England's morality has been one-sided and has not adequately represented working-class culture where, in fact, sexual relationships were more fluid and much less likely to be formalized in law.[19] The Sandles were clearly members of this working class, and Hannah may well have formed a long-term *de facto* relationship and had children as a result. Her daughter was one of her most important contacts, as her regular correspondence with her from Chailey – via the pen of Charlotte Simmons, a fellow workhouse inmate – suggests. So why should little Thomas Sandles have caused his mother such a dilemma in her relationship with her daughter? Why had she avoided letting her daugher know of her pregnancy? Under cross-examination, Charlotte Simmons explained: 'This was a love-child, and she wished her daughter not to know it.'[20] It seems that Hannah Sandles may have felt acutely that there were limits to what was acceptable, that children from a stable union, whether or not it had been formalized in marriage, were legitimate, whereas those resulting from a love affair of a widow

Court Sessions Papers (CCCSP), 6th session (1843–44), pp. 955–9; Sarah Briden (1845), CCCSP, 5th session (1844–45), pp. 644–6; Hannah Brumwell (1856), CCCSP, 5th session (1855–56), pp. 630–33; Elizabeth Ann Harris (1856), CCCSP, 6th session (1855–56), pp. 726–31; Sarah Price (1857), CCCSP, 6th session (1856–57), pp. 719–23; Sarah Gaunt (1872), CCCSP, 12th session (1871–72), pp. 452–4.

[18] 'The Chailey murder', *Supplement to the Brighton Guardian* (28 March 1849), p. 3, col. 2, evidence of Charlotte Simmons.

[19] John Gillis, *For Better and for Worse: British Marriages, 1600 to the Present* (Oxford, Oxford University Press, 1985)

[20] 'The Chailey murder', *Supplement to the Brighton Guardian* (28 March 1849), p. 3, col. 2.

in her forties were not. If she did not think that her daughter could accept her with an illegitimate child, with her limited and fragile support networks, it is quite possible that she truly felt there to be no place for herself, even in working-class culture.

On 20 July 1848, at the age of forty-four, Hannah Sandles gave birth to a male child whom she named Thomas.[21] At the birth, she was assisted by one of her fellow inmates. During the following few weeks while she remained in the workhouse, the women with whom she lived were of considerable assistance to her. The new child entered a communal culture where responsibilities were shared. A number of the women bathed and dressed Thomas on a regular basis. Someone else made clothes for him from a number of aprons donated by the wife of the superintendent. While such intimacy would have been of great benefit to the mother of a new-born baby, it proved the demise of Hannah Sandles. One of the most crucial parts of their testimony was the result of their intimacy with the body of the child. This enabled them to give evidence as to the identity of the infant's body found in a well, whereas the medical officer of the Chailey Union who had attended the child when alive was unable to identify the body.[22]

On 8 September, Hannah Sandles left Chailey Union workhouse. Despite the urging of the superintendent for her to stay, she was determined to take responsibility for her own life again. She wanted to return to London to find work, presumably as a laundrywoman, and to find a situation for her daughter, Eliza. It is probable that Hannah had decided that in order to cope with the baby, she would have to find employment for Eliza, then somewhere between eight and ten years of age.

There was no system of provision for people leaving workhouses. She left with sixpence and some bread, given to her out of charity by the wife of the superintendent. She had a babe-in-arms, two young children, and a forty-mile journey ahead of her to London. The fact that under such straitened circumstances she did not turn to her sister, who lived just three or four miles from Chailey, is further evidence of the fact that her daughter was her only meaningful support.

Hannah cut across Chailey Common and was seen with her two children and a baby in her arms by a woman who lived near where the path entered the main road. Several miles further along the road to London, she entered a public house at lunchtime, by which time she no

---

[21] Evidence of Thomas Awcock Bull, registrar of births, deaths and marriages for the Chailey Union, depositions for the inquest, September 1848, PRO ASSI 36/6.

[22] 'The Chailey murder', *Supplement to the Brighton Guardian* (28 March 1849), p. 3, col. 2.

longer had the baby. Eight days later, on 16 September, Mrs Jane Manners – who lived in an isolated cottage along the route which must have been taken by Hannah Sandles – found the body of an infant floating in her well.

Inquest and trial

The possibility of foul play of some kind was clear enough for the coroner to commence enquiries on the day the body was discovered by Mrs Manners. Although Hannah may have felt that she had put a safe distance between herself and her deceased infant, she was quickly accused and charged with the murder by the coroner's inquest, and later tried at assizes and convicted for the murder of Thomas Sandles.

The body was found at eight o'clock on the morning of 16 September. At two o'clock in the afternoon a post-mortem was performed by Mr Walker, the surgeon. Various parties would have been contacted to identify the body before it was dissected by the surgeon, so by lunchtime suspicion had already fallen on Hannah Sandles. On this first day of the inquest, Elizabeth Park, the wife of the governor of Chailey Union workhouse, and Charlotte Simmons, an inmate of the Union who had tended Hannah and the baby as nurse and written letters to Hannah's sister for her, gave evidence. The workhouse, as the place where pauper women went to give birth, was a logical place to make early enquiries. Sandles's poverty and her need to resort to the notoriety of institutionalization made her vulnerable from the start.

After the evidence of Park and Simmons, the inquest was adjourned until 19 September. Henry Harper, police superintendent for East Sussex, went to London with Mr Park, the governor of Chailey Union, by desire of the coroner, on Monday 18 September. East Sussex had had a modern police force for nine years at this stage. Modern policing was in its early days and consequently appropriate policing practices were still being defined. So it is not surprising that Hannah Sandles was the victim of what we would now certainly consider suspect police methods. In the mid-1850s, not long after this case was decided, abuses of police power were so widespread as to cause a detailed inquiry into complaints. Superintendent Harper went to London with a warrant for Sandles's arrest in his pocket. Instead of identifying himself and explaining his purpose clearly, he managed to confuse her and consequently cause her to give conflicting stories which, when repeated at both the coroner's hearing and during the trial, contributed significantly to the construction of her guilt. According to the defence attorney, even in 1849 he should simply have located her, apprehended her and brought her back to be heard before the coroner and the coroner's jury. Indeed, during the trial, Justice Parke upheld an objection raised by defence counsel, Mr Clarkson, and refused to admit as evidence anything said by Sandles after a particular threat was made to her by the police superintendent.[23]

Harper, in plain clothes, located where Sandles lived and used a messenger, also in plain clothes, to call her into the street where he questioned her without identifying himself. She answered him freely, explaining that she had come from Chailey last Friday week, bringing two children with her. After going with Harper to the school to get the children, and leaving them with her landlady (at which stage we wonder that she was not getting suspicious about the motives of this man) he persuaded her to go with him to a pub. Sandles was confronted with Mr Park, and apparently was much distressed. In the presence of both men, she was again asked how many children she brought with her from Chailey. Now she replied "Three", but explained that she had left the baby with a sister in Sussex. It was at this stage in the questioning that Harper threatened her that, unless she informed him of the location of the sister, or the third child, it was his duty as a constable to detain her. This was the threat that both defence counsel and judge considered unreasonable at the trial.

At last, Harper apprehended her and they returned to the coroner's hearing in Chailey, where she was the main suspect for the murder of Thomas Sandles. A constable was sent to her lodgings to take charge of her children and her property. He located a bundle with baby's clothes in it, which also became crucial evidence in the trial. When Sandles stood before the coroner's jury, she wore an apron made from the same workhouse-issued material as the dead infant's frock, which served as a powerful visual link between Hannah and the body.[24] To the historian this can be read as poignant symbolism for her vulnerability. As a very poor woman she had no choice about how she dressed the child, probably little choice about what she wore herself, and it was probably poverty that drove her to salvage the baby clothes in order to make a few pennies – an act that resulted in the discovery of this evidence in her room in London. The coroner's jury returned a verdict of wilful murder against Hannah Sandles, and she was committed under a coroner's warrant to Lewes gaol. Sandles's desperate effort to take control of her life by leaving the workhouse had failed dismally. She stayed in the Lewes gaol for six months awaiting trial at the 1849 Lent assizes.

[23]   Ibid., p. 3, col. 3.
[24]   This was mentioned in the evidence of Charlotte Simmons given at the assize trial, *Sussex Agricultural Express and County Advertiser* (24 March 1849), p. 4, col. 6.

Sandles's trial appears to the twenty-first-century reader as a rather one-sided contest. No defence lawyers were appointed before the trial. As was common at this time, counsel was appointed by the judge and handed the depositions as the case came to trial, therefore providing no opportunity to summon witnesses on the defendant's behalf. However, the trial was no more nor less 'just' than any number of similar contemporaneous trials, and as such can provide us with a useful snapshot of the mid-nineteenth-century criminal-justice system at work. It could be argued that, in the end, Sandles was convicted on the grounds of a prosecution story that accorded with contemporary narratives of female weakness and shame.

So what was the basis of the prosecution case? Medical jurisprudential testimony was becoming increasingly important in criminal trials, especially those involving deaths by violent means, poisoning and drowning, as well as all deaths of new-born infants. The deposition of William Walker, surgeon, taken before the coroner's inquest seems, on first reading, to contain conclusive evidence that Thomas Sandles died by drowning:

> I examined the Body and supposed it must have been in the Water three or four Days at least. Decomposition had commenced in the Face and Mouth. There was an appearance on the Forehead which seemed to me to be an Accumulation of Dirt – there were no external Marks of Violence. There was an Oozing of Mucus from the Mouth and Nostrils. The Hands were partially open – The Palms of the Hands and the soles of the Feet were completely sodden, caused no Doubt by the Body having been some Time in the Water. The Eyelids were closed – the Skin was hard and pitted under the Pressure of the Fingers owing probably to long Immersion. I have this Evening made a post Mortem Examination of the Body – The whole of the Viscera are healthy – There is no Water in the Stomach, which contains a small quantity of milky fluid resembling milk. The Brain was a little congested but otherwise healthy – There was no Water in the Lungs – In my Opinion the Death of the Child was caused by suffocation produced by Drowning – There is no appearance of Disease about the Child ... The Lungs were considerably congested.[25]

In mid-nineteenth-century England, it was not considered necessary for water in the lungs to be present for drowning to be determined as the cause of death.[26] Indeed, leading medical jurists noted in the 1840s that

---

[25] Evidence of William Gambier Walker at the coroner's inquisition, held at the dwelling house of John Kenning known by the sign of the King's Head, 16 September 1848 before Francis Harding Gell, coroner, PRO ASSI 36/6.

[26] Alfred S. Taylor, *A Manual of Medical Jurisprudence* (London, John Churchill, 1844), pp. 501 and 514; Theodoris Romeyn Beck and John B. Beck, *Elements of Medical Jurisprudence*, 7th edn, (London, Longman, Brown, Green and Longmans, 1842), p. 671.

there was considerable contention regarding signs of death by drowning.[27] However, the surgeon's categorical statement that death was caused by drowning must have carried some weight in determining the verdict of the coroner's court. Certainly, it would seem as if the press considered medical evidence of central importance: the *Brighton Gazette*, in briefly paraphrasing the events during the coroner's hearing, placed medical testimony first and misrepresented this evidence so that it appeared more damning than it actually was: 'Mr Walker, surgeon, examined the body, and found external marks of violence and also congestion of the brain and lungs, such as would have been produced by suffocation. To all appearances the child was perfectly healthy.'[28]

But at the trial a considerably more ambiguous picture emerged as to the cause of death. The surgeon was clear that from the physical signs in the body, death had resulted from suffocation, but it could not definitely be said that this had resulted from drowning. Under cross-examination it emerged that:

> the actual sign of death from convulsions is also suffocation ... His conclusions that suffocation was caused by drowning were arrived at from the fact that the body had been found floating on the water. He did not think it was possible to determine whether this child had been suffocated before being immersed in water or afterwards.[29]

Even after being recalled and re-examined by His Lordship and the defence, the possibility of death by convulsions prior to immersion remained. There was no possibility at all that Sandles had strangled the child before throwing it in the well because there were no signs of external violence. On summing up to the jury on the question of the cause of death, the judge had this to say:

> There was no doubt that the child died of asphyxia ... They would have to consider whether or not it was seized with a sudden convulsion in which it died before it was thrown in. There was no evidence of its being subject to convulsions. The notion of its having fallen into the well could scarce be entertained ... It was not improbable that prisoner had gone to the house, found no one at home, saw the well, and was struck by a sudden idea that it would be a good means of getting rid of her illegitimate child.[30]

The lack of certainty surrounding signs of death by drowning amongst medical jurists did not deter Mr Walker from stating categorically that the child had died from drowning, but it provided ammunition for the defence. Crucially, however, although the defence

---

[27] Taylor, *A Manual*, p. 514; Beck, *Elements*, p. 660.

[28] *Brighton Gazette*, (21 Sept. 1848), p. 8, col. 2.

[29] *Sussex Agricultural Express and County Advertiser*, (24 March 1849), p. 4, col. 5.

[30] *Supplement to the Brighton Guardian*, (28 March 1849), p. 4, col. 1.

emphasized medical uncertainties, they failed to affect the verdict. In Sandles's case it seems to have been presumed from the surrounding evidence that Hannah threw her child down the well while alive. This presumption was made all the easier by the fact that Sandles fitted the stereotype of an infanticidal mother: she was unmarried and of the very lowest of the servant class.

Even the evidence as to the identity of the body was suspect. While one witness was prepared at the trial to positively swear to the identity of the body, this was done on the basis of its having scurvy and sore thighs, from which many children suffered, and on the basis primarily of its long arms and large hands, because by the time the body was shown to witnesses resident in the workhouse, considerable decomposition had set in around the face. According to the defence summing-up 'it was impossible to identify it', yet the prosecution story held sway with the judge who noted that 'a deal of testimony had been given tending to prove that it was [her child]. If it was not, what had become of her child? Where had it gone to? He would read the evidence tending to prove the identity.'[31] The rhetorical questions here appealed to the common sense of the jury rather than to clearly defined rules of evidence.

Sandles was further linked with the crime by additional circumstantial evidence. The body was found naked, and a set of baby clothes was found in a bundle in Hannah's room. The woman who had made the clothes gave evidence that the stitching was her own. Sandles's own story that she had left her baby with her sister, denied by the sister, also threw suspicion on her. But central to the prosecution story – the glue which somehow made it coherent – was the establishment of motive. The prosecution had to tell a story connecting Sandles with the crime. In order to tell a story which made sense, which convinced the jury, it had to be told within established parameters. And that which made most sense was that she was the mother of legitimate children, and did not want anyone to know about the illegitimate one, so murdered it. The judge summed up the case in a letter to the Home Secretary:

> The case was very clear. The Prisoner, a widow of 47 [sic] years of age, had been an inmate of the Chailey Union for some months. She had 2 children of 8 and 6 years of age born in Wedlock, and while in the union she was pregnant and delivered of a child, illegitimate .... The notes however will hardly be required, as the case was established by the clearest evidence, so as not to have a shadow of a doubt .... The crime no doubt was committed, partly from the state of destitution in which she was, and partly for the purpose of concealing her shame.[32]

---

31 Ibid.
32 Letter from Parke J. to Home Office, 24 March 1849, PRO HO 18 252/34.

So the prosecution sought to establish the picture of a poor struggling woman weighed down with shame. Considerable emphasis was placed upon evidence establishing that she wished no one in London to know about the child and on her statements that she hoped the child would die at birth. Conflicting evidence as to the legitimacy of Eliza and William and the fact that she had told her sister-in-law of the approaching birth were both glossed over in the final construction. All Sandles's children born before Thomas became legitimate in the story. Despite the judge's closing comments that '[t]he desire of prisoner to hide from her daughter the fact of her having the illegitimate child was no proof of her guilt; neither was the expression that she "wished God would take her child"',[33] this evidence was crucial in the construction of the prosecution case.

After deliberating for only a few minutes, the jury returned a verdict of guilty, with a recommendation to mercy on the grounds of the care she had previously shown her children. The arbitrariness of the conviction was criticized in a *Times* leader comparing the evidence in the Sandles case with that in another case reported at the same time and asked scathingly, 'such is the evidence upon which one jury acquits, and such the evidence upon which another jury condemns. Which of the two is the more damning and conclusive?'[34]

The arbitrariness of conviction can be better understood if the contradictory nature of reactions to infanticide is considered. Certainly, as already suggested, there was considerable sympathy for the plight of women in poverty with children to support. Juries were loath to condemn women to the gallows when lamentable social conditions over which the women had little control, were perceived to be important contributory factors to the crime. But at the same time, infanticide was something horrible, 'other' and 'unnatural', requiring action of some kind to eliminate it. This characteristic of the crime could lead to sensationalism potentially dangerous to a woman indicted for the crime. At the time of the Sandles inquest the *Brighton Herald* ironically called for a more measured view:

> The *Times* has been lately exposing with great zeal and, we have no doubt, as far as the writer of the articles is concerned, with great honesty, the enormous amount of infanticide in this country. Abundant evidence exists which must be familiar to a large portion of our readers, and which proves that infanticide is almost as common here as it is said to be in China itself ... These murders are not confined to towns, but they are rife also in the country – in retired villages, and among a population supposed to be

---

[33] *Supplement to the Brighton Guardian* (28 March 1849), p. 4, col. 1.
[34] *The Times* (26 March 1849), p. 4, col. 5.

superlatively innocent – such as Bartolozzi, in the last century, delighted to exhibit, in his imaginative pictures, as Shepherds piping a reed, and Shepherdesses, in pretty straw bonnets, with gay ribbons, gracefully flaunting in the wind or wound around the necks of charming-looking pet lambs. All this was false, unnatural, and mischievous. But we believe that, till of late years, the labouring agricultural classes were a plain, hardworking, virtuous, and sober people. The existence of infanticide to such a frightful extent proves that our country, as well as town population, is deteriorating, notwithstanding Bible Societies, Agricultural Associations, and Cricketing Clubs, to which no one is admitted as a member who does not pledge himself to celibacy; and that it is high time that our legislators should begin to think of some remedy for these astounding and frightful evils.[35]

Another local paper, however, was so convinced of Sandles's guilt at the time of the inquest that the medical evidence was misquoted as proving violence had been done to the body.[36] An evangelizing press may well have influenced the views of jury members. Then, when the Lent assizes opened in Lewes, the assize sermon at St Michael's Church was delivered on the text of the 34th verse of the 14th chapter of Proverbs: 'Righteousness exalteth a nation, but sin is a reproach to any people.'[37] The jury in Sandles's case did not wish to be reproached for the sin of Hannah Sandles. She was convicted on the basis of circumstantial evidence, her own muddled story elicited from her as the result of dubious police methods, and the construction of a prosecution story that fitted a conventional narrative of infanticide.

The quality of mercy

Yet the people of Sussex were strongly against the execution of the capital sentence. Hannah's conviction was a drama which provided an opportunity for voicing opinions about the proper definition of justice. At the same time as there was clearly a belief that Sandles should be punished for what was generally believed to be her transgression of woman's natural maternal role, there was also an enormous reservoir of sympathy for her. Her sentence of death was an excuse for this to burst its banks in a public campaign. Four petitions were sent to the secretary of state, George Grey, together with a number of individual letters asking Grey to recommend the queen to show mercy. Two petitions, one

---

[35] *Brighton Herald* (23 September 1848), p. 2, col. 1.
[36] *Brighton Gazette* (21 September 1848), p. 8, col. 2.
[37] *The Sussex Advertiser, Surrey Gazette & West Kent Courier* (20 March 1849), p. 5, col. 4.

each from the inhabitants of Brighton and Lewes, were so heavily and impressively supported that the signatures were removed for convenient Home Office storage. Signatories included members of the magistracy and legal profession.[38] The covering letter for the Lewes petition was actually written by one of the solicitors for the prosecution; and one of the counsel for the prosecution wrote personally to Sir George Grey on behalf of Sandles, which suggests that the prosecution may have been somewhat surprised that conviction resulted at all.[39] The Society of Friends also petitioned on Sandles's behalf, as did the governors of the Chailey Union.[40]

Nobody spoke about the justice of the case in terms of the evidence or verdict. There seemed to be a broad consensus that Sandles was rightly convicted; the prosecution story had made sense to the community at large. Even the judge described the case as 'established by the clearest evidence, so as not to have a shadow of a doubt'.[41] And only the Quakers presented an argument that the death penalty was wrong in principle. So what was under discussion? For some, previous administrative practice in granting clemency in cases of infanticide was a consideration in the granting of justice in this case. But the clearest trend was the widespread opinion that the justice of the case could not be met without consideration of the person of the offender and the social circumstances surrounding the act. Where life was in danger of being taken away, it seems that people felt driven to give that life some integrity. The words of the petitioners and individual letter writers, both relatively humble and of high education, expressed a belief (if usually implicit) that the criminal justice system was mostly concerned with matters such as the person and the circumstances, rather than with achieving 'just' sentences commensurate with the crime committed.

In this case the person of Hannah Sandles was constructed as having some identifiable essence, communicated in phrases such as 'excellent character', 'honest, hard-working', 'motherly affection' and 'respected'.[42] V.A.C. Gatrell's monumental study of the criminal justice

---

[38] 'The Memorial of the Magistracy, Clergy, Gentry, Bankers, Merchants, Solicitors, Tradesmen, and other Inhabitants of the Town and neighborhood of Lewes', PRO HO 18 252/34.

[39] Letter from Stephen Hale to home secretary, 30 March 1849, PRO HO 18 252/34.

[40] 'Memorial of the undersigned Members of the Society of Friends, commonly called Quakers, residing at Brighton and Lewes', received Home Office 31 March 1849, PRO HO 18 252/34; 'Petition from the Chairman, Vice Chairman and Guardians for Union of Chailey', 28 March 1849, PRO HO 18 252/34.

[41] Letter from J. Parke to home secretary, 24 March 1849, PRO HO 18 252/34.

[42] All from the letter from John M. Cobbett, counsel for prosecution, to secretary of state, 24 March 1849, PRO HO 18 252/34.

system in this period points to the importance of the question of 'character' to both sentencing practice and the appeal process, and Sandles's petition file supports his point.[43] One petitioner thought it essential to tell the secretary of state that he felt 'assured that it was no innate heartlessness that prompted her.'[44] 'Humanitas', the anonymous correspondent who wrote to the *Brighton Herald*, also sought to establish an individual identity for Sandles. James Park, governor of Chailey workhouse wrote of how 'good' she had been while there; the governor of Lewes gaol wrote to say how 'good' she had been in gaol; and the gaol chaplain wrote of Sandles's 'deep anguish ... and her attention to instruction'.[45] Most petitioners believed there to be a basic definable core of personality upon which adverse environmental factors could wreak temporary havoc. The Chailey governors expressed this well:

> We cannot but think therefore that the fact of the approaching discovery of her shame and wretchedness of her condition may have induced her in a moment of bodily and mental depression to commit that dreadful crime which from her generally kind conduct to her other children would seem to have been alien to her nature.[46]

There was another consideration deemed important in determining the justice of the case: the sex of the convicted prisoner. At least in debates over capital punishment, the notion of justice was clearly gendered, which could result in the criminal justice system operating to women's advantage.[47] Of interest in this context are some comments made in the *Brighton Herald* in an article pleading for action to be taken on behalf of Sandles:

> There is something so horrible – so revolting – so opposed to all the feelings of our heart – in the bare idea of a woman being hung that we can scarcely bring ourselves to think that such a thing can be done at our very doors, within a day or two ... The crime of Hannah

---

[43] V.A.C. Gatrell, *The Hanging Tree: Execution and the English People 1770–1868* (Oxford, Oxford University Press, 1994), p. 540.

[44] Letter from Stephen Hale to the home secretary, 30 March 1849, PRO HO18 252/34.

[45] All letters in PRO HO 18 252/34.

[46] Ibid.

[47] Peter King has found a pattern of greater lenience in the punishment of women in the late eighteenth and early nineteenth centuries, Peter King, 'Gender, Crime and Justice in Late- Eighteenth and Early Nineteenth-Century England', in Margaret L. Arnot and Cornelie Osborne (eds), *Gender and Crime in Modern Europe* (London, UCL Press, 1999), pp. 44–74. The author has found that in cases where men were tried by the Central Criminal Court between 1840 and 1880 for murdering young children they were more likely to be convicted than women and more likely to hang once convicted, Margaret L. Arnot, *Gender in Focus: Infanticide in England 1840–1880* (unpublished PhD, University of Essex, 1994), pp. 156–70.

Sandles was a dreadful one; but, to throw aside all hypocritical scruples, there *were* circumstances connected with it which lessen its magnitude, and raise a doubt how far a woman in the situation of Hannah Sandles, turned adrift upon the world with sixpence in her pocket, a long and painful journey of forty miles before her, and three children dependent upon her – no husband, no friends, no helping hand – it becomes a matter of speculation how far desperation may have driven the wretched woman into momentary madness and led her to commit a crime, which, to all appearance, she afterwards bitterly deplores ... we do not believe that is necessary [*sic*] to protect the children of the most wretched, to hang Hannah Sandles. Mothers do not require such a horrible example. Heaven forbid they ever should in this country! Let her be punished – let her be removed from society – but let her life be spared, and let us be spared the dreadful spectacle of beholding a woman deprived of life in such a manner.[48]

The people of Sussex were spared this tragic spectacle. Although the newspapers congratulated the petitioners on their successful campaign to save Sandles's life, Sir George Grey and Justice Parke had already decided the outcome before a single petition file hit the home secretary's desk. By this time a great deal of discretion was left in the hands of the judges and the opinion of the trial judge about capital convictions, communicated to the home secretary, held great sway. The Sandles case is interesting in this respect, for Parke genuinely passed to the home secretary the prerogative of mercy. With a reputation for bullying defendants, his passing of the death sentence in court had undoubtedly carried terror to Sandles's heart:

His Lordship then put on the black cap, and passed sentence of death upon the prisoner, and he at the same time told her not to place any reliance upon the recommendation of the jury, as he was afraid, from the dreadful character of the offence, the law must inevitably take its course. He would, however, transmit the reommendation to the proper quarter, but he again entreated her not to imagine that it would be of any avail in procuring a mitigation of her sentence.[49]

Parke's letter to Grey equivocated: he expressed his view that the facts of the case were indisputable, but also noted that the motives of destitution and shame were evident. He explained to Grey: 'I have in compliance with the promise I made to the Jury, to forward their request [for mercy] to you and leave you to judge whether it is a case, in which it can, with a due regard to Justice, be granted.'[50] On the very day that

---

[48] *Brighton Herald* (31 March 1849), p. 2, col. 6.

[49] *The Times* (24 March 1849), p. 7, col. 4. For a critical view of Parke, see Gatrell, *The Hanging Tree*, p. 504.

[50] Letter from J. Parke to home secretary, 24 March 1849, PRO HO 18 252/34.

this letter was received, Grey summoned Parke for a face-to-face discussion about the case. We can never know what was said, but Grey noted the decision to issue a respite during Her Majesty's pleasure on the same day, several days before the first petitions were received.[51]

Sandles remained in Lewes gaol for two years after her sentence was finally commuted on 8 May 1849. The commutation was to two years' imprisonment with hard labour, followed by transportation for life.[52] During this two years, Hannah had to put up with extremely overcrowded conditions and 'violent and abandoned' female prisoners using 'awfully profane and obscene language.'[53] At one period during her imprisonment all the prisoners experienced 'the failure of health, strongly marked by the loss of constitutional power and depression of Physical energies' and at another, there was a cholera epidemic.[54] Her hard labour consisted of pumping water to supply the female prison, washing prisoners' linen and bedding, mangling and ironing, making and mending prison clothing and cleaning the female prison. She worked between seven and ten hours a day depending on the season.[55] Despite the extra rations provided for prisoners on hard labour, Hannah must have experienced exhaustion under this punishing regime for she was ordered by the visiting justices to be provided with a better diet than the ordinary diet of the prison.[56]

She survived her two years' imprisonment, and on 4 October 1851 left England on the *Anna Maria* bound for Van Diemen's Land, where she arrived on 26 January 1852, together with her two youngest children, Eliza, by then aged twelve years, and William, aged ten. It is very likely that she never again saw her beloved adult daughter, Louisa. In the colony she kept on the right side of the authorities, her record remaining clear of further offences. After several months working on probation as a member of a convict gang she was probably sent out to service. In 1854 her application to marry was granted. On 12 June 1854 she was married in Hobart in the Church of England to Henry Entwhistle, also a convict, thirteen years her junior, bachelor and carter. She received her ticket of leave in October the same year. In April 1856,

[51] File note, ibid.

[52] PRO HO 18 252/34. See also Lewes, gaol and house of correction, 'Visiting justices report', 2 July 1849, East Sussex Record Office, QAP/2/E4/6.

[53] Report of John Sanders, governor of gaol, to justices in general quarter session, 1 January 1849, in East Sussex Record Office, QAP/2/E4/6.

[54] Surgeon's report, 15 October 1849, in ibid.; governor's report, 15 October 1849, in ibid.

[55] Annual return to the secretary of state for the Home Department, Michaelmas, 1849, Schedule B, qq. 25 & 26, in ibid.

[56] Quarterly report of the visiting justices, 9 April 1849, in ibid. For detailed prison diet, see annual return, q. 23, in ibid.

seven years after her conviction, she was recommended for a conditional pardon, which was granted in February 1857.

At some time during the next decade Entwhistle deserted her. At the age of fifty-nine, still in Hobart, where she had obviously chosen to make her home as a freed convict, she married again, probably bigamously, a man called Benjamin Rushbrook, a grocer aged sixty-four. Entwhistle died only in 1879. Her extended encounters with structures of authority had not thwarted her will to survive, and her memory of her tragedy when struggling as a widow probably strengthened her resolve to find men to buffer her against the world. Marriage to a grocer (even though he, like her, could not write) was undoubtedly a step up in the world. Hannah Sandles, sometimes Mansfield, *née* Tingley, later Entwhistle and Rushbrook died from 'apoplexy' in Liverpool Street, Hobart on 3 January 1879 in her seventy-fifth year.[57]

Conclusion

In some respects, Hannah's story reveals a good deal more about infanticide than an aggregated analysis of a large sample of cases ever could. The value of 'microhistory' for crime history has long been recognized by a number of crime historians, although its richest rewards seem to be gleaned most consistently by early-modern European historians.[58] This chapter has barely approached the laudable goals of the genre, partly because Hannah's life and the events were bound up in two different places – London and Sussex – making the rich evocation

---

[57] Biography of life in Australia put together from the following records, all in the Archives Office of Tasmania: conduct record of Hannah Sandles per *Anna Maria* Feb. 1852, CON 41/32; indent for same prisoner, CON 15/7; marriage registration of Henry Entwistle and Hannah Sandals [sic] RGD 520/1854; marriage registration of Hannah Entwistle to Benjamin Rushbrook, RGD 182/1863; death registration of Henry Entwhistle [sic] RGD 36/1879; convict records for Henry Entwistle, CON 33/107; 52/7; convict records for Benjamin Rushbrook, CON 33/53; 14/27; death registration of Hannah Rushbrook, RGD 595/1879. Note that the death of Henry Entwhistle registered in 1879 may have been for a different person, but considering the uncommon name, the small population and the absence of a registration of death for a Henry Entwistle before that date, the probability of a bigamous marriage is high. Other English records: coroner's inquisition and indictment, PRO ASSI 35/289/9.

[58] Carlo Ginzburg, *The Cheese and The Worms* (London, Routledge, 1980); Carlo Ginzburg, 'Microhistory: two or three things that I know about it', *Critical Inquiry*, 20 (1993), 10–35; E. Le Roy Ladurie, *Montaillou* (Harmondsworth, Penguin, 1980); Giovanni Levi, 'On microhistory', in Peter Burke (ed.), *New Perspectives on Historical Writing* (Cambridge, Polity Press, 1991), pp. 93–113. A notable exception in the modern historiography can be found in Gatrell, *The Hanging Tree*, Chapter 17.

of locale a tall order in a short chapter. On the other hand, determination to find out about Hannah has enabled a fuller portrait of a 'lost person'[59] than would ever emerge without 'microhistorical' questions being pursued.

The narrative has also highlighted a number of important themes in the history of infanticide. These include Hannah's poverty and her vulnerability in the face of authority, the strong pressures that she felt to conceal her pregnancy, the mobilization of a stereotypical notion of the murdering mother at the trial in a way that strongly contributed to her conviction, and the ambiguous and contradictory ways in which she was treated as suspect and convict, being first hounded and then almost honoured as an 'honest, hard-working but very poor woman'.[60] As other chapters in this volume clearly demonstrate, the emergence of such themes at the trial of Hannah Sandles in the middle of the nineteenth century must be understood within the context of broader continuities and transitions in the social, cultural, medical and political construction of child murder.

---

[59] E. Muir and R. Ruggiero, *Microhistory and the Lost Peoples of Europe* (Baltimore, Johns Hopkins University Press, 1991).
[60] Letter from John M. Cobbett to home secretary, 27 March 1849, PRO HO 18 252/34.

CHAPTER NINE

Getting away with murder?
Puerperal insanity, infanticide and the defence plea

Hilary Marland

In May 1867, the *Warwick Advertiser* reported to its readers on the 'Sad Death of a Child'.[1] The newspaper account, which included a summary of the inquest proceedings, described how a local woman, Elizabeth Barnwell, had drowned her infant boy in the Warwick and Napton Canal while out walking. The story of the rescue of mother and infant from the water and the unsuccessful attempt to revive the child was recounted with dramatic effect. It was agreed that Elizabeth was attempting to destroy the infant, but the surgeon who had attended at the scene after the drowning explained to the coroner how the mother was at the time suffering 'great mental excitement'. After evidence was presented by various witnesses, it was agreed by coroner, surgeon, newspaper reporter and witnesses to the crime that, at the moment when Elizabeth plunged into the water, she was suffering from mental derangement resulting from her recent childbirth. This was confirmed by the fact that there was no attempt at subterfuge or concealment on her part.

Elizabeth Barnwell neither confessed nor hid her crime, nor tried to disguise it as an accident. Her story was related as one where her state of mind was responsible for an action which was totally out of character; prior to this sad occurrence Elizabeth had been an orderly, respectable woman and loving mother. The plea went undisputed. The coroner expressed particular sympathy for the accused who, he declared, had suffered a good deal of distress before and after the incident. The defence of temporary insanity appears to have been clearly understood by medical, legal and lay participants. Elizabeth's defence, which led to her committal to the local asylum, was her state of mind, taken by all to be sufficient explanation for the murder of her child.[2]

The drowning of Elizabeth's Barnwell's young son occurred during a

---

[1]   *Warwick Advertiser* (11 May 1867), 2.
[2]   Ibid.

period of considerable concern locally and nationally about the ease with which women were concealing their pregnancies and births, and then doing away with their new-born infants. Together with maternal ignorance on infant feeding, the poor supply of cow's milk and the problems of wet-nursing, infanticide contributed to a mortality rate amongst children that, according to *The Lancet* in 1858, 'out Herods Herod'.[3] During the mid-1860s the public outcry about the high incidence of infanticide reached a peak. Infanticide was declared as prevalent in 1864 as at any previous time in history: 'no one who sees the newspapers can have failed to observe almost daily, instances of new-born children found, it may be at a railway station, it may be on a door step, but always under circumstances leading to the belief that the child so found had been destroyed during birth, or immediately afterwards'.[4] 'It has been said of the police, with too much truth', reported Mrs Baines in the *Journal of Social Science* in 1866, 'that they think no more of finding the dead body of a child in the street than of picking up a dead cat or dog'.[5]

Such horrors were summarized in evidence presented to the Royal Commission on Capital Punishment in 1866, and coincided with the furore over baby-farming which also erupted in the late 1860s.[6] Illegitimate children were seen as being most at risk, particularly when born to young servant girls. Moreover, it was recognized that only a very small proportion of murders reached a coroner's inquest or the courtroom.[7] 'But who shall declare the number of infants murdered in secret?', questioned the *Social Science Review*, 'Who shall tell how many cases of infanticide are never brought into the light of day? We fear their name is legion.'[8] There were few expressions of concern about women

---

3   *The Lancet*, 1 (1858), 346, cited in G.K. Behlmer, 'Deadly motherhood: infanticide and medical opinion in mid-Victorian England', *Journal of the History of Medicine*, 34 (1979), 403–27, at 403.

4   Anon., 'Child-murder and its punishment', *Social Science Review*, new series, 2 (1864), 452–9, at 452.

5   Mrs M.A. Baines, 'A few thoughts concerning infanticide', *Journal of Social Science*, 10 (1866), 535–40, at 535.

6   M.L. Arnot, 'Infant death, child care and the State: the baby-farming scandal and the first Infant Life Protection legislation of 1872', *Continuity and Change*, 9 (1994), 271–311; G.K. Behlmer, *Child Abuse and Moral Reform in England, 1870–1908* (Stanford, Stanford University Press, 1982), esp. ch. 2; Lionel Rose, *Massacre of the Innocents: Infanticide in Great Britain 1800–1939* (London, Routledge & Kegan Paul, 1986).

7   A.R. Higginbotham, '"Sin of the age": infanticide and illegitimacy in Victorian London', in K.O. Garrigan (ed.), *Victorian Scandals: Representations of Gender and Class* (Athens, Ohio University Press, 1992), pp. 257–88.

8   'Child-murder and its punishment', 452.

being wrongly accused, but frustration and anger was provoked by acquittals on the most slender of grounds. Women were getting away with murder because of a failure to detect the crime in the first place, but also in the context of events taking place in the courtroom itself.

In 1803, Lord Ellenborough's Act had overturned the harsh Stuart law of 1624, which decreed that the mother of a bastard child was guilty of murder and liable to the death penalty if she had tried to conceal the birth by hiding the body of the infant. The onus fell on the mother to prove that the child had been still-born or had died of natural causes. After 1803 infanticide was dealt with like other murders, with the mother assumed innocent until proven otherwise. If a murder charge failed, as it often did, the jury could return a verdict of 'concealment of birth' with a penalty of up to two years' imprisonment. To prove murder, the prosecution had to establish that the infant was fully born and existing independently of the mother's body at the moment that the crime took place. In 1828, concealment of birth became a separate offence with which any woman could be charged, irrespective of whether or not the child had been still-born. The 1861 Offences against the Person Act further extended the offence to include any person involved in concealing the birth.[9] In practice, no woman was hanged for the murder of her new-born child after 1849, and few were convicted of murder by mid-century, most being acquitted or found guilty of the lesser offence of concealment.

The legal situation was deemed highly unsatisfactory as public revulsion at the number of infanticides mounted during the 1850s and 1860s. The severity of the penalty for infanticide, death by hanging, compared with the mildness of the punishment for concealment was picked out as a particular failing of the law. Meanwhile, the difficulties of establishing separate existence and of proving that murder had taken place, which even the growing body of forensic science failed to address adequately, made juries less likely to find mothers guilty of infanticide. The punishment was also deemed 'unequal': 'it falls on the wretched mother, who may have been more sinned against than sinning, while the equally or more guilty father cannot even be brought under the power of the law'.[10]

The position of medical men in the debate on infanticide was an ambiguous one. They were often at the forefront of the intense public reaction against infanticide, exposing the problem and searching for

---

[9] For more details on legislation, see N. Walker, *Crime and Insanity in England, vol. 1: The Historical Perspective* (Edinburgh, Edinburgh University Press, 1968), ch. 7 'Infanticide'; Rose, *Massacre of the Innocents*, esp. ch. 8.

[10] 'Child-murder and its punishment', 453.

solutions, with *The Lancet* being particularly prominent in this campaign. Doctors were also closely associated after 1864 with the taking-up of the issue by the National Association for the Promotion of Social Science. In 1865 the Harveian Society undertook a survey of the social aspects of new-born child murder, led by Charles Drysdale of the Malthusian League, Ernest Hart, later editor of the *British Medical Journal*, and the former military surgeon and supporter of the Contagious Diseases Acts, J.B. Curgenven. George Greaves, a Manchester obstetrician, William Burke Ryan, author of a socio-medical study of infanticide,[11] and Edwin Lankester, coroner to Central Middlesex, were also closely connected to a campaign which was to enhance the image of the medical profession, dealing as it did with such a critical social issue.[12]

Yet at the same time doctors were accused of offering support to already lenient judges and juries, and showing a lack of responsibility in presenting their medical evidence conscientiously.[13] The role of doctors in the witness stand was to become more significant during the nineteenth century, particularly as the forensic evidence that they were required to present became more complex. As Roger Smith's work has demonstrated, medical evidence was increasingly required on the state of mind of the accused at the time the crime was committed, and the insanity defence was used more frequently.[14] Individual and social problems were described in terms of medical concepts, and questions of 'irresistible impulse' and 'responsibility' played a greater part in legal debates.[15] The vested interests of asylum doctors and alienists, an emerging group who were engaged in establishing asylums and urging lunacy reform, fitted into this, as the courtroom became a place where they could claim status and expertise.

---

[11] W.B. Ryan, *Infanticide: Its Law, Prevalence, Prevention and History* (London, J. Churchill, 1862).

[12] Behlmer, 'Deadly motherhood'; Rose, *Massacre of the Innocents*, esp. chs 5 and 6; C.L. Krueger, 'Literary defenses and medical prosecutions: representing infanticide in nineteenth-century Britain', *Victorian Studies*, 40 (1997), 271-94.

[13] Baines, 'A few thoughts concerning infanticide', 536.

[14] R. Smith, 'The boundary between insanity and criminal responsibility in nineteenth-century England', in Andrew Scull (ed.), *Madhouses, Mad-Doctors, and Madmen: The Social History of Psychiatry in the Victorian Era* (London, Athlone, 1981), pp. 363–84; R. Smith, *Trial by Medicine: Insanity and Responsibility in Victorian Trials* (Edinburgh, Edinburgh University Press, 1981).

[15] J.P. Eigen, '"I answer as a physician": opinion as fact in pre-McNaughtan insanity trials', in M. Clark and C. Crawford (eds.), *Legal Medicine in History* (Cambridge, Cambridge University Press, 1994), pp. 167–99; J.P. Eigen, *Witnessing Insanity. Madness and Mad-Doctors in the English Court* (New Haven and London, Yale University Press, 1995).

A particular form of mental disorder was implicated in connection with infanticide: puerperal insanity, which was 'not a rare disease, and it may take the form of homicidal mania, threatening the life of the child'.[16] Women suffering from this form of insanity were deemed either to be unaware of what they were doing or to have temporarily lost control of their actions. There was little new in the idea of female vulnerability, with child-bearing testing 'both the strength and weakness of femaleness'.[17] Puerperal insanity represented total breakdown. Robert Gooch, one of the earliest and most influential authors on puerperal insanity, pointed to two periods of particular susceptibility in a constant cycle of threat to the delicate female form:

> During that long process, or rather succession of processes, in which the sexual organs of the human female are employed in forming, lodging, expelling, and lastly feeding the offspring, there is no time at which the mind may not become disordered; but there are two periods at which this is chiefly liable to occur, the one soon after delivery when the body is sustaining the effects of labour, the other several months afterwards, when the body is sustaining the effects of nursing.[18]

Infanticide represented the antithesis of female nature, a total rejection of maternal ties, duties and feelings. Puerperal insanity could explain this, with the mother becoming, as a result of her mental disorder, confused, despondent or driven to a murderous fury. As childbirth was deemed ever more dangerous during the nineteenth century, the idea that child-bearing women were likely to fall prey to puerperal insanity became increasingly acceptable.[19] As will be seen later, the plea of puerperal insanity could fit different infanticide scenarios, including that of the unmarried mother who quickly destroyed her new-born infant and the married women, often exhausted by breast-feeding, who murdered an older child. Judges and juries appear to have been convinced by this explanation of the mother's madness and crime, while other witnesses eagerly took it up and added to it.

---

[16] W.A. Guy and D. Ferrier, *Principles of Forensic Medicine*, 7th edn, rev. by W.R. Smith (London, Henry Renshaw, 1895), p. 153.

[17] Smith, *Trial by Medicine*, p. 144.

[18] R. Gooch, *On Some of the Most Important Diseases Peculiar to Women* (London, The New Sydenham Society, 1829), p. 54.

[19] For ideas on female vulnerability in the nineteenth century, see A. Digby, 'Women's biological straitjacket', in S. Mendus and J. Rendell (eds.), *Sexuality and Subordination: Interdisciplinary Studies of Gender in the Nineteenth Century* (London and New York, Routledge, 1989), pp. 192–220; O. Moscucci, *The Science of Woman: Gynaecology and Gender in England 1800–1929* (Cambridge, Cambridge University Press, 1990), esp. chs 1 and 4.

This chapter will examine the use of puerperal insanity as a defence plea in cases of concealment and infanticide. It will describe the emergence and classification of puerperal insanity as a distinct form of mental disorder in the early nineteenth century, and show how this quickly extended into its use as a defence plea, with puerperal insanity contributing to the ongoing medico-legal discussions about insanity and responsibility. Using material drawn from Quarter Sessions papers and the local press for the 1850s and 1860s, the impact of the insanity plea will be explored in the case of the Warwickshire assize sessions. While assize judges were also locked into the debate on how to reduce the shocking level of child murder, once in court they expressed rather different views on culpability, including the role of mental derangement. Finally, the case of Elizabeth Barnwell will be discussed in more detail. Her story unfolds from childbirth through to the crime and inquest, her committal to the asylum and her subsequent recovery and release. The case illustrates the important role of medical and lay witnesses, and demonstrates why, when the insanity plea was applied, it was so difficult to pursue through the courts mothers who murdered their children. In Elizabeth Barnwell's case no attempt at pursuit was made. It will be suggested that the use of puerperal insanity as a defence plea satisfied some of the ambiguities surrounding infanticide. It mediated between the wrath provoked by high levels of child murder and the sympathetic approach to mothers who committed the crime.

Puerperal insanity and infanticide: a close relationship

The phenomenon of erratic and even harmful behaviour on the part of mothers following childbirth had been recognized long before the nineteenth century by midwives, doctors, courts and inquest juries.[20] Following the trial of giving birth, involving intense physical effort, pain and disruption of the delicate reproductive organs, and in many cases increased strain on family resources, mothers were seen as liable to become deranged, neglectful or violent. They came to represent a risk to themselves and other family members, particularly the new-born child. During the early nineteenth century this idea was refined and developed. The labelling of this set of mental conditions as 'puerperal insanity' or 'puerperal mania' led to more refined descriptions of its causality and

---

[20] M. Jackson, *New-Born Child Murder* (Manchester, Manchester University Press, 1996), esp. pp. 120–23.

expected course.[21] At the same time, puerperal insanity began to be used with increasing authority as a defence plea in cases of infanticide or concealment, and this in turn bolstered the position of doctors presenting themselves as experts on the disorder.

In 1820 the London obstetrician, Dr Robert Gooch, produced the first detailed account in English of puerperal insanity.[22] Just two years later, in 1822, a trial taking place at the Old Bailey is cited by Joel Peter Eigen as the first instance of a 'gender-specific psychophysiological debility: puerperal insanity', being used in a defence plea, in the trial of a married woman for infanticide.[23] Rather than 'announce' that the woman was simply deranged, insane or delirious, the medical witness, the surgeon Joseph Dalton, sought to provide a context and explanation for the crime: hereditary predisposition to insanity, the birth itself, and irritation caused by 'the breast extremely full of milk' at weaning. Combining the role of medical and character witness, which many doctors were to take on in such trials, Dalton testified that 'she was an affectionate wife, and had correct parental feelings'.[24]

Puerperal insanity, together with its sister disorders of insanity of pregnancy and lactational insanity, was to become a popular area of enquiry in the decades to follow, with numerous accounts appearing in medical journals, treatises and textbooks. By the mid-nineteenth century, obstetricians and alienists were describing and commenting on the condition, suggesting how to cure it and offering case histories to their readership. General practitioners and surgeons also appear to have been well aware of the liability of women to develop mental disorders after giving birth. It was these men, like Dalton and the surgeon in Elizabeth Barnwell's case, who were frequently called to the witness stand, as well

---

[21] There are few studies to date of puerperal insanity, but see N.M. Theriot, 'Diagnosing unnatural motherhood: nineteenth-century physicians and "puerperal insanity"', *American Studies*, 26 (1990), 69–88; S. Day, 'Puerperal insanity: the historical sociology of a disease' (DPhil thesis, University of Cambridge, 1985); I. Loudon, 'Puerperal insanity in the 19th century', *Journal of the Royal Society of Medicine*, 81 (Feb. 1988), 76–9; H. Marland, '"Destined to a perfect recovery": the confinement of puerperal insanity in the nineteenth century', in J. Melling and B. Forsythe (eds), *Insanity, Institutions and Society, 1800–1914* (London and New York, Routledge, 1999), pp. 137–56; H. Marland, 'At home with puerperal mania: the domestic treatment of the insanity of childbirth in the nineteenth century', in P. Bartlett and D. Wright (eds), *Outside the Walls of the Asylum: The History of Care in the Community 1750–2000* (London and New Brunswick, NJ, Athlone, 1999), pp. 45–65.

[22] R. Gooch, *Observations on Puerperal Insanity* (London, 1820), extracted from 6th vol. of medical transactions, Royal College of Physicians (read at the College, 16 Dec. 1819).

[23] Eigen, *Witnessing Insanity*, p. 142.

[24] Ibid. This case is taken from the *Old Bailey Sessions Papers* (1822), case 811, 5th session, 331.

as eminent forensic experts. During the nineteenth century, birth was described increasingly as dangerous and pathological rather than normal and natural.[25] All women, the obstetrician Robert Lee declared in the opening to his *Lectures on the Theory and Practice of Midwifery*, were 'exposed to great suffering and danger during pregnancy and childbirth'.[26] Not surprisingly, alongside the dangers of infection and haemorrhaging, prolapse and diseases of the breasts, mental distress following childbirth was accepted as a further and far from rare threat to new mothers.[27] As descriptions and discussion of puerperal insanity passed from obstetric and psychological literature into forensic texts, it became a common and often successful defence strategy in infanticide and concealment trials during the mid-nineteenth century.[28]

Descriptions of puerperal insanity abound with stories of unseemly, disruptive behaviour, and violence to self, husband, attendants and particularly the new-born infant, in normally peaceful and caring women. Robert Gooch referred to the rumbustious behaviour which would accompany the disorder: 'the patient swears, bellows, recites poetry, talks bawdry, and kicks up such a row that there is the devil to play in the house'.[29] In 1848 James Reid, physician to the General Lying-in Hospital in London, an author on puerperal insanity who was much cited in forensic texts, described how 'the mother is urged on by some unaccountable impulse to commit violence on herself or on her offspring', while at the same time being 'impressed with horror and aversion at the crime'.[30]

> The infant is usually the object ... in puerperal insanity; an impulse to destroy, haunts the mind continually, and struggles with maternal tenderness, which as strongly checks the act. The sufferer, in some

---

[25] See Digby, 'Women's biological straitjacket'.

[26] R. Lee, *Lectures on the Theory and Practice of Midwifery* (London, Longman, Brown, Green, and Longmans, 1844), p. 1.

[27] The proportion of female asylum admissions attributed to puerperal insanity varied greatly. In 1858 Bucknill and Tuke gave a range of 5 to 25 per cent for insanity of pregnancy, childbirth and lactation together. In 1872 James Young Simpson suggested that about 10 per cent of all females in lunatic asylums were suffering from puerperal insanity. J.C. Bucknill and D.H. Tuke, *A Manual of Psychological Medicine* (London, J. & A. Churchill, 1858), pp. 236–7; J.Y. Simpson, *Clinical Lectures on the Diseases of Women* (Edinburgh, Adam and Charles Black, 1872), p. 556.

[28] See Eigen, *Witnessing Insanity*; Smith, *Trial by Medicine*, esp. ch. 7; Walker, *Crime and Insanity in England*, vol. 1, ch. 7 'Infanticide'; Day, 'Puerperal insanity'.

[29] *A Practical Compendium of Midwifery; Being the Course of Lectures on Midwifery, and on the Diseases of Women and Infants, Delivered at St. Bartholomew's Hospital by the Late Robert Gooch, M.D.*, ed. G. Skinner (London, Longman, Rees, Orme, Brown, and Green, 1831), p. 290.

[30] James Reid, 'On the causes, symptoms, and treatment of puerperal insanity', *Journal of Psychological Medicine*, 1 (1848), 128–51, 284–94, at 135.

cases, implores that the infant may be removed from her, lest she
should altogether lose her self-control, and is heard praying to
Heaven to prevent her from yielding to the temptation.[31]

All authors on puerperal mania described the potential to harm on the
part of mothers, though some, like Fleetwood Churchill, who remarked
that the mother became 'forgetful of her child', played this down.[32] They
warned those dealing with such cases to remove all dangerous items
down to spoons, bed sheets and handkerchiefs, and certainly all sharp
objects: 'and the patient should never be left for a moment alone, or
especially with her infant'.[33]

The language of misrule and danger changed little over the decades.
As late as the 1880s the eminent psychiatrist, Thomas Clouston, was
still describing how childbirth,

> One of the most joyous times of life is made full of fearful anxiety,
> and the strongest affection on earth is then often suddenly converted
> by disease into an antipathy: for the mother not only 'forgets her
> suckling child', but often becomes dangerous to its life.[34]

Puerperal insanity was a slippery condition to define, and great
uncertainly existed as to its cause, duration and impact.[35] Doctors seem
to have been prepared to agree that puerperal insanity had a strong
association with childbirth, and that it was a distinct form of mental
disorder. There was also general consensus about its sub-division into
two categories: melancholia, a form of intense misery which was likely
to result in permanent insanity and a lapse into drollery or dementia;
and mania, distinguished by overexcited, disruptive and deviant
behaviour, but usually curable within a few months.[36] Both could lead
to infanticide, the former through hopelessness and neglect, the latter
through a marked, though often short-lived, loss of reason.

It was mania which appeared most frequently in infanticide cases
with its 'temporary' nature and sudden onset, typified by the struggle
that mothers felt, referred to by Reid above, between not wanting to
harm their infants and an inability to prevent themselves from doing so.
The alienist and author on medical jurisprudence, James Cowles
Prichard, cited such a case. In 1824 the mother of two children in

---

[31] Ibid., p. 135.
[32] Fleetwood Churchill, *On the Diseases of Women; Including those of Pregnancy and Childbed*, 4th edn (Dublin, Fannin and Co., 1857), p. 739.
[33] Ibid., p. 424.
[34] T.S. Clouston, *Clinical Lectures on Mental Diseases* (London, J. & A. Churchill, 1887), p. 502.
[35] See Marland, 'At home with puerperal mania', also for a discussion of claims to expertise by competing medical groups.
[36] See, for this optimistic approach, Marland, '"Destined to a perfect recovery"'.

humble circumstances applied to the Hitchin Dispensary 'in consequence of the most miserable feelings of gloom and despondency, accompanied by a strong, and, according to her account, an almost irresistible propensity, or temptation, as she termed it, to destroy her infant'. The feeling came on a month after the birth, and she begged to be 'constantly watched'. She recovered but, when she had another child a few years later, again she 'was assailed by the propensity to destroy it'. During the worst phase of the illness 'she is perfectly aware of the atrocity of the act to which she is so powerfully impelled, and prays fervently to be enabled to withstand so great a temptation'. She retained a great affection for the child, at the same time even identifying the instrument that she would use to destroy it, fearing to handle a knife even at mealtimes.[37]

Aside from agreement on the broad categories, for the rest puerperal insanity was an untidy, elusive disorder. Despite being pursued by many 'experts' in the fields of psychiatry and obstetrics, no firm conclusions could be reached, regarding its onset, preconditions, causes, prevalence, precise timing or duration, where it should be treated (at home or in the asylum), how it should be treated, if it was more likely to affect first-time mothers or women who had borne many children, the chances of re-occurrence, and whether it would prevail most amongst undernourished, mistreated and deserted poor women or amongst well-do-do, feebly-constituted ladies for whom childbirth was considered a massive physical and mental shock.[38] The latter were considered less likely to kill their children, as they would not be left unattended particularly if the illness was detected, and the child would be protected from harm by domestic servants and nurses. It was reported time and again how women suffering from puerperal mania had taken the opportunity to murder the infant during moments of carelessness. The new-born, sometimes against the advice of a doctor who had warned of such an outcome, had been left alone with the mother, in some cases for just a few minutes.

Grave concerns were expressed, particularly given the looseness of the definition of puerperal insanity, that the insanity plea would be made indiscriminately, for example, on behalf of women murdering older

---

[37] J.C. Prichard, *On the Different Forms of Insanity in Relation to Jurisprudence, Designed for the Use of Persons concerned in Legal Questions Regarding Unsoundness of Mind* (London, Hippolyte Baillière, 1842), pp. 123–4. This case was also cited in Isaac Ray, *A Treatise on the Medical Jurisprudence of Insanity*, 4th edn (Boston, Little, Brown and Company, 1860), pp. 235–6.

[38] See, for an example of the struggle to provide an organic explanation for the condition, F.W. Mackenzie, 'On the pathology and treatment of puerperal insanity: especially in reference to its relation with anaemia', *London Journal of Medicine*, 3 (1851), 504–21.

children long after they had given birth, or even that the disorder would be related to a previous confinement. In 1854 John Charles Bucknill, superintendent of the Devon County Lunatic Asylum and author on the relationship between crime and insanity, referred to a woman currently under his care after making a recent attempt on her child's life, who had had an attack of puerperal mania twenty-two years previously. Though he attributed the exciting cause of the act to an argument with her aunt and to ill-treatment by her husband, her much earlier bout of mania was considered to have a bearing on her crime.[39]

Puerperal insanity, responsibility and medical evidence

Confidence in puerperal insanity and its use as a defence was not on the whole to be swayed by anxieties about the elasticity of its definition. By the mid-nineteenth century Alfred Swaine Taylor, in his *Principles and Practice of Medical Jurisprudence*, was describing cases distinguished from 'deliberate child-murder by there being no motive, no attempt at concealment, nor any denial of the crime on detection. Several trials involving a question of puerperal mania have been decided, generally in favour of the insanity, within the last few years.'[40] Citing as his authorities Samuel Ashwell, a well-known author on the diseases of women,[41] and the alienist, George Man Burrows,[42] Taylor described the 'sudden impulse' prompting women to commit the act of murder, 'so that the legal test of responsibility cannot be applied to such cases'.[43] He went on to cite the case of Mrs Ryder, tried in 1856:

> There was an entire absence of motive in this as in most other cases of a similar kind. The mother was much attached to the child, and had been playing with it on the morning of its death. She destroyed the child by placing it in a pan of water in her bedroom. The medical evidence proved that she had been delivered about a fortnight previously – that she *had had an attack of fever*, and that she had *probably* committed this act while in a state of *delirium*. She was acquitted on the ground of insanity ... it was *evidently* a case in

---

[39] J.C. Bucknill, *Unsoundness of Mind in Relation to Criminal Acts* (London, Samuel Highley, 1854), pp. 91–2.

[40] A.S. Taylor, *The Principles and Practice of Medical Jurisprudence*, 8th edn (London, John Churchill, 1865), p. 1122.

[41] S. Ashwell, *A Practical Treatise on the Diseases Peculiar to Women, Illustrated by Cases, Derived from Hospital and Private Practice* (London, Samuel Highley, 1845).

[42] G.M. Burrows, *Commentaries on the Causes, Forms, Symptoms, and Treatment, Moral and Medical, of Insanity* (London, Thomas and George Underwood, 1828), Commentary VI, 'Puerperal insanity'.

[43] Taylor, *Medical Jurisprudence*, p. 1122.

which the insanity was only *temporary*, and the prisoner might be restored to her friends on a representation being made in the proper quarter.[44]

This case combines a very loose description of the disorder with a certainty about its attribution. This was to typify the use of the insanity plea in infanticide trials. Emphasis on the lack of subterfuge or denial also became a defining characteristic of the disorder as did, for married women at least, comments on the mother's attachment to the child and lack of a motive. They were consistently referred to as being 'good mothers'. In the case of Mrs Ryder, it is possible that the delirium associated with puerperal fever was being confused with puerperal mania. It is not at all clear which condition she was suffering from.[45]

This elasticity of definition stands in sharp contrast to the increasing precision employed in seeking to establish criteria to prove when and how the deaths of new-born infants had occurred and whether they had been born alive, questions which occupied some forty pages in Alfred Swaine Taylor's textbook, for example. Proof of whether the child had breathed independently of the mother, whether strangulation was accidental (caused by the umbilical cord being wrapped around the child's neck) or deliberate, whether bruising had been purposely inflicted or had resulted from the birth, or whether the child had died while a part of its body was still undelivered was difficult, if not impossible, to ascertain. 'Proof' of the existence of insanity, meanwhile, was readily accepted often on the slimmest of evidence. Reading through accounts of trials it is possible to detect a palpable sigh of relief amongst judges, juries and witnesses if the woman could be declared insane. It relieved the medical witness from the burden of working out exactly how the infant had died, as the woman was likely to be acquitted in any case.

In some cases, however, witnesses, juries and judges could be left in little doubt that a murder had taken place, but were still prepared to consider the role of insanity. A trial which was well-publicized by both the lay and medical press took place at the Essex Lent assizes in 1848, when a thirty-seven-year-old married woman Martha Prior was tried for the murder of her infant by almost decapitating the baby with a razor.[46] *The Lancet* reported that all the evidence went to show the existence, at

---

[44] Ibid.[my emphasis]

[45] See, for the potential difficulties of separating out the delirium of puerperal fever from puerperal insanity, and the recording of puerperal insanity as a cause of death, Irvine Loudon, *Death in Childbirth: An International Study of Maternal Care and Maternal Mortality 1800–1950* (Oxford, Clarendon, 1992), pp. 143–6.

[46] 'Chelmsford – Friday, March 10. Charge of Murder – Acquittal on the Ground of Puerperal Insanity', *Journal of Psychological Medicine*, 1 (1848), 478–83; *The Lancet*, 1 (1848), 318–19.

the time of the murder, of puerperal mania, which came on a few days after delivery. One of Prior's neighbours, Mary Portway, when giving evidence, described the prisoner's restlessness, pains, discomfort and distracted behaviour. Prior told Portway that 'she was going to die, and wished me to tell her sister to be a friend to her children; she said that her breasts were very bad ... She seemed to me not quite right in her mind; she was flushed in her face'.[47] Prior persisted in telling Portway 'that she was going to die; she said I might shoot her, or get some one else; that she was going to hell, and might as well go at once'. When she saw her again later the same week, Portway described, in remarkably muted tones which seem to typify many trial testimonies, how 'the child lay by her with its throat cut. I said, "Mrs Prior, what have you been doing?" She said, "What I meant to do, and you may serve me the same". I removed the child to the cradle; I thought her mind was not as it should be.' Mary Portway also stated that the prisoner was a peaceable, well-conducted woman. No professional man, claimed The Lancet, summing up the case, would have had a moment's doubt concerning the existence of insanity.[48]

Mr Thomas Bell, the surgeon who delivered her and then prescribed medicines to treat her pains and disorders, declared Prior to be labouring under puerperal mania. Bell complained that he had not been sent for earlier, when Mary Prior became prostrated following heavy bleeding. Yet he had cautioned her friends and relatives against trusting her with her child, and wanted a nurse to be procured. 'I ordered that the child should not be taken to her, and she should not be left alone; her countenance was haggard and vacant; there was a great tendency to irritation of the body'.[49] Bell's instructions were clearly not observed, and Prior obtained the murder weapon, a razor, under the pretext of wanting to cut her nails. Prior was declared conscious of what she was doing, but unable to control her own actions.[50] She was reportedly calm and collected after she had destroyed the child, claiming it was what she intended to do all along.[51] In this case credence was given to the testimony of a neighbour, which was not unusual. Nor was

---

[47] The breasts often bore the brunt of blame in infanticide trials as the precipitating cause of the insanity, with medical witnesses claiming the mother to be in a state of temporary insanity because of an excessive flow of milk, or because the milk was suppressed, or simply because the mother had 'bad breasts'. In many cases the mother's continued efforts to breast-feed her child when she herself was debilitated and starving were seen as triggering mental breakdown.

[48] The Lancet, 1 (1848), p. 318.

[49] Ibid.

[50] Ibid., p. 319.

[51] 'Chelmsford – Charge of Murder', p. 481.

Portway's confidence in declaring that Prior's 'mind was not as it should be'. Signs of insanity included 'irritation of the body' and 'prostration'. Prior had also bled heavily, she looked vacant, and made no attempt to hide or deny what she had done. Bell's evidence perhaps also shows signs of an eagerness to escape any accusation of negligence or lack of care on his part.

Many infanticide trials did not depend upon the evidence of a forensic expert or medical man experienced in treating insanity, but on the opinion of a surgeon or general practitioner and a collection of witnesses – neighbours, friends and passers-by – all of whom found it appropriate to comment on the woman's state of mind and felt equipped to testify to the existence of insanity. Medical witnesses were often giving evidence on a one-off basis.[52] They might have come across a couple of similar cases during their practices, but could not claim expertise in treating mental disorders or in obstetrics. Yet they had no qualms about firmly ascribing child murder to puerperal insanity.

Other trials involved well-known experts, specialists in mental disorder and asylum superintendents, who were brought in to examine the accused and pronounce on the case, without prior knowledge of the defendant's medical history or circumstances. This led to further complications. Puerperal insanity was deemed a temporary condition, which could mean that the accused woman was recovered by the time she reached the courtroom, or even before she had been examined by the doctor. The suggestion of 'temporary insanity' meant that it was impossible to be sure of the mental state of the accused at the actual moment of the crime and whether she was 'responsible' for her actions, and this could lead to unpredictable judgements. Doctors, as well as judges, were not always convinced, but they do seem to have erred on the side of accepting the insanity plea. Trial proceedings, judges' addresses to the jury and their verdicts suggest the willingness of judges and jurors alike to support the idea that the effects of giving birth left women in a state of mental excitement, which was sufficient to explain their crime.

In summing up the Prior case, however, Lord Chief Justice Denman, in the words of *The Lancet*, threw unjust imputations upon the reputation and professional ability of the surgeon Mr Bell and doubt on the insanity plea. Denman declared Bell's opinion 'rashly formed. How could one human being speculate upon the mind of another ... I don't understand how any man, with reasoning powers and scientific acquirements, can say that she acts upon a sudden impulse, when there

---

[52] See Eigen, *Witnessing Insanity*, Appendix 2, 'Medical witnesses who testified at the Old Bailey about the mental condition of the accused, 1760–1843', pp. 195–205.

is nothing that shows alienation of mind, and a great deal that shows a deliberate purpose'.[53] Yet the jury, responding as Denman predicted and acting 'upon the testimony of the medical gentleman', returned a verdict of 'not guilty' on the grounds of insanity. Denman concluded by remarking that 'such opinions were too often given by scientific men upon too slight foundation for the safety of the public'.[54] However, medical men too could be left in considerable doubt in such cases, even those as experienced as John Charles Bucknill in treating insanity and acting as a medical witness. He expressed concern about the Prior trial, finding Denman's comments not unreasonable and objecting to the loose usage of the term 'uncontrollable impulse', which was, he argued, the root cause of every crime.[55]

The Warwickshire evidence

In Warwickshire, as elsewhere, pleas based on puerperal insanity featured in cases involving the epitome of the infanticidal woman: the young domestic servant, accused of concealing her pregnancy and destroying the infant at birth or soon after. Between 1860 and 1865, twenty-one women were tried for infanticide or concealment in Warwickshire, sixteen of whom were domestic servants.[56] The idea of the act of either abandonment or infanticide taking place while the woman was in a frenzy of pain and shock was given credence by descriptions of a transient form of puerperal mania, which could take place at the moment of birth itself.[57] This phenomenon proved particularly useful in explaining the actions of frightened young women giving birth alone, as it was ostensibly linked to first confinements. Such women often declared ignorance of the fact that they were pregnant at all, or claimed that they did not realize that they had given birth or that

[53] *The Lancet* reminded its readership that Judge Denman was the son of the esteemed obstetrician Thomas Denman who, standing in direct opposition to his famous father, when writing on insanity had given his opinion that the behaviour of the patient varied greatly: 'even in very bad cases there are lucid intervals, or a reasonableness on certain subjects, where the disorder would not be suspected', *The Lancet*, 1 (1848), p. 319.

[54] 'Chelmsford – Charge of Murder', p. 480.

[55] Bucknill, *Unsoundness of Mind*, pp. 86–7, 101. In this same account, Bucknill was also linking a recent case of child murder to a bout of insanity some 22 years previously.

[56] *Warwick Advertiser*, (21 October 1865).

[57] In 1856 William Tyler Smith explained how this would occur in first labours or if the head of the child was unusually large: at the point of birth women could 'lose their self-consciousness, or self-control, and commit, if allowed, extravagant acts, in these brief intervals of insanity': W. Tyler Smith, 'Puerperal mania', Lecture XXXIX: 'Lectures on the theory and practice of obstetrics', *The Lancet*, 2 (1856), 423–5, at 423.

the baby had come too soon. The single mother was also more likely to conceal her birth, but often in a very flimsy, distracted way, hiding the child under the bed, in a box or in piles of clothes, or abandoning it in the privy, the scene of many Warwickshire births.[58]

The insanity plea was also used in cases, which tended to feature rather less in the national debate, where the accused was a married women, often with older children. In these cases the crime would take place usually when the child was several weeks or even several months old. The stakes were higher, as these were clear cases of infanticide. It was generally agreed that the onset of puerperal insanity was within the six-week 'puerperal' period, and most likely to occur between a few days and two weeks after delivery, but it could also manifest itself much later, when it blurred into lactational insanity. The two periods of intense danger for women, when they were most liable to become mentally disturbed, had been defined by Robert Gooch and others as shortly after birth and then again several months later, when their health had been broken by continued efforts to breast-feed and when they themselves were in a weakened state. The risks of lactational insanity were deemed greater for married women, as they were more likely than single mothers to nurse their infants. These women were usually described as being devoted mothers who were fond of their children.

A plea of mental derangement was more often than not tied in with a 'poverty defence'. The women were penniless, malnourished, had borne too many children in quick succession, were sometimes physically disabled or particularly sickly, or were victims of bad husbands who maltreated them or did not provide properly for their families. In other cases, like that of Elizabeth Barnwell, the circumstances were not regarded as particularly difficult, and the women were described as simply acting out of character and as being afflicted with a temporary loss of reason. The mothers did away with their children quickly and cleverly, while they had been carelessly left alone. Often they had begged not to be left unguarded, having felt a compelling urge to destroy their infants. Again, hardly any attempt was made to hide the crime, which was soon discovered by the neighbours or family.

In 1865, *The Lancet* published a brief report on the Warwickshire Quarter Sessions, pointing to the great increase in infanticide in the

---

[58] The phenomenon of birth into excrement also featured in forensic textbooks: see, for example, J.L. Casper, *Handbook of Forensic Medicine* (London, New Syndenham Society, 1864), which also gave credence to the idea that the parturient could be completely ignorant of the act of delivery, and even married women could feel the urgent need to pass faeces with the infant consequently being born into excrement and suffocated.

locality, and to the general reluctance of judges to condemn and juries to convict.[59] The local newspaper, summarising the recent spring assizes in March of that year, described how Baron Martin had endeavoured to impress upon the grand jury the necessity of altering the law respecting infanticide.[60] The points he made fitted with national concerns during the 1860s. Martin pointed out that the number of cases reaching court bore little relation to the crime. He also related the number of infanticides to the demographic imbalance between males and females, resulting in there being more unattached young women to be seduced, and to the increased ferocity of the reaction to unchaste women. However, more than anything else he blamed deficiencies in the law for the current increase in infanticides. Juries could not bring themselves to convict mothers for murdering their children; the penalty was too heavy. If women were convicted, it was on the trivial charge of concealment. Baron Martin understood that most of the women charged were servants, whose livelihood 'depends upon their concealing the evidence of their shame', and that greater moral guilt attached to the seducer, 'who turns away and leaves her to her fate and the child to her mercy'. Yet he still demanded proper punishment to 'terrify', while not being too severe to inflict.[61] In October 1865, the case was taken up by the local MP, Sir Robert Hamilton, who argued for a separation of the crime of concealment from infanticide, for more 'usable' penalties for infanticide, and for single women to be enabled to obtain support through the law prior to their confinement.[62]

While the view that most infanticides never reached court was likely to have been correct, the perception of the high rate of acquittals – at least in the 1850s – was not borne out by the Warwickshire evidence. Out of eight cases of infanticide recorded in the calendars of prisoners for Warwickshire between 1839 and 1857, only a cluster of three appearing together in court in the summer of 1856 were acquitted.[63] This cluster sparked a burst of interest in the local press. In one case a verdict of accidental poisoning was reached. Regarding the other two cases, in his opening remarks Mr Justice Cresswell was already advising that the prisoners should be acquitted, on the ground that the acts resulting in the death of their infants were not 'wilful'.[64] The case which attracted most attention was that of an eighteen-year-old domestic

[59] *The Lancet*, 2 (1865), 471.
[60] *Warwick Advertiser* (11 March 1865).
[61] Ibid.
[62] Ibid., (21 October 1865).
[63] Warwick County Record Office (WCRO), County of Warwick, Calendar, Summer Assizes, 1856. QS 26/1/61.
[64] *Warwick Advertiser* (2 August 1856).

servant, Sarah Harris, described as being deranged at the time that the crime took place.

Sarah Harris had given birth at her place of work in Birmingham while her mistress was also in the house, apparently unaware of what was going on. After a detailed account of the movements of the accused around the house and her complaints of feeling 'unwell', and her even being tended by her employer, she gave birth alone. Harris then suffocated the baby in her skirt before hiding him under the bed. Her employer's suspicions were aroused by strange noises 'like cats', and she raised the alarm and called a midwife, Mary Durnell, to the house. Durnell testified that Harris was 'in a wild state like a mad person', and she had great difficulty keeping her in bed, 'she was so frantic'. For a long time, she was unable to utter a sound but when she did speak it was to declare 'Oh dear, I have murdered the baby'. The midwife found the baby under the bed wrapped in a black skirt, and an examination confirmed that Harris had recently been delivered. The defence lawyer declared that the prisoner could not be held responsible for what had occurred during her 'furious delirium', and the forensic examination could not draw any firm conclusions. The child had suffocated and had lacerations around the mouth, but these, it was pointed out, could have occurred during delivery. Justice Cresswell in his pre-trial remarks had already expressed the same view and Sarah Harris was duly acquitted.[65]

In terms of outcome as well as interest the 1856 acquittals appear to have represented a blip rather than a pattern. The assize records for Warwickshire are incomplete, and no calendars have survived for the years between 1859 to 1869. An attempt has been made to bridge this unfortunate gap by reading the reports of assize proceedings in the local press, but it is likely that many cases went unrecorded, while in others scant information is given.[66] Apart from the three women acquitted at the summer assizes of 1856, between 1839 and 1857 the five other infanticides reaching court were found guilty of murder, manslaughter or concealment and sent to prison for terms of up to two years' hard labour.[67] For the eleven women charged with the lesser crime of concealment between 1850 and 1855, four were acquitted. The rest received custodial sentences, ranging from three days' gaol to six months' hard labour.[68]

---

[65] Ibid.

[66] Up until 1859, when it is possible to compare the calendar records with newspaper reports, it becomes evident that some cases are covered only briefly by the press, others not at all. Crimes of property and other violent crimes attracted more avid reporting.

[67] WCRO, Calendar of prisoners, 1839-57, QS 26/1/3-63.

[68] Ibid., QS 26/1/39-58.

As the momentum of the campaign to tackle infanticide grew locally and nationally during the 1860s, it attracted more detailed press coverage. The year 1865 saw another cluster of local cases, and the interest these caused was further fuelled by accounts of more distant infanticides, in London or even the continent.[69] The case of Esther Lack, a London woman who had murdered her three children, sparked a cynical response in the *Warwick Advertiser* in September 1865, under the caption 'Insanity and crime'.[70] Lack had cut her children's throats at night while her husband was working. Lack claimed that she feared that they would die of starvation. Her crime was attributed 'to debility of constitution, caused by the delivery of three infants at a birth some seven or eight years ago'. Since then her eyesight and strength had failed her. The *Warwick Advertiser* concluded its report by stating that the case 'would probably be resolved by psychologists into an abnormal action of the brain'.[71]

The borderline between madness and a range of other mental symptoms suggested as manifesting themselves around the time of childbirth was shaky. These symptoms included distress, nervous terror, shock, anguish caused by pain, despair and euphoria, all reported in infanticide cases. The plea of mental disorder extended to cases where the accused was clearly not insane but was very upset, behaving oddly, facing the distress of destitution, or was feeble-minded.[72] Some of the ways mental distress could influence the outcome of a trial were summed up by Baron Martin in 1865:

> Human nature revolts against pronouncing the doom of death against some ruined creature seduced into vice, perhaps by some one far more guilty than herself, and then hurried into crime at the last moment by the bewildering, maddening influences of agony, shame, and terror.[73]

One of the cluster of three prisoners appearing in court in the summer assizes of 1865 accused of concealment or attempted murder, was seventeen-year-old Caroline Russell. She was charged with attempting to

---

[69] For literary representations of infanticide, see Krueger, 'Literary defenses and medical prosecutions', and, more generally, for explanations of female crime, L. Zedner, *Women, Crime, and Custody in Victorian England* (Oxford, Oxford University Press, 1991), ch. 2.

[70] *Warwick Advertiser* (2 September 1865).

[71] Ibid.

[72] Roger Smith cites cases of insanity being substituted for poverty as a plea. He also cites the case of Emma Lewis, sent to Bethlem in 1854 after murdering her new-born baby. No medical evidence was produced at the trial, only an account of how the bastard child had resulted from a cruel seduction. Smith, *Trial by Medicine*, pp. 148–50.

[73] *Warwick Advertiser* (11 March 1865).

strangle her illegitimate female child. She gave birth in secret at the home of her employer. Long after the suspicions of another servant had been aroused, the cries and blood on the floor were correctly interpreted and a doctor called. Dr Tibbets found the child with an apron string around its neck, tied tightly, laid in a box in Russell's room. The child was successfully revived. It was concluded that Russell had tied the child up but had probably not intended to take its life. She was discharged, her youthfulness and erratic behaviour apparently influencing the jury in reaching their verdict.[74]

An absence of forensic clarity could also be seen in cases where the woman's state of mind was in doubt, making it extremely difficult to obtain a conviction. In May 1860 Catherine Malins was brought before the Warwickshire coroner so weak and exhausted from the birth of her child that she was considered unable to participate in the proceedings.[75] Malins, a young woman who lodged with Mr and Mrs Blackwell in Warwick, claimed that she had unwittingly delivered the child in a privy. The surgeon who was summoned to the scene believed that the infant had not been still-born but had died shortly after being delivered. It was unclear whether the child had been born in the privy or had been put there subsequently by Malins. Malins denied knowing that she was pregnant, and described how the child had 'cried and cried while it was falling'. The case, it was concluded, could not be brought to trial, there being insufficient evidence to show how the infant had died.[76]

Ignorance and feeble-mindedness were also grounds for acquittal or the imposition of a lighter sentence. In a much earlier case, in 1850 a Warwick woman, Bridget Tameney, was brought to court accused of poisoning her child with sulphate of copper while she was recovering from her delivery in the lying-in ward of the local workhouse. Tameney claimed that she had been informed by a navvy's wife that the substance would benefit the child. The surgeon observed that the mother was kind and affectionate to her other child but 'rather below the standard of intellect': not insane, but easily led. A verdict of manslaughter was returned with a six-month prison sentence. In this case, Tameney appears to have been punished as much for her lack of care, and for not informing the workhouse surgeon of her action, as for accidentally taking the child's life.[77]

---

[74] Ibid., (15 July 1865).
[75] Ibid., (26 May 1860).
[76] Ibid., (28 April, 12 May and 26 May 1860).
[77] Ibid., (6 April 1850).

The case of Elizabeth Barnwell

Of the trials reported in Warwickshire during the 1850s and 1860s, it was those involving mental derangement that stand out. It was the cases of the young frenzied servant Sarah Harris in 1856 and then that of Elizabeth Barnwell in 1867, married and respectable but suffering from temporary insanity, that offered a complete narrative of the events leading up to the crime and an explanation for what had taken place. In the case of Sarah Harris, the forensic evidence did not prove whether the child had died during or after delivery, whereas for Elizabeth Barnwell there was little doubt how the child had met its end. In both cases the insanity plea was eagerly embraced. That the two women were deemed insane seems also to have satisfied the need for retribution, the women being seen to have suffered greatly – particularly Elizabeth Barnwell, who was to reflect on her dreadful act during her four-month long incarceration in the local asylum.

In June 1867, Elizabeth Barnwell was admitted to the Warwick County Lunatic Asylum, recorded as suffering from 'mania, puerperal'. On her order for admission, Thomas William Bullock, surgeon of Warwick, stated 'I have attended her for a month past when her child was drowned in the canal. She has since that time told me she would commit suicide ... she maintains at this time that she shall do away with herself if someone does not prevent her'. Her friends and neighbours testified that she had been seen with a rope trying to hang herself; she had a deep red mark around her neck from the attempt. Elizabeth (or Eliza, as she seems to have been known) had also asked for poison. She was said to walk about the house wringing her hands and crying.[78]

Eliza's route to the asylum had begun some six weeks previously with the opening of the inquest into the death of her child.[79] The first witness to be called, John Berry, a boatman, reported that while working on the canal he saw Eliza Barnwell out walking. Shortly afterwards, he heard a splash and on running to the spot saw her struggling in the water. He managed to pull her out, by putting a boat hook through her clothes. Once out of the canal Eliza said, 'Oh my baby is in the water. I was going for a walk up to Mrs Seywell [a friend], for I have been very bad'. John Berry stated that after she had said this Eliza Barnwell appeared not to know what she was doing. The witness rushed to the water, saw blood on the surface, and fished the baby out with a net. The infant bled at the nose, but was still alive. Frantic efforts were made to revive the

---

[78]   WCRO, Warwick County Lunatic Asylum, CR 1664/280. Orders for admission, 1867, no. 1504: order for admission of Elizabeth Barnwell.

[79]   *Warwick Advertiser* (11 May 1867).

infant: he was rubbed vigorously, given brandy, wrapped in a blanket and rushed to the nearest doctor, but was dead on arrival.

Mr Bullock, the surgeon, was called to see the child, and concluded that the body revealed no signs of violence except for a small bruise to the head. He then turned to the mother:

> She was very ill, with cold extremities and suffering under great mental excitement. I have attended her ever since. She is now better but still in a low nervous state. She is quite unable to attend here to-day. In my opinion the child died from suffocation by drowning. The child was little over a month old. I had not attended her [EB] previously. She is better to-day than she was yesterday. She sits up in bed and talks very wildly about the child and asks for it. She was attended by a midwife, and a nurse was with her for a fortnight.

Eliza's husband, a carpenter, added in his evidence that she had seemed to be 'going on well since her confinement'. Yet in the days leading up to the incident she had said she felt 'very low spirited'. 'She was particularly fond of the child', her husband added, 'it being a son, and the other child being a girl'. The coroner explained to the jury that he thought it unnecessary to adjourn the inquiry so that the mother could attend. He wished to avoid causing her the pain and upset that this would inevitably entail. He also strongly advised the jury to return a verdict of accidental death, as the 'mother did not have any bad feeling against the child, but was very fond of it'. The jury duly returned this verdict.

On being admitted to the asylum six weeks later, Eliza's condition had deteriorated. The case book reported how, 'On May 3rd while doubtless under the influence of some morbid impulse she threw herself and her infant which she was carrying into the canal. The infant was drowned'.[80] The word 'infanticide' does not appear in the record. It was concluded that the attack of insanity had commenced after Eliza's confinement in April. Since then she had been in a melancholy condition and had threatened suicide. On admission it was remarked that Eliza had a peculiarly sad expression. She was disruptive and fancied that she could see her child. Her appetite was poor, her bowels costive, and she complained of pains in the head. She cried a good deal, but was willing to employ herself. Eliza was dosed with morphine and aperients. By August she was starting to show a slow improvement, and had lost much of her depression. Her demeanour was cheerful but 'not natural'. She employed herself by sewing, slept well, but was still constipated. By October she was making good progress, was cheerful and her expression

---

[80] Warwick County Lunatic Asylum, CR 1664/621. Case book of those admitted 13 May 1867 – 25 January 1870: no. 1504, Elizabeth Barnwell, admitted 29 June 1867.

was considered 'normal'. She was very industrious at sewing and also assisted on the ward. Eliza was released on a month's trial, which was standard practice at Warwick, and on 1 November was discharged 'recovered'.[81]

I have dwelt on Eliza Barnwell's story at length, partly because it is a complete account – which we can follow through from childbirth to the crime, inquest, diagnosis, verdict, committal and recovery – but also because her case typifies many of the features of the puerperal mania–infanticide link, in particular showing how readily this association was accepted, not only by medical men, but also by the family and neighbours whose reports and opinions feature so strongly in the evidence presented at inquests and trials. What was more unusual was that the three key witnesses in Eliza's case were men: the surgeon, the boatman and her husband. More often it was female neighbours, female servants, the lady of the house or the local midwife who were telling the story as they saw it in court. Such women would be far more likely to be involved with the accused at the time of birth or shortly afterwards. They might also have been seen as more appropriate witnesses, being better able to pronounce on the woman's state of mind and on her generally good behaviour before the crime and being able to attract the sympathy of judges and juries.

Eliza was described as being low spirited and the incident was deemed unmeditated, a spur-of-the-moment action. The mother had no motive – indeed she was said to like the child more than his sister – and she did not attempt to hide what she had done, or even to pretend that she had fallen into the water by accident. The surgeon who was called was unlikely to have had much expertise in treating mental illness, but he had no hesitation in attributing the event to the 'great mental excitement' that the mother was experiencing. Bullock could not resist the aside that a midwife had attended the mother, rather than a medical man. Her husband pointed to Eliza's fondness for the child. The coroner was sympathetic and did not want to subject Eliza to further suffering. The case was deemed 'sad' in the newspaper account, but neither tragic nor shocking. On entering the asylum, Eliza was described as suicidal and melancholic, repentant too and under the sad delusion that her child still lived. Her pathway to good health was typical of puerperal mania: slow improvement, an eventual restoration of a natural and cheerful demeanour, the desire to work, and finally recovery and discharge back to her husband and remaining child.

---

[81] Ibid.

Conclusion

Even at a time when there was so much concern about the problem of infanticide and about mothers getting away with destroying their infants, this account shows above all the ease with which the label of insanity could be applied or accepted by medical men and laymen, judges, witnesses, jurors, neighbours and the public. There was an almost formulaic explanation of the crime, described as being a result of temporary derangement coupled with a lack of wilful intent or subterfuge, with witnesses reflecting on the mother's affectionate nature, and love of her child or children in the case of married women. For medical men, puerperal insanity was depicted as an almost 'normal' side-effect of giving birth, strengthening the notion that pregnancy and childbirth were fraught with danger for the mother and others. Infanticide was an end-station on the route of puerperal mania, which was linked to harmful behaviour of many kinds (including self-harm and suicide, and threats to husband and birth attendants) and might or might not end in the death of the infant. The story of Eliza Barnwell ended penultimately in the asylum. But many of the women acquitted were seen as being in need of neither punishment nor a cure, since doctors testified that, though insane when the crime had been committed, the women were fully recovered by the time the case came to trial. In cases where women were taken to asylums the story was played out in full: they were physically restored to health, encouraged to work and to prepare themselves once again for their roles as wives and mothers.[82]

As Christine Krueger has argued, during the 1860s heightened concern about the perceived epidemic of infanticide dovetailed with sympathy for infanticidal women.[83] This sometimes divided opinion. When the subject of infanticide came up at the annual meeting of the Social Science Association in 1866, for example, there was a rift between those advocating compassion and sympathy towards infanticidal women and those who felt they 'represented the very antithesis of womanhood'.[84] This conflict was also evident in medical approaches to infanticide. The appointment of Thomas Wakley, editor of *The Lancet*, as coroner to West Middlesex in 1839 led to higher numbers of convictions in cases of infanticide, and Wakley and other London physicians were prominent leaders of the anti-infanticide campaign.[85]

[82] Marland, '"Destined to a perfect recovery"'.
[83] Krueger, 'Literary defenses and medical prosecutions'.
[84] *Transactions of the National Association for the Promotion of Social Science (NAPSS) 1866*, pp. 293–4; Zedner, *Women, Crime, and Custody*, p. 29.
[85] Krueger, 'Literary defenses and medical prosecutions', pp. 282, 284.

Yet the same journal, for example in the case of Mrs Prior, also supported the views of medical witnesses giving evidence in infanticide trials. *The Lancet* on more than one occasion refuted the views of judges who questioned the idea of temporary insanity and who challenged the validity of medical testimony, pointing to the fickleness of legal opinion on the insanity plea, which allowed it 'a certain run' and then rejected it altogether.[86]

Judicial views were equally complex and ambiguous. Judges abhorred the crime of infanticide and expressed concern about its unchecked increase but also, as in the Warwickshire assizes, advised juries to take on board evidence explaining the woman's state of mind and to acquit. More significant perhaps than these complexities was the fact that the use of the insanity plea could satisfy these conflicting views. It explained how the terrified servant girl was pushed in her frenzy to destroy her new-born child or why naturally good mothers for a short time became murdering demons. While verdicts involving puerperal insanity could reinforce beliefs that women accused of infanticide represented the very antithesis of womanhood, they also allowed such women to be treated with compassion.

Acknowledgements

The research on which this article is based was carried out as a Wellcome University Award Holder, and I am grateful to the Wellcome Trust for funding my project on puerperal insanity. My particular thanks go to Mark Jackson for his detailed comments and advice.

---

[86] *The Lancet*, 1 (1848), 318–19.

CHAPTER TEN

Images and impulses: representations of puerperal insanity and infanticide in late Victorian England

Cath Quinn

During the second half of the nineteenth century, psychiatry increasingly replaced obstetrics as the authoritative medical body pronouncing upon the insanity of child-bed. This process tended to locate infanticide as a symptom of an illness, routinely referred to as 'puerperal insanity'. The relatively recently established psychiatric profession saw an opportunity to legitimate its usefulness to society by addressing the concerns raised by the 'infanticide crisis' of the 1860s.[1] These concerns were accompanied by an increased number of cases receiving medical attention as more doctors attended 'problem' deliveries,[2] following which it was believed that puerperal insanity was more likely to occur. The psychiatric profession functioned as an ostensibly 'objective' and 'scientific' body, providing sanitized explanations for the spectre of the mad mother. As psychiatry expanded and became increasingly professionalized, individual doctors colonized particular areas to create their own specialisms.[3] Some doctors chose to make insanity their speciality and worked in the numerous county lunatic asylums or as private specialists. However, there were many general medical practitioners, such as family doctors, who also treated cases of insanity. Significantly, in the mid-Victorian period, psychiatry was not a coherent, authoritative body of

---

[1] See: G.K. Behlmer, 'Deadly motherhood: infanticide and medical opinion in mid-Victorian England', *Journal of the History of Medicine*, 34 (1979), 403–27; M.L. Arnot, 'Infant death, child care and the state', *Continuity and Change*, 9 (1994), 271–311.

[2] Especially in the hinterlands of the London teaching hospitals, where the population was densely concentrated.

[3] The introduction of Kraepelin nosology in the 1890s and the discovery of the role played by chemical hormones in the early twentieth century resulted in the reconceptualization of insanity around the event of childbirth and the decline of the disease label 'puerperal insanity'.

knowledge.[4] There were no authoritative diagnostic manuals, no set text-books and no recognized qualifications. Rather, psychiatrists or alienists were simply conversant with a particular body of knowledge and made use of this knowledge to treat cases of insanity. In this chapter, I shall use the term 'psychiatric profession' to refer to those employing and contributing to this knowledge, whatever their professional qualifications.[5]

The middle classes, who dominated Victorian society both economically and politically, constructed idealized social identities for women in terms of their maternal potential.[6] The 'natural' role for a male was in the aggressively constructed public sphere, whilst 'naturally' passive woman was thought to be more suited to the private domestic domain.[7] All women were presumed to have innate maternal 'instincts', whether or not they had children.[8] These scientific ideas, of natural instincts, were heavily informed by religious rhetoric which suggested that if a woman did not aspire to maternity like the Virgin Mary, she was in danger of falling as Mary Magdalena had done. How then did a society which held ideals of maternity as synonymous with the role of women, react to the potential rupture in its fabric presented by cases of puerperal insanity and infanticide?

This chapter investigates this tension by examining the words and photographs that the psychiatric profession employed to represent puerperal insanity. In the first section, I shall explore how puerperal insanity was described in the medical journals held in the Manchester Medical Collection, which survives in remarkably preserved form and which is reasonably indicative of what was being read by nineteenth-century medical practitioners.[9] British medical journals, due to their

---

[4]   See Roy Porter, *The Greatest Benefit to Mankind* (London, HarperCollins, 1997), p. 493.
[5]   It is of course important to recognize the potentially large disparity between psychiatric theory and every day practice. For a discussion of this difference see E.H. Ackernecht, 'A plea for a "behaviourist" approach in writing the history of medicine', *Journal of the History of Medicine and Allied Sciences*, 22 (1967), 211–14.
[6]   See L. Davidoff and C. Hall, *Family Fortunes* (London, Hutchinson, 1987), pp. 335–43.
[7]   It is questionable how far these idealized roles were enforced in practice. For a discussion of this point, see Mary Poovey, *Uneven Developments* (Chicago, Virago, 1989), particularly Chapter One.
[8]   The idea of 'natural instincts' was heavily informed and supported by evolution theories which were prominent at this time.
[9]   Medical journal articles were supplemented by the key texts to which they most frequently referred. The bibliography for my MA thesis consisted of nine key texts and forty-two journal articles. Articles in foreign journals, if explicitly cited in British journals and contained in the collection, were also included. I would like to thank Pat Cummings for her help, expertise and time spent in introducing me to the Manchester Medical Collection.

rapidity of publication and facility of reply, provided an important forum for discussion. They allowed unusual cases to receive a national audience, and often promoted consensus by repetition. However, they also revealed how limited that consensus could be in the arguments and debates that they facilitated.

In the second section, I shall examine psychiatric photography – which became popular about the same time that the puerperal insanity diagnosis was salient – the impact of which can be studied in a variety of photographs and other contemporary illustrations from medical archives and art galleries.[10] Puerperal insanity appeared particularly suited to photographic illustration, which supposedly offered an objective image, free from human intervention. In the conclusion, I shall consider how similar conceptions and prejudices ran through both forms of representation, written and visual, and how these were used to resolve conflict between the idealization of mothers and the social exclusion of lunatics.

Puerperal insanity in the journals

The term 'puerperal insanity' strictly referred to insanity which began during the puerperal period, that is, from birth up to a few weeks afterwards. In the late nineteenth century, the psychiatric profession extended this usage to include insanity occurring in pregnancy, whilst breast-feeding, and even during the birth itself. The insanities manifested included mild disturbances, such as the food cravings and disconcerting dreams of pregnancy, as well as more extreme behaviour, such as dashing the abdomen against a wall to encourage the expulsion of the baby in labour and the, albeit rare, occurrence of infanticide. A case of puerperal insanity was defined as such if it occurred between conception and the end of lactation, suggesting that it was considered to be a consequence of the maternal state, rather than a distinct disease following a particular pathology. This construction served to emphasize the disruptive potential, and unstable nature, of *all* women.[11]

Insanity which began in pregnancy was usually described in terms of despondency, and medical commentators often suggested that in these cases the pregnancy might be unwelcome:

---

[10] My final collection consisted of over thirty photographs and other illustrations of puerperal insanity.

[11] For a more wide-ranging discussion of this point see: O. Moscucci, *The Science of Woman: Gynaecology and Gender in England, 1800–1929* (Cambridge, Cambridge University Press, 1990).

During the fifth month of her first pregnancy she became very low spirited and depressed. She attempted suicide by drowning, but did not succeed in her intention from the shallowness of the water ... Eleven weeks after the birth she deliberately strangled it [her baby], and then attempted to poison herself with laudanum ... She said that her impression at the time was that it would be happier if it was dead, and that she attempted suicide so that her husband might not be tainted by having a murderess for his wife.[12]

Dr John Batty Tuke, Medical Superintendent of the Fife and Kinross District Lunatic Asylum, listed the case above and the following one as examples of the insanity of pregnancy: 'B.E., age 35, wife of a tradesman, mother of several children, during the third month of her last pregnancy she took morphia with the intention of committing suicide'.[13] Whilst attempts to induce an abortion were considered to be rational acts, and therefore deplorable, the accompanying propensity to suicide in these two cases was taken as evidence of the deranged state of the women's minds. In view of this, any attempt to harm an unborn infant was considered not as murder but as the result of an evident illness from which such women were suffering.

Insanity occurring at parturition was a relatively rare occurrence, but received considerable discussion in medical journals as doctors, although not psychiatrists, were more likely to be present at the time of the birth. Insanity at parturition was supposed to be characteristically intense and brief, disappearing shortly after the child was born.[14] This description of puerperal insanity provided a perfect context within which to define infanticide as an irresistible impulse, since the unconscious nature of the act could be easily sustained. When individual cases of insanity of parturition were described, signs of insanity had often been clearly manifested in the later stages of pregnancy.

Insanity beginning in the puerperal period, that is up to six to eight weeks after the birth, was understood to be either of predominantly a maniacal or predominantly a melancholic type. Mania was believed to be characterized by inflamed, animal-like thoughts and actions, whilst melancholy was characterized by despondency, lethargy and a lack of will.[15] When mania predominated, the onset of the illness was believed to be sooner after the birth and the insanity more severe than in

---

[12] Dr Skae and Dr Clouston, 'The Morisonian lectures on insanity for 1873', *Journal of Mental Science*, 20 (1874–75), 2–7, at 6.

[13] J.B. Tuke, 'Cases illustrative of pregnancy, puerperal mania and insanity of lactation', *Edinburgh Medical Journal*, 12 (1866–67), 1083–1101.

[14] A.C. Clark, 'The sexual and reproductive functions', *Journal of Mental Science*, 34 (1888–89), 390–93, at 392.

[15] H. Maudsley, *The Pathology of Mind* (London, Macmillan, 1895), pp. 418–19.

predominantly melancholic cases. However, maniacal cases were also believed to be more easily and more rapidly cured.

The insanity of lactation was not discussed in terms of infanticidal impulses as it was considered to be essentially an insanity of exhaustion, characterized by melancholic symptoms, rather than the mania required to commit infanticide. However, cases of insanity were still recorded as puerperal in origin up to a year after the birth, and were thought to be caused by the weakened bodily systems of breast-feeding mothers. The danger of the patient committing infanticide was believed to diminish with time from the birth.

The pregnant, puerperal and lactational states were believed to be the most significant 'causes' of puerperal insanity. The illness was regarded as a form of general insanity occurring around a particular event, rather than a distinct disease with its own pathology. By grounding the disease in female biology, doctors could express their sympathy to sufferers whose illness had been caused merely by seeking to fulfil their maternal role. A sympathetic image of the woman as a mother was thus maintained. All mothers did not fall victim to the disease, as the predisposed state then had to be acted upon by an external cause that inflamed their vulnerable state into an insanity. When these external causes showed deviation from the maternal ideal, such as increased age, heredity, poverty or illegitimacy, moral censure could be invoked against the woman. These beliefs were so strongly held that some doctors were willing to state them as fact even though they themselves had never encountered such cases.[16] When a doctor was concerned to protect the moral reputation of a patient, he would take care to stress that the exciting causes in her case were physical, such as another physical illness, the shock of the first birth, or a particularly difficult labour, and therefore not her fault.

Whilst the causes of puerperal insanity were fairly unanimously agreed upon, different doctors often championed quite different symptoms as being characteristic of the disease. Some of these characteristic symptoms were chosen for their notoriety, rather than their prevalence, as the predominant symptoms of the disease. The only common point of agreement was that 'there is no end to the variety of the symptoms of puerperal insanity'.[17] Physical symptoms

---

[16] George H. Savage, an assistant physician at Bethlem Royal Hospital, in 'The prevention and treatment of the insanity of pregnancy and the puerperal period', *The Lancet*, 1 (1896), 164–5, stated: 'No doubt my cases, being nearly all taken from respectable married women, do not include those in which shame and grief play the chief part in causation. It is in the lower orders and after illegitimate births that we should find the most instances of that kind.'

[17] R. Boyd, 'Observations on puerperal insanity', *Journal of Mental Science*, 16 (1870), 153–65, at 157.

were generally conceptualized within an economy of fluidity.[18]
Within this system, illness was believed to be caused by blockages or
overflows. Blockages could poison both the body and the mind,
whilst overflows could debilitate them. For example, the suppression
of breast milk was believed to lead to a blockage which poisoned the
mind; conversely over-lactation was believed to be a fluid overflow
leading to debilitation. Concern was also directed to the blockage, or
flow, of the lochia[19] and bowels. Dr Valentine Bird, Physician to the
South London Dispensary for Women and Home for Sick Children,
Sydenham Park, described the case of Mrs C., whose insanity he
believed was contributed to by an injudicious train journey which
she undertook:

> As prolonged railway travelling, amongst other evils, necessarily
> occasions irregularity of diet, and prevents proper attention being
> paid to the evacuation of the bowels and bladder, its avoidance
> during the pregnant state, of course, cannot be too much insisted on,
> no matter how strong the subject of it may be.[20]

Many doctors believed that the onset of the illness was indicated by
sleeplessness to the point where it defined the disease. Other distinctive
symptoms carried much stronger moral overtones. A woman's chastity
was often equated with her ability to hold her tongue. Her 'verbal
chastity' was considered especially important in the areas of sexual
relations and blasphemy. Medical journal accounts are full of incredulity
at the garrulousness of the women, the subject matter they discussed and
the words they used. Dr M.D. MacLeod, Medical Superintendent, East
Riding Asylum, reported that:

> It is characteristic of the disease that obscenities are almost always a
> marked feature in the ravings, and that there continues, even into
> convalescence a tendency to obscene and salacious conversation.[21]

Dr Daniel Hack Tuke, physician and distinguished writer on the mental
sciences, agreed that 'it is true that, in mania, modest women use words
which in health are never permitted to issue from their lips'.[22] Although
Dr Savage was willing to diagnose a case 'from the mincing gait and

---

[18] See S. Shuttleworth, 'Female circulation', in M. Jacobus, E.F. Keller and S.
Shuttleworth (eds), *Body/Politics*, (New York, Routledge, 1990), pp. 47–68.

[19] Lochia referred to the discharge of cellular debris, mucus and blood following
childbirth.

[20] V. Bird, 'Induction of labour and delivery by forceps in puerperal mania', *British
Medical Journal*, 1 (1879), 544–5.

[21] M.D. MacLeod, 'An address on puerperal insanity', *British Medical Journal*, 2 (1886),
239–42, at 239.

[22] J.C. Bucknill and D.H. Tuke, *A Manual of Psychological Medicine* (Philadelphia,
Blanchard and Lea, 1858), p. 238.

lascivious looks of the patient',[23] most doctors found it hard to accept that mothers would indulge in masturbation. Despite frequent reference being made to the practice by patients, it was usually attributed to irritation of the genital organs.

A woman's delusions towards her husband and child could be the most disconcerting symptoms of the illness for her medical attendant. A doctor entering a middle-class household occupied an uncertain position if he attempted to challenge the authority of the male head of household.[24] If the female patient believed the doctor to be her husband, or condemned her husband in front of the doctor, his position became even more precarious. Henry Maudsley, neurologist and one of the most influential thinkers in the mental sciences in the latter half of the nineteenth century, cautioned doctors that a patient might be found to be 'addressing her medical attendant, whom she may believe to be her husband disguised, in terms of unbefitting endearment'.[25]

The most notorious, and potentially the most dangerous 'symptoms' of puerperal insanity – suicide and infanticide – were listed together as 'irresistible impulses'. Dr John Batty Tuke stated that:

> As a rule such patients have no memory of their action and rarely attempt to hide the evidence of their crime. Cases occur in which the child is murdered and the mother is found sleeping quietly with the blood-marks unwashed from her person and her clothes.[26]

In such cases, the shock of killing the child was thought to have brought the woman to her senses, whilst clearing the actual event from her mind. In focusing on the impulse overwhelming the woman's mind, rather than the legal profession's concern about the death of the child, the psychiatric profession could separate the woman concerned from the act committed and so portray the mother as a victim of illness, rather than as a murderer. The lack of any attempt to conceal the infant's body or the blood on her own body or clothes was taken as proof of the woman's deranged state and as evidence that she had been

---

[23] J.C. Bucknill and D.H. Tuke, *A Manual of Psychological Medicine* (London, J. & A. Churchill, 1874), p. 359. Dr George Savage was an assistant physician at Bethlem Royal Hospital and published figures and case studies from Bethlem. His report was particularly useful because of the detailed records that had been kept and was often referred to for its comprehensiveness.

[24] See: A.D. Wood, '"The fashionable diseases" : women's complaints and their treatment in nineteenth-century America', *Journal of Interdisciplinary History*, 4 (1973), 25–52; and a critique of the article by R.M. Morantz in ibid., 641–60.

[25] H. Maudsley, *The Pathology of Mind: A Study of its Distempers, Deformities and Disorders* (London, Macmillan, 1895), p. 417.

[26] J.B. Tuke, 'On the statistics of puerperal insanity', *Edinburgh Medical Journal*, 10 (1864–65), 105.

overtaken by irresistible impulses, rather than having rationally planned the deed.[27]

The pathologization of the disease saw the 'crime' of infanticide being reduced to a 'symptom' of puerperal insanity.[28] The classification of infanticide as an 'irresistible impulse' allowed doctors to argue in court the non-conscious nature of the act. However, the language and labels that doctors used to fulfil a legal agenda were very different from the concerns they expressed when discussing the illness within the medical community. Rather than being interested in the 'crime' of infanticide that had been committed, doctors were concerned with the mental impulses that might lead a person to commit such an act. These impulses were, they believed, present from pregnancy, through the birth and up to a year afterwards. Whilst legal discourse could examine infanticide only in terms of the death of an infant shortly after birth, the psychiatric profession could discuss insanity and infanticidal impulses throughout the whole period in which the body might be said to be in a 'maternal' state.

Doctors' accounts of married patients showed a great deal of variation from the image of the 'typical' infanticidal mother which appeared in the popular press – that of a young, single servant girl. Medical accounts often mentioned the woman's other children[29] and also included information on their more general rejection of a domestic role. Legal records and newspaper accounts recorded only those cases where the woman had been successful in committing infanticide. Medical accounts, however, were concerned with intent rather than results, and included those who talked of, or attempted, infanticide, but did not actually succeed. Doctors treating cases where the 'irresistible impulse' had become an infanticidal fact continually asserted that no woman could really intend to kill her child, whatever her social or economic circumstances.[30] In cases where doctors met with a lack of remorse they concluded that the patient was still obviously insane.[31]

Heroic therapeutics were not usually employed in attempting to treat puerperal insanity. Puerperal insanity was noted for its tendency to cure itself in time. The disease was considered a by-product of a 'natural' process that would eventually correct itself. In treating puerperal

---

[27] See R. Smith, *Trial by Medicine* (Edinburgh, Edinburgh University Press, 1981), Chapter 7.

[28] For a fuller discussion of this transition see Smith, *Trial by Medicine*, and T. Ward, 'The sad subject of infanticide: law, medicine and child murder, 1860–1938', *Social and Legal Studies*, 8 (1999), 163–80.

[29] Boyd, 'Observations on puerperal insanity', 160–64.

[30] Skae and Clouston, 'Morisonian lectures on insanity', p. 6.

[31] Ibid.

insanity many of the usual treatments for 'general insanity' were employed, and special attention was paid to the reproductive organs and the breasts. The limited range of treatments open to medical practitioners is reflected in the limited space devoted to therapeutics in the articles. The majority of treatments were directed towards physical symptoms: purgatives were used to unblock the system, particularly of milk and blood; sedatives were used to calm patients down and encourage sleep; and stimulants were used to invigorate lethargic patients.[32] Recovering patients were encouraged to employ themselves in light domestic tasks and were fed nutritious foods to regain the maternal 'ideal' of a 'stout and rosy' figure.[33] To be 'cured' meant to be able to resume one's social role. Physically, the return of menstruation was accepted as a sign that one had resumed one's role as a biological 'woman'. The gaining of an affectionate interest in one's husband and child was taken as final proof that a woman was ready to resume her position in society and was therefore cured.

In reading beyond the medical accounts of classification, causation, symptomatology and therapeutics, women suffering from puerperal insanity can be seen within the wider context of their social and familial lives, rather than just as patients. Adrian Wilson has suggested that 'other' voices, conventionally considered missing from the historical record (such as the actors and social structures involved in calling for the doctor), can be inferred from doctors' accounts.[34] From this perspective, medical articles on puerperal insanity reveal how problematic even the supposedly simple category 'doctor' was. The authors of the accounts include alienists, obstetricians and family doctors. These doctors attended a case at the request of a variety of people including the patient, her husband, her nurse, her family, her friends and even her husband's employer.

The case studies in the journals also provide a variety of information about the patients themselves, often including a woman's age, her obstetrical history,[35] whether she was literate, and her husband's – or occasionally even her own – employment. The cases that many doctors presented in medical articles reveal that they had often known both the patients and their families very well for long

---

[32] J.T. MacLachlan asserted that 'the mind recovers when the body is put right', in 'Clinical essays on insanity', *Glasgow Medical Journal*, 47 (1897), 266.

[33] See L. Napier, 'Case of puerperal pyrexia', *The Lancet*, 1 (1890), 346–7.

[34] A. Wilson, 'Participant or patient? Seventeenth century childbirth from the mother's point of view', in R. Porter (ed.), *Patients and Practitioners* (Cambridge, Cambridge University Press, 1986), pp. 129–44.

[35] Many women did not include miscarriages in such accounts, especially those which occurred in early pregnancy.

periods of time and felt particular compassion for such unfortunate cases occurring at what should have been a very happy time. The relationship and the potential complications between male doctors and their female patients have been discussed above.[36] What becomes evident, on careful reading of these case studies, is the wide variety of other voices present in these narratives.

Loudest amongst the other voices was the woman's husband. Doctors were generally compassionate towards their suffering and praised the loving attention that they continued to give their wives. Dr Valentine Bird praised the husband of Mrs C. as being a 'most excellent nurse'.[37] Such praise usually occurred in middle-class cases, where the husband had probably paid the doctor's fees. Richard Perry, house-surgeon to the General Lying-in Hospital, Lambeth, went so far as to perform a post-mortem to prove, against neighbours' gossip, that Mr Roberts had not contributed to his wife's insanity and subsequent demise.[38] If a husband was neglectful of his duties, doctors were quick to admonish him and express sympathy for the wife. Where a husband was not available to take care of his wife, through death, desertion or her rejection of his company, parents or parents-in-law often stepped in.[39] Frequently it was the parents, or other members of the family, who took the woman to an asylum.[40] Doctors complained that families often sought to hide a history of insanity and related illnesses among the patient's relations, and thereby hindered treatment of the patient.[41]

Friends and neighbours could exert a strong influence, especially if the woman was without a husband or a family. It was to friends and neighbours, who had undergone the trials of childbirth themselves, that many women turned for advice. Friends and neighbours also supported the continuance of 'traditional' treatments disapproved of by the established medical profession.[42] One, albeit declining, practice

---

[36] A particularly balanced approach to this two-dimensional relationship can be found in C. Smith-Rosenberg, *Disorderly Conduct: Visions of Gender in Victorian America* (New York, Alfred A. Knopf, 1985).

[37] V. Bird, 'Induction of labour', *British Medical Journal*, 1 (1879), 544–5.

[38] R. Perry, 'Case of puerperal mania, with the post-mortem examination', *The Lancet*, 1 (1842–43), 394.

[39] For a discussion of the role of the family and its influence on asylum admissions see; R. Adair, J. Melling and B. Forsythe, 'Migration, family structure and pauper lunacy in Victorian England', *Continuity and Change*, 12 (1997), 373–401.

[40] Dr T. Smith, 'St. Mary's Hospital', *The Lancet*, 2 (1851), 415–16.

[41] J.T. Dickson, 'A contribution to the study of the so-called puerperal insanity', *Journal of Mental Science*, 16 (1871), 379–90.

[42] The conflict between women's and medical understandings of women's bodies is discussed in V. Bullough and M. Voght, 'Women, menstruation, and nineteenth-century medicine', *Bulletin of the History of Medicine*, 47 (1973), 66–82.

advocated that a woman would not be 'right' after giving birth until she had been bled of the excess blood her body now contained. For example, J. MacCormack, physician to the Mullinahore Dispensary in County Tipperary, described a fatal case in which a woman 'was bled by some horse doctor, and took some medicine, ordered by the midwife, previous to my seeing her'.[43]

The nurse, as a figure outside the family, was often considered by doctors as a more objective and reliable witness than the family. The nurse occupied an uneasy middle ground between community and doctors and acted for both, dependent upon the circumstances and her judgment of the situation. Family doctors continued to see patients and their families after the period of puerperal insanity. Unlike alienists working in asylums, they would maintain contact with their patients even if the insanity did not recur. Therefore they can, and do, inform us that many women who suffered from puerperal insanity – even some of those who committed, or attempted to commit, infanticide – went on to be what they considered 'good' mothers.

Puerperal insanity in photographs

The influential disciplines of physiognomy and phrenology postulated that insanity was rooted in biology and could therefore be 'read' on the body, especially the face.[44] In the late 1830s, when these theories dominated psychiatry, the new technology of photography was being developed in Britain and France. Photographic images were automatically reproduced and therefore supposedly an accurate representation. All previous methods of reproduction had required the impressionistic aid of the artist's hand. Amateur photography became popular in the 1860s, with the introduction of the paper negative. This made it possible to reproduce illustrations in books and journals more easily and cheaply. Thus photography became more accessible to those wishing to explore its possibilities, including members of the expanding psychiatric profession. The introduction of snap-shot[45] speeds in the 1880s allowed psychiatric photography finally to achieve its main aim: to capture a patient's expression and stance at a single instant.[46]

---

[43] J. MacCormack, 'Cases of puerperal mania, with a dissection and remarks', *The Lancet*, 1 (1838–39), 549–50. The doctor blamed her death on the injudicious bleeding.

[44] See R. Cooter, 'Phrenology and British alienists', *Medical History*, 20 (1976), 1–21, 135–51.

[45] That is, 1/60th of a second or faster.

[46] For a more systematic and theoretical discussion of this development, see J. Tagg, *The Burden of Representation* (Basingstoke, Macmillan, 1988).

Psychiatry, rather than the more empirically based 'higher' sciences, made the first systematic, 'scientific' use of photography.[47] The profession had long based its claim to a special understanding of madness on being able to see what others could not. Photographic images brought an exciting new potential to psychiatric practice, the opportunity to diagnose patients from photographs. Theoretically, there was no need for a doctor to meet or interact with a patient; their illness would be entirely 'readable' from the image produced. Thus doctors could 'introduce' their patients to other medical practitioners in books, journals or private correspondence. Photographs also presented therapeutic implications. Doctors could compare their stricken patients to photographs of them when they were healthy[48] and convalescent patients could be shown photographs of themselves in deranged states in the hope of speeding their recovery.

The psychiatric profession was not uniformly enthusiastic in its adoption of photography. Some doctors questioned whether such images could be realistic likenesses, given that patients had to pose for several seconds at the direction of the doctor. Charles Darwin found the photographs by Sir James Crichton Browne fascinating,[49] but did not reproduce them in *The Expression of the Emotions in Man and Animals* (published in 1872) because he was concerned how far Crichton Browne had directed the patients.[50] Some doctors, such as Alexander Morison, author of the influential *The Physiognomy of Mental Diseases*,[51] maintained that photography would never provide the movement and emphasis required, and continued to use lithographs for illustrations. Photography was thus never completely embraced by all of the psychiatric profession, even when exposure times were reduced.

Puerperal insanity presented itself as a particularly suitable subject for Victorian psychiatric photography. Photography was limited to reproducing the image placed before it; psychiatry welcomed such apparent transparency. Photographs allowed psychiatry to reproduce images of patients in a particular 'state' or sequence of states. Psychiatrists had previously found themselves limited to describing insanity as either maniacal or melancholic. Puerperal insanity, unlike many other mental

---

[47] An account of which is given in S. Gilman, *The Face of Madness: Hugh W. Diamond and the Origin of Psychiatric Photography* (New York, Brunner/Mazel, 1976).

[48] As suggested by J. Shaw, 'Facial expressions as one of the means of diagnosis and prognosis in mental diseases', *Medical Annual* (1894), 344–74.

[49] Browne was perhaps the most famous mid-century British alienist.

[50] For a discussion of the professional relationship between Darwin and Browne, see J. Browne, 'Darwin and the face of madness', in W.F. Bynum, R. Porter and M. Shepherd (eds), *The Anatomy of Madness: Volume 1* (London, Tavistock, 1985), pp. 151–66.

[51] A. Morison, *The Physiognomy of Mental Diseases* (London, Longman, 1843).

diseases, contained examples of both states, occasionally in the same patient. The tendency to recovery of those suffering from puerperal insanity also made it particularly suitable for contrasting photographs of the patient as 'deranged' and then 'recovered'.

The wide-ranging illness of puerperal insanity was often misnamed 'puerperal mania', reflecting the frenzied killing with which it was associated in the popular mind. Mania – characterized as active, aggressive, almost bestial behaviour – was viewed as an exaggerated form of stereotypical male behaviour. Conversely, the passive, quiet, despondent symptoms of melancholia were considered to be an exaggeration of stereotypically female behaviour. When males were visually represented in allegorical paintings as melancholic they were often feminized,[52] whilst depictions of maniacal females frequently attempted to 'unfeminize' them, usually by attacking their chastity. This loss of virtue resulted in a loss of social status. They were no longer 'proper' women as prescribed by middle-class Victorian ideals. Photographs of puerperal insanity, in emphasizing the maternal nature of a woman, allowed women to be depicted in a maniacal state without a corresponding loss of social status, as they were still characterized in essentially maternal terms.

Hugh W. Diamond, Superintendent of Surrey County Lunatic Asylum, pioneered psychiatric photography in the early 1850s.[53] He was the first to use photography in a systematic and scientific manner. His interest in photography stemmed from his antiquarian exploration of inventions and how they operated. Dr Diamond exhibited his 'Types of insanity' at the first public exhibition devoted entirely to photographs, organized by the Society of Arts in 1852. At the exhibition, the title of the collection overshadowed the content of the photographs and they were treated as scientific curiosities, not as portraits of people. The first three illustrations presented here are reproduced from a collection of photographs held by Bethlem Royal Hospital Archives. Although they have the name 'Henry Hering' inscribed on them, they are generally assumed to be the work of Diamond.[54]

Living in the grounds of the asylum, Diamond could photograph patients with as much ease (and, it has been suggested, as much familiarity)[55] as he photographed his friends and family. He followed the

---

[52] For a more detailed discussion of this point see L.S. Dixon, *Perilous Chastity* (Ithaca and London, Cornell University Press, 1995), pp. 198–201.

[53] See Gilman, *Face of Madness*.

[54] Various explanations have been put forward to account for the appearance of Hering's name on the collection. It is possible that Hering provided a set of prints for Diamond.

[55] A. Burrows and I. Schumacher, *Portraits of the Insane: The Case of Dr Diamond* (London, Quartes, 1990).

contemporary conventions of portrait photography and posed his patients in a studio which he had set up in the asylum. Diamond used photographs in his treatment of patients in the asylum. He showed patients photographs of themselves in order to demonstrate the falsity of their delusions, such as proving to them that their head was attached to their body and that they did have two arms. Diamond also used photographs with convalescent patients to show them how far they had 'improved'. It is significant that Diamond had trained at a time when psychiatry was extolling the benefits of 'moral treatment'[56] and 'talking patients sane' and so was particularly receptive to such practices.

Figures 10.1 and 10.2 demonstrate how Diamond used photographs to aid the convalescence of his patients. Figure 10.1 depicts a women suffering from puerperal mania. The position adopted by the patient, seated with her hands crossed, could be taken as typical of a melancholic posture. However, the photograph is clearly posed and closer examination reveals that the woman's left hand is being held down by a second party, whose shoulder can be seen to the left of the picture.[57] This 'third hand' highlights the difficulties encountered in getting mentally ill patients to sit still for the required exposure times.[58] In Figure 10.2, taken during the convalescent stage of the illness, the woman can be seen to have progressed to a standing position, and is now dressed in 'respectable' clothing and even marking her place in the book she is holding.

The element of 'recovery' depicted in these photographs included the outcome of a process of socialization, in which the patient had shown progress in her clothing, her hair and her posture from one who was 'manifestly' insane to one who was ready to resume the society of others. Medical men would have 'read' these indicators as clearly as they would have read any other 'marks' of insanity. This is not to suggest that the insanity did not exist, but that the deviation from expected social conventions was considered as much a symptom of the disease as any psychological or organic disturbances.

---

[56] 'Moral treatment' arose out of a more humane attitude towards insane patients and emphasized psychological and environmental therapeutics over medicinal ones.

[57] I am grateful to Patricia Allderidge, Archivist and Curator of Bethlem Royal Hospital Archives and Museum, for pointing this out to me.

[58] The patient is not wearing a strait-jacket, but a loose quilted smock. This institutional clothing provided padding and prevented patients from damaging their own clothes. The photograph also shows that the woman is wearing a girdle, something that would not usually have been worn with a loose quilted smock. It is likely that the girdle was being used to tie her to the chair. This does not, necessarily, mean that she was being coerced into sitting. The girdle may, like the 'third hand', have been used to help keep a possibly highly agitated or nervous patient still in order to produce a clear image.

Figure 10.1 This three-quarter-length portrait of 'E.R.' – who was being treated for puerperal mania – reveals more than is first apparent.

Figure 10.3, from the same collection, shows a woman who was labelled as having committed infanticide. Women who were deemed to be guilty of this crime are the only patients in this extensive collection to be consistently portrayed at domestic tasks. In order to be accepted as

Figure 10.2   In convalescence, 'E.R.' is shown unattended. Both photographs
were taken by Hugh Diamond, Superintendent of Surrey County
Lunatic Asylum.

authoritative in the courts, psychiatrists had to show that these women
were essentially 'good' mothers, but that circumstances and irresistible
impulses had overwhelmed them. The domesticity of the photographs

Figure 10.3   Diamond's caption attributes infanticide by 'M.B.' to melancholia, a form of extreme behaviour seen as typically female.

reinforced the notion that these patients were primarily domestic – and therefore maternal – women, when circumstances allowed them to be. The suggestion offered in photographs such as Figure 10.3 is that only the asylum can provide those circumstances. The photographing of individual women in this way broke with the tradition of asylum paintings in which the 'mad mother' was shown with either a blanket wrapped around a log to symbolize her lost baby[59] or her child abandoned carelessly beside her.[60] The 'empirical' photographic portrait replaced the allegorical painting and was thus believed to make the image more 'scientific'. The holding of dolls or other baby-like objects was then used to symbolize delusions or childlike simplicity.[61]

As photographic apparatus became more widely available, many doctors who had the necessary time, knowledge and money, took up an amateur interest in the pastime. Drs Barker and Parker were two such enthusiasts and worked at Bethlem Hospital in 1888.[62] Rather than follow any particular system, or attempt to illustrate any particular states, stages or illnesses, they merely brought their equipment into the hospital and over a period of several days photographed most of the patients as an extension of their amateur interest in the hobby. No reference is made to the photographs, or their usefulness, in the case notes in which they appeared. One of the most striking features of these portraits is the lack of background. Figure 10.4 depicts a patient suffering from puerperal insanity, in the early stages of her convalescence. The blank background gives the portrait a stark, detached feel and offers a striking contrast to many contemporary paintings, in which mothers were generally situated in rural, pastoral settings, emphasising the 'naturalness' of motherhood.[63] The lack of background in these patient photographs heightens the sense of their dislocation from society.

Towards the end of the nineteenth century, photography became easier and cheaper, and thus more widely used. At the same time, increasing numbers of individuals found themselves in institutions such as asylums, and the use of photographs in institutional records became common.[64] John Tagg has used a Foucauldian analysis of power to suggest that this new system of documentation produced a new kind of knowledge, which could then be used as a system of surveillance. Figure 10.5, which

---

[59] S. Gilman, *Seeing the Insane* (New York, Brunner/Mazel, 1982), pp. 138–9, 211.

[60] See Wellcome Institute Library, London, photographic collection, ref: MOO17213BOO.

[61] The Hering collection contains such an illustration: 'H.S. Chronic mania with delusions', holding a doll. Hering Collection, ref. 7.

[62] 'Messers. Barker and Parker, during their residence, made a very complete series of photographs of the patients then in the hospital', *Bethlem Annual Report* (1888), held at Bethlem Royal Hospital Archives and Museum.

[63] Manchester City Art Gallery holds numerous examples of such 'pastoral' portraits, including: 'Mother and Child', by P.F. Poole; 'Osier Peeling', by R.W. McBeth; and 'Mrs Scott Elliot and Children', by A. Swynnerton.

[64] Tagg, *Burden of Representation*, p. 59.

Figure 10.4 This austere head-and-shoulders portrait of 'Louisa L.S.' was taken at Bethlem Hospital on 16 February 1888, one of a series showing most of the patients at the time.

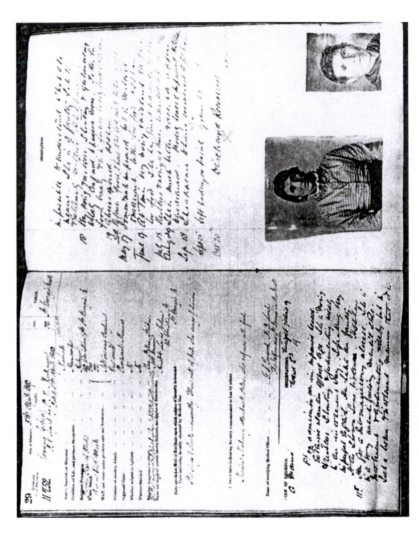

Figure 10.5 Part of the records of 'Joanna C', typical of the Colney Hatch Asylum case books.

includes a photograph of a patient suffering from puerperal mania, is a reproduction of two pages from the Colney Hatch Asylum case books and illustrates this form of institutional record-keeping. The photograph is not with the admission notes, at the beginning of the case notes, introducing the patient. Rather, the photograph appears in the main body of the information about the patient, communicating their condition and aiding their identification.

According to Sander Gilman, photographs have been used to address society's fears about 'deviant' groups through a process that he refers to as 'otherization',[65] in which certain groups are highlighted as being both distinct and more vulnerable to a particular disease. The perceived characteristics of the group then become synonymous with the symptoms of the disease.[66] 'The portrait of the sufferer, the portrait of the patient, is therefore the image of the disease anthropomorphized'.[67] That may have been a factor in the way photographs were recorded at Colney Hatch, apart from the obvious purpose of recognition if the patient escaped or transgressed again after being discharged.

At the start of the twentieth century, moving images began to replace static ones. When psychiatric theory turned its attention from reading expressions to motor dysfunctions, such as nervous tics, it looked towards the new technologies to represent them. Apparently new diseases, such as shell shock and its attendant motor dysfunctions, were exhibited in these moving images which claimed to be even more objective than their predecessors.

Conclusion

Separate consideration of journal and photographic sources allows the explicit examination and comparison of the concepts and prejudices informing them. The medical journal articles and the photographs both demonstrate the variety of ideas about puerperal insanity being consciously asserted by the psychiatric profession, and the less self-consciously social preconceptions underlying them. The inclusion of visual representations is important in studies such as this not only to examine the politics of their production, but also to

---

[65] For a discussion of the theory of 'otherization' see S. Gilman, *Disease and Representation* (Ithaca and London, Cornell University Press, 1988), Chapter One.

[66] See M. Jackson, 'Images of deviance: visual representations of mental defectives in early twentieth-century medical texts', *British Journal for the History of Science*, 28 (1995), 319–37.

[67] Gilman, *Disease and Representation*, p. 2.

provide a contemporary point of comparison with more conventionally accepted sources.

The construction of puerperal insanity in terms of 'nature gone astray' helped to make the illness more acceptable, a consequence of the maternal state rather than the result of any particular fault on the part of the woman. Medical journals treated puerperal insanity as a general insanity rather than a distinct disease with its own particular pathology. Psychiatric photography emphasized the domesticity, and therefore the maternity, of the puerperal – and particularly the infanticide – cases. The women were depicted as 'naturally' maternal but overwhelmed by adverse circumstances. The widespread acceptance of the theory of maternal instincts made the concept of insane and infanticidal impulses more acceptable.

The psychiatric profession subsumed puerperal insanity and infanticide into a medical model of behaviour and claimed that it could thus identify, control and possibly cure the disease. The increasing classification and analysis of puerperal insanity in medical journals gave the impression that the psychiatrists were gaining an improved understanding and command of the illness.[68] The lack of background in psychiatric photographs – rather than the pastoral settings in contemporary paintings of mothers – emphasized the patients' removal from society, and thus reduced the threat that they posed to that society. By constructing images of puerperal insanity both in photographs and in medical language, the psychiatric profession were claiming greater authority over treatment of the disease.

The emergence of infanticide as a symptom of puerperal insanity, of which women were merely passive victims, allowed the reconciliation of the contrasting images of mother and lunatic. Insane and infanticidal mothers became subjects suitable for sympathy rather than censure. As the conceptualization of infanticide shifted from a rational strategy for the concealment of unwanted pregnancies to an irresistible impulse as the result of an illness linked to the maternal state, so the focus moved from the morally fallen single woman to highlighting a potential instability in all women. This process further constructed, and constricted, women in terms of their maternal role. Their potential for maternity had become a potential for insanity. This preoccupation with the state of mind of the mother, and with the conscious or non-conscious nature of her actions, continued to dominate debates about infanticide well into the twentieth century.

---

[68] A.C. Clark, 'Aetiology, pathology and treatment of puerperal insanity', *Journal of Mental Science*, 33 (1887–88), 169–89, 372–9, 487–96.

Acknowledgements

This chapter is based on work undertaken for my MA thesis 'Representations of puerperal insanity in England and Scotland, 1850–1900', (University of Manchester, 1998). I would like to acknowledge the financial support of the British Academy and the intellectual support of my supervisor, Dr Mark Micale, in the completion of the thesis. My current doctoral work on the history of puerperal insanity is supported financially by the ESRC.

CHAPTER ELEVEN

The boundaries of Her Majesty's Pleasure: discharging child-murderers from Broadmoor and Perth Criminal Lunatic Department, *c.*1860–1920

Jonathan Andrews

Recent literature on the history of infanticide in nineteenth-century Britain has tended to focus on the crime, trial and punishment of offenders. The historiography has generally concentrated on the meaning of the crime for Victorian society, the evolution of medico-legal defences and discourse about infanticide, and the changing relationship between lay and professional ideologies.[1] Historians have also been especially preoccupied with the way in which societal and professional judgments were mediated by gendered views of women, their behaviour and their bodies, and of their roles as mothers and wives, as well as by differences in the way women's crimes were evaluated as against those of male offenders.[2] In regard to offenders adjudged insane, historians have given most attention to the ways in which the insanity defence was adjusted to provide exculpation, the professionalization of forensic psychiatric testimony, and the medicalization of the crime, while concurrently exploring the influence of socio-economic explanations for infanticide, such as poverty, abandonment and spousal

---

[1] R. Sauer, 'Infanticide and abortion in nineteenth-century Britain', *Population Studies*, 32 (1978), 81–93; G.K. Behlmer, 'Deadly motherhood: infanticide and medical opinion in mid-Victorian England', *Journal of the History of Medicine and Allied Sciences*, 34 (1979), 403–27; T.R. Forbes, 'Deadly parents: child homicide in eighteenth- and nineteenth-century England', *Journal of the History of Medicine and Allied Sciences*, 41 (1986), 177–99; R.J. Kellett, 'Infanticide and child destruction: the historical, legal and pathological aspects', *Forensic Science International*, 53, 1 (Feb. 1992), 1–28.

[2] M.L. Arnot, 'Gender in focus: infanticide in England 1840-1880' (PhD diss., Essex, 1994); A.R. Higginbotham, '"Sin of the age": infanticide and illegitimacy in Victorian London', in K.O. Garrigan (ed.), *Victorian Scandals: Representations of Gender and Class* (Athens, University of Ohio Press, 1992), pp. 257–88; L. Zedner, *Women, Crime, and Custody in Victorian England* (Oxford, Clarendon Press, 1991), pp. 29–30, 38–9, 88-90; J.A. Bars, 'Defining murder in Victorian London, an analysis of cases 1862–1892' (DPhil diss., Oxford, 1994).

abuse/unreliability.[3] Most of the existing literature, however, has confined itself primarily to the initial medico-legal and penal arbitration and disposal of offenders. Seldom have historians considered in much depth the longer-term disposal of infanticides, their evaluation whilst under detention within asylums (or prisons), and their discharge and restoration to families and communities.[4]

John Baker, Broadmoor's deputy superintendent, referred to infanticides in 1902 as 'the bulk of the female population'[5] and they similarly represented over half of the female admissions to Perth Prison's criminal lunatic wing. Baker, like most other contemporary authorities, defined infanticide as the murder of infants, typically within days or months (and certainly within a year) of their births. Yet such cases represented but a portion of child murders, and moreover a significantly smaller proportion of those child-murderers designated insane. In a 1999 article, Tony Ward seems to have been the first historian to have thoroughly addressed the paradoxical situation whereby the 'medical' defence up to the Infanticide Act of 1922 was constructed primarily around the murder of new-born infants, despite that fact that 'this kind of infanticide was much less likely to be seen as a product of mental disease than the killing of older babies'.[6]

In this chapter, like Ward, I shall examine (insane) infanticide within the broader setting of violent assaults against children of all ages up to

---

3   T. Ward, 'Psychiatry and criminal responsibility in England, 1843–1939' (PhD diss., De Montfort University, Leicester, 1996); R. Smith, *Trial by Medicine: Insanity and Responsibility in Victorian Trials* (Edinburgh, Edinburgh University Press, 1981); R. Smith, 'Defining murder and madness: an introduction to medicolegal belief in the case of Mary Ann Brough, 1854', in R.A. Jones and H. Kuklick (eds), *Knowledge and Society: Studies in the Sociology of Culture Past and Present. A Research Annual*, vol. 4 (Greenwich, Connecticut: JAI Press, 1983), pp. 173–225; R. Smith, *Criminal Responsibility, Psychiatry and History: Three Essays*, 2nd edn (Lancaster, Centre for Science Studies & Science Policy; Paris, Cité des Sciences et de l'Industrie, 1988).

4   The main exception is Janet Saunders, although her work concentrated on criminal lunatics and mentally defective criminals in general sent to county asylums and other institutions, and on their hereditarian and eugenically motivated quarantining. J. Saunders, 'Magistrates and madmen: segregating the criminally insane in late nineteenth-century Warwickshire', in V. Bailey (ed.), *Policing and Punishment in Nineteenth-Century Britain* (London, Croom Helm, 1981), pp. 217–41; Janet Saunders, 'Criminal insanity in 19th-century asylums', *Journal of the Royal Society of Medicine*, 81 (1988), 73–5; J. Saunders, 'Quarantining the weak-minded: psychiatric definitions of degeneracy and the late Victorian asylum', in W.F. Bynum, R. Porter and M. Shepherd (eds), *The Anatomy of Madness: Essays in the History of Psychiatry*, 3 vols, (London, Tavistock, 1985-88), vol. 3 (1988), pp. 273–96.

5   J. Baker, 'Female criminal lunatics: a sketch', *Journal of Mental Science* (Jan. 1902), 13–25, at 15.

6   T. Ward, 'The sad subject of infanticide; law, medicine and child murder, 1860–1938', *Social and Legal Studies*, 8 (1999), 163–80.

fifteen. However, I shall concentrate on the detention and release of insane offenders. This survey restricts itself to a sample of child-murderers admitted to Broadmoor Hospital and Perth Criminal Lunatic Department (Perth CLD) before 1914. These institutions offer interesting and viable material for comparison, being the main state-sanctioned receptacles for the criminally insane in England and Scotland respectively. However, Perth CLD was much smaller than Broadmoor and, largely because it was not a separate asylum but was physically and administratively attached to Perth's general (convict) prison, it remained more suffused with penal ideologies.[7] While men represented a significant group amongst those 'criminal lunatics' who had murdered or assaulted children, attention will mostly be directed here to women, who constituted the great majority of such offenders.

Some recent historical research on asylums in general, baulking at an over-preoccupation with incarceration in existing historiography, has begun instead to explore excarceration.[8] Yet the dynamics of discharge from institutions like Broadmoor and Perth have rarely been looked into. Well over half of these institutions' child-murderers were discharged as recovered, female offenders being especially likely to obtain their release.[9] An investigation of discharge may reveal a great deal about the relationship between medical, legal and lay attitudes to crime and insanity, and about how more specific medical, moral, gendered and class-mediated constructions of crime and mental disease impacted on the policies of authorities and the attitudes/actions of the wider community. Focusing on the discharge of those convicted of infanticide also enables us to question the extent to which various types of offender could be reintegrated into communities. Roger Smith observed how 'the Home Secretary's power to authorise releases was

---

[7]   For general background on these institutions, see P.H. Allderidge, 'Criminal insanity: from Bethlem to Broadmoor', *Proceedings of the Royal Society of Medicine*, 67 (1974), 897–904; R. Partridge, *Broadmoor: A History of Criminal Lunacy and its Problems* (London, Chatto & Windus, 1953); J.A. Baird, 'The transfer of Scottish prisoners: a historical and descriptive study of convicted prisoners transferred to psychiatric hospitals' (MD diss., University of Edinburgh, 1984).

[8]   D. Wright, 'Getting out of the asylum: understanding the confinement of the insane in the nineteenth century', *Social History of Medicine*, 10, 1 (1997), 137–55; David Wright and Peter Bartlett (eds), *Outside the Walls of the Asylum: The History of Care in the Community* (London, Athlone Press, 1999). See also, J.K. Walton, 'Casting out and bringing back in Victorian England', in Bynum, Porter and Shepherd (eds), *Anatomy of Madness*, vol. 2 (1985), pp. 132–46.

[9]   Broadmoor's Junior Deputy MS, J.S. Hopwood, calculated that for the period 1900–25 'of the 166 cases admitted, 94 [57 per cent] have been discharged recovered'; J.S. Hopwood, 'Child murder and insanity', *Journal of Mental Science* (Jan. 1927), 95–108, at 99. I have found a similar (if slightly smaller) proportion in my own 1863-1914 sample.

exercised more with puerperal maniacs than any other group' but he did not go much further in explaining this than to surmise that 'a major factor' was that post-menopausal women 'could no longer commit the same murders'.[10] This chapter will explore such issues in considerably more depth, through a sustained examination of a wide range of documentation relating to discharge proceedings.

The issue of discharge was closely linked to facts and opinions determined during a patient's trial or at the time of admission, and therefore a patient's ultimate disposal was also related to the trial and the admission process. In the main, this chapter is devoted to distinguishing the major rationales behind patients' discharges, and to contextualizing deliberations over this matter against wider processes of socio-historical change. Although appreciative that the outcome or response to treatment could, of course, have a bearing on medical deliberations over discharge, I am not concerned primarily here with treatment. In the first section, I shall briefly delineate the demographic profiles of child murderers and their victims, more precisely focusing on the women's marital status and the ages of the children, and what these suggest about the distinctive characteristics of insane infanticide. The second section explores the administrative structures within which decisions about discharge were made. The next section addresses the more significant biological and risk factors which determined the arbitration of discharge, such as relapse, re-impregnation, heredity, racial degeneration, puerperal and lactational insanity, and menopause. The chapter concludes by exploring the economic and socio-moral profiles of child murderers, including domestic or spousal abuse and the culture of female 'fallenness', the respectability of the family, and the hygienic and socio-economic suitability of the domiciliary environment.

Marital status of child murderers and age profiles of their victims

The ages of child victims may have significant implications for our understanding of infanticide, and of the distinctive character of lunatic infanticides in Victorian times. Out of 35 child victims – in a sample of 27 child-murdering or assaulting patients admitted to Perth CLD during 1857–1914 – 15 (43 per cent) were infants of under a year old, 11 of whom (31 per cent of the total) were under six months old. Yet even more victims (49 per cent) were two years old and above, while a large contingent (17 per cent) were between five and fifteen.

---

[10] Smith, *Trial by Medicine*, p. 154.

Table 11.1 Child victims murdered/assaulted by patients admitted to
Perth CLD 1857–1914.

Nos.	Age
11	<6 months
4	<1 year
3	<2 years
11	<5 years
4	<10 years
2	<15 years
Total 35	

Table 11.2 Child victims murdered/assaulted by patients admitted to
Broadmoor 1863–1914.

	Victims		Perpetrators	
	Nos.	Age	f	m
	55	<6 months	51	4
	18	<1 year	15	3
	15	<2 years	9	6
	42	<5 years	30	12
	17	<10 years	13	4
	7	<15 years	2	5
Total	154		120	34

Of the 154 child victims – in a sample of 136 patients[11] who committed infanticide or assaulted children and were admitted to Broadmoor in the period 1863–1914 – 47 per cent were under a year old, three-quarters of whom (36 per cent of the total) were under six months. Yet once again older children are significantly represented, 43 per cent in this sample being from two to fifteen years old, and 16 per cent in the five to (under) fifteen age range.

The presence of older children amongst the victims of lunatic infanticides contrasts interestingly with statistics on ordinary ('sane') infanticides, where, as Behlmer and others have shown, infants under one predominated as victims.[12] Possibly, the insanity defence was more likely to succeed (and, no doubt, more commonly pursued) in the case of older children. Moreover, very few (relatively speaking) of the lunatic infanticides in my sample involved new-born infants, or indeed infants

---

[11] Of these patients, 13 had murdered/assaulted more than one child.

[12] Behlmer cites Registrar-General statistics for 1863 which record that 63 per cent of all homicides involved infants under the age of one; G.K. Behlmer, *Child Abuse and Moral Reform in England* (Stanford, California, Stanford University Press, 1982), p. 18.

of less than three months. This clearly reflects the clemency with which crimes against the new-born were prosecuted after 1849 (the date of the last execution for infanticide) and the rarity with which, if prosecuted, they were treated as ordinary homicides (rather than misdemeanours) – and thus the limited utility of an insanity defence in such cases.

As Ward has stressed, insanity was strikingly less preferable as a defence than still-birth or accident.[13] Higginbotham's study of Old Bailey trials of 132 women accused of involvement in illegitimate infant deaths in the period 1839–1906 found only 3 per cent adjudged insane and less than 1 per cent sent to an asylum (although 42 per cent were charged with murder or manslaughter).[14] Where younger infants were involved, courts seem to have found it easier to establish that the mother was sane and responsible, especially where abandonment, desertion, concealment of pregnancy or shame over illegitimacy might be seen as 'rational' motives. Conversely, severe and capital punishments for homicide were more likely in cases where older children were the victims, and it is here that the insanity defence tended to come more into its own.

In only one of the Broadmoor cases in my sample had the mother been convicted of concealing the pregnancy. Although concealment figured to some extent in the trials of quite a number of these infanticides, as Baker found, most such cases involved 'single women who endeavour to hide their shame'.[15] Illegitimacy was somewhat more common amongst the child victims of Broadmoor's patients: case notes, case files and other records show that at least 22 (14 per cent) out of 153 child-murders or assaults (by women) had involved illegitimate children. Yet, while this figure is probably a significant under-registration, since the legitimacy of murdered and assaulted children was not always recorded in available (especially asylum-based) records, it is still likely that illegitimate victims were substantially fewer than ordinary 'sane' infanticides.

Some cases offer poignant testimony to the vilification and mental anguish that women suffered as the result of bearing children out of wedlock. Such cases also reiterate the close relationship historians like Behlmer and Arnot have traced between baby-farming and infanticide, especially in the period of agitation about infant life protection legislation during the early 1870s.[16] The case of Ann O., who was

---

13 Ward, 'Sad subject', 166.
14 Higginbotham, 'Sin of the age'. Baker's 1902 study identified only 16 women who had murdered illegitimate new-borns.
15 Baker, 'Female criminal lunatics', 15, 19.
16 M.L. Arnot, 'Infant death, child care and the state: the baby-farming scandal and the first infant life protection legislation of 1872', *Continuity and Change*, 9/2 (1994), 271–311; Behlmer, *Child Abuse*, ch. 2.

admitted to Broadmoor in 1873 for the murder of her illegitimate four-year-old child, offers a good example.[17] According to her own statement, Ann had given birth to two illegitimate children before her marriage, only one of whom she had evidently told her husband about; the other – reflecting a common contemporary practice[18] – had been 'put out' to private keeping, probably with a relative or hired nurse. What allegedly led to the filicide was the return of this child to stay with her and the resultant shame and familial conflict it aroused, as Ann's former indiscretions were thrust under the nose of her mother-in-law and her husband, who

> when he came to know about the other which was sent from its former keeping to stay with them the fact prayed upon her [Ann's] mind & he was vexed & his mother 'nagged' her about it. This led to her destroying it.

As emerges clearly from the larger Broadmoor sample, there was an important gender disparity in the statistics regarding child victims. Older children were much more prominent as victims of lunatic men than of lunatic women. This suggests that men were more apt than women to murder or assault older children, whereas women's violent impulses were much more focused around problems with the new-born and babies. As well as socio-environmental differences in the responsibilities and stresses of child-rearing, this must also reflect a genuine and predictable epidemiological difference between the sexes, and the strong influence of pre- and post-partum depression and psychosis in determining the violent acts of women.

Typically, murdered and assaulted children in my Broadmoor and Perth samples were the youngest in large families, where parents (women, in particular) already had a number of children to look after. This could be seen to reflect, to some degree, the sense in which infanticide might be a response to difficult, if not intolerable, psychological and socio-economic pressures experienced by women caring for large families. Sometimes, indeed not uncommonly, adults murdered or assaulted more than one child at the same time, and many (women more especially) attempted suicide concurrently (or soon after) a violent assault on their children.

The Harveian Society and most contemporary authorities agreed that 'infanticide was usually the act of single women abandoned by their

---

[17] Broadmoor cases will be identified henceforth by their register number (RN), which links them to their register and case file records in Broadmoor Hospital's Medical Records Centre, in Crowthorne, Berkshire. Ann O.'s number is RN288.

[18] See, for example, the notorious case of Mary Harris discussed by Behlmer, *Child Abuse*, pp. 20–22, and the discussion in Ch. One, above.

lovers'.[19] By contrast, murdering mothers sent to Broadmoor and Perth were typically married women, from poor or lower middling families. Baker's 1902 study calculated that unmarried mothers comprised just 22 per cent of infanticidal women (defined in Baker's study as those who had killed infants under two months old).[20] In my survey of 107 women sent to Broadmoor before 1914 who had murdered or assaulted children under fifteen, 79 (74 per cent) were married, whereas just 25 (23 per cent) were single and 3 were widows. (Married men also predominated amongst a sample of 27 male child murderers or batterers, only 3 being recorded as single, with 3 widowed and 21 married). Although these figures quite evidently constitute an under-registration of those offenders who were separated, abandoned, divorced and widowed, the stark disparity with ordinary infanticide cases is still worthy of emphasis. Indeed, insanity was apparently more likely to be imputed to the infanticidal acts of married mothers than to the same crimes committed by single women. Perhaps married women were more apt to, or be seen to, commit their crimes irrationally because they were regarded as acting in spite of some degree (however variable) of financial and emotional support from their spouses, whereas single mothers were more commonly found to be (or culturally constructed as) the abandoned, the destitute and the isolated.

Structures of authority and bureaucracy

Fundamentally, all decisions whether to discharge patients from Broadmoor and Perth rested with the secretaries and under-secretaries of state for England and Scotland and their departments. The main concern of the Home Office and the Scottish Office in making assessments was (and indeed remains) the continuing risk to the public presented by such cases. Yet the secretary of state's decision was mediated by other authorities, in particular by reports on patients' condition which were forwarded to the department periodically by the medical superintendent and his staff at both institutions. These reports were delivered annually as a requirement of on-going assessment and monitoring, whether a patient was being actively considered for discharge or not. In addition, the medical superintendent was normally asked to submit a special report on a case virtually whenever an application for discharge had been made.

---

[19] Behlmer, *Child Abuse*, pp. 22–3.

[20] Baker, 'Female criminal lunatics', 20. In Hopwood's sample for the period 1900–25, single women comprised 26 per cent of 166 child murderers; Hopwood, 'Child murder', 101.

The sheer amount of work involved in reviewing cases is worth emphasising. It might be assumed that this would have encouraged a rather cursory investigation of cases, but on the contrary it is the thoroughness and efficiency of the authorities that impresses. Evidence from Broadmoor and Perth, nevertheless, shows that families were often ignorant about procedures governing discharge, especially at the start of an admission. Families often did not know whom to apply to, and in what form. Some saw the medical superintendent as 'all powerful in the matter' and bombarded him with letters and appeals, as did the relatives of the Broadmoor infanticide, Rose L.[21] Gradually, however, there tended to be a process of education. Many families persisted in all kinds of strategies to obtain the release of their loved ones, and some displayed tremendous resourcefulness in doing so. While most appeals proved in vain, infanticide cases (females, at least) plainly had a better prognosis in terms of conditional discharge than any other category of murderer admitted to Broadmoor and Perth. Out of a sample of 92 infanticidal women whose outcomes are known, 68 per cent (63) were conditionally released from Broadmoor (7 being removed to other asylums, 21 dying and 1 committing suicide). Men fared considerably worse, only 45 per cent (10) of my sample being discharged to relatives or guardians, 9 dying and 3 being transferred.

Discharge from either institution was a lugubriously bureaucratic business. Broadmoor discharges required sanctions from the Home Office and the medical superintendent (or his staff), but also from the Lunacy Commissioners. They would agree only after detailed investigations into the circumstances of the patients' relations, investigations which could involve a whole host of references from interested parties – from families, friends, neighbours, employers and other acquaintances, to local clergy and parish officers. Discharge applications might also entail the local constabulary being conscripted to vet the suitability and social respectability of the places and persons to which it was planned to return prisoners. Procedures at Perth were even more complicated, its status as a prison meaning that the additional sanction of the Prison Commissioners and their medical advisers was required.

It is an obvious but important point to make that, by contrast with fixed sentencing for ordinary crimes, detentions at 'Her/His Majesty's Pleasure' were by definition unfixed, indeterminate sentences. They were to be legally prolonged for as long as the offender was deemed to be a risk to the public (or themselves), and this tended also to mean for as long as they were still judged insane and unable to take care of

---

[21] RN368.

themselves, or to be safely looked after by others. It should be emphasized, furthermore, that the standard contemporary prison term for 'sane' infanticide in both England and Scotland was itself only about two years, considerably less than the average stay of Broadmoor and Perth infanticides. Even excluding those who never fully recovered, those conditionally discharged in my sample endured average detentions of over four times this duration.

Biological and risk determinants of discharge

The most prominent anxiety amongst officials on both sides of the border in assessing discharge was the risk involved or, as Baker put it in 1902, 'the safety of the public at large'.[22] Home Office officials and prison commissioners took their public responsibilities in this respect very seriously. Often, however, the prime concern of clinicians appears to have been less with the patient re-offending than with the patient relapsing.

While a prime concern in all cases, relapse tended to have a specific meaning for many infanticide cases. Because the majority of such cases after about 1870 were ascribed to puerperal or lactational insanity, relapse was regarded as highly dependent on whether a patient became pregnant again. Yet, as we shall see, the authorities were generally unwilling to take the radical practical steps required to prevent this possibility. Thus fears of relapse could have only a limited impact on policy towards such cases.

Apart from liability to relapse, emphasis was also placed on the hereditary history of insanity in the family as a whole, clinicians often being prepared to investigate the matter deeply and to provide detailed evidence to the Home Office. Baker noted in 1902 that heredity appeared as a factor in 24 per cent of Broadmoor's infanticide cases, and saw this factor as one of six which 'militate against the chances of recovery'.[23] Evidence of heredity appears to have become more detailed and conspicuous in Broadmoor and Perth records towards the end of the nineteenth century, when anxiety about hereditary transmission and the propagation of the mentally unfit was at its height in the psychiatric profession.[24] Broadmoor's Medical Superintendent (MS), William Orange (Deputy Superintendent 1863–70; MS 1870–86), was in no doubt that 'crime is, in many cases, traceable to degeneration, and to

---

[22] Baker, 'Female criminal lunatics', 13.

[23] Ibid., 23.

[24] Hopwood found a family history of insanity in 32 per cent of his 1900–25 sample; Hopwood, 'Child murder', 102.

physical conditions similar to those associated with insanity'.[25] Predictions abounded about the possible degeneration of the race, as did eugenically mediated recommendations for containment measures. Even more than ordinary asylums, these institutions whose inmates combined in one individual the two transmissible vices of crime and insanity were seen by a number of contemporary alienists as providing the quarantine essential for people unfit to breed. Heredity was less commonly accepted as significant evidence in the actual trial process for insanity. Yet alienists were better able to assert their hereditarian views of insanity within the confines of the institutional setting, and other officials were by no means dismissive of the importance of such evidence.

The profundity of medical concerns with hereditary transmission of mental disease clearly impacted on infanticide cases and on society at large during this period. Families themselves appreciated that clinicians placed particular weight on evidence concerning this matter. Speaking on the family's behalf, a sister of the infanticide, Rose L., addressed herself to the subject of heredity in a 1902 letter to the Broadmoor MS 'as it seems to me to have an important bearing on the case'.[26] This family and others were at pains to deny or conceal the evidence of hereditary taint, but asylum officials were equally concerned to expose such obfuscation, which they saw as undermining the accuracy of their own science and against the wider interests of society. For example, when Rose's sister testified that 'we can say with absolute truth that we have no insanity in our family. My father was always most emphatic on this point', Richard Brayn, the Broadmoor MS (1895–1910) was careful to contradict her testimony. He informed the Home Office at some length that the 'statement ... is not correct', that her 'sister died in Banstead Asylum a few years ago. A paternal Aunt is also said to have been insane. Mrs L's father drank to excess & some of her sisters were intemperate'. Such discrepancies were not merely a case of deceit and ignorance on the family's part, but also arose from genuine disparities between lay and medical views of insanity. Many families would not have conceived of intemperance, insanity or eccentricity in distant relations as evidence of hereditary taint, and their interests were only ambivalently served by doing so.

Medical anxieties about hereditary transmission continued to figure in decisions about patients' guardianship after discharge, especially when it came to questions of marriage or the likelihood of relapse. There

---

[25] W. Orange, 'Criminal responsibility in relation to insanity', in D.H. Tuke (ed.), *Dictionary of Psychological Medicine*, 2 vols (London, Churchill, 1892), vol. 1, pp. 294–320, at 320.

[26] RN368.

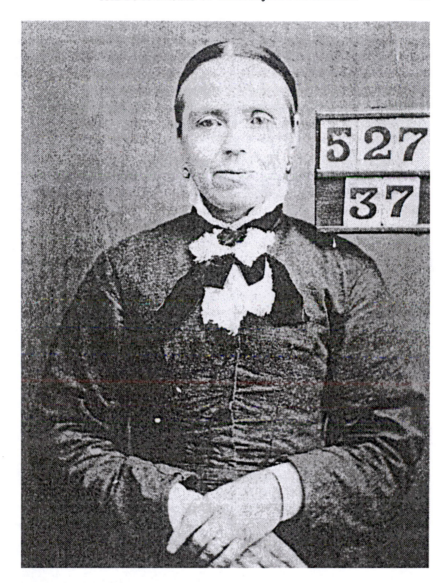

Figure 11.1 The infanticide 'Mrs Marjory M.' sought conditional discharge from Perth prison in 1877 so that she could marry. After two relapses, she was finally set free unconditionally in 1909.

is evidence in the records – from Broadmoor, Perth and other asylums – of families experiencing deep anxiety about the issue, and of some actually breaking off marriage contracts if a history of insanity was discovered. In the case of the conditionally liberated Kilmarnock infanticide, Mrs Marjory M. (see Figure 11.1), who wished to marry another conditionally discharged criminal lunatic from Perth CLD, her guardian wrote a memorandum to the Home Secretary in 1877, stating in terms highly redolent of medical language that she had

> no fear that she will ever relapse into her former condition, & as she is nearly 50 years of age, there does not appear to be any likelihood of her transmitting a diseased organism to another generation.[27]

Occasionally, testimony from patients' guardians and other lay folk is highly suggestive of the adoption of – or engagement with – medical models as to hereditary transmission. Sarah E.D.'s mother responded to one of her daughter's letters from Broadmoor, pointing out that there was more insanity in her blood than Sarah had herself recognized:

> Her mother writes (today) "You say that only your Aunt Ann committed suicide but my aunt Jane cut her throat, your uncle Joe of Sheffield committed suicide by throwing himself in the canal".[28]

The medical staff at Perth and the Scottish Prison Commissioners were sometimes fastidious in noting in case files any information about hereditary taint. Crombie, secretary to the Scottish Prison Commissioners, recorded that Sarah C.S.'s husband, for example, 'never heard of insanity shewing itself in any members of either his own or his wife's family'. However, Crombie subsequently noted a communication from the local police,

> stating that one of the lunatic's uncles Andrew ... died in Gartnavel Asylum. He believed that he would lose all his money and that he would die in poverty – a similar phase of insanity which exhibited itself in Sarah.[29]

The original communication from the constabulary was even more detailed on the subject, but was itself heavily reliant on local knowledge in the community. Indeed, it is arguable to what extent medical experts and other officials were imposing hereditarian views of criminal insanity, and to what extent they were merely codifying and extending the meaning of popular, folk judgments that had long prevailed in families and communities. As Zedner argues, Victorian alienists 'continued to operate entirely within the bounds of their moral world', so that 'their

---

[27] Perth cases will be mostly identified henceforth by their case book reference or else by their case file number. For Marjory M., the references are HH21/48/1, 93–6 and HH18/51. James Thomson was her intended spouse. Perth CLD and related criminal records are housed in West Register House, Charlotte Square, Edinburgh, EH2 4DF (part of the National Archives of Scotland, HM General Register House, formerly the SRO).

[28] RN384.

[29] HH17/104; HH21/48/3, 457–9.

resulting definitions were almost as much a product of contemporary values as were earlier explicitly moral and social interpretations'.[30]

In some cases, however, such as Mary B.C.[31] – admitted to Perth in 1865 after drowning the youngest of her several children – it was their hereditary history most of all that appears to have persuaded clinicians to consider them too dangerous to be at large. Mary was said to have full cousins for parents and an insane sister, whilst her parish minister informed the Perth Medical Superintendent that 'her uncle was in an asylum, also that several ... are regarded as of weak mind in their locality'. She was recorded to have been adjudged sane by medical witnesses at her trial, despite evidence of a previous bout of insanity at the puerperal period, but they 'agreed that she was unsafe to be liberated on the ground chiefly of hereditary Insanity'. Mary was conditionally liberated after twelve years at Perth.

Despite such evidence, it nevertheless seems unlikely that the Home Office itself, either in England or in Scotland, placed much weight on heredity in coming to a decision, the subject rarely being cited in Home Office minutes. When it was mentioned, it generally appears to have had considerably less bearing on the fact or timing of release than did other diagnostic and socio-moral criteria. Moreover, if there was a form of insanity in this period in which heredity was seen as of less significance it was probably puerperal insanity, the very diagnosis that may be seen as making infanticide cases more distinctive. Most contemporary medical investigations of puerperal insanity – in looking for its aetiological basis in the transient generative, or time-of-life, physiological processes that were common to all women around pregnancy, childbirth, lactation or menopause – tended to offset the emphasis on heredity normally found in explanations of mental disease. Indeed, it is notable how much less frequently cases were ascribed to such physiological factors in analyses of the causes of insanity in ordinary prison populations, where hereditary taint was seen to abound.[32]

---

[30] Zedner, *Women, Crime, and Custody*, p. 90.

[31] HH21/48/1, 165–7.

[32] A study of English local prisons by John Baker in the 1890s showed factors such as heredity, congenital and previous attack accounting for 26 per cent of female cases of insanity as against just 9 per cent ascribed to specifically female physiological processes; Baker, 'Insanity in English local prisons, 1894–5', *Journal of Mental Science* (April 1896), 294–302, at 299. Even so, hereditarian and more general organic interpretations of child murderers' insanity were sometimes cited by clinicians in contradiction of puerperal (and even lactational) explanations, especially in the case of mothers who had murdered older infants and children. Although on her admission to Broadmoor in 1874, for example, the cause of Caroline E.'s infanticide had been registered as 'puerperal', in her case notes this was rejected on the ground that the child had been nine months old, and heredity recorded instead: 'Not puerperal – child nine months of age. Hereditary tendency – mother's brother was insane & cut his throat'. See RN237.

Lurking beneath and beyond the extra risk of relapse that a strong heredity was perceived to endow patients with, were medico-legal concerns about the possibility that patients would again become pregnant. The vast majority of infanticides committed to Broadmoor and Perth in this period were young women, of child-bearing age (less than 8 per cent out of 155 admitted to Broadmoor before 1914 were aged forty-five or over), whose murderous acts were commonly ascribed to puerperal or lactational insanity, or other gender-specific biological factors. Puerperal and lactational insanity were also understood by contemporary medical men to be conditions peculiarly liable to relapse. The danger of releasing women of child-bearing age was a frequent concern in deliberations over discharge, and was a crucial factor in actively delaying the discharge of some women from both institutions. Furthermore, this concern seems to have become more prominent towards the end of the period, as the psychiatric community grew more preoccupied with hereditary and organically rooted mental disease. For example, out of a sample of 52 infanticidal women admitted to Broadmoor during 1880–1902, 63 per cent (33) were over 40 and 44 per cent (23) were over 45 when discharged to their families or guardians, whereas of 30 admitted during the earlier period 1863–79 only 40 per cent (12) were over forty and only 10 per cent (3) over forty-five when discharged.[33]

Sarah E.D. – admitted in 1885 aged twenty-three, after murdering her only child and subsequently giving birth to another in the asylum – was not conditionally discharged to the care of her nephew until 1907, when she was forty-five.[34] Mary J.H., admitted to Broadmoor in 1891 aged twenty-eight, after drowning both her children, did not gain her discharge until she was forty years old, in 1913.[35] After years of recurrent depression and religious mania, her case notes record a prolonged period of mental tranquillity, her only reported symptoms during the last decade of her stay being headache, migraine and 'malaise' (often during menstruation), 'irregularity' of menstrual periods and occasional 'religious exaltation'. Yet frequently the Broadmoor and Perth authorities appear to have had little other option than to detain such patients, given their continuing symptoms of acute derangement.

Cases examined at Perth CLD appear to imply that concern with future pregnancies in discharging criminal lunatics was no more nor less prominent in Scotland. Mary S.B.[36] – sent to Perth in 1881 aged thirty-five, after the murder of one child and attempted murder of two others

---

[33] This is only partly explained by a disparity in the average age on admission of these samples, the earlier group being aged 30 on average, and the later group 33.

[34] RN384.

[35] RN468.

[36] HH21/48/2, 231–4; HH17/13.

– waited seventeen years for her discharge. By this time – as John MacNaughton, the Perth Superintendent, reported – her acute phase and 'tendency to violence' had long 'passed away'. The Scottish Lunacy Commission concurred with this verdict, John Sibbald observing that 'her homicidal condition ceased more than 12 years since' and that 'as it was connected with pregnancy and subsequent nursing it is not likely to recur, she being now past the age for childbearing'.[37] In 1898 Mary was transferred to Ayr District Asylum.

Concern about future child-bearing was rarely a decisive factor on its own in justifying patients' continuing detention. And despite the percolation of heightened anxieties about degeneration and hereditary taint, the impact of such issues on discharge policy seems rather limited. The authorities, bowing no doubt to the weight of community interest in achieving the early restoration of family members, seem to have been more concerned with the simple matter of relapse than with any risk to the race as a whole presented by infanticides. Worries about child-bearing were evidently less to do with the question of the transmission of disease to future generations, than with the possibility of the mother again becoming insane and therefore a threat to her own, or to other, young children. While puerperal insanity was seen as a form of mental disease very apt to recur, it also tended to be regarded as a somewhat temporary condition. Whereas the majority of infanticide cases gained their release only in their late forties or older, a significant proportion of women were conditionally discharged while still young and fertile, after detentions of less than ten years. Medical superintendents and Home Office officials were reluctant to accept the implications of a policy of eliminating all risks in discharging infanticides. This would have meant detaining some young women for twenty-five years or more, after they had to all intents and purposes recovered. Neither Broadmoor nor Perth, nor any other contemporary British institution, ever seems to have been used for an especially strict policy of procreative quarantine.

In the case of Lucy K., admitted to Broadmoor in 1878, for example, William Orange reported to the Home Office in 1885 that

> she is 35 years of age; and although ... there would be considerable risk of her relapsing if she were discharged ... this risk would not be materially lessened unless she were detained [*and here he crossed out the phrase* 'for a period of perhaps fifteen years or more', *substituting*] until she had passed the child bearing age.[38]

---

[37] Notably, Sibbald had been one of those commissioners who had championed the closer supervision in Scotland of single patients in private dwellings and removing the inadequately supervised to asylums, partly on the ground of preventing them from propagating the mentally unfit.

[38] RN284.

Lucy was discharged in 1886.

Some women were discharged with striking speed, despite explicit concerns about future impregnation. Emma L. – admitted to Broadmoor in 1876 aged twenty-two, after cutting her three-week-old infant's throat and attempting suicide, was discharged conditionally to her friends within two years, despite prominent fears about the consequences that might occur with a subsequent pregnancy. Ellen A. – a twenty-year-old servant who had strangled her child – was conditionally liberated within a year of her admission to Perth in 1896, and was unconditionally liberated two and a half years later, marrying a farm servant.[39] On the one hand, Ellen's case underlines the continuing preparedness of psychiatric and penal authorities to regard puerperal insanity as a temporary condition. On the other hand, concerns about future impregnation and the need for adequate supervision were still prominent in granting her full liberation: as the under secretary of state put it, 'she may again become pregnant, in which case some supervision might be expedient'.[40]

Ellen's case may have been slightly exceptional. She was considered sane from the time of her admission, and discharged to the supervision and employ of the Pilkingtons, relatives of the Perth Medical Superintendent, MacNaughton; and it was there that she met her future husband, another of the Pilkingtons' employees. Yet it is a striking example of the sympathetic way medico-legal supervision could function in this period, and of the relatively relaxed assessment of the dangers of release, re-impregnation and relapse. However, one should not exaggerate this sympathy, for the special concern that interested persons displayed in such cases is not necessarily a good guide to attitudes in the wider community. For example, in 1877, eighteen months after her conditional discharge from Perth CLD, Marjory M.'s guardian testified to being 'induced to apply for her release, by the solicitations of my sister, Mrs Eliza Brown', herself a conditionally discharged child murderer who had spent six years in Perth.[41] This guardian also referred to 'the hope of settling Mrs M. in a comfortable way of living thus doing good to her & carrying out the

---

[39] For Emma L. see RN252; for Ellen A., see HH21/48/3, 304–306; HH17/2.

[40] It was largely on this ground that a request for liberation was initially refused by the secretary of state department, and then her conditional liberation was relaxed first to quarterly reports and annual visits, before she was unconditionally liberated. By law (the 1871 Criminal and Dangerous Lunatics Act), conditional liberation normally required 6 monthly reports to be made on the prisoner by the Perth Superintendent to the Prison Commissioners, and monthly reports by the guardian. The continuance of this licence was very much dependent on the prisoner's continuing good conduct.

[41] HH21/48/1, 93–6; HH18/51.

benevolent intentions of the law in regard to such persons'. Yet, despite continuous years of mental health since her admission, Marjory's own family had been decidedly unwilling to take her home, while her discharge had been long delayed due to the difficulty of finding a suitable guardian. She was to go through a host of different guardians and two further readmissions before she was unconditionally discharged in 1909.

Alienists had long connected insanity amongst women in their forties with the menopausal cycle, and Baker estimated that 13 per cent of Broadmoor's female infanticides had killed 'under the influence of climacteric insanity'.[42] It is not remarkable therefore that, quite apart from medical concerns about future pregnancies and child rearing, discharge was also subject to delay out of anxiety about the impact of the menopause. Eliza T., for example – admitted to Broadmoor in 1877, after drowning her youngest in a tub – was refused her discharge in 1880 in part because she was deemed at forty-five years old to be 'approaching a time of life when a relapse is not unlikely'.[43] This was despite her having been free from relapse since admission. Of a sample of 65 infanticidal women admitted to Broadmoor during 1866–1902 and discharged to relatives or guardians, two-thirds (44) were over forty and 39 per cent (26) were over forty-five. However, in many cases, as in Eliza's, concerns about future impregnation and the menopause were often aired only to be shelved quite quickly afterwards. Following further pressure from an MP, parish rector, surgeon and her own husband, Eliza was discharged in 1881.

Occasionally, important diagnostic distinctions had a crucial bearing on the deliberation of infanticidal cases, and they signal substantial impact for psychiatric understandings of puerperal and lactational insanity in influencing politico-legal authorities. In Emma L.'s case, the visiting justices of Warwick County Prison had applied for her release within a couple of months of her admission on the specific grounds that she had been suffering from puerperal fever and had recovered. However, the asylum and Home Office officials responded that Emma had been suffering on the contrary from puerperal mania and that such a condition required more caution. Periodic reports from Orange expressed explicit anxieties that

> as she is a young & married woman, and ... might ... again & again
> ... bear children ... Should she be discharged to the care of her friends
> we would recommend that the strictest attention & watchfulness ...
> should be provided ... particularly during those periods when her

[42] Baker, 'Female criminal lunatics', 23.
[43] RN270.

morbid feelings are especially likely to be attended with risk of harm,
namely, not only during pregnancy but also up to the time of the
weaning of the child.[44]

Even so, the conditions of discharge for Emma and other child
murderers rarely stipulated much more than that relations and local
authorities maintain the patient 'under careful supervision' and
immediately report any symptoms of a recurrence of the malady, and
this may imply a limited role for after-care by doctors.

In both the treatment and the on-going assessment of infanticidal
women in the asylum, particular emphasis was generally placed on the
restoration and maintenance of putatively 'normal' menstruation and
lactation. To some degree this was the case for other categories of female
patients too. Yet such concerns were especially prominent for female
child murderers. This was mainly due to prevailing medical
understandings of most female infanticide as arising from gender-
specific biological imbalances – from the insanity of pregnancy, and
puerperal and lactational insanity – and the conviction that patients'
mental problems would ease once such imbalances were corrected.
Similarly, patients' continuing emotional and behavioural problems in
the asylum, as well as reports of physical sickness and pain, were often
related to ovarian and gender-specific biological origins, as when Sarah
E.D. was regularly recorded as 'very depressed & irritable at times' as a
result of 'uterine problems' and given a pessary to wear.[45] Often such
diagnoses were made by clinicians at the cost of more prosaic emotional
and psychological causes. Yet there is some, if often rather scanty,
evidence from patients' notes and letters that women themselves may
have shared these views of their illnesses, as when it was recorded of
Mary J.H. in 1897–98 that she was 'subject to recurrent attacks of
melancholia of an ovarian and hysterical colouring' and also that she
herself 'complains of slight ovarian pain left side'.[46]

Patients' sexual propensities were also seen as peculiarly associated
with such conditions. An additional stumbling block to Mary J.H.'s
earlier discharge was quite evidently her relationships with other
patients, seen by her doctors as unhealthily intimate. Mary herself
accused other patients of having 'unholy passions' towards her. Similar
anxieties about patients' morbid sexual impulses were prominent in
other infanticide cases as well, and clearly hindered their early discharge.
Agnes D., for example, was said to display 'undesirable peculiarities' in
her relations to other females:

---

[44] RN252.
[45] RN384.
[46] RN468.

> Once or twice she has gone to ward 5 to have tea with another patient named Doyle. Their demeanour towards one another partakes somewhat of a morbidly affectionate character. They endeavour to shut themselves in a room together & the whole circumstances are not above suspicion.[47]

Patients were seldom considered healthy and discharged unless 'morbid' sexual feelings had abated, and unless abnormal gynaecological or urogenital signs were absent or radically reduced. This was more especially the case in Broadmoor, where medical treatments such as binding the breasts and drug therapies aimed at modifying production of menses and breast milk were deployed. At Perth, however, records of such concerns are much sparser, and are prominent rather later in the period, again reflecting perhaps the more limited influence of psychiatric approaches on the institutional environment.

Social, moral and environmental determinants of discharge

Amongst the most important criteria for the restoration of offenders to their families were the social and moral condition of the family itself, criteria highly prone to various cultural, class, gender and educational biases. Asylum superintendents, Home Office officials, and prison commissioners put considerable emphasis on the social respectability of patients' relations in the assessment of suitability for discharge, or relaxations of the conditions of discharge. Thus the husband of Sarah A.B., described in Broadmoor records as 'a man occupying a respectable position as a school board Visitor', was profiled more positively than the significantly poorer engineer husband of Lucy K., whose residence in India was initially seen as a severe impediment to his wife's discharge.[48] Officials and medical officers from other institutions which had dealings with Broadmoor also often remarked on the degree of respectability of patients' backgrounds. The Newgate medical officer, for example, noted the connection of Sarah's husband 'with the School board and [that] they were moving in respectability'. Similar examples may be found at Perth. Almost identically, Sarah C.S.'s speedy discharge in 1903 and subsequent relaxations of her supervision were repeatedly referred to her family's respectability, while her father was observed to have 'a large dairy farm and ... a seat on the Parish Council and School Board'.[49]

Assessments by clinicians and officials of social respectability often

---

[47] RN472. It was later recorded as 'noticible [sic] that she is generally in company of the younger patients'.

[48] RN316 and RN284.

[49] HH17/104; HH21/48/3, 457–9.

appear to accord with those of families and other opinion at the local
level, on which officialdom was anyway very much reliant for its
information. In Sarah C.S.'s case, her local parish minister had
provided the Home Office and Prison Commissioners with a detailed
endorsement of her family's respectability. He put considerable value
on the wholesome moral virtues of a previously harmonious and
loving marital life, and on Mr S.'s honourable, upright, honest and
kind character. Yet there is also substantial evidence of criteria and
standards being imposed by authorities that were significantly at
variance with those of certain sectors of the community, and more
especially families themselves.

Patients' levels of education, judged in particular in terms of their
literacy, were recorded on admission, and assessments of the educational
backgrounds of their family and kin on the same grounds had real
bearing on patients' suitability for discharge, and on their kin's
acceptability as guardians. It seems unlikely that educated officials at
either the Edinburgh or the London Home Office would have had the
same standards as patients' families and communities in this respect. If
sometimes they were able to encourage higher standards, at other times
their attitudes may have over-valued education and undervalued
emotional bonds, and lacked appreciation of the socio-economic
contexts of poor families. It is not surprising that the Broadmoor
infanticide, Emma L., had a number of applications for discharge
refused and was ultimately discharged in 1878 to her friends rather than
her husband when her case files recorded that

> her husband ... does not appear to be in sufficiently good
> circumstances, or to possess the necessary degree of intelligence
> which would enable him to have his wife properly taken care of, and
> to prevent for the future the possibility of violence.[50]

This contrasts with the local newspaper report, which had
characterized Thomas L. as 'a hard-working respectable man' although
'rather short of work at the time' of the crime, and his wife as a
'woman [who] has always borne a character amongst her neighbours
for industry and respectability'.

Similar evaluations were also prominent within the criminal-lunatic
asylum and amongst government officials subsequently, and were often
key in deliberations over discharge. While many relatives were criticized
for not visiting or writing to patients enough, many others were
censured for interfering too much, for communicating selfishly or
excessively emotively to patients. Husbands who were working or living
away from home were seen as in positions of quasi-abandonment of

---

[50] RN252.

their wives, even though the narrow employment opportunities and economic circumstances of some seem to have given them few options. And relatives themselves attempted to counter such concerns in their appeals to the authorities. Edward, the husband of Lucy K., for example, wrote to the Broadmoor Superintendent:

> There is no use my coming to England to seek Employment as I could not get a situation Railway Companies bringing up their own Drivers from lower scales. Therefore you can see how I am situated.[51]

Not infrequently, clinicians appear rather judgmental of relatives, whose moral values they often found wanting and whose interventions were seen as damaging to progress in patients' mental health. In attempting to preach healthy conduct in order to prevent mental ill health, late Victorian psychiatry had increasingly tended to posit as a moral sin behaviour that appeared to contravene the laws of health. If relatives appeared negligent in the circumstances of the crime's original commission, a negative impression was often formed in the minds of the authorities. Contemporary asylum clinicians were particularly damning of relatives who deferred placing women displaying signs of puerperal insanity in asylums 'owing', as Baker put it in 1902, 'to some perverse reasoning'.[52] Similar judgments appear in Broadmoor clinical notes. Lucy K.'s husband was noted to have been absent in India when she killed her child. The husband of Mary J.H. had said on an initial visit that 'he noticed nothing wrong as he was very busy day and night at his trade (a hatter)'.[53] His subsequent translation to America to get work, and the emotional letters he wrote to his wife, did little to improve his standing in the eyes of Broadmoor's Superintendent, who observed that 'her husband ... is apparently wandering aimlessly about the United States & not doing much good'.

On the other hand, despite reservations and judgmentalism on the part of officials and medical men, it was often the will of the family that eventually prevailed in the restitution of offenders to their communities. About nine years after her admission, Lucy K. was indeed allowed to go to her husband in Bombay, the conditions of her discharge stipulating that her brother transfer her

> to the care of Mr and Mrs Merrony and Mrs Little during a voyage to Bombay, where, upon arrival, she shall be by him placed without delay under special supervision in an Asylum in the event of a relapse into insanity.

The key role women played in child care and household work obviously

---

[51] RN284.
[52] Baker, 'Female criminal lunatics', 22.
[53] RN468.

meant that many families were keen to get mothers back as soon as they could. Indeed, it was these more pragmatic, if not selfish, motivations that are often in evidence in the negotiation of discharge as much as, if not more than, the interests of affection. It was only when feeling the strain of domestic cares upon him, three years after his wife's stroke, that the father of Mary J.H. wrote to Broadmoor in 1894:

> asking about patient's liberty says "her mother my wife has had a stroke since three years ago". Wants daughter out to assist in house work.

Within a few years of this application, however, the widowed father had remarried, and seems to have been much less inclined to have his daughter back, Mary complaining in correspondence at the apparent change in her father's 'manner' towards her, which she attributed to the influence of his new wife. Mary was eventually discharged conditionally to the care of her sister in 1913, twelve years after her admission.

This is not to deny that abuse, abandonment and other forms of domestic strife and hardship are regularly in evidence, and often cited in infanticide cases. It was frequently just these sorts of histories to which particular attention was drawn, both during and after the trial. The recent historiography on infanticide has observed repeatedly the tendency in trial proceedings, judgments and social commentary for blame to be shifted from female offenders to their husbands or other 'responsible' males, more especially those who could be shown to have neglected their social duties or obligations.[54] Similar evaluations are also very prominent within the criminal-lunatic asylum and amongst government officials subsequently, and were often key in deliberations over discharge. Mary A.H., for example, was admitted to Broadmoor in 1891 with a head injury, the result of a blow to the head received from her husband about twelve years previously.[55] The insanity of Agnes L.B. – wife of a Glasgow engraver and the youngest of a family of eleven, admitted to Perth CLD in 1902 after drowning her six-month-old baby and attempting to drown herself – was attributed explicitly by her siblings

> to the harsh & cruel treatment of her husband. After her return from the Asylum he subjected her to continued abuse, pulling her out of bed by the hair of her head, & attempting to throw her over the window.[56]

---

[54] Ward, 'Sad subject', 169, 176.

[55] RN462.

[56] HH21/48/3, 481–3, 437; HH17/58. Evidence of spousal abuse was not always verifiable for, as in Agnes's case, it was sometimes provided by the alleged victim alone: Agnes's siblings 'did not see this done, but were told it by Agnes herself'.

Agnes herself ascribed her crimes directly to her husband's (mental) cruelty: 'She gave the cause that her husband had said he would be in a better position were it not for her'.

The history of Agnes D.'s 'domestic trouble' (she was admitted to Broadmoor in 1892 after drowning a three-and-a-half-year-old child),[57] combined a whole gamut of ingredients that one finds routinely in infanticide cases: a large family, infant mortality, illegitimacy, post-partum depression, poverty, marital disharmony and spousal abuse or desertion. Having lost two of her four children (the first stillborn, the second within a week of its birth) by the time she was just twenty years old, a second marriage had required her to take on three more stepchildren, while the illegitimacy of her eldest child was the source of constant strife with her new husband. It was this illegitimate child that she murdered. She was recorded (in the patient register) to have confessed 'not [to have] felt well since birth of second last child only a year ago', complaining that her 'husband [had] ... caused her much worry and unhappiness while she was not feeling strong'. Indeed:

> she seems to have led a miserable and unhappy married life. Husband treated her badly when she was 'carrying' the last child and though he never actually used violence towards her his conduct made her very unhappy. An illegitimate child from before marriage seems to have been the cause of his ill treatment of her.

While such histories were commonly cited as exculpatory and as explicatory of a perpetrator's mental affliction, they might also be highly pertinent to the negotiation of the prisoner's length of stay in a special institution and the appropriate circumstances for discharge. A significant proportion of women detained in Perth and Broadmoor had patently come from abusive domestic situations, with drunken, violent or negligent husbands, or other miscreant relations. Yet, for the very reason that their domestic situations were so unfavourable, unless alternative means of support could be found, their discharge could be delayed, and their return to their former situations rendered highly unlikely. Evidently unsuitable for a return to her husband's domicile, it was ten years before Agnes D. was discharged to her brother's care. And, significantly, only 22 out of a sample of 52 married women discharged to non-institutional settings from Broadmoor were returned to their husbands' care, 18 being sent to their parents, siblings or children, and the rest to other relatives or unrelated guardians deemed more responsible.

Similar instances of ill-treatment and domestic trouble appear frequently in Broadmoor and Perth records, making up about 17 per

---

[57] RN472.

cent of my infanticide sample thus far. Such cases plainly won extra sympathy from clinicians, their stories resonating with standard Victorian constructions of distressed or fallen women and of virtually blameless crime seen as springing – in part at least – from ineluctable environmental degradation.[58] In some cases, such gendered sympathy seems to have disposed male clinicians and Home Office officials quite positively towards a rapid release, if alternative support could be found. Hannah J.C. – admitted in 1891 aged twenty-eight, after drowning two of her children in the canal – was said in clinical notes to have

> had [a] very unhappy married life – husband a drunkard & treated her very cruelly – were evicted for non-payment of rent, husband bullied and cursed her – got into a state of despair.[59]

She was discharged conditionally to her brother's care after a stay of just over five years.

A case worthy of deeper consideration is that of Emily H.W., an eighteen-year-old unmarried domestic servant, who was discharged to her friends' care just one and a half years after her admission for murdering her illegitimate baby six hours after its birth. Her insanity was attributed in case notes in relatively uncomplicated terms to 'childbirth and seduction mental worry in consequence'.[60] Ward's account of her trial underlines how much more controversial her case was than appears on first inspection in her notes: her open admission of the murder, having concealed the pregnancy, nullified the possibility of a defence citing still-birth or accident. Ward points out how clinical concepts such as 'transient delirium' (as introduced in Emily's case) occasionally served to muddy the waters and how it was 'medical uncertainty' over the accused's state of mind which enabled Emily's acquittal on grounds of insanity.[61]

Ward mostly confined his consideration of this and other cases to trial documents, however, and for any complete view of such cases it seems important to examine both trial and institutional records. Other more lay-mediated factors, such as what the judge called her 'innocent and prepossessing appearance' (clinicians too referring to her as 'a rather pleasant looking girl with a childish expression of face'), also clearly played their part in this case. Even more telling no doubt was sympathy surrounding the circumstances of her impregnation, through rape by her step-father. There seems little doubt that the apparent lack of definitive

---

[58] A. Anderson, *Tainted Souls and Painted Faces: The Rhetoric of Fallenness in Victorian Culture* (Ithaca, Cornell University Press, 1993); Ward, 'Sad subject', 165-6.

[59] RN590.

[60] RN485.

[61] Ward, 'Sad subject', 166–7.

signs of insanity pre-trial, which had provoked a judicial recommendation that she be 'sent to a home or refuge', also helped post-trial to ensure that her detention in Broadmoor was a short one. Emily's 'wretched', if not ashamed, feelings about her pregnancy are stated quite explicitly in case notes and would probably have been just as significant and comprehensible to the assembled court as they were subsequently to clinicians in the asylum. She was described in case notes as having

> not been feeling well during the 9 months she had been 'carrying the baby' feeling ill and wretched suffering much from headache sleeplessness and lowness of spirit. The night before her baby was born she did not sleep at all feeling so wretched and miserable.

Not dissimilarly, Harriet R.H., another unmarried domestic servant (or cook) admitted to Broadmoor in 1895 after brutally killing her new-born baby, was discharged about two and a half years later to her sister's care. She was described as having 'led a sober industrious life herself, till she unfortunately got into trouble ... was very miserable & melancholic at the time of birth of the child', the cause of her malady ascribed to 'love affairs (seduced?) & puerperal [state]'.[62] Such histories of seduction and victimization of respectable poor women were apt to engender compassion on the part of medical and lay authorities. Nevertheless, those who displayed emotional, unseemly or forward conduct whilst in the asylum could provoke serious doubts as to their fitness for the outside world. Three months before her discharge, Harriet was said to be 'though rational & tranquil at present, with her gushing & somewhat flaunting manner it is a question if she would not get into trouble again if discharged'.

Mary J.W. – admitted in 1902 after drowning one of her children, and discharged to her aunt's care after a detention of less than six months – gives us the classic history of fallenness.[63] Abandoned by her lover, a married man who had seduced her by deception and then hanged himself, her condition was likewise attributed to 'domestic troubles': to this desertion and to the 'grief' and shock at his suicide and her father's death soon after. Her rapid discharge was clearly expedited by sympathy for her fallenness and by the fact of her having a new baby to look after, originally born in Warwick prison. Such cases imply that the circumstances surrounding the crime were far from irrelevant to the rapidity of a discharge.

In a larger proportion of female infanticide cases than in other female admissions insanity was attributed by clinicians – and, even more so, by families and by offenders themselves – to domestic troubles. This was an

---

[62] RN507.
[63] RN618.

ascription that tended to free the perpetrator from the blame commonly associated with other mental pathologies such as general paralysis of the insane, masturbatory insanity and alcoholically induced states. Insanity attributed to moral causes also promised higher hopes of recovery and restitution than organically rooted conditions. This fact cannot have been lost on perpetrators and their relations, and clinicians often appear content to credit their explanations. Clinical notes for Rebecca L., admitted to Broadmoor in 1884 after drowning the youngest of seven children, certainly suggest acceptance of her version of events and her ascription of her condition to 'ill usage on part of her husband'.[64] They record that she gave 'a calm & rational account of herself & the circumstances connected with her offence', claiming she 'had "slaved" very hard to keep things going with her intemperate husband who was very exacting thoughtless & unkind'. Not all such women had alternative places to go, however, while the needs of remaining children often proved compelling. Although her history may have helped to elicit sympathy and to shorten her period of detention, irrespective of her marital problems, Rebecca was discharged to her husband's care within two years of her committal.

Not all lunatic infanticides received such sympathy towards their stories. The language used by clinicians to record patients' own accounts of themselves was sometimes disposed to be dubious and rather dismissive, if not overtly disparaging of them. The case notes of Annie P., for example – she was admitted to Broadmoor in 1883 and described repeatedly as maniacal, troublesome and annoying to other patients and staff – record as follows:

> 25/05/1885 ... gives a long gabbling account of her former history. How her husband had given up his former way & married her 'under a cloak'. That when she threw the child out of the window her husband had approached her with the view of assaulting her. How she had typhoid fever, a 'miscarry' & a 'stroke' (left side) all about the same time. It was all thro' the illtreatment of her husband, & his mother who was not carrying on right.[65]

Versions of events from different actors were not always identical and they pose problems for the social historian in identifying bias, misunderstanding or incomplete knowledge: yet they may also reveal something about prevailing ideologies within, and disparities between, lay and medical attitudes. While Annie P. blamed her husband's ill treatment, he himself denied the charge, alleging that it was she who had been abusing him with bad language and had also got into 'intemperate habits'. Clinicians, meanwhile, more disposed towards physiological

---

[64] RN365.
[65] RN364.

than socio-moral explanations, adjudged the alleged history of spousal abuse and intemperance as 'doubtful', placing emphasis instead on an attack of typhoid and pleurisy after the birth of her last child.

Rose L., who spent over thirty years in Broadmoor before being discharged to her sister's care in 1914, complained repeatedly about the 'bad treatment she received from her husband' and was convinced that he was to blame for her plight, refusing to have anything much to do with him or her sisters whilst in the asylum.[66] Yet her case notes suggest a chronic pattern of pathological persecutory delusions and paranoia. Her husband, meanwhile, offered a very different story, alleging that she had succumbed to drink due to the bad influence of her elder sisters, as a result of which she had 'became a different person' and been admitted to an inebriates' home. Before killing the child, he claimed, she had already attempted to drown it once before, to commit suicide by drinking chloroform, and to suffocate him also, while – as he emphasized further – he had 'ample proof that his wife was unfaithful'.

The willingness or ability of patients to maintain contacts with relations, and the family's and community's willingness to receive them back, were plainly highly significant factors in the negotiation of discharge. Patients were generally encouraged to sustain communication with ('respectable') families by asylum staff, clinicians stressing the importance of socialization as both a diagnostic and a remedial aid, as when Mary J.H. was 'asked to write to her friends who are enquiring after her said she would try & do so'.[67] Many required especial coaxing, however, on-going familial strife making them unwilling or else their mental conditions making them unable. When Mary attempted to write, for example 'she felt so lost & miserable that she was unable to continue however she hopes to be able to write soon'.

Some child murderers clearly had more difficulties dealing with the correspondence and visits of their families and other friends or relations; and asylum authorities were not slow in restraining or secluding such patients, or banning disturbing or 'unrespectable' visitors, when necessary. Often, however, it was the success and patience of families in maintaining bonds through such visits and in taking back convicted child murderers that is striking. For years after her admission to Perth CLD in 1902, Agnes L.B. was described as 'perverse', 'insolent' and 'quarrelsome', and initially refused to communicate with her sister: 'She cannot be got to write to her sister, who keeps her child, seems to take no interest in her friends'.[68] Yet, it was ultimately to this sister's care that

---

[66] RN368.
[67] RN468.
[68] HH21/48/3, 481–3, 437; HH17/58.

she was conditionally removed in 1912. And there she remained, on and off, despite regular frictions with her sister and her other guardians, despite repeated (and unauthorized) changes of residence and of employment, as reported by the Inspector of Prisons, and despite the fact that she was often found 'excited', 'troublesome' or 'impertinent & dissatisfied with everything'.

Some communities and families were less tolerant of the presence or return of allegedly recovered mad infanticides into their midst. Crimes like infanticide were sometimes quite major dramas for a tightly-knit local community, and neighbourhood memories could be resilient and uncompromising. Lunatic infanticides were occasionally – if far from commonly – sensationally reported in the local press, and prodigious lists of witnesses at trials indicate how wide an involvement a local community might have in the adjudication and sharing of knowledge about a crime, particularly a capital offence. The trial itself might become a veritable theatre for local interest. The press report on the (Broadmoor) case of Emma L., for example, recorded how:

> Great excitement was aroused in the neighbourhood when the tragical affair was known, and the court in which the woman was tried was largely visited during the day.[69]

Partly as a result of this, families were sometimes so worried about the stigma that might attach to a returning offender that they made special efforts to get them relocated to an area where the history of the crime was unlikely to be known, so that their own and the former patient's good name might be preserved and a new start made. The family of one Perth patient, for example, anxious to preserve a certain anonymity and freedom from stigma, removed her to a parish over thirty miles from her previous settlement.

Yet asylum, Home Office and police supervision of conditional discharge might still occasionally endanger the identity of such individuals and render such arrangements a less than discreet matter. The guardians of the Perth infanticide, Ellen A., complained bitterly about being checked up on by their local constabulary in 1897, and they were backed up by their brother-in-law, the Perth Medical Superintendent, McNaughton. He also pointed out to the Home Office 'that in England ... the Police are asked to make inquiries as to conditionally liberated Lunatics only when suspicions are excited'. It is unlikely that every discharged patient received such powerful protection. In ordinary circumstances, however, as McNaughton remarked, the police never undertook 'active supervision' in such cases.

---

[69] RN252.

And even in this case the constable involved had not visited solely to enquire after Ellen and thought it 'impossible that any one in the district can know anything about the girl'.[70]

As with supervision of guardianship for ordinary lunatics, the authorities were also very much concerned with the physical conditions in the domiciles to which patients were to return. Apart from issues such as the ease and stresses of employment, child-care situations, and the support structure within the home, medical opinion tended to place particular emphasis on matters of hygiene and creature comforts. Thus, in reporting on the case of the infanticide Sarah C.S., quite apart from her mental condition, the Perth Medical Superintendent was careful to ensure that 'The house is clean & tidy, and she has every comfort & attention that could be desired'.[71] From their arrest and trial to patients' subsequent detention, discharge and death, asylum and other authorities gathered an enormous range of knowledge about patients' circumstances. In Sarah's case, her file even includes a precise plan of her farmhouse home and a map of its location in relation to the local village, that was used at her trial.

Conditional discharges invariably specified that ex-patients were not only to remain, but to spend every night, at the addresses to which they had been first discharged; and any change in such circumstances, even one night's absence, required written authorization. Thus, when Sarah's husband wanted to take her on a holiday to Saltcoats, or on a temporary visit to some near relations, he was obliged to ask permission to do so. Other cases where families' houses were deemed impoverished or demoralizing were generally assessed negatively for discharge, a police report in 1900 on Eleanor J.'s parents' home declaring it 'very poor ... cheerless & depressing'.[72] Eleanor was to die in Broadmoor thirty years later.

Once again, such issues were common to all discharges. Yet greater emphasis seems accorded to them in female and in infanticide cases. In this connection, the quality of companionship available in the household was another subject adverted to. Significantly, the act of infanticide itself was often related to the absence of support within the home. The lack

---

[70] For Ellen A., see HH21/48/3, 304–306; HH17/2. In Ireland, as ongoing work by Pauline Prior on Dundrum Criminal Lunatic Asylum is showing, discharged prisoners were commonly sent to Australia and other colonies. Although some of them clearly had families in such regions, such measures also appear to have something in common with the motives of banishment and ostracism detectable in the contemporary transportation of Irish convicts. However, there seems considerably less evidence of such practices when it came to infanticide cases from Broadmoor and Perth.

[71] HH17/104.

[72] RN444.

of reference to such matters in male cases indicates how profoundly prevailing contemporary models of women as weaker vessels, more dependent on support and social interaction within the domicile, were affecting the arbitration of discharge.

The local constabulary was also enlisted to monitor patients, and to ensure that the conditions of their discharge were upheld. Though motivated by preventive concerns with after-care, this close supervision of discharges suggests a considerable expansion of psychiatric involvement into areas of community policing, a development that was in part to presage the twentieth-century expansion of social work and welfare activities. Such special conditions seem to have been imposed more frequently at the end of the nineteenth century than previously. Historians have stressed the wider expansion of police supervision of parturient women (and their carers) in this period, relating it to moral panics about baby-farming and infanticide that intermittently reared their heads,[73] while in general this was a time of intensified social and medical concern about child welfare. Psychiatry, furthermore, was seeking to develop an enlarged brief of its own to attend to the mental hygiene of the community.

Conclusion

This chapter has been only a selective survey of the discharge of mad infanticides and of the various evolving criteria that dictated the timing and conduct of discharge. I have not had space to discuss in detail, or in some cases even mention, all the actors and intermediaries involved in this process. Most attention has been given to the rationales of the main arbiters: the asylum authorities and government officials – including the Home Office, the Prison Commission and the Lunacy Commission – as well as the offenders' relations. Little, however, has been said about patients' employers and more distant relations, about MPs and other political figures, parochial and police authorities, privately hired medical practitioners, or legal advisers and solicitors, let alone about philanthropists or religious and voluntary organisations (such as that icon of contemporary respectability, the Salvation Army).

Apart from the various actors involved, this study has tended to stress the tremendous range of factors influencing discharge of the criminally insane, and moreover the distinctiveness of deliberations when it came to (female) child murderers. Socio-moral and socio-economic issues, such as the respectability of the offender and her family and the integrity

---

[73] Arnot, 'Infant death', 287.

of the home, were especially prominent. For women whose crimes had often been so closely linked with issues such as exhaustion, spousal abuse, abandonment, isolation and lack of domiciliary support, the ability of relatives to provide a respectable, secure home, as well as affectionate companionship, was also at a considerable premium in assessing suitability for discharge. This chapter has additionally emphasized the extent to which medicalized causal explanations for female child murder, such as pregnancy or the puerperal and lactational states, encouraged frequent and early discharge. At the same time, it has outlined growing concerns at the time with the menopause, re-impregnation and the transmission of hereditary taint of insanity, which evidently delayed the release of some women patients.

Nevertheless, I have shown that medical and political authorities were generally rather restrained in sanctioning or advocating the use of the asylum for the prolonged quarantine (and effectual sterilization through internment) of child murderers. Writing in 1901, the Broadmoor MS, Richard Brayn, claimed that there was universal agreement 'as to the undesirability of these women having any more children'.[74] However, he was also well aware of 'the difficulty' of 'how to prevent it'. Appreciating the strength of societal sympathy for such cases, he recognized that 'if the woman is young and recovers, and appears to be able to maintain her sanity, she can hardly be detained in an asylum until past the child-bearing age'.[75] The majority of families were keen – and agitated actively – to see these women returned to them, most being wives, housekeepers and mothers. While eugenic views were bringing the issue of sterilization more steadily to the fore by the beginning of the twentieth century, and forensic psychiatrists and medical criminologists were often more favourably disposed to such radical interventions, most still recognized, as did Brayn, that 'public opinion is not yet educated up to the idea of having ... [female child murderers] sterilised'.[76]

Zedner has stressed the tendency for Victorian evaluations of women's crime to concentrate on socio-moral issues such as reputation, respectability, status and past conduct, rather than on the consequences of crime.[77] Yet the questions she posed as to how far such biased preoccupations affected judgments during trials have not yet been adequately answered by historians, while just as importantly few have even asked how they affected offenders' subsequent disposal. This study

[74] R. Brayn, 'A brief outline of the arrangements for the care and supervision of the criminal insane in England during the present century', *Journal of Mental Science*, (April 1901), 250–57, at 256.

[75] Ibid., 256–7.

[76] Ibid., 257.

[77] Zedner, *Women, Crime, and Custody*, p. 30.

has confirmed the tendency to see infanticidal women as victims of their environments as much as victims of their biology. Circumstances of destitution or male seduction, violence, vice or irresponsibility, were often deciding factors, not only in the disposal of insane child murderers, but also in their continuing evaluation while under detention and supervision.

Acknowledgements

This work forms part of a five-year research project, supported financially by the Wellcome Trust, to whom grateful acknowledgement is made. Thanks also to Anne Shepherd for her contributions to the project as a part-time research assistant for a year, to Mark Jackson and John Stewart for detailed comments on earlier drafts, and to staff at Broadmoor Hospital and West Register House, Scottish National Archives, for providing study facilities and assistance.

CHAPTER TWELVE

Legislating for human nature: legal responses to infanticide, 1860–1938

Tony Ward

'The movement in legal scholarship known as Critical Legal Studies has much to contribute to general historians', remarks Martin Wiener.[1] In discussing the late nineteenth- and early twentieth-century law on infanticide, I want to return the compliment by suggesting that critical legal studies has a lot to learn from the kind of history that sets criminal justice in its cultural context.

I use the term 'critical legal studies' loosely to refer not just to the American academic movement of that name,[2] but more generally to a current of legal scholarship which, rather than striving to present the law as a coherent body of doctrine, seeks to expose its fundamental contradictions or incoherences. These contradictions are often portrayed as reflecting fundamental tensions within liberalism or post-Enlightenment individualism.[3] The leading study of English criminal law in this vein is Alan Norrie's *Crime, Reason and History*. Norrie argues that common-law doctrines of criminal liability contain deep contradictions, which must be understood as a product of their formative period in the early nineteenth century. He discerns a fundamental conflict between the law's ideology of 'abstract individualism', which envisages a world peopled by rational, calculating responsible subjects, and 'the concrete, social individuality of human beings operating within a conflictual society'.[4] 'Legal form is created and

---

[1] M.J. Wiener, *Reconstructing the Criminal: Culture, Law and Policy in England, 1830–1914* (Cambridge, Cambridge University Press, 1990), p. 9 n. 26.

[2] For a dispassionate history of the movement see N. Duxbury, *Patterns of American Jurisprudence* (Oxford, Oxford University Press, 1997). For an introduction to its ideas see M. Kelman, *A Guide to Critical Legal Studies* (Cambridge, Mass., and London, Harvard University Press, 1987).

[3] A classic exposition is D. Kennedy, 'The structure of Blackstone's Commentaries', *Buffalo Law Review*, 28 (1979), 205–382, at 209. From a feminist perspective, the contradictions exposed by Critical Legal Studies may be viewed as characteristic of *male* experience in modern societies, which is crucially shaped by men's non-experience of pregnancy and motherhood: R. West, 'Jurisprudence and gender', *University of Chicago Law Review*, 55 (1988), 1–72, at 1.

[4] A. Norrie, *Crime, Reason and History*, (London, Weidenfeld & Nicholson, 1993) p. 31.

maintained against the persistent "threat" of social and political "leakage" into the process of state justice and punishment'.[5]

The Infanticide Act 1938, which is still in force, appears to provide a clear illustration of Norrie's thesis. In abstract individualist terms, a mother's killing of her baby is simply the murder of one individual by another; but the law cannot completely ignore the 'social and emotional pressures' which drive flesh-and-blood mothers to kill. However, 'there are clear limits to the law's abilities to recognise such pressures without its denying its own rationale as a punitive mechanism relying on individual responsibility'. The result is a compromise, which allows a mother who kills her baby under the age of one year, while the 'balance of her mind' is 'disturbed' as a result of the birth or of subsequent 'lactation', to be convicted of infanticide rather than murder. In this way the law is able 'to maintain a generally punitive stance to a social problem, laced with an unthreatening show of compassion'.[6]

On the whole Norrie's analysis is persuasive, but I am uncomfortable about his portrayal of legal individualism coming repeatedly into collision with an external 'reality' of crime. One does not have to embrace any very radical form of epistemological scepticism[7] to recognize that the 'reality' which manifests itself in criminal trials is not something 'out there', but is constructed through a complex interplay between legal and scientific discourses and 'common sense' knowledge.[8] For example, the 'social and emotional pressures' which led to infanticide were perceived by the 'enlightened' sensibilities of the late eighteenth century in a way they had not been before.[9] Indeed, the legal 'abstraction' that treated infanticide just like any other murder developed in response to precisely this humanitarian understanding, replacing the earlier law which had presumed that unmarried mothers whose babies had been born in secret and found dead were guilty of murder.

Both the criminal law's 'abstract individualism' and the countervailing humanitarian understanding of crime developed in the same social and cultural context. As Haskell argues, the (male,

---

[5] Ibid., p. 26.

[6] Ibid., p. 189.

[7] My position is, I think, quite consistent with the 'critical realism' to which Norrie subscribes: see W. Outhwaite, 'Realism and social science', in M. Archer, R. Bhaskar, A. Collier, T. Lawson and A. Norrie (eds), *Critical Realism: Essential Readings* (London, Routledge, 1998).

[8] See T. Ward, 'The sad subject of infanticide: law, medicine and child murder, 1860–1938,' *Social & Legal Studies*, 8, 2 (1999), 163–80.

[9] M. Jackson, *New-Born Child Murder: Women, Illegitimacy and the Courts in Eighteenth-Century England* (Manchester, Manchester University Press, 1996).

bourgeois) individual in a market society was expected to be rational and calculating, but also to cultivate a strong sense of obligation and an awareness of the long-term consequences of his actions. These characteristics facilitated an awareness of the social causes of human suffering and a sense of obligation to do something about it.[10] Thus the 'compassionate' understanding of the infanticidal mother's suffering and its social causes, and the individualistic view of the murderess as a responsible subject, were closely related 'modes of subjectification'.[11]

In the Victorian period, the compassionate view of infanticide combined two main elements. One was sympathy for the physical pain of a mother giving birth unattended: as Roger Chadwick points out, at a time when women of all classes normally gave birth at home, accounts of the mental consequences of the pain of childbirth 'could unite both sympathy and personal experience'.[12] The other element was the conception of the 'fallen woman' as a subject heavily determined by social forces, the antithesis of the autonomous, rational masculine self.[13] A rational woman, argued William Acton, knowing the disastrous social consequences of pregnancy, would never allow herself to be 'seduced' (except, perhaps, in a situation where marriage was a realistic prospect). 'She must, therefore, be either temporarily insane, or permanently weaker minded' than the male. The consequence of the seducer's 'coarse, deliberate villainy' was 'to force the mother to take to prostitution, and to tempt her to make away with her child'.[14] Although the mother is not entirely excused – she is 'tempted' but not 'forced' to kill – the stronger-minded father bears a large share of the moral responsibility for her crime. In this respect Acton's account is very close to those of eighteenth-century humanitarians such as William Hunter.[15]

Of all sane, adult individuals, the fallen woman driven to

---

[10] T.L. Haskell, 'Capitalism and the origins of humanitarian sensibility,' *American Historical Review*, 90 (1985), 339–61, 547–66; T. Laqueur, 'Bodies, details and the humanitarian narrative,' in L. Hunt (ed.), *The New Cultural History*, (Berkeley, University of California Press, 1989), pp. 176–204; Jackson, *New-Born Child Murder*.

[11] Nancy Fraser's term (inspired by Foucault) for 'the ways in which various discourses position the people to whom they are addressed as specific sorts of subjects endowed with specific sorts of capacities for action': N. Fraser, *Unruly Practices: Power, Discourse and Gender in Contemporary Social Theory* (Cambridge, Polity Press, 1989).

[12] R. Chadwick, *Bureaucratic Mercy: The Home Office and the Treatment of Capital Cases in Victorian England* (New York and London, Garland, 1992), p. 294.

[13] A. Anderson, *Tainted Souls and Painted Faces: The Rhetoric of Fallenness in Victorian Culture* (Ithaca, Cornell University Press, 1993).

[14] W. Acton, *Prostitution, Considered in its Moral and Social Aspects*, 2nd edn (London, Churchill & Sons, 1870, repr. Frank Cass, 1972), pp. 272, 274, 284–5.

[15] Jackson, *New-Born Child Murder*, pp. 116–19.

infanticide was perhaps the hardest to equate with the responsible subject of the criminal law. As Wiener argues, however, the crucial assumption underlying Victorian legal doctrine was not that offenders *really were* rational, autonomous subjects, but rather that by strictly upholding a system of rules which treated people *as if* they were such subjects, the population could be educated and disciplined to become more rational and self-controlled in reality. 'Reformers were doing more than bringing the law into closer accord with human nature and social realities; they hoped to use the law to *change* that nature and those realities.'[16]

In Wiener's view, this stress on the educative and disciplinary value of strict definitions of criminal liability was particularly a feature of the early Victorian period. From the 1870s onwards, according to Wiener, a shift in emphasis away from denunciation and deterrence was reflected in 'a general acceptance of a psychiatric view of women who killed their infants'.[17] I have argued elsewhere that to see the Infanticide Acts as a belated recognition of late Victorian psychiatry's successful 'medicalization' of female deviance considerably over-simplifies the relationship between medicine and law.[18] Moreover, it seems debatable whether the weakening of Victorian assumptions about will and character in the latter part of the nineteenth century affected legal thinking quite so profoundly as Wiener's account suggests.[19] For this very reason, Wiener's insights into the moral agenda of early Victorian criminal justice remain pertinent in seeking to understand the (lack of) development in criminal-law doctrine in the twentieth century, not to mention the twenty-first.

This chapter is not primarily concerned with the psychiatric aspects of the debate (although these will be briefly discussed in the penultimate section) but rather will concentrate on the tensions within legal thinking which made the redefinition of infanticide as a non-capital offence so difficult to achieve, despite its clear pragmatic attractions as a means of securing consistent punishment for the crime. The structure of the chapter reflects the episodic nature of the debate. It will first consider the calls for reform in the 1860s and early 1870s, which were stimulated by a perception that infanticide was alarmingly increasing. As this alarm subsided, infanticide slipped out of the political limelight until a series of parliamentary debates in 1909–10. After a further hiatus around the

---

[16] Wiener, *Reconstructing the Criminal*, pp. 54–5.

[17] Ibid., p. 268.

[18] Ward, 'Sad subject'. Cf. L. Zedner, *Women, Crime, and Custody in Victorian England* (Oxford, Clarendon, 1991), pp. 88–90.

[19] Cf. D. Garland, 'Designing criminal policy', *London Review of Books*, 13 (10 Oct. 1991), 13–14.

time of the Great War, a renewal of parliamentary interest led to the passage of the Infanticide Act 1922. Although many of the arguments of the inter-war years recall those of the late Victorian period, infanticide was no longer seen as a widespread social problem, and attention was drawn only to a few well-publicized individual cases. The three cases which most directly influenced the development of the law – those of Edith Roberts (1921), Edith O'Donoghue (1927) and Brenda Hale (1936) – will be discussed in some detail.

Infanticide, concealment and capital punishment, 1860–74

'[E]very newspaper and gaol delivery and coroner's court shows that infanticide is an absolute custom among English society of the present day...[and] is frightfully increasing,' the *Daily Telegraph* claimed in 1865.[20] George Behlmer has suggested three reasons why such expressions of alarm about infanticide became common in the 1860s. Firstly, 'stories of mass infanticide provided grist for the mills of an expanding press'.[21] The *Daily Telegraph* itself speculated 'whether the universal dissemination of intelligence, with the excessive publicity now given to the minutest transactions of daily life from one end of the Empire to the other, may not be calculated to direct public attention to every single case of child-murder brought before our coroners or our magistrates'.[22] Secondly, such stories contrasted disturbingly with 'our boast to have extirpated infanticide in India'.[23] At a public meeting in London in 1865, the Recorder of Rangoon claimed that '[i]n Bengal, Ceylon and Burmah, he had seen children thrown to the pigs, and those pigs afterwards used for human food; but things even more intolerable than that had come to his knowledge since he had been in London'.[24]

Thirdly, concern about infanticide was fanned by a new breed of populist coroners.[25] A long struggle between coroners and magistrates over the payment of coroners' fees came to a head in 1859–60 and,

---

[20] Editorial, *Daily Telegraph* (5 Aug. 1865), p. 4.
[21] G.K. Behlmer, 'Deadly motherhood: infanticide and medical opinion in mid-Victorian England', *Journal of the History of Medicine*, 34 (1979), 403–27, at 406.
[22] Editorial, *Daily Telegraph* (13 Sep. 1865), p. 6.
[23] Editorial, *Daily Telegraph* (5 Aug. 1865), p. 4.
[24] *The Times* (5 Sep. 1865), p. 9.
[25] On the populist coroners, see: O. Anderson, *Suicide in Victorian and Edwardian England* (Oxford, Clarendon, 1987), pp. 15–40; I.A. Burney, *Bodies of Evidence: Medicine and the Politics of the English Inquest, 1830–1926* (Baltimore, Johns Hopkins University Press, 2000).

along with poisoning, the issue of infanticide was central to the coroners' case against the magistrates' 'interferences' with their discretion over the holding of inquests.[26] By revealing the 'true' incidence of infant murder, coroners also revealed the need for a thorough inquiry into all unnatural deaths.

Behlmer specifically attributes the increase in the number of murder verdicts to the Coroners Act 1860, which effectively freed the coroners from the magistrates' control.[27] In general, however, this legislation appears to have made little immediate impact on the number of inquests held.[28] It seems rather to have been the crusading zeal of a few individual coroners that led to an alarming increase in the number of murder verdicts on infants in certain districts. The most prominent of these was Dr Edwin Lankester, who as coroner for Central Middlesex not only recorded far more verdicts of 'willful murder' – and fewer of 'found dead' – than most of his colleagues, but regularly publicized the fact through an annual report.[29] The *Medical Times and Gazette* held Lankester, and the coverage of his inquests and reports in the 'cheap press', largely responsible for what it considered a 'panic' over the supposed increase of infanticide.[30]

Lankester derived statistics from his inquest verdicts and used them to support an explanation of infanticide which could be regarded as an early instance of 'routine activities theory' in criminology.[31] The geographical distribution of infanticide, he claimed, reflected the social distribution of opportunities for concealment. Lankester assumed concealment of pregnancy and

---

[26] J.T. Smith, *The Right Holding of the Coroner's Court, and Some Recent Interferences Therewith* (London, Henry Sweet, 1859); J. Sim and T. Ward, 'The magistrate of the poor? Coroners and deaths in custody in nineteenth-century England', in M. Clark and C. Crawford (eds), *Legal Medicine in History* (Cambridge, Cambridge University Press, 1994), pp. 245–67.

[27] Behlmer, 'Deadly motherhood', pp. 408–409; see also J.D.J. Havard, *The Detection of Secret Homicide* (Cambridge, Cambridge University Press, 1960) p. 64.

[28] Departmental Committee on Coroners, *First Report*, Part II, Cd. 4782, House of Commons Parliamentary Papers (hereafter *PP*), (1909), XV, 385, Appendix 2. I am grateful to Don Prichard for bringing these figures to my attention.

[29] See L. Rose, *Massacre of the Innocents: Infanticide in Victorian England* (London, Routledge, 1986), pp. 62–9; M.P. English, *Victorian Values: The Life and Times of Dr Edwin Lankester* (Bristol, Biopress, 1990).

[30] Editorial, 'Asserted increase of infanticide', *Medical Times and Gazette*, 1 (28 Apr. 1866), 445. See also 'A coroner's arithmetic', *British Medical Journal*, 2 (1866), 341 (reprinted from the *Pall Mall Gazette*).

[31] See M. Felson, *Crime and Everyday Life* (Thousand Oaks, Calif., Pine Forge Press, 1994). Felson predicts that crimes will occur where three necessary elements converge: 'a motivated offender, a suitable target, and an absence of capable guardians'.

birth was generally possible only for women in domestic service.[32] This explained why, within Lankester's jurisdiction, Paddington had the highest rate of infant murder (1 per 4,000 of population) and Clerkenwell the lowest (1 per 25,000):

> It is not so much that in Clerkenwell there are no servants, as the fact that in Clerkenwell, what servants there are, are more directly under the control of the mistress of the house. In the West End of London, the servants are more numerous, more independent of the mistress, and the fact of their condition is seldom discovered before the opportunity occurs for the pregnant woman to deliver herself and make away with her offspring.[33]

The remedy for infanticide therefore lay chiefly in 'the kindly and sisterly superintendence' of female servants by their mistresses.[34]

Lankester also complained that the law was 'almost criminally lenient' in its treatment of infanticidal women.[35] Evidence which convinced a coroner's jury often proved insufficient to obtain a conviction in those cases where the mother's identity was known. In Ann Higginbotham's sample of Old Bailey child-murder trials from 1839–1906, fewer than half of the neonaticide cases were fully tried, usually because – despite the verdict of the coroner's jury – the murder indictment was either dismissed by the grand jury or dropped by the prosecution.[36] The legal basis of these decisions, as Mr Justice Willes explained, was

> the almost impossibility of proving that the child, at the time of coming to its death, was, in the language of the law, 'a reasonable being in the Queen's peace' – a definition which applied only to a child having had entire birth. The evidence failed to establish in the great proportion of cases that the child was the subject of a complete and separate existence.[37]

In William Burke Ryan's view, this obstacle to conviction was 'a "legal fiction"—a backdoor for the escape of the guilty and bloodstained

---

[32] 'Third annual report of the coroner for Central Middlesex', *British Medical Journal*, 1 (1866), 448–50.

[33] E. Lankester, *The Sixth Annual Report of the Coroner for the Central District of Middlesex* (London, Robert Hardwicke, 1869), p. 29.

[34] 'Third annual report', *Medical Times and Gazette*, 1 (7 Apr. 1866), 369.

[35] Lankester, *Sixth Annual Report*, p. 32.

[36] A.R. Higginbotham, '"Sin of the age": infanticide and illegitimacy in Victorian London,' in K.O. Garrigan (ed.), *Victorian Scandals*, (Athens, Ohio University Press, 1992), pp. 257–88, at 271–2. Although it was possible to try a defendant for murder on the basis of the coroner's inquisition alone, those accused were normally indicted for murder and brought before a grand jury.

[37] Charge to the grand jury at Wells, quoted in 'State of the law in relation to infanticide', *Lancet*, 2 (1865), 237–8

mother'.[38] Lankester, Ryan and other commentators[39] attributed acquittals to the sympathy of judges and juries for fallen women and their sense (perhaps prompted by their own sexual guilt)[40] of the injustice of sentencing the woman to death while her seducer went free.

Those women who did face trial for killing new-born babies were usually convicted only of concealment of birth. Though the maximum sentence for concealment was two years,[41] in practice sentences rarely exceeded six months.[42] Judges showed no inclination to use a concealment conviction as a pretext for punishing a murder that had not been proved.[43] Baron Bramwell had 'no doubt the Legislature meant the judges to give a very severe sentence when there had been foul play with the child, and a nominal sentence when there was no suspicion of anything wrong. But the Judges WON'T be parties to this kind of Fraud – one can call it nothing else.'[44]

Even those who saw the sympathies of jurors as misplaced could accept that they created a strong pragmatic case for distinguishing the killing of a new-born child from capital murder.[45] 'An apparent remission in severity', a committee of the Harveian Society argued, 'would really increase and ensure the punishment and prevention of infanticide'.[46] As the leading criminal jurist of the period, Sir James Fitzjames Stephen, put it, 'you have to legislate for human nature as you find it'.[47] For Stephen, the function of the criminal law was not merely

---

[38] W.B. Ryan, *Infanticide: Its Law, Prevalence, Prevention and History* (London, J. Churchill, 1862), p. 6.

[39] E.g. 'Infanticide', *Lancet*, 2 (1863), 426–7; 'S.G.O.', letter to *The Times*, (5 Aug. 1865); J.B. Curgenven, *The Waste of Infant Life*, (London, Faithfull & Head, 1867); H. Humble, 'Infanticide: its cause and cure,' in O. Shipley (ed.), *The Church and the World: Essays on Questions of the Day* (London, Longmans Green, Reader & Dyer, 1866).

[40] 'Their views are perverted by their own actions': Humble, 'Infanticide', p. 58. 'S.G.O.' also hints at this.

[41] Offences Against the Person Act, 1861, s. 60.

[42] Higginbotham, 'Sin of the age', p. 274.

[43] For a proposal to increase sentences for concealment, see *Daily News* (12 Aug. 1865), p. 4.

[44] Letter to Frederick Pollock, 3 Sep. 1865, in C. Fairfield, *Some Account of George William Wilshere, Baron Bramwell of Hever, and his Opinions* (London, Macmillan, 1898), p. 37.

[45] See, for example, Rev. Lord Osborne's evidence to the Royal Commission on Capital Punishment, *Report, Minutes of Evidence and Appendices*, No. 3590, PP (1866) XXI, 1; Curgenven, *Waste of Infant Life*, p. 14.

[46] W.T. Smith, 'Address on infanticide and excessive infant mortality', *British Medical Journal*, 1 (1867), 721–5. Smith chaired the Committee, whose members included Lankester and Curgenven.

[47] Royal Commission, *Minutes*, Q. 2,293.

to deter offenders but to reinforce public morality;[48] this made it important to avoid too sharp a conflict with 'public sentiment'.[49]

In 1866, the Royal Commission on Capital Punishment recommended the creation of a new offence of inflicting grievous bodily harm on a baby during or within seven days of its birth, where the baby subsequently died. This would have removed both the unreal threat of capital punishment and the legal difficulties of proving that the baby was born alive. From the moral-disciplinary perspective there were two major objections to this proposal. First, even though the threat of capital punishment was not always carried out, it might be a deterrent; and 'the greater the temptation' faced by an unmarried mother, 'the greater the necessity for punishment'.[50] Secondly, the proposed law appeared to put a lesser value on infant life. Stephen, ever the hard-headed utilitarian, readily admitted as much: 'You cannot estimate the loss of the child itself; you know nothing about it at all.'[51] To opponents this was quite unacceptable. Lord Redesdale put the point starkly in opposing one of a series of unsuccessful Bills[52] which sought to enact variants on the Royal Commission's recommendation: it was 'far better that all the murderesses in the country should be acquitted' than to 'have it declared by Act of Parliament that the wilful or the malicious killing of a child was not murder'.[53]

Lord Alverstone's dilemma, 1908–1909

After the defeat of a series of reform attempts in the 1860s and 1870s, there was a long hiatus in the debate over the law on infanticide. With the crime apparently in decline, 'references to infanticide were becoming increasingly rare in the English press'.[54] In 1908, however, the Society for the Abolition of Capital Punishment revived the humanitarian arguments for reform, citing a series of cases where young single mothers had been convicted either of manslaughter or murder. While accepting that the death penalty had been 'practically abolished' in such cases, the Society protested against the mental 'torture' which 'an ignorant girl must go through' when the sentence was pronounced. The

---

[48] This is a central theme of J.F. Stephen's magisterial *History of the Criminal Law of England*, 3 vols (New York, Burt Franklin, facsimile reprint, n.d.; orig. publ. 1883).

[49] Royal Commission, *Minutes*, Q. 2,294.

[50] Baron Bramwell, Royal Commission, *Minutes*, Qq. 134, 137.

[51] Ibid., Q. 2,193.

[52] See D.S. Davies, 'Child-killing in English law', *Modern Law Review*, 1 (1937), 203–23.

[53] *House of Lords Debates* (hereafter *H.L. Debs.*), 221 (28 July 1874), col. 847.

[54] Behlmer, 'Deadly motherhood', p. 427.

'seduced young servant-girl' was the victim of 'a callous society', and the very fact that she showed no 'maternal instinct' indicated that she was virtually insane.[55]

Such views did not commend themselves to the Home Office: 'adult women are scarcely to be treated like children or lunatics in the matter of murder', the head of the criminal division commented in 1909.[56] But the Liberal Lord Chancellor, Lord Loreburn, did move an amendment to the 1908 Children Bill which would give the judge discretion to pass a sentence of penal servitude rather than imprisonment where a mother was convicted of the murder of her infant under the age of one year. Loreburn accepted that 'public opinion was shocked at the idea of the death sentence being passed where it was manifestly inhuman to carry it out'.[57] Just as excessive taxation led to smuggling, excessive punishments led to acquittals of the guilty.[58]

The successful opposition to Loreburn's amendment in the House of Lords was led by the Lord Chief Justice, Lord Alverstone, who 'feared that if the clause as it stood were adopted the worst murders of infants – the killing of infants of three or six months old by deliberate starvation and ill-treatment – would become of much greater frequency'.[59] Alverstone was a former Conservative MP with a long-standing interest in child protection issues[60] and the way he linked infanticide by distraught mothers with 'infanticide by neglect', and by implication with 'baby-farming' (of which there had been several sensational cases in the preceding few years),[61] recalled a common tactic by public-health reformers of the 1860s and 1870s.[62] Like W.B. Ryan in 1866,[63] Alverstone accepted that a compassionate response was appropriate to some cases that fitted the humanitarian story of seduction and desertion, but he feared that such compassion would erode restraints against child

---

[55] C. Heath, *Some Notes on the Punishment of Death* (London, S.A.C.P., 1908), pp. 9–11.

[56] Minute by H.B. Simpson, PRO HO45/10573/176819/1.

[57] *H.L. Debs.*, 195, 4 Nov. 1908, col. 1178. On this occasion the amendment was withdrawn, to be re-introduced at the report stage of the Bill.

[58] *H.L. Debs.*, 196, 12 Nov. 1908, col. 485.

[59] Ibid., col. 486.

[60] G.K. Behlmer, *Child Abuse and Moral Reform in England, 1870–1908* (Stanford, Stanford University Press, 1982), pp. 135, 158–9.

[61] H.L. Adam, *Woman and Crime* (London, T. Werner Laurie, 1911); J. Knelman, *Twisting in the Wind: The Murderess and the English Press* (Toronto, University of Toronto Press, 1998), Ch. 6; A. Ballinger, *Dead Woman Walking: Executed Women in England and Wales, 1900–1955* (Aldershot, Ashgate, 2000).

[62] M.L. Arnot, 'Infant death, child care and the state: the baby-farming scandal and the first infant life protection legislation of 1872', *Continuity and Change*, 9 (1994), 271–311.

[63] Ryan, *Infanticide*, p. 26

murder more generally. He also feared that if judges had discretion there would be inconsistencies in the use of the death penalty.[64] Lord Ashbourne supported him, arguing that in a Bill designed to protect children nothing should be enacted 'which might take away that solemnity and sanctity which should be applied to life'.[65]

The view that the death penalty communicated a necessary message about the value of human life also underpinned the policy of the Home Office that no mercy should be shown to 'baby farmers' convicted of killing other people's babies. In refusing a reprieve for Leslie James in 1907, despite circumstances which left room for doubt whether she had killed her victim deliberately or through drunken carelessness, the Home Secretary wrote:

> Having regard to the widespread laxity which exists as regards infant life, the extent to which the abominable system of baby farming prevails, and the difficulty which usually exists in proving an intention to kill, it appears to me of the utmost importance to do nothing to weaken Home Office practice in connection with baby farming practices.[66]

Alverstone returned to this theme the following year, when, following the defeat of the Lord Chancellor's amendment, he introduced his own Bill to reform the sentencing of infanticidal mothers:

> A most careful examination of this question has led me to the conclusion, in which I am supported by those who are working every day for the protection of child life, that the number of child murders is so great – I will not trouble the House with statistics, though they are alarming – that we ought to do nothing to in any way spread the feeling that there is to be any less punishment in cases of child murder.[67]

Had he wished to trouble the House with statistics, he might have mentioned that in 1906, 55 recorded deaths from homicide – 19 per cent of all such deaths – were of infants under a month in age, and 134 infants of the same age were found to have died of neglect.[68]

Alverstone's Bill would have allowed the judge to record, rather than pronounce, the sentence of death in cases where a mother murdered her child when she had not recovered from the effects of giving birth. The power to record rather than pronounce the sentence of death had been

---

[64] *H.L. Debs.*, (4th Series) 196, (12 Nov. 1908), col. 486; see also Earl of Halsbury, col. 487.

[65] Ibid., col. 489.

[66] Quoted by Ballinger, *Dead Woman Walking*, p. 94.

[67] *H.L. Debs.*, 1 (4 May 1909), cols. 722–3.

[68] *69th Annual Report of the Registrar-General of Births, Marriages and Deaths*, PP (1908), XX, 1, p. cxxxiv.

removed from judges in murder cases in 1861, but still applied to piracy and the burning of ships in the royal dockyards: it amounted to a public recommendation to mercy, which was invariably followed by the Home Secretary. Alverstone's proposal aimed to maintain the symbolism of the mandatory death penalty for murder while recognising the need for mercy in a limited class of cases; but it satisfied no-one. The defendant would still face the anguish of knowing she had been sentenced to death,[69] and in the Lord Chancellor's view this would still make juries reluctant to convict.[70] The former Tory Lord Chancellor, the Earl of Halsbury, turned Alverstone's argument against him: 'To any one who knows the statistics of infanticide, it is very unwise to take away from that crime the terrors that follow upon it.'[71]

Alverstone eventually accepted an amendment from the Lord Chancellor which would allow the jury in infanticide cases to return a verdict of manslaughter rather than murder. The amended Bill fell because the government could not make time for it in the House of Commons. In 1910 the Home Secretary, Winston Churchill, 'received representations from a woman prison visitor as to the bad effect of undue lenience in infanticide cases' and wrote to Alverstone asking him if he would re-introduce his amended Bill. Alverstone expressed willingness and discussed the drafting of the Bill with the Home Office, but he took no further action.[72] Later the Bill would form the basis for the Infanticide Act 1922.

The defence of the old order in infanticide sentencing (which apparently had the support of most of the judges)[73] is a striking example of the 'as if' quality of the criminal law's 'abstract juridical subject'. Alverstone did not suppose that every mother who killed her child was a rational, calculating individual who deserved to be hanged (we shall see later that he took a very lenient view of one emotionally distressed mother whom he tried). But he and other traditionalists thought that 'the law' in its impersonal majesty should treat such women *as if* they were fully responsible, thereby symbolically upholding a simple set of moral precepts (a person is a person, murder is murder) and maximizing

---

[69]   *H.L. Debs.*, (5th Series) 1, (4 May 1909), col. 727 (Lord James).

[70]   Ibid., col. 725.

[71]   Ibid., col. 726.

[72]   These events were related in 1922 by the Home Office civil servant Alexander Maxwell, in a note on the background to the Child Murder (Trial) Bill, PRO LCO 2/476.

[73]   Alverstone said he had consulted all the judges who were in London (he did not say how many they were) and they all agreed with his position with the exception of Mr Justice Coleridge (*H.L. Debs.*, 196, [12 Nov. 1908], col. 490). Coleridge (speaking in his capacity as an hereditary peer), argued that, in the particular context of infanticide, fears of an unseemly variation in judicial practice were unrealistic. (Ibid.)

the sentence's deterrent impact on those who did coolly calculate whether to kill. By insisting that 'the law' rather than the judge should determine the sentence, leaving it to the Home Secretary to show mercy, the judges also, ironically, absolved themselves from individual moral responsibility for the cruel spectacle they enacted as well as avoiding personal criticism as 'hanging' or 'non-hanging judges'.[74] Reformers on the other hand thought that the 'mockery'[75] of passing the death sentence merely undermined the law's deterrent and educative goals. They had to wait until 1922 before this view prevailed.

The trial of Edith Roberts

Edith Roberts, a twenty-one year old factory hand from Hinckley, stood trial at Leicester assizes in 1921 for the murder of her new-born baby girl. Roberts had concealed her pregnancy from her family and had apparently managed to give birth without disturbing her sister, with whom she shared a bed.[76] The baby was found with a camisole tied tightly round her mouth. Roberts told her stepmother 'that she suffered great agony through the night, that the child was born early in the morning, that she did not hurt it and that it never breathed'. A local doctor considered that the baby had had a separate existence; her lungs floated in water, a standard test to establish that a nenonate had breathed, although breathing did not conclusively establish the 'separate existence' required to sustain a charge of murder.[77] He conceded it was 'perfectly possible that the girl was unconscious through the pain she suffered, and that she might not realise what she was doing.'[78]

Counsel called no witnesses but relied on the two usual defences in cases of new-born child murder. He argued that the evidence that the baby had had a separate existence was unsatisfactory; and he appealed to the jury 'to say that whatever the girl had done was done in the frenzy and agony of pain through which the girl was passing, and therefore hardly conscious of her own acts, and consequently not responsible.'[79]

A novel and controversial feature of the 1921 assizes was that

---

[74] Ibid., col. 486.

[75] H.L. Debs., (5th Series) 1, (4 May 1909), col. 424.

[76] Leicester Mercury (7 June 1921), p. 1.

[77] J.D. Mann, Forensic Evidence and Toxicology (4th edn, London, Griffin & Co., 1908), pp. 142–8; S.B. Atkinson, 'Life, birth and live-birth', Law Quarterly Review, 20 (1904), 134–59.

[78] Leicester Mercury, (7 June 1921).

[79] Leicester Mercury, (8 June 1921), p. 5.

women were called for jury service;[80] but Edith Roberts's counsel had used his right of peremptory challenge to remove all prospective women jurors. Mr Justice Avory commented in his summing-up that counsel probably thought an all-male jury would be more sympathetic to the prisoner than a mixed one.[81] Counsel later protested to the Court of Criminal Appeal against this remark: 'I think that women are unfair towards members of their own sex. My motive was not to get sympathy but a fair jury.'[82] The jury he got took only fifteen minutes to find Edith Roberts guilty, but with a strong recommendation to mercy.

It was 'said of Mr Justice Avory that he has no feelings and that he is incapable of any emotion';[83] that 'his face was expressionless and his voice ... was toneless'.[84] He donned the black cap to impose on Edith Roberts 'the only sentence the law allowed'. A less austere judge might have made some attempt to convey the reality that there was no prospect of the death sentence being carried out. Mr Justice McCardie, in a similar case in 1916, declined to wear the black cap and told the prisoner: 'It would be a hollow pretence for me to suggest in any way that your life will be forfeit'.[85] Edith Roberts showed no awareness that the death sentence was a pretence. She 'collapsed and uttered loud cries and moans, which continued as she was being carried from the court. Several ladies who were in court were also much affected by the painful scene.'[86] Six days later the sentence was commuted.[87]

The *Leicester Mercury* called Roberts's case 'one of those tragic stories in which a girl momentarily goes wrong ... [and] is apparently too ashamed to throw herself upon the affection of those who would have befriended her despite her lapse'.[88] But for a young woman in Roberts's position to throw herself on her family's affections would have been no easy matter. Oral testimonies from the 1920s and 1930s describe a working-class culture in which any discussion of female sexuality was taboo ('there was no word for

---

[80] Women became eligible for jury service under the Sex Disqualification (Removal) Act 1919; the first women jurors were called at the winter assizes of 1920–21. See P. Horn, *Women in the 1920s*, (Stroud, Alan Sutton, 1995).

[81] Quoted in the report of Roberts's unsuccessful appeal: *Leicester Mercury* (25 July 1921), p. 1.

[82] Ibid.

[83] G. Lang, *Mr Justice Avory* (London, Herbert Jenkins, 1935), p. 26.

[84] S. Hicks, *Not Guilty, M'Lord* (London, Cassell, 1939), p. 122.

[85] G. Pollock, *Mr Justice McCardie* (London, John Lane the Bodley Head, 1934), p. 162.

[86] *Leicester Mercury* (8 June 1921), p. 5.

[87] On 13 June 1921: see *The Times* (26 July 1921), p. 4.

[88] *Leicester Mercury*, (8 June 1921).

"pregnant"')[89] and in which having an illegitimate child was 'a totally shameful thing ... a bigger crime than stealing'.[90] A factory worker like Roberts would also have had a strong incentive to hide any sign of pregnancy in order to keep her job.[91] Despite some temporary softening of attitudes towards unmarried motherhood during the Great War, the pressures from parents, respectable opinion and the poor laws which led either to abortion or to neonaticide remained much as they had been in the Victorian era.[92]

As in the Victorian era, however, there was also a sense of unease at condemning a woman in Edith Roberts's situation while the father of her child went free.[93] A meeting of 500 people in Leicester Market Place unanimously demanded Edith Roberts's immediate release 'in the interest of justice and humanity' and called for the law to be changed so that the father should 'take his full share of the responsibility' and so that women would not be excluded from juries.[94]

The Infanticide Act 1922

When the demand for reform in the light of Roberts's case was taken up in parliament by the local MP Henry McLaren, the Home Secretary offered to provide him with the revised text of Alverstone's Bill.[95] The Home Secretary's invitation to re-introduce the measure was taken up by the general secretary of the Labour Party, Arthur Henderson. The Bill had a fairly easy passage through the House of Commons[96] but in

---

[89] S. Alexander, 'Becoming a woman in London in the 1920s and the 1930s', in D. Feldman and G.S. Jones (eds), *Metropolis. London: Histories and Representations Since 1800* (London, Routledge, 1989), p. 263. See also C. Dyhouse, *Girls Growing up in Late Victorian and Edwardian England* (London, Routledge & Kegan Paul, 1981), pp. 20–21.

[90] Quoted in R. Hood and K. Joyce, 'Three generations: oral testimonies on crime and social change in London's East End,' *British Journal of Criminology*, 39, 1 (1999), 136–60, at 149.

[91] Horn, *Women in the 1920s*, p. 115.

[92] N. Middleton, *When Family Failed* (London, Gollancz, 1971), Ch. 12; J. Lewis, *Women in England, 1870–1950* (Hemel Hempstead, Harvester Wheatsheaf, 1984), pp. 11, 65; A. Holdsworth, *Out of the Doll's House* (London, BBC Books, 1988), pp. 133–4; C. Haste, *Rules of Desire* (London, Chatto & Windus, 1991), p. 72.

[93] See, for example, J.W. Jeudwine, *Observations on English Criminal Law and Procedure* (London, King & Son, 1920).

[94] *Leicester Mercury* (19 July 1921).

[95] *H.C. Debs.*, (5th series), 143 (20 June 1921), cols 924–5.

[96] The only real debate occurred in the standing committee, where an amendment by the Home Secretary to limit the measure to 'newly born' children was withdrawn in the face of 'strong objections': *Report and Proceedings of Standing Committee A* (HC 61) *PP* (1922), IV, 963; Memo by A. Maxwell, 13 May 1922 in PRO LCO 2/476.

the Lords there were sharp exchanges between Lord Birkenhead, the Conservative Lord Chancellor in the coalition government, and Lord Parmoor, the Labour peer who sponsored the Bill. Birkenhead criticized the wording of the Bill on two seemingly contradictory grounds. On the one hand, the power of the jury to return a verdict of manslaughter added nothing to the existing law, since the jury in a murder trial could always do this 'if they think it proper on the facts'; on the other hand, the formula (originally Alverstone's) that the mother 'had not recovered from the effect of giving birth to the child' was too wide, and would cover a woman suffering from 'some minor indisposition' months after the birth.[97]

Birkenhead's permanent secretary, Sir Claud Schuster, drafted an amendment to meet these objections, and Birkenhead successfully piloted it through the Lords.[98] Instead of a verdict of manslaughter, the amendment created a new offence of infanticide, subject to the same penalty as manslaughter (that is, anything up to life imprisonment). A mother would be guilty of infanticide rather than murder only where the baby was 'newly born' and where the effects of giving birth were such that 'the balance of her mind was disturbed'. As I have argued elsewhere,[99] this form of words had little to do with the medical diagnosis of puerperal insanity, which was typically made several days or weeks after the birth. Its purpose was to meet Birkenhead's insistence that the mother's condition must be 'such as to have deflected her will, [or] her realisation of what is right and what is wrong'.[100]

Lord Parmoor was unhappy with the use of terminology which 'would necessitate consideration of medical evidence ... A poor woman does not want to get into the midst of a technical discussion of that kind',[101] but the wording was strongly defended by Birkenhead and by Lord Carson:

> We have to take great care that no woman should be allowed to be under the impression that the law mitigates her crime merely because she has gone through the process of giving birth to a child ... [T]o make the language more general, and to allow it to be thought that mere natural infirmity should be allowed as a defence would, I think, be a calamity.[102]

The nuances of drafting which Carson thought would have such a

---

[97] *H.L. Debs.*, 50, (16 May 1922), cols 440–41. Similar objections were set out by parliamentary counsel in PRO LCO 2/476.

[98] PRO LCO 2/476.

[99] Ward, 'Sad subject'.

[100] *H.L. Debs.*, (5th Series) 50, (16 May 1922), col. 441.

[101] Ibid.

[102] Ibid., col. 765.

salutary effect on a woman contemplating infanticide proved quite beyond the comprehension of Josiah Wedgwood, the Labour (formerly Liberal) MP who had the task of steering the Lord Chancellor's amendment through the Commons after it was passed by the Lords. Having cruelly exposed Wedgwood's complete inability to explain what difference the amendment made, the Conservative MP Sir Frederick Banbury aptly remarked that 'A great deal of legislation is passed because honourable members ... do not in the least know what they are doing.'[103] Nevertheless it was now up to the courts to interpret the 'intention of parliament'.

Insanity and infanticide: R. v. O'Donoghue

In 1927 Mary O'Donoghue found herself unemployed, penniless, with an abscess on her breast and nothing to feed her 35-day-old baby except a tin of condensed milk. She strangled the baby with a napkin and put the body in a cardboard box under her bed. When she was taken to Holloway prison, the medical officer there noticed 'nothing abnormal about the girl's mental condition ... but her physical condition was very poor'.[104]

This was just the kind of case that Birkenhead had carefully excluded from the scope of the 1922 Act. She might have some 'minor infirmity' connected with the birth, but her child was not 'newly born'. And ought mere starvation to have clouded her judgment of right and wrong? True, there was some medical evidence to support an insanity defence but, as the judge remarked 'there are always to be found medical men ready to come forward for the defence'.[105] Accordingly, O'Donoghue was sentenced to death for murder and reprieved a few days later.

O'Donoghue's lawyer appealed, claiming (quite wrongly) that the Act had been designed to meet cases of puerperal insanity, which might appear 'from two to six weeks after childbirth'. He argued that the words 'newly born' should be broadly interpreted to cover any birth from which the mother had not recovered. The Lord Chief Justice pointed out that on this reading the words 'newly born' would be 'otiose and meaningless'. The appeal was dismissed – a result which certainly reflected the intentions of Lord Birkenhead, if not of parliament.[106]

---

[103] *H.C. Debs.*, (5th Series) 155, (30 June 1922), col. 4288.

[104] J.H. Morton, 'Female homicides', *Journal of Mental Science*, 80 (1934), 64–74, at 66.

[105] This remark was quoted by the medical man concerned, Dr Finucane, in the discussion following L. McIlroy, 'The influence of parturition upon insanity and crime', *Transactions of the Medico-Legal Society*, 22 (1928), 53–73, at 69.

[106] *R. v. O'Donoghue*, *Criminal Appeal Reports*, 20 (1927), 132.

Although most doctors probably would not have considered Mary O'Donoghue insane,[107] the case re-opened a long running debate about the relationship between puerperal insanity and the law. Cases in which mothers killed their children – *not* new-borns, but children from a few weeks to a few years old – were the most discussed examples of the phenomenon of 'irresistible impulse'.[108] Critics complained that such impulses, which reduced the mother to 'the helpless spectator of her own insane conduct',[109] were excluded from the M'Naghten Rules laid down by the judges in 1843, under which insanity was a defence only where it prevented the defendant from knowing the 'nature and quality' of an otherwise criminal act or that it was (legally) wrong.[110] In practice, however, the courts were usually willing to stretch the Rules to cover distressed mothers.

Take, for example, what Lord Alverstone called 'one of the saddest cases I ever heard of', which he tried in 1902. The defendant, Mary Worley, had been married for nearly five years – or so she believed – to a man named Askew, and had borne three children by him. When Askew turned out to be a bigamist, Mary left him. Mary's father then went to Askew's house where, after quarrelling with Askew, he shot himself. When Mary received the summons to attend her father's inquest she threw herself into a canal with two of the children, one of whom drowned. The court readily accepted that she had been temporarily insane, although she had left a note which clearly implied that she intended her own and the children's deaths and knew that killing them was wrong (though she sought to cast the blame on Askew). In ordering her to be detained during His Majesty's Pleasure, Alverstone told her 'she must not feel that this cast any censure on her at all'.[111]

The terms of the debate over the insanity defence were very similar to those in the discussion of infanticide.[112] Lawyers on both sides (and many medical writers) accepted that the insanity defence needed to be carefully circumscribed to serve the law's aims of deterrence and moral discipline, but that some account needed to be taken of the (possibly

---

[107] McIlroy, 'Influence of parturition'.

[108] R. Smith, *Trial by Medicine: Insanity and Responsibility in Victorian Trials* (Edinburgh, Edinburgh University Press, 1981), Ch. 7; S. Day, 'Puerperal insanity: the historical sociology of a disease' (PhD diss., Cambridge, 1985). See also Chapters 9 and 10 above.

[109] W.C. Sullivan, *Crime and Insanity* (London, Edward Arnold, 1924), p. 98.

[110] *Daniel M'Naghten's Case, Clark and Finelly's Reports*, 10 (1843), 200.

[111] PRO HO144/579/A63301 (including cuttings from the *Birmingham Daily Post* and *Birmingham Daily Mail*).

[112] For more detailed discussion see Ward, 'Sad subject', and T. Ward, 'Law, common sense and the authority of science: expert witnesses and criminal insanity in England, c.1840–1940', *Social & Legal Studies*, 6 (1997): 343–62.

misplaced) humanitarian sympathies of juries and the general public. Some – notably, once again, J.F. Stephen[113] – argued that the law should explicitly recognize 'irresistible impulse' as a defence so as to regularize the verdicts which juries in practice returned on parents who killed.[114] Others thought it was important to keep legal rules clear, strict and simple, while accepting some flexibility in their application.[115] The Atkin Committee, in its report on insanity and crime published in 1923,[116] took the former position, but when its proposals were debated in the House of Lords, the Law Lords who spoke unanimously took the latter view.[117] The opposing views were succinctly put by two judges in a discussion of the issues raised by O'Donoghue's case. Mr Justice Humphreys praised the English jury's 'extraordinary capacity for doing justice by perhaps illogical means', but Lord Atkin thought it 'a reproach to the law that it can ever be reasonable in practice only by being violated in theory'.[118]

It was Mr Justice Humphrey's efforts to do justice by perhaps illogical means that eventually brought about the extension of the Infanticide Act. Brenda Hale was a middle-class married woman who bore two children. Two to three weeks after each birth she showed what her doctor and her husband considered to be signs of mental illness and expressed fears that she would hurt the baby. In the case of the second child, born in May 1936, her fears were realized and she cut the baby's throat and her own.[119] At her trial for murder and attempted suicide in July 1936, Lord Dawson of Penn, the president of the British Medical Association, testified that she had not recovered from the effects of giving birth and that from a medical point of view a child was 'newly born' up to the age of four weeks. Strictly speaking this was compatible with the decision in the O'Donoghue case, where Lord Hewart had declined to define 'newly born' but said it could not extend to a child of

---

[113] J.F. Stephen, *A General View of the Criminal Law of England* (London, Macmillan, 1863), p. 95; Stephen, *History*, vol. 2, Ch. 19.

[114] The courts were less consistent in dealing with homicidal fathers than with mothers, but some such men benefited from a very generous interpretation of the M'Naghten Rules. See Ward, 'Sad subject', 168–9.

[115] See, for example: Lord Bramwell, 'Insanity and crime', *The Nineteenth Century*, 18 (1885), 893 (discussing a hypothetical mother who kills her children to send them to heaven, 'indifferent to their own fate'); H. Oppenheimer, *The Criminal Responsibility of Lunatics* (London, Sweet & Maxwell, 1909).

[116] Cmd. 2005, PP 1923, XII/1, 787.

[117] *H.L. Debs.*, 57, (15 May 1924), cols 443–76.

[118] Discussion of McIlroy, 'Influence of parturition', 62, 73 (Atkin's comment is in a letter read out by McIlroy).

[119] J.C.M. Matheson, 'Infanticide', *Medico-Legal and Criminological Review*, 9 (1941), 135–52, at 139–40.

'more than a calendar month in age'. Humphreys, however, considered himself bound to direct the jury that the child was not 'newly born' and instead elicited a verdict designed to soften the stigma of being found 'guilty but insane': Mrs Hale was *'Not Guilty* of murder, but *Guilty* of the act charged, for which she was not responsible in law'.[120]

In the course of his summing-up, Humphreys suggested that legislation should be introduced to define 'newly born', and this suggestion was taken up by Lord Dawson. After consultation with his medical colleagues Dawson introduced a Bill which instead of redefining 'newly born' replaced it with a provision covering a mother's killing of her baby under a year old when she had not recovered either from the birth or from lactation.

'Lactational insanity' was typically a condition of 'overworked and poorly fed women',[121] often suffering from anaemia.[122] Overwork, malnutrition and anaemia were all common conditions among working-class mothers of the 1930s.[123] Indirectly, therefore, the Bill took account of the social conditions which probably lay behind the violent acts of some depressed mothers.[124] But by putting the defence on a medical footing the Bill reassured those like Lord Atkin who were concerned lest 'it should be thought that taking the life of an infant child is not as serious a form of murder as taking life of anybody else'.[125] The Bill was passed unopposed and received the royal assent on 23 June 1938.

Conclusion

At the time of writing, the 1938 Act remains in force, and the non-custodial sentences which were usual from 1924 onwards[126] remain the norm.[127] The reference to 'lactation' in the Act has come to seem archaic; in practice the Act is applied in circumstances of social and emotional stress.[128] The Criminal Law Revision Committee has

---

[120] *The Times* (22 July 1936).

[121] McIlroy, 'Influence of parturition', 60.

[122] J.S. Hopwood, 'Child murder and insanity', *Journal of Mental Science*, 73 (1927), 95–108, at 97; Morton, 'Female homicides', 70.

[123] M.S. Rice, *Working-Class Wives: Their Health and Conditions* (Harmondsworth, Penguin, 1939).

[124] Such as the cases described by Hopwood, 'Child murder'.

[125] *H.L. Debs.*, 108, (22 Mar. 1938), cols 299–300.

[126] N. Walker, *Crime and Insanity in England*, vol. 1. (Edinburgh, Edinburgh University Press, 1968), p. 269. When prison sentences were passed under the 1922 Act they were often merely nominal, see Matheson, 'Infanticide'.

[127] See R. v. *Sainsbury*, *Criminal Appeal Reports (Sentencing)*, 11 (1990), 533.

[128] A. Wilczynski, *Child Homicide* (London, Greenwich Medical Media, 1997).

recommended amending the Act to bring it in line with this reality, but their recommendation has not been implemented.[129] It is still occasionally argued that in some symbolic way the Act encourages child abuse[130] – a criticism voiced most forcefully by Judge Hanophy of New York in defending his system's insistence that neonaticide is murder just like any other: 'We aim to protect the children rather than excuse the killer ... any law that grants a blanket exemption ... to those who kill their children when their children are under the age of one is a law that is primitive and uncivilized.'[131]

The debate as to whether or not infanticide is really different from murder reflects a continuing tension between two 'modes of subjectification' in criminal law. While criminal-law doctrine addresses itself to an autonomous juridical subject, the lay and medical narratives through which reality is reconstructed in the courtroom[132] often depict a very different, much less autonomous subject. One of the abiding features of criminal justice, from the Victorian era to the present, is that the resolution of this tension varies according to the gender of the defendant: courts are more likely to accept portrayals of women offenders as 'sad' or 'mad' rather than 'bad', and less inclined to treat them as rational, autonomous agents.[133] In confronting us with this invidious dichotomy – *either* compassion *or* respect for the offender's autonomy and the victim's rights – criminal law still shows some of the characteristics of the Victorian rhetoric of fallenness, 'opposing an illusory ideal of autonomy to an extreme determinism characteristically gendered as feminine'.[134]

Acknowledgements

I am grateful to Mark Jackson, Gerry Johnstone and Liz Rogers for their comments on an earlier draft of this chapter.

---

[129] Criminal Law Revision Committee, *Offences Against the Person* (London, HMSO, 1980, Cmnd. 7844), paras 102–105.

[130] See A. Payne, 'Infanticide and child abuse,' *Journal of Forensic Psychiatry*, 6, 3 (1995), 472–76.

[131] *Independent* (8 March 1996), quoted by J. McDonagh, 'Infanticide and the nation, the case of Caroline Beale,' *New Formations*, 32 (1997), 11–21, at 16.

[132] W.L. Bennett and M.S. Feldman, *Reconstructing Reality in the Courtroom* (New Brunswick, N.J., Rutgers University Press, 1981); A. Worrall, *Offending Women, Female Lawbreakers and the Criminal Justice System* (London, Routledge, 1990).

[133] H. Allen, *Justice Unbalanced: Gender and Psychiatry in Judicial Decisions* (Milton Keynes, Open University Press, 1987); K. Daly, *Gender, Crime and Justice* (New Haven, Yale University Press, 1994); Wilczynski, *Child Homicide*, Ch. 5.

[134] Anderson, *Tainted Souls*, p. 19.

CHAPTER THIRTEEN

'Nothing in between': modern cases of infanticide

Julie Wheelwright

On 20 May 2000 an American university student, Kelly Angell, aged twenty, was *en route* to Britain from her parents' home in Portland, Maine, when the plane made a scheduled stop at Logan Airport, Boston. While waiting for her flight to the UK, she gave birth in the ladies' washroom to a baby boy, then severed the umbilical cord with her fingers. The *Daily Mail* reported that, 'in her distress, she allegedly left the 8lb baby boy in a toilet bowl and covered him with tissue paper, believing him to be stillborn'. Kelly Angell then returned to the airport waiting room for her flight. In the meantime, a cleaner found the baby and the police were immediately called to investigate.[1] The lengthy newspaper article featured no direct quotes from Kelly Angell herself, although there were comments from friends of her British boyfriend, Graeme Clifton, aged twenty-one, and from her brother, Jeremy Angell, aged eighteen. Her defence lawyer was quoted as saying that Kelly's parents were traumatized by the events and concerned about their daughter.

This news report of a near-neonaticide reveals one of the most striking features of how modern society continues to perceive women who have concealed their pregnancies and then experienced an unassisted delivery. These women rarely have a public voice, their actions are shrouded in a silence that suggests guilt, and those who surround them – their parents, their infant, their partners – are portrayed as the real victims. In the absence of clearly articulated motives and experience, the only framework for a contemporary understanding of the infanticidal woman is constructed from the medical and legal discourse and bolstered by the fickle morality of the press. As 'Kate', the pseudonym of a woman who was convicted of infanticide in England in 1994, said in a BBC television programme on the subject, those who commit infanticide are considered in the public, legal, or medical discourse as either 'mad or bad'. In all three arenas there is, as she said, 'nothing in between', no space for alternative,

---

[1] 'Girl dumps Briton's baby after airport birth drama', *Daily Mail* (1 June 2000).

more sophisticated explanations.[2] Furthermore, the issue is closely framed by a contemporary, and indeed historically rooted, conundrum about what motherhood means and what our maternal expectations have become. Expectant mothers must very often weigh the fine balance between the need to continue making a financial contribution against the need to give the child the best of their care and attention. The mother's needs must be subsumed by those of the new family, and depression can result for those who feel the lack of a viable alternative; a 'nothing in between' the traditional home-maker and the working professional woman.[3] Especially with the added pressures of poverty and ill-health, some find the job becomes too much. Despite the reams written by feminist writers and others about the yawning gap between these divergent expectations, the framework in which motherhood is viewed remains muddled.[4]

Obviously there is far more at work in cases of modern infanticide than an individual woman's ambivalence about the challenges that contemporary motherhood entails. However, given that contraception and abortion are now accessible and (generally) morally acceptable alternatives to pregnancy, it is important to consider why, even in developed countries like Britain and the United States, the number of women each year who conceal a pregnancy before abandonment or infanticide has remained stable.[5] The media, as the coverage of the Angell case and others will illustrate, remains fascinated with the macabre details and the haunting question of motive in such cases. The subject attracts attention partly because it evokes the same extreme reactions and deep emotions that surround debates about access to abortion.[6] It has been suggested that the women themselves may regard the baby as an extension of the mother/self and that therefore the violence is perpetrated, not against what they can identify as another human being, but against themselves. Josephine McDonagh, for example, has recently suggested that contemporary debates about abortion and infanticide revolve around the tangled issue of whether the mother's rights can be regarded as independent from those of the

---

2   Interview with author, 2 March 1998, for 'Deadly Secrets', *QED*, BBC1.

3   Ibid.

4   M. Benn, *Madonna and Child: Towards a New Politics of Motherhood* (London, Jonathan Cape, 1998); R. Coward, *Our Treacherous Hearts: Why Women Let Men Get in Their Way* (London, Faber and Faber, 1993).

5   M.N. Marks and R. Kumar, 'Infanticide in England and Wales, 1982–1988', *Medicine, Science and the Law*, 33 (1993), 329–39; S.J. Creighton, 'Fatal child abuse – how preventable is it?', *Child Abuse Review*, 4 (1995), 318–28.

6   S. Schwarz, 'Is abortion a form of infanticide?', in S. Schwarz, *The Moral Question of Abortion* (Chicago, Loyola University Press, 1990).

child before, or soon after, birth.[7] This dilemma about whose rights must be considered more important may begin at conception but it continues as a powerful theme and much-debated issue in contemporary writing on motherhood.

These are questions that women who commit infanticide or experience a concealed pregnancy struggle to answer themselves. In interviews, they rarely provide explanations that appear rational. 'Kate' described how she concealed her pregnancy because she 'didn't want to bother anyone' and smothered her infant to prevent discovery. Caroline Beale both did and did not realize she was pregnant and wanted to avoid upsetting her boyfriend and his family who were mourning another woman's death. Amy Ellwood told the district attorney in New York State where she was prosecuted that she had smothered her new-born son because, 'I just thought my parents wouldn't find out that way'.[8] Twyana Davis, a college student in Ohio who took great care to ensure that her new-born baby girl would be found after she put her in a rubbish bin on campus, provided the most lucid explanation. She was living with her maternal grandparents at the time and 'didn't want them to know that I messed up' because she feared that they would send her back to live with her alcoholic mother.[9] Dr Margaret Spinelli, the psychiatrist who treated Caroline Beale and who has interviewed several neonaticidal mothers, argues that these women convince themselves that the baby is dead before they deliver it.[10]

Unlike the other historians included in this collection, I have had the opportunity to interview women who have concealed a pregnancy and either abandoned an infant or committed infanticide. However, the thought processes of these women during pregnancy, in labour and in the aftermath are often impossible to access. At the time, many seem to have been in a dissociated state and to have erased their memories in order to protect themselves from the physical and emotional pain of the labour and its aftermath. Dr Spinelli's research suggests that many of these women are 'in a trance' when they deliver the baby and cannot accept its reality.[11] Others could not return to face the reality of their newborn's existence. When I interviewed Caroline Beale at Rikers' Island prison in May 1995 while she was awaiting trial for the murder of her new-born daughter, I

---

[7] J. McDonagh, 'Infanticide and the nation: the case of Caroline Beale', *New Formations*, 32 (1997), 11–21.

[8] P. Pearson, *When She Was Bad: How Women Get Away With Murder* (London, Virago, 1999), p. 70.

[9] Interview with author, 8 Mar. 1998, for 'Deadly Secrets', *QED*, BBC1.

[10] 'Prom baby's mom indicted,' *Ashbury Park Press* (18 Sep. 1997).

[11] J. Wheelwright, 'A moment as a mother', *The Guardian* (13 May 1995); and 'Prom baby's mom indicted'.

was unable to question her directly about the events surrounding her labour for legal reasons. But when I touched too closely on a sensitive subject, she was unable to speak. As Beale told a BBC Radio interviewer in 1997 about her experience of giving birth: 'It's like looking back at a photograph. I can hardly remember anything that happened about it.'[12] Dr Susan Elmhurst, a London paediatrician who has treated several women with concealed pregnancies, has suggested that her patients regarded the baby as an unacceptable part of themselves and that the neonaticidal mothers always had a reason for their actions. They could not understand the baby as 'real' or separate from themselves.[13]

Significantly, modern discourse on infanticide, if the press can be used as a guide, rarely includes any account of the men who father these infants. While historically public sympathy has sometimes sided with the women who were often considered to be the victims of male vice, women accused of infanticide are now assumed to be acting out of free will. As a result, even a very young woman who falls pregnant is still assumed in such news reports to be operating on a basis of conscious, adult decision-making when she commits neonaticide. Even in cases like those of Caroline Beale or 'Kate', who both had boyfriends during their pregnancies, there is no discussion about the father's attitude to the pregnancy.[14] There is an assumption that the woman is suffering from an emotional and psychological condition in which she feels compelled to hide her pregnancy, but there is no analysis of the psychological state of her partner who colludes in the process. Similarly, contemporary research on neonaticide focuses on the mother and tends to neglect the dynamic between the couple. The father appears to be an unimportant factor in understanding the mother's condition.

The roots of contemporary debates in Britain about infanticide are to be found largely in the circumstances leading to the Infanticide Act of 1938, which specified that a lesser charge than murder would apply to mothers who had not recovered from the birth or lactation and who killed their own infant under the age of twelve months. As earlier chapters in this book make clear, for much of the eighteenth and nineteenth centuries, new-born child murder was treated in legal terms as an idiosyncratic crime. According to McDonagh, the need to have a separate law for new-born child murder rested on two central problems which persist today: firstly, the problem of forensic evidence and the difficulty of determining whether the baby was born alive or still-born;

---

[12] Wheelwright, 'Moment as a mother'; and Caroline Beale interview, *Woman's Hour*, BBC Radio 4, 5 July 1997.

[13] In conversation with author, 25 Oct. 1997.

[14] J. Marleau et al., 'Paternal filicide: a study of 10 men', *The Canadian Journal of Psychiatry*, 44 (1999), 57–63.

and secondly, the mental stability of the mother. 'In 1861 the offence [of concealment] was extended further to include 'any person' not merely the mother, and it is the Offences Against the Person Act 1861, s. 60 which continues to govern the law on concealment to this day.' According to some historians, the introduction of the new offence of infanticide in 1922, and its clarification in 1938, led to more sympathetic and lenient treatment of women while bolstering the perceived connection between mental instability and motherhood. As McDonagh has argued, this 'relieved women of criminal agency in infanticide cases, but it also tended, less specifically, to pathologize maternity, institutionalising an expectation of female insanity'.[15]

In contemporary debates in Britain about infanticide, the thinking has moved on again: there is now an unwillingness to accept an automatic relationship between motherhood and mental disturbance. Where the early twentieth-century Infanticide Acts treated childbirth as a normal condition and pathologized its occasional 'abnormal' consequences, our modern tendency to view it as a communal, medically-controlled condition has further pathologized it. In earlier historical periods, a woman who was forced by circumstance to have an unassisted delivery was not considered anomalous; now, however, it has become unthinkable. Modern approaches have medicalized delivery while romanticizing pregnancy and mothering. This has led to failure to acknowledge the emergence of problems relating to pregnancy and mothering to the extent that women find it difficult to seek appropriate treatment for a range of post-natal illnesses.[16]

Modern understandings of infanticide

However anomalous these cases at first appear, the number of women convicted of infanticide in Britain has remained relatively stable since the 1940s.[17] In addition, the presumption under English law that infanticide is a crime that requires special legal consideration has also endured since it was first enshrined in law in the seventeenth century.[18] What appears to have changed, however, is that historical or traditional stereotypes concerning the economic, class and social profile of victims are no longer adequate to explain modern infanticide. It is not a crime associated exclusively with poverty, nor does it occur only among very young women who have little knowledge or conscious awareness of

---

[15] McDonagh, 'Infanticide and the nation'.
[16] M. Smith, Health Visitors' Association, in conversation with author, 12 Oct. 1997.
[17] Marks and Kumar, 'Infanticide in England and Wales'.
[18] McDonagh, 'Infanticide and the nation', 14-16.

their ability to conceive. Even more confusing, these women also defy clear categories of mental illness since they appear to have been fully functional before and after their pregnancies. Another important difference between early modern and modern anxieties about the suspicious deaths of children, is that while there certainly are recent cases of single and unsupported women committing neonaticide, as in the past, there are also a large number who are either involved in a relationship, or cohabiting, with the child's father.[19]

Although it would be entirely understandable that these women would wish to erase painful memories, another obstacle to accessing their experience is one of language. The paucity of language relates to the absence of a philosophical framework for understanding infanticide beyond the 'mad/bad' dichotomy. The reality inevitably lies somewhere between the two poles of criminality and insanity, where women must accept responsibility for having committed a murder, yet should be treated sympathetically because of their mental confusion. Equally, it is important to remember that these women have endured an unassisted delivery and risked their lives either to continue denying their pregnancy or to protect what they perceive as a shameful or damaging secret.[20]

The contemporary testimonies of infanticidal mothers (the discussion in this chapter is limited to those who committed, or were prosecuted for, the murder of their infant after a concealed pregnancy and within the first twenty-four hours of its life) suggests that, as in earlier centuries, the fear of losing an already fragile identity is paramount. Women fear their parents' reaction and they are ashamed that they have transgressed boundaries of sexual propriety: they have committed an act that will tarnish their reputation and possibly ruin their future. Their thinking seems similar to those teenage girls who refuse to use contraception because that would mean admitting that they have been having sex; they cannot deal with the consequences of their actions so the baby becomes a problem that can only be 'solved' through being 'unborn' again. Alternatively, the women may feel so alone or vulnerable themselves that they cannot accommodate a baby or even admit to a pregnancy in the first place. Often they are so unaware of their bodies that they notice the symptoms of pregnancy far too late for a termination and are so terrified that their denial of reality becomes even more profound.[21]

---

[19] Author's review of recent cases of neonaticide as reported in British press, 1975–98.

[20] Results from a 1998 survey of the clients of 'Project Cuddle', a voluntary organisation based in Los Angeles that 'rescues' the infants of women who have a concealed pregnancy or are about to abandon a baby, suggest that pregnancies that result from rape or from mixed-race teen relationships are factors in abandonment.

[21] Dr Margaret Oates, interview with Clare Richards, 5 March 1998, 'Deadly Secrets', QED, BBC1.

Although abortion now has wide legal and social acceptance in the UK and although the law on infanticide is still generally supported, unease about the wider implications for women persist. In her 1997 book, *When She Was Bad: How Women Get Away with Murder*, journalist Patricia Pearson argued that the persistence of infanticide reflects a deep cultural anomie among young women. 'For the post-Sexual Revolution generation, raised on a rhetoric that celebrated sexual freedom but had no memory of what the revolution was for, there are no links between intimacy and commitment, pregnancy and childbirth, sex and the beginning of a bright, constructive love.'[22] Pearson remains suspicious of what she labels a 'vocabulary of motive' for infanticidal mothers who attempt to rationalize their experience. She comments on the case of an American woman, Paula Sims, who allowed her two daughters to drown in the bathtub and then buried their bodies in the woods near her home: '[M]aybe it is just simpler to believe that she'd been insane, that she hadn't taken action in order to wrest herself free of a stifling life.'[23] British journalist Yvonne Roberts argued along similar lines in the *Sunday Telegraph*, commenting on the North American practice of treating infanticide as a crime of homicide: 'In my view American rules are clearer, unmuddled by prejudices or unproved beliefs about biological destiny. They caused Caroline Beale pain but that might be the price to be paid if justice is to be extended not just to the increasing numbers of women who fail the test of conformity but also to those babies who otherwise have no voice; the victims of murder committed by a rational hand.'[24] Both writers argue that the infanticidal mother must be regarded as an adult who has made a conscious decision to end her baby's life and caution against allowing the mitigating factor of mental confusion in determining a sentence.

However, the psychiatric experts who treat infanticidal mothers have argued that, with neonaticide in particular, the phenomenon *is* unique and cannot be compared to other crimes of homicide. According to Drs Spinelli and Oates, following the pain of labour a woman may well be in a mental state where she cannot act rationally and is confused. The normal mental process may have been interrupted for several months before the delivery, which is often the point at which a woman begins to dissociate from the reality of her pregnancy. As William Hunter did many years ago, modern psychiatrists question the woman's rationality and her mental state when she has chosen to risk endangering her own life as well as the baby's to prevent anyone knowing she was pregnant

---

[22]   Pearson, *When She was Bad*, p. 67.
[23]   Ibid, p. 86.
[24]   Y. Roberts, 'Are the Americans right?', *Sunday Telegraph* (10 Mar. 1996).

in the first place. From the psychiatric perspective, the fact that these women have an unassisted delivery must be taken as testimony to their irrational thought process. Neither is there any suggestion that their behaviour is consistently aggressive. This is aberrant behaviour: they are not 'killers'.[25]

In spite of extensive medical research, the problem of the women's subjectivity persists and is reflected in media coverage. Since the women seem unable to articulate their actions and there is a powerful disincentive for them to speak to the press after the event, in media accounts they are often reduced to an infant-like state themselves and their experience is shaped by the professionals who must judge and treat them.[26] 'Kate' described in an interview how she came to believe that she was 'bad' while on remand at Risley prison, because that was preferable to the label of 'madness'. Infanticidal women represent the antithesis of our culturally accepted notion of being a mother, because in these cases the bodily function of producing a child is completely divorced from the experiencing of mothering the infant. As Dr Spinelli argues, the infant is dead to them, even before its delivery.[27]

I would suggest that it is precisely the ambivalence that so many mothers feel about their children and the unacceptability of expressing contradictory feelings that serves to generate public and media interest in these cases. Although I have interviewed only three women who have concealed their pregnancies, it was their ambivalence and their desperation to deny an unbearable reality that struck me most profoundly. In the remainder of this chapter, I shall describe the details of a recent neonaticide case which led to the arrest and conviction for infanticide of a woman whose identity will remain anonymous. She appeared in a television programme that I produced in association with Clare Richards for BBC television in 1998. Using the testimony of Kate and drawing upon other cases, I shall then explore how women themselves understand their own psychological motives for concealing a pregnancy and for killing or abandoning their new-born baby.

---

[25] Dr Margaret Spinelli, interview with author, 12 Mar. 1998, 'Deadly Secrets', *QED*, BBC1; J. Wheelwright, 'A life given and taken', *The Guardian* (28 July 1998); M.N. Marks, 'Characteristics and causes of infanticide in Britain', *International Review of Psychiatry*, 8 (1996), 99–106.

[26] During the 1997/98 research for 'Deadly Secrets', in *QED*, a BBC1 documentary, we contacted via their solicitors more than 30 women who had been convicted of infanticide. The majority refused to answer our letters while several others said they wished to remain anonymous. 'Kate' was the only one who agreed to meet and discuss the project with us.

[27] 'Prom baby's mom indicted'.

Kate's story

The following details are based on interviews conducted in 1998 with 'Kate', a woman in her twenties who responded to a letter we had forwarded to her probation officer concerning our programme for BBC Television. 'Kate' agreed to have her interview used in our programme on the understanding that her identity would remain completely anonymous. 'Kate's name and other identifiable details have been changed to maintain that protection.

On a warm autumn evening in 1994, twenty-one-year-old Kate was at home with her boyfriend with whom she was living. There was a knock at the door and her boyfriend went to answer it. Two plain-clothes policemen stood on the doorstep, but looked past him to Kate. They took her into a bedroom where one of the officers mumbled something about a baby's body being discovered in a ditch. 'I can't remember their exact words,' says Kate, 'it's a blur to me now.' But minutes later she was led away from her home to a police car and driven to the local police station. There, she was charged with the murder of her new-born infant daughter, born seven weeks earlier.

Kate had been with her boyfriend for just over six months. But shortly before she met him, she had had a brief affair with a man from the office where she worked. Since her menstrual periods had always been irregular, she was six months pregnant before she understood the disastrous consequences of the affair. It was then too late to have an abortion and she was terrified to confess to her new boyfriend that she was carrying someone else's child. She told no one and managed to disguise her pregnancy by wearing baggy clothes and making excuses for symptoms. Three months later, alone in an empty room in a rented house, she gave birth to her baby and, in a moment of panic, smothered her.

'If somebody had told me the year before that this was going to happen to me, I'd have just laughed', says Kate. There was nothing remarkable about this small woman except her waist-length reddish hair and her quick wits. She rattled off words nervously, admitting that she found the experience distressing to talk about – then paused, groping her way towards an understanding of it. 'When I realised I was pregnant, there wasn't a day that I didn't think, "I've got to do something about this", but time was running out, and it just got later and later.' Her relationship with her mother was volatile, and she did not feel that she could confide in any of her friends, insisting that she did not want to 'bother' people. She coped by pretending that nothing had happened: telling someone, she now admits, would have made the pregnancy real and would have forced her to act. 'I wish somebody had come up to me and said quietly, "Look, you're pregnant, but there's nothing to worry about. You're going to be okay."'

During the day, Kate carried on as usual, but at night she could barely sleep and felt exhausted by the effort of keeping her secret. 'When I was six or seven months pregnant, it was awful. I felt drained and worn out. But I kept getting up, going to work and coming home', she explained. 'It was as though there was something preventing me from being aware of what was happening.' An only child of divorced parents, Kate had grown up keeping her emotions to herself. She had no desire to upset either her now-remarried father or her mother. She believed that her relationship with her new boyfriend was too fragile for such a difficult problem and so, she repeated, 'I just didn't want to bother anyone.' But when she was full term, Kate was forced to confront reality. She got up for work early in the morning, went to the bathroom and her waters broke.

'I think the labour started right away. I didn't know what was happening. I knew I was in labour but I didn't know what stage it was.' For the next seventeen hours, Kate lay in bed, drifting in and out of consciousness as her contractions grew stronger. 'I was so tired but I kept thinking that I had to wake myself up.' As she lay there, she could hear noises in the street but felt so disconnected from reality that she could not call for help. 'I was thinking, "I wish I was dead, I wish it would stop, I wish I could die and that would be it."' Kate delivered the baby alone without injury despite the fact that the infant was breech. Had she been in hospital, it is likely that she would have had a caesarean section.

It is estimated that every year about twenty women in England and Wales conceal a pregnancy and deliver a baby on their own, before abandoning or killing it.[28] On occasions, the baby has been abandoned outdoors and has died of exposure rather as the result of any intent on the mother's part to commit a deliberate murder. According to psychiatrists, these women use a psychological mechanism called 'splitting' to blank out the knowledge that they are pregnant. By refusing to tell anyone, or even work out their due date, they hope the birth will never happen. 'Splitting' enables a woman to stop feeling anxious about her condition. However, according to Dr Oates, by removing the element of fear, any incentive to act on the situation is also removed. 'The main thing these women have in common is the capacity to keep their own counsel. Most of the women I've met have known that they were pregnant. They say things like, 'Well, I didn't want to think

---

[28] Marks and Kumar, 'Infanticide in England and Wales'.

about it,' or 'I thought it might go away'. If they admitted it to other people and to themselves, it would become real and they would have to do something about it.'[29]

Dr Oates explained that women who keep the birth of their baby a secret tend to have easy labours and rapid deliveries. 'Perhaps that's one of the reasons that the concealment actually proceeds. After all, if anything goes wrong early on or during the labour, many of them would be found out.' Even after her daughter was born, Kate explains that the feeling of unreality persisted. 'I was reeling from the whole process of the labour, but it didn't seem any more real when the baby was born.' Rationality seeped through briefly as Kate realized that the umbilical cord was still attached. With the baby in her arms, she staggered down the stairs to the kitchen where she found a sharp knife to cut the cord. 'All I really remember was the bedroom. It was horrific – there was blood all over the floor and all over the bedding. It looked as though someone had been murdered. As if someone had had their head chopped off.'

Kate felt overwhelmed by her predicament even as she recalled an attempt to breast-feed her daughter. 'It was just her and me in the world. Nobody else was there,' she says. When the baby began to cry, Kate panicked at the thought that someone might hear her and, on impulse, she put her hand over the baby's mouth and pinched her nose until the noise stopped. Kate then wrapped the baby's corpse in a pillowcase and some plastic bags. Yet she could not bear to dispose of the body so she kept the bundle in her bedroom.

According to Dr Oates, the trigger to kill a baby following a secret delivery is almost always the infant's crying. 'It signals the beginning of life, so the mother wants to kill the baby before it has started to live. The mode of death is almost always gentle – it's not hitting, strangling or stabbing – and is usually asphyxiation within minutes or certainly within an hour or two of birth.' The women believe it is 'less bad' to kill an infant that has yet to draw breathe and both Caroline Beale and Kelly Angell insisted they believed their babies were still-born. In Angell's case, the infant lived.[30] However, Kate stated during her interview that she had breast-fed her baby before smothering her, though the pathologists' report denied this.[31]

For the next few weeks, Kate was in a state of severe emotional shock, robotically going to work and pretending that everything was normal.

---

[29] Dr Margaret Oates, interview with Clare Richards, 5 Mar. 1998, 'Deadly Secrets', *QED*, BBC1.

[30] See: Wheelwright, 'Moment as a mother'; 'Prom baby's mom indicted'; and 'Girl dumps Briton's baby'.

[31] Conversation with author, March 1998.

Eventually, when it came time to move in with her boyfriend, she took the plastic bundle from her bedroom and walked down to the local playing fields where she left it in a water-filled ditch. A witness saw Kate from her window nearby and, thinking her actions were strange, went to look inside the bag. The woman immediately informed the police who tracked Kate down to her new home. After giving a full statement describing how she had smothered her daughter, she spent five days in police custody before being transferred to Risley prison where she spent six months on a hospital ward.

Kate suggested that immediately after her arrest it was easier to see herself as a wicked, evil woman than as mentally unstable. 'After all, I murdered my own child, so I felt I should be there.' But she remains angry that she was offered no psychotherapy, and was told by her solicitor to present herself as either 'wicked or bonkers, as there was no in-between. I was crying and was told by this barrister, "That's good, because a jury will be more sympathetic if you're in tears." The police saw me as a cold-blooded murderess, and were only concerned about the events leading up to the labour and afterwards. They didn't want to know what was going through my mind or how I was feeling.' Eventually the charge was reduced to infanticide, and Kate was sentenced to three years' probation. 'Women who have killed an infant should have psychiatric treatment and be dealt with by the courts,' says Dr Oates. 'But in the majority of cases, neither the interests of the woman or society would be served by a custodial sentence.' Women who commit infanticide rarely re-offend and usually go on to be caring mothers with subsequent children.

For Kate, the media played a particular role in her realization of how her crime was viewed by the public. 'There was six line lines [about my case] in the Today [newspaper] ... that could have been a six-month-old child, it was that little piece that made me feel it. In prison they saw me as a cold-blooded murderess ... I was pregnant and suddenly there was a baby ... they wanted to know what I was doing, not how I was feeling.' Moreover, Kate felt that in her interviews with the police, with her solicitor and with the prison psychiatrist, she was being asked to perform according to a script without anyone expressing a genuine interest in what she had experienced and why. 'I had to retell the story over and over. I got really blasé to rationalise it to myself ... They didn't see past the event, the murder charge, they didn't see me.' Kate identified a feeling of invisibility that is also discernible in the media reports of other recent cases. Although in Britain the infanticide law recognizes the importance of a mother's mental stress, the notion of wilful murder continues to dominate our understanding of infanticide. This phenomenon may reflect a persistent unwillingness to accept the reality of maternal mental illness and its consequences for those very infants whose rights and welfare we are vociferous in protecting.

Societal rage towards the infanticidal mother was something that Kate experienced during her second night on the hospital ward at Risley prison. There, the other inmates shouted, 'You're going to hell' and issued death threats. Kate's boyfriend also received 'hate mail' while she was on remand and following press reports in the local media.[32] In the United States, Twyana Davis agreed to appear on an episode of the 'Leeza Show' to discuss her concealed pregnancy and the abandonment of her baby, following extensive local coverage of her case. After Davis described her experience, women in the audience were invited to give their comments. One shouted the following at her: 'I have two small children and there are times when I want to say, "Get away from me". I can't name one person who isn't stressed as you're claiming. But what right do you have to just say, "I'm so stressed out" and throw that baby away.' Another accused her, 'You threw your baby in a trash can for God's sake ... You could leave it in a basket on a door step but not throw it in a trash can.'[33]

There is a common thread that runs through the comments from outraged women at Risley, the hostile chat-show audience, and the views of columnists such as Patricia Pearson and Yvonne Roberts mentioned earlier. There is genuine anger at any woman who abuses a child or endangers its life. But there is also in these comments perhaps an underlying feeling of jealousy that the infanticidal mother has committed an act that runs through the mind of every parent who is anxious, over-tired and drained of energy. Particularly with infants, there is often a recognition not only of our vulnerability but also of our power to end an infant's life. The boundary preventing us from over-stepping that mark can, at times, appear precarious. The infanticidal mother arouses rage because many mothers know how close they may have come to acting out the same desperate fantasy.

The complexity of modern cases

While Dr Oates argues that women who abandon or kill their children carry within them 'a core of sadness' ever after, she believes that their behaviour during their pregnancies is an aberration in their overall life experience. A recent Canadian longitudinal study of filicidal mothers came to similar conclusions. Dr Renee Roy, a psychiatrist at the Institut

---

[32] Conversation with author, March 1998.
[33] 'The Leeza Show', ABC Television, 11 Aug. 1997.

Pinel Philippe de Montreal has treated thirty mothers who have been convicted of filicide in Quebec. These women, she discovered, are often loving mothers, often living without emotional support, who become overwhelmed by circumstances. The majority of women Dr Roy treated were suicidal at the time of the murder and believed their children would be better off dead rather than doomed to repeat their own cycle of deprivation and emotional abuse.

'Mercy killing' is among the reasons women gave for their actions, says Dr Roy. 'It looks like a mercy killing but that's a superficial answer; beneath it there's something related to extended suicide or a depressive illness. You need to go further.' The women are usually affectionate mothers who would sacrifice their own comfort for the comfort of their child. The murder usually occurs when the mother's thinking becomes so distorted that she believes homicide is the only solution. 'A few months afterwards', says Dr Roy, 'she begins to think, "My God, what have I done?" When they get in touch with those feelings, they become very suicidal.'[34]

However, many of the women in Dr Roy's study showed little outward sign of emotion, little remorse or regret for their actions, even to the staff at the psychiatric hospital where they were serving out their sentence. Staff members reacted badly to the mothers who refused to show pain and sadness, while in the safe confines of psychotherapy sessions the women would pour out to Dr Roy a bottomless well of grief and sadness. 'It's as if being alive is a punishment in itself', she says. 'They stay fragile for a long, long time and often choose not to have other children, which is part of the punishment they give themselves.'

Sometimes these women find the burden of guilt and loss unbearable. 'I've seen a couple of cases of women who committed suicide during incarceration', says Dr Roy. 'The reaction of all the staff members who were in contact with them was that they were in so much pain, [the women] felt it was the only solution.' Diane Yano, a thrity-seven-year-old Calgary engineer who drowned her two children in a bathtub at Fairmont in June 1999, is beginning her sentence. Dr Elizabeth Zoffman, the forensic psychiatrist who was the expert witness at Yano's murder trial testified that she had a history of chronic depression and had made several suicide attempts. She is currently being detained for further treatment because Dr Zoffmann believes that without medication and therapy, Yano is a threat primarily to herself. Although Yano was clearly psychotic when she committed the murder and is suffering from breast cancer, an unidentified witness at Yano's trial seemed to crystallize public ambivalence about her actions. 'She

---

[34] J. Wheelwright, 'Mothers who kill', *Vancouver Sun* (4 December, 1999).

definitely had a history of mental illness, but I just don't understand how someone could do something like that. I'm still thinking it just doesn't excuse it.'[35]

The comments from this anonymous witness reflect the intense discomfort that these cases provoke. We can sympathize with the mother only if she is mad. The only alternative contemporary framework of reference for her actions is to consider her as criminal. To accept the notion of mental illness implies that these women cannot take responsibility for the death of their infant. To accept a verdict of criminality, on the other hand, forces us to overlook the mental distress and physical pain that led to such actions. As Dr Roy herself suggests, these women do feel guilt and continue to condemn themselves for their actions, a sentiment supported by Dr Margaret Oates's statement that the women 'never really recover'. Experts who work with these women often argue that the moral and medical issues are complex, and that they need to be untangled and understood as an interweaving of individual action, mental distress, and reaction to social pressures.

Conclusion

The BBC film that featured an interview with 'Kate' affords us the rare opportunity to gain a degree of insight into the thinking process of a woman who has committed neonaticide and been convicted for infanticide. Her experience begins to fill the gap left by the usual press reports about such cases, where the woman's voice is rarely heard and her story is shaped by concerns for the baby, the parents and the baby's father. Kate's anxieties about not wanting to 'bother' friends or family with her problem parallel those identified by Twyana Davis and Caroline Beale. They are further bolstered by current research with neonaticidal mothers conducted by Dr Margaret Spinelli, who concluded that the women are in a dissociated state during and after their labour. The women are typically incapable of rational thought at this stage.

For many contemporary feminist writers, such accounts force womanhood back into a position where women's biology over-rides their rational faculties. Patricia Pearson and Yvonne Roberts believe that the law should reflect women's equality as rational beings, should treat them as fully responsible adults, and should punish women for committing a crime. Yet much recent research suggests not only that neonaticidal mothers are incapable of rational thought but also that, if

---

[35] Ibid.

the antiquated dichotomy of 'mad or bad' is to be avoided, a more sophisticated alternative framework for understanding concealment and infanticide is required.

It is undoubtedly appropriate that a woman who has killed her child is regarded as having committed a criminal act and is dealt with, at least in the first instance, by the criminal-justice system. Nevertheless, the recognition that mental instability can trigger overwhelming despair and may lead to the subsequent death of a child should be regarded not as an excuse, but as the sign of a tolerant society that appreciates that condemning crimes must be balanced with compassion for those whose illness or circumstances overwhelm their judgments and their own fragile sense of humanity. As the testimony of modern infanticidal mothers makes evident, living – for these women – may well be the heaviest punishment anyone could give them.

Acknowledgements

This article was written with the assistance of a Non-Fiction Writer's Grant from the Canada Council.

Index

abandonment of children 17, 23, 26, 32, 131–2
abduction 53
abortion 131–40 *passim*, 145–7, 196, 263, 271, 276
Abraham and Isaac 23
'abstract individualism' 250
acquittal rates, *see* conviction rates
Act for the due execution of divers laws and statutes heretofore made against rogues, vagabonds and sturdy beggars, and other lewd and idle persons (1610) 39–40
Act for the further Prevention of malicious shooting, etc. (1803) 6–7, 11, 40, 50, 78, 89
Act to prevent the Destroying and Murthering of Bastard Children (1624) 5–7, 11, 35–6, 43, 48, 61, 65, 73–80, 83, 88–91, 170, 250
Acton, William 251
Addison, Joseph 64–5
Affair of the Placards (1534) 21
ages of child victims 219–20
Alberti, Michael 121–2
Allen, Sarah 85
Alverstone, Lord 258–60, 264, 266
Ambrook, Elizabeth 86
Amery, George 40
Anderton, Ellen 43
Angell, Jeremy 270
Angell, Kelly 270, 280
Anhalt, Countess 124
Anna Amalia, Duchess of Saxe-Weimar 106
Anna Karenina 107
Anna Wilhelmine von Anhalt-Dessau, Princess 124
Arkansas 108
Arnot, M.L. 221
Ashbourne, Lord 259
Ashwell, Samuel 178
Atkin, Lord 267–8

Atwood, Margaret 93
Augustine of Hippo 21, 24–5, 27
Austen, Jane 118–19
Avory J. 262

baby-farming 10–11, 14, 169, 221–2, 246, 258–9
Baker, John 217, 221–5, 233, 237
Ball, William and Elizabeth 41–2
ballads 111–12, 127
Banbury, Sir Frederick 265
Barnes, Esther 39
Barnwell, Eliza(beth) 168, 173, 183, 188–91
Barrat, James 46
Bason, James 45
Bateman, Pleasant 85–6
Baxter, Elizabeth 40
Beale, Caroline 3, 11, 272–3, 276, 280, 284
Beattie, John 49
Becker, Susanne 95
Beckett, Elizabeth 40
Behlmer, George 220–21, 253–4
Bell, Thomas 180–81
Bernard of Luxembourg 27
Berry, John 188
Bethlem Royal Hospital archives 205
Bettilly, Thomas 41
Beza, Theodore 21, 31
Bird, Valentine 198, 202
Birkenhead, Lord 264–5
Blackstone, William 78
'blood libel' 18–34 *passim*
Bluebeard character 93–6
Boshof, Martha 134–6, 144–8
Bossen, Johanna Dorothea 120–21
Boswell, John 23, 26
Bracegirdle, Isaac 44
Bramwell, Baron 256
Brandt, Susanna 101–102, 115–16
Brayn, Richard 226, 247
Brentano, Peter von 123
Brighton Gazette 158
Brighton Herald 150–51, 160–64

Broadmoor Hospital 17, 218, 222–44
Brown, Eliza 232
Buckham, Isabella 86
Bucknill, John Charles 178, 182
Bullock, Thomas William 188, 190
burning of infants 24–5
Burrows, George Man 178
Bush, Barbara 133

Calvinism 20–21, 29
Canning, Elizabeth 16, 52–61, 65–71
Carson, Lord 264–5
Carter, Angela 93–6
Carter, Isidore 12
Castro, Alphonso de 27
Chadwick, Roger 251
Chailey Union workhouse 152–4, 162–3
'character' 163
Charles IX 34
Charlotte, Queen 79
Châteaubriant, edict of (1551) 20
Chester Court of Great Session, records of 37–51
Children Bill (1908) 258
Churchill, Fleetwood 176
Churchill, Winston 260
Clerkenwell 255
Cliff, Margaret 45, 48–9
Clifton, Graeme 270
Clouston, Thomas 176
Codwell, Elizabeth 35
Colley, Alice and Thomas 52
Colney Hatch asylum 212–13
common law 6, 249
Compiègne, edict of (1557) 20
concealment of pregnancy and birth 1–11, 17, 18, 36, 43, 48, 61, 74–5, 78, 96–100, 126, 131, 170, 184, 221, 256, 271–4
Condé, Prince of 33
Constantine the Great 24
conventicles 22
conviction rates 4, 6, 11, 16, 73, 81–2, 91–2, 102, 184
Coroners Act (1860) 254
Court of Criminal Appeal 262
Cox, Daniel 68–70
Crespin, Jean 30

Cresswell J. 184
Creuzer, Friedrich and Sophie 105–107
Crichton Browne, Sir James 204
Criminal Law Revision Committee 268–9
'criminal lunatics' 218
critical legal studies 249
Crouzet, Denis 19, 26
Curgenven, J.B. 171

Daily Telegraph 253
Dalton, Joseph 174
Damm, Sigrid 123
Darwin, Charles 204
Davies, Alice 41
Davis, Natalie 26
Davis, Twyana 272, 282, 284
Dawson, Lord 267–8
de l'Hôpital, Michel 34
de Mouchy, Antoine 30–31, 33–4
de la Popelinière, Lancelot du Voisin 32
de la Roche-Chandieu, Antoine 30–31
Dean, Sarah 39, 45–6
Defoe, Daniel 63–4
Dehne, Johann 121
denial of pregnancy 103, 113, 115
Denman LCJ 181–2
des Gallars, Nicolas 30
detention at Her/His Majesty's Pleasure 224
Diamond, Hugh W. 205–209
'diminished responsibility' pleas 81
discharge from mental institutions 217–19, 223–6, 231–4, 239–47
   social, moral and environmental determinants of 235–46
Dixon, Mary 76–7
Dodd, James Solas 68–9
Dodd, John and Hannah 44
Dodd, Richard 41
Dolan, Fran 60
domestic servants 1–2, 8–9, 14, 45, 60–67, 71–2, 169, 182, 184, 255
Dooling, Wayne 140
double standard of morality 104
drowning 157–8

Drysdale, Charles 171
du Toit, Gabriel 139, 142
du Val, Antoine 29
Duff, Elizabeth 10
Durand, Nicolas 28
Durnell, Mary 185
Dutch East India Company 129

eating of children 23–4, 30, 32–3
Eigen, Joel Peter 174
Ellenborough, Lord 6–7, 170
Ellis, Sarah 14
Ellwood, Amy 272
Elmhurst, Susan 273
Entwhistle, Henry 165–6
Enwright, Margaret 1–2
Epiphanius of Salamis 24
Erasmus, Desiderius 28–9
'erotic plot' 16, 94–5, 100–109
Essex 49
Eucharist, the 20–21
eugenics 226, 247
executions for infanticide 39, 49, 64,
    98, 102

Fairbrother, Dorothy 41
family involvement in infanticide 43
Faust (play) 111, 116–17
Fielding, Henry 58, 66–7, 69
Fisbie, Elizabeth 43–4
Fisher, R.B. 131–2
folklore 111
foundling hospitals 101
Frances, Joan 40
François I 21
François II 20, 33
Frankfurt am Main 101, 115
Frederick the Great 100
Frederick William I of Prussia 100
Fulda 26

Gascoyne, Sir Crisp 55, 71
Gatrell, V.A.C. 162–3
gender disparity in child victims 222
Gilman, Sander 213
Glaffey, Annette von 125
Gnosticism 24
Goethe, Cornelia von 123
Goethe, Johann Wolfgang von 106,
    111, 114–16, 123
Gooch, Robert 172, 174–5, 183

Goodwyn, Frances 41
Gouge, William 35
Graaff-Reiner 128, 135–6, 141, 148
Greaves, George 171
Greer, Germaine 109
Grey, Sir George 161–2, 164–5
Grimm, Brothers 111
Grosvenor, Sir Richard 35
Guibert of Nogent 25
Guise, duc de 31
Günderrode, Karoline von 104–107

Habermas, Rebekka 101, 114–15
Hale, Brenda 253, 267
Hale, Matthew 75–7, 88–9
Halsbury, Earl of 260
Halwood, Elizabeth 45
Hamilton, Sir Robert 184
Hancocke, John and Amy 43
Hanophy J. 269
Harper, Henry 155–6
Harris, Elizabeth 87
Harris, Mary Jane 11–15
Harris, Sarah 184–5, 188
Hart, Ernest 171
Harveian Society 171, 222, 256
Harvey Darton, F.J. 58
Haskell, T.L. 250–51
Hayes, Esther 44
Hayward, P.A. 26
The Heart of Midlothian 111,
    113–14
Heilbrun, Carolyn 108
Henderson, Arthur 263
heredity 225, 228–31
heresy 18–34 passim
Herrup, Cynthia 59
Hewart, Lord 267–8
Heyden, Susanne von 105–106
Higginbotham, A.R. 221, 255
Highfield, Emma 40
Hill, John 67
Hobson, Mary 47
Hodgkin, Jane 40
houses of correction 40
Hozius, Stanislas 28–9
Humphreys J 267–8
Hunter, Sarah 86
Hunter, William 3–4, 65, 79–81, 88,
    251, 276

illegitimacy 6–9, 114, 132, 140, 147, 169, 221–2
Infant Life Protection Act (1872) 14
Infant Life Protection Society 14
infanticide, use of term 10–11, 36
Infanticide Act (1922) 10, 17, 217, 253, 260, 263–5, 274
Infanticide Act (1938) 10, 17, 250, 268, 273–4
'infanticide craze' 36
inquests 47–8, 254
insanity, pleas and diagnoses of 10, 16–17, 74–92, 164, 168–205 passim, 213–14, 220–23, 229–34, 265–8

Jackson, Elizabeth 46–7
Jackson, Mark 36
James, Leslie 259
Jarvis, Elizabeth 87
Jews and Judaism 18, 21–6, 33
Jones, Mary 40
juries 4, 6, 12, 92, 160, 184, 261–2, 266–7

Kendricke, Elizabeth 41–2
Kent, David 62
kidnapping of children 25, 33
Klettenberg, Remigius de 124
Klettenberg, Susanna von 123–4
Koss, Thea 117
Krueger, Christine 191

La Roche, Maximiliane von 123
La Roche, Sophie von 123
Lack, Esther 186
Lancaster, John 44
The Lancet 169–71, 179–83 passim, 192
language of emotion 83, 85, 89–91
Lankester, Edwin 171, 254–6
Laqueur, Thomas 80
Lateran Council (1215) 27
Lavater, Johann 124
law reform 6 , 17, 96–7, 252
Lee, Robert 175
Leicester Mercury 262
Letjou 129, 138–9, 142
Levertov, Denise 109
Lord, James 52–3
Loreburn, Lord 258

Lorraine, Cardinal of 31–2
Lunacy Commissioners 224, 231
Lutheranism 27

McCardie J 262
MacCormack, J. 203
McCrory, Helen 107
McDonagh, Josephine 271, 273–4
Machen, Arthur 58
McLaren, Henry 263
MacLeod, M.D. 198
M'Naghten Rules 92, 266
MacNaughton, John 231–2, 244
Maddock, Dorothy 47
Magdeburg 120
Malins, Catherine 187
Manchester Medical Collection 194
Mandeville, Bernard 64–5
mania, puerperal 176–82 passim, 196–7, 205
Manicheism 25, 27–8
Manners, Jane 155
manslaughter 187
married men 223
married women 74–6, 183, 223
Martin, Baron 184, 186
martyrdom 29–30
'Mary Hamilton' (ballad) 112
Massey, Thomas 40–41
masturbation 199
Matthisson, Friedrich von 125
Maudsley, Henry 199
medical evidence 121–2, 157–8, 161, 171, 173, 181–2, 192
medical journals 194–8, 201, 213–14
Medical Times and Gazette 254
Médicis, Catherine de 20, 31–2, 34
melancholia 176, 196–7, 205, 234
men accused of infanticide 18, 41–2
microhistory 166–7
middle-class status 123
midwives 142
Millet, Mary 87
Millett, Kate 109
Mina 139–43, 148
mitigating circumstances 101
Moloch 22–3
Montanism 24
Moore, Judith 58
Morison, Alexander 204

Morris, Alice 41
Mosigkau 124–5
Muller, Regina 145
Muller, Theodorus 129–31, 135–7, 144–7

new-born infants, deaths of 9–10, 18, 35–6, 42–3, 217, 222, 267–8, 273
Nicaea, Council of 27
Norrie, Alan 249–50
Northern Assize Circuit 50

Oakes, Frances 69
Oates, Margaret 276, 279–84
O'Donoghue, Edith 253, 267
O'Donoghue, Mary 265
Offences against the Person Act (1828) 7, 170
Offences against the Person Act (1861) 170, 274
Ohnmais, Anna Maria 117–18
Old Bailey Sessions Papers 50, 64
Olenschläger, Johann Daniel von 124
Orange, William 225–6, 231
orgies 22, 31–2
'otherization' 213

Paddington 255
Park, Elizabeth 155
Park, James 163
Parke J. 164–5
Parker, Diana 86
Parkins, Elizabeth 86
Parmoor, Lord 264
Parsons, Daniel 44
Pearson, Edmond 57
Pearson, Joan 43–4
Pearson, Patricia 276, 282, 284
Perfect, Hannah 87
perjury 71
Perrault, Charles 93
Perry, Richard 202
Perth Criminal Lunatic Department 17, 218, 222–35, 239, 244
Pestalozzi, Johann Heinrich 122
Philida 128–31, 137–43 passim
photography, use of 195, 203–14
Pinch, Adela 89–90
Pixey, Hester 47
Plath, Sylvia 108–109, 127

poisoning 187
Poissy, colloquy of (1561) 21
poor law 8–9, 263
Portway, Mary 180–81
'poverty defence' 183
Pratt, Selina 12–15
'preparation defence' 77–8, 82–3, 87–8, 92
Prichard, James Cowles 176
Priest, Margery 42
Prior, Martha 179–82, 192
Prison Commissioners 224, 228
prosecution rates 11
prostitution 53–4
Protestants, persecution of 20–21, 33–4
psychiatric profession 193–4, 204, 207–208, 213–14
puerperal insanity/mania, see insanity; mania

Quakers 162

Radford, Mary 83, 85
Ramecker, J.M. 111
Ramsay, Allan 55, 70–71
Raw, Emilie 2
Redesdale, Lord 257
Reid, James 175–6
relapse in mental conditions 225–33
religion 18–23, 124, 194; see also heresy
Rich, Adrienne 109
Richards, Clare 277
ritual murder 18, 22–7 passim, 34
Roberts, Edith 253, 261–3
Roberts, Martha 46
Roberts, Penny 32
Roberts, Yvonne 276, 282, 284
Robinson, Elizabeth 46
Rogers, George 144
romance 114
Ross, Robert 135
Rothman, Christoffel 129, 144–8
Roy, Renee 282–3
Royal Commission on Capital Punishment 4, 169, 257
rue Saint Jacques affair (1557) 29–31
Rushbrooke, Benjamin 166
Russ, Joanna 122–3

Russell, Caroline 186–7
Ryan, William Burke 171, 255–6, 258

säcken 100
sacrifice of children 22–3
St Bartholomew's Day massacre (1572) 19
Sandles, Eliza 154, 160, 165
Sandles, Hannah 16, 149–67
Sandles, Louisa 151–2
Sandles, Thomas 153–9
Sandles, William 160, 165
Sant, Sarah 39
Saturn 22–3
Sauer, Anna 128–31, 134–43, 146–8
Sauer, J.N. 135, 138, 140, 144
Savage, George 198–9
Savigny, Friedrich von 105–106
Sayers, Dorothy L. 108
Schlosser, Johann Georg 123
Schmidt, Michael 98–9
Schuster, Claud 264
Scott, Sir Walter 111–14
Select Committee on Infant Life Protection 14
Semple, Robert 134–5
Sense and Sensibility 118–19
sensibility, concept of 89–92
Sexton, Anne 108–109, 127
Shell, Robert 132
Shrewsbury, Mary 86
Sibbald, John 231
Simmons, Charlotte 153, 155
Sims, Paula 276
single women 2–9, 17, 41, 61–5, 74–7, 94, 100, 123–4, 182–4, 222–3, 263
Smith, Roger 92, 171, 218–19
Smollett, Tobias 55
Social Science Association 191
Social Science Review 169
socialization 206
Society for the Abolition of Capital Punishment 257
Society of Arts 205
Society of Friends 162
Soissons 25
Somerset, Lord Charles 137
Spinelli, Margaret 272, 276–7, 284
spinsters, *see* single women
Squires, Mary 54–6, 66

Steinem, Gloria 109
Stephen, Sir James Fitzjames 256–7, 267
Stockenstrom, Andries 144–6
Straub, Kristina 58–9
Strickland, Martin 1
Strong Poison 108
suicide 104, 106, 108, 196, 222, 283
Surrey 49–50
Symonds, Deborah 111–14

Tagg, John 210
Tailor, Mary 41
Tameney, Bridget 187
Taylor, Alfred Swaine 178–9
Taylor, Elizabeth 47
Terling (Essex) 35
Terry, Ann 85
Tertullian 23, 30
Tey, Josephine 58
Thomas, Mary 44
Thomasius, Christian 119
The Three Riders 111
The Times 160
Tingley, James and Jane 151
Today (newspaper) 281
torture, use of 98, 100, 119–20
'traditional' treatments 202–203
Treherne, John 58
Trekow, Johane von 125
Trent 26
Trevor, Anne 45, 47–8
Troyes 32
Truter, J.A. 132
Tuffnel, Sarah 87
Tuke, Daniel Hack 198
Tuke, John Batty 196, 199
Turner, Elizabeth 77

Valentinians 28
van Dülmen, Richard 98
van de Kaap, Hester 133
van de Kaap, Rosalyn 128–31, 137–44
Vassy massacre (1562) 19
Vawdrey, John 45–6
Vincent of Lérins 27
virginity of children 26
Vooght, Harriet 1–3, 7
vulnerability of women 4, 9, 14, 16, 172

Wagstaffe, Lydia 42
Wakley, Thomas 191
Walker, Isobel 112–13
Walker, William 157–8
Ward, Tony 217, 221, 240
Warwick Advertiser 168, 186
Warwickshire 173, 182–92
Waters, Margaret 14
Weber, Beat 109
Webster, Phoebe 76
Wedgwood, Josiah 265
Wells, Susannah 54, 60, 66
wet-nursing 14, 133
Whicksted, Robert 41
Whitfield, Robert 87–8
Whoretopp, Jonathan and Sarah 42
Wiener, Martin 249, 252
Willes J. 255
William of Norwich 25–6

Wilner, Arlene 58
Wilson, Adrian 201
Winsor, Charlotte 11–13
witchcraft 35–6, 97–9, 119–20
Witzel, George 27–8
Wolff, Christa 105, 107
Wolff, Johann Tobias 121
Woolf, Virginia 118
working mothers 9, 15, 271
Worley, Mary 266
Worrall, Sarah 41
Wright, Ursula 41
Wrightson, Keith 35
Wyatt, Margaret 40

Yano, Diane 283–4

Zedner, L. 228–9, 247
Zoffman, Elizabeth 283